Dance, Spectacle, and the
Body Politick, 1250–1750

Dance, Spectacle, and the Body Politick, 1250–1750

Edited by Jennifer Nevile

Indiana University Press

Bloomington & Indianapolis

This book is a publication of

Indiana University Press
601 North Morton Street
Bloomington, IN 47404-3797 USA

http://iupress.indiana.edu

Telephone orders   800-842-6796
Fax orders   812-855-7931
Orders by e-mail   iuporder@indiana.edu

The paper used in this publication meets the minimum requirements of American National
Standard for Information Sciences—Permanence of Paper for Printed Library Materials,
ANSI Z39.48-1984.

Manufactured in the United States of America

Library of Congress Cataloging-in-Publication Data

Dance, spectacle, and the body politick, 1250–1750 / edited by Jennifer Nevile.
   p. cm.
 Includes bibliographical references and index.
 ISBN-13: 978-0-253-35153-1 (cloth : alk. paper)
 ISBN-13: 978-0-253-21985-5 (pbk. : alk. paper) 1. Dance—Europe, Western—History. 2. Dance—Social aspects—Europe, Western. 3. Europe, Western—Social life and
customs. 4. Europe, Western—History. I. Nevile, Jennifer.
 GV1643.D36 2008
 793.3094—dc22
                        2007045268
1 2 3 4 5 13 12 11 10 09 08

In Memory

David R. Wilson

(d. 2006)

Friend and colleague

For all his work in promoting and furthering scholarship in early dance

Contents

Acknowledgments

For a number of years I have felt there was a need for a collection of scholarly essays that focused on early dance pre-1750. I would like to thank all the contributors for their enthusiasm and support of this project, and for their belief in the importance of such a collection. The success of this collection is entirely due to the efforts of all the contributors in writing essays of such distinguished scholarship that are also a delight to read. The clarity and flow of the narrative of chapter 1 was improved, and errors eliminated, by the comments of Jennifer Bain, Mary Chan, Ken Pierce, Jennifer Thorp, and Tim Wooller. Any errors that remain are solely my responsibility. I am very grateful for their generosity in terms of their expertise and their time. As an editor I also benefited greatly from the advice I received on various aspects of baroque dance practice from Ken Pierce, John Powell, and Jennifer Thorp, and on the medieval period from Randall Rosenfeld, who also kindly provided translations of the Latin quotations in chapter 2. The collection as a whole benefited from the comments of Indiana University Press's anonymous readers. Thanks are also due to all those who helped with the illustrations, in particular Sarah Adams from Isham Memorial Library, the librarians at Isham Memorial Library and Houghton Library, Harvard University, as well as Sylvie Minkoff (Éditions Minkoff) and Sheila Noble (Edinburgh University Library), who graciously granted permission to reproduce the images whose copyright they held. Special thanks to my mother, Fay Nevile, for drawing the illustration of the garden compartment and the floor patterns of the hay in *Dolce Amoroso Foco*. I also wish to thank Jane Behnken, music editor at Indiana University Press, for all her assistance with this project.

Editorial Note

Throughout the five hundred years covered by these essays, spelling varied considerably. For the sake of consistency the spelling of names has been regularized in this volume. Thus, while the dance master Pierre Beauchamps's name is spelled both with and without the final -s in modern scholarly literature, in this volume the former spelling is used. For discussion on the inconsistent spellings of Beauchamps's surname in the seventeenth century, see John S. Powell, "Pierre Beauchamps, Choreographer to Molière's Troupe du Roy," *Music and Letters* 76, no. 2 (1995): 169n7. Likewise, on the two wills of Raoul-Auger Feuillet his signature appears as "Raoul-Anger." Throughout this volume, however, his first name will be spelled "Raoul-Auger," as this is how it is spelled in all reference works, scholarly monographs, and articles.

The glossary at the end of the volume provides brief definitions of key terms in the dance practices of the time, as well as musical and dance terms that are not generally known outside of specialist areas. Foreign language terms that only occur once are provided with a translation in the body of the text.

Dance, Spectacle, and the Body Politick, 1250–1750

Part 1

Introduction & Overview

❧

Introduction

For most of the 500 years from 1250 to 1750 art and politics were not seen as two separate and distinct activities. As F. W. Kent insists in his study of Lorenzo de' Medici's patronage of the arts, "Lorenzo and his contemporaries would not have distinguished, indeed could not have distinguished, between the world of the arts and politics in this way; they did not find it strange . . . that a talented person might have a refined knowledge of both."[1] The same lack of distinction applied to dance and politics during this period: dance was part of the political process in a way that is often difficult to appreciate today, when the two are viewed as distinct worlds. Dance, especially when combined with music and poetry, was seen as a reflection of the harmony of the universe, harmonies which "lay behind the spatial relationships of architecture and sculpture, the colours and proportions of painting, and of course behind the measures of poetry and the movement of dance. It was even the basis, as it had been for Plato, of moral behaviour, helping to attune the soul to God."[2] Since choreographies embodied the same harmony as ordered the universe, they too had the power to order or "harmonize" the souls of those who watched. It was hoped that the combination of dance, music, and poetry not only exercised its harmonic powers on the bodies and souls of those watching a danced spectacle, but also on the "body politic," the political state or entity, to restore it to peace and harmony.[3] Dance had a close relationship with, and participation in, the contemporary intellectual, political, and artistic milieu, and its many roles are explored in the essays in this collection.

While dance was ever-present in the lives of western Europeans from the late medieval period to the middle of the eighteenth century, it has not fared so well as an academic discipline. Its relatively late entry into the modern higher education institutions has meant that even much basic research has yet to be done, and many of the scholarly tools for furthering research which are available in other disciplines have not been developed in the area of dance history. This is especially true for dance history prior to 1800. This collection of essays is one contribution toward filling these lacunae in dance history scholarship. The aim of the collection is to present a picture of dance in society from the late medieval period to the middle of the eighteenth century, and to demonstrate how the dance practices during these five centuries participated in the intellectual, artistic, and political cultures of their day. The essays present a wide-ranging perspective on dance, as the contents not only include structural analysis of differing dance genres and their relationship with the accompanying music, but also the social and intellectual context of dance, its function in society, its relationship with other contemporary artistic practices, and its place in the moral and theological debates, both in terms of the earthly human condition and also in wider cosmological terms. The essays are divided into sections centered around a particular theme, with the essays in each part ordered chronologically. The collection of essays are arranged so that the book progresses from the general to the more specific, before broadening once more in the final section, part 6, where a picture is presented of how dance was so enmeshed in the fabric of western European society during this period that it permeated all facets of life: the intellectual and artistic cultures, the moral or theological perspective, even philosophic and scientific thought.

Chapter 1 provides an overview of the entire period and across the whole of Western Europe, including in its discussion examples from Spain, Germany, and Scandinavia, as well as from France, Italy, and England, the three countries which are the focus of individual essays. The purpose of this chapter is to provide the necessary background to the individual chapters for readers who may not be familiar with this period of history, and its dance practices in particular. Thus, woven into a narrative, the reader will find in this chapter a discussion of the context of the dance practices, whether as private entertainments, court balls, or dancing as part of court spectacles, and later in commercial theatrical productions; a discussion of the dance masters and their treatises; the various forms of dance notation, and the music that accompanied the dances; as well as a brief overview of the main dance genres of the period, and the spaces in which the dance performances took place. Part 2 is more specific, focusing on dance in late thirteenth-century Paris, the courts of fifteenth-century Italy, and in France during the sixteenth and early seventeenth centuries, while part 3 discusses dance as part of public theatrical events in late seventeenth-century France and in England during the first half of the eighteenth century. Parts 4 and 5 are more technical and specific, concentrating on choreographic structures of different genres and their relationship with the accompanying music in part 4, and in part 5 on the interaction between dance and the political process in sixteenth-century Italy, seventeenth-century France, and early eighteenth-century England. An introduction at the start of each part highlights connections between the essays, and each part concludes with a list of further reading.

Key Terms

As a term for a period in European history, the "Renaissance" dates back to at least 1860 when the Swiss historian Jacob Burckhardt first published *The Civilization of the Renaissance in Italy: An Essay*, a work that has subsequently influenced generations of historians, right up to the present day. The word itself means "rebirth," and the period is closely associated with the rediscovery of the ancient world, particularly in Italy. Scholars have argued over its appropriateness, even over the period covered by the term. Some have rejected it altogether, preferring alternatives such as "early modern." It is not the purpose of this book to enter into all the current debates over the use and meaning of this term, as this has been done elsewhere, as, for example, in the recent anthology, *The Renaissance: Italy and Abroad*.[4] In this volume the word "Renaissance" is used solely as an alternate way to refer to the fifteenth and sixteenth centuries.

In the eighteenth century the word "baroque" was used in writings of art and music criticism in the general sense of bizarre, irregular, and extravagant. It was not used in English language scholarship to refer to a specific period in music history until the 1940s, and debate continues over the validity of the term for music composed circa 1600 to 1740–65. In dance history the term "baroque" is commonly used to refer to dance practices from circa 1650 to 1725–50. This is how the term is used in this collection of essays. The use of this term to refer to the dance practices of this period is not meant to imply that every dance conformed to the original meaning of the word as bizarre, extravagant, or excessively ornamental.

The terms "social" and "theatrical," "amateur" and "professional," occur constantly in writings on early dance, with very little consensus on the precise definition of each term. The difficulty in defining these terms is not new. The debate over "amateur" and "professional" was flourishing in the sixteenth and seventeenth centuries, with dance masters and courtiers arguing the issue.[5] Descriptions of dancing from circa 1500–1700 repeatedly stress the virtuosity expected and demanded of courtiers when dancing, yet other writings counseled against extravagant steps and gestures by noble performers. Whether noble dancers were equal in ability to professionals—those who earned their living by teaching, performing, and composing dances—is now probably unanswerable, and must have varied from individual to individual. What is important to emphasize is that when the term "amateur" is used in this volume it does *not* have the connotations often associated with it today, that is, unskilled, inexpert, clumsy, or downright incompetent. The gulf in ability between the noble dancers and the professionals did not arise until the very end of the period covered by this volume. The debate over the ability of noble dancers is important, as it affects how researchers view the primary sources, both choreographic descriptions and records of dance performances in letters, diaries, newspaper reports, and so on. If the assumption that amateur equals unskilled is adopted, then judgments are already being made about the choreographies performed by these courtiers, and what was, or was not, possible, even before one bar of notation is analyzed.

The same fluidity and lack of distinction also applies to the terms "social dance" and "theatrical dance," as there is no agreement as to where the line between the two should be drawn. Choreographies that were regularly danced in a ballroom setting were also performed as part of theatrical productions, while dances that were composed for a specific theatrical event could and did migrate to the ballroom.[6] Dance masters choreographed dances for a small number of couples to be performed at a court ball, for a wedding, or at an official state occasion, just as they composed new choreographies to be performed by courtiers as part of a theatrical production. The assertion that social dances were composed of stock formulas, while theatrical dances consisted of newly invented, elaborate patterns and figures, does not fit the choreographic evidence. As Jennifer Thorp has commented: "It is rather a myth that all early eighteenth-century theatrical dances were ipso facto more complex or technically demanding than ballroom dances; any study of the extant repertory reveals that both genres contained examples ranging from the dull and simple to the sophisticated and technically brilliant."[7] Similar analyses of the sixteenth-century Italian choreographies reveal that the surviving theatrical dances are very similar to the recorded social dances.[8]

With these qualifications in mind it is possible to make some general observations on what characterized social and theatrical dances during this period. Social dances were definitely performed for enjoyment and entertainment at both informal, private occasions and at more formal, public events. The performers were not disguised or masked and were not representing historical characters or mythological figures. Social dances were also a moving depiction of the relationships between men and women, as happened on a daily basis at court. (This is particularly clear in the fifteenth-century Italian choreographies.) Theatrical dances can be said to involve the performers wearing elaborate costumes and disguises while representing famous historical or mythological figures, or fabulous animals such as centaurs. Often theatrical dances were accompanied by mime where the story or moral being represented by the dancers was acted out, and vocal pieces further explained the narrative behind the dances. Stage props and scenery, ranging from the simple to the highly complex, were also a part of theatrical dances. Thus it is important to note that the distinction between "social" and "theatrical" is not based on the location of the performance, nor on who were the performers, but on the circumstances of the performance, the presence or absence of scenery and stage props, and whether an element of the exotic was present.

In his listing of "all the most renowned dancers of his day" which begins his treatise *Le gratie d'amore*, Cesare Negri describes some of them as a "maestro di ballare" (dancing master), while others are noted as being "excellent in the profession of dance" ("qual è nella professione del ballare eccellente"). These were all men who conducted dance schools, taught private pupils, were paid to perform and choreograph dances, and who wrote treatises. In short, these were men who made a profession, in the modern sense of the word, of teaching dance. Thus from the mid-sixteenth century onward this is what the term "dancing or dance master" represents. In the fifteenth century the exact parameters of the term "dance master" and what was meant by the "profession" of dance is not so clear-cut. As Douglas Biow has pointed out, the discourse about, and formation of, professional identity in Italy "experienced a profound shift" between the mid-fifteenth century and the end of the sixteenth century.[9] The Italian humanists who "assisted in constructing professional identity in the Renaissance" had a flexible attitude in this regard, as they themselves moved between professions and they felt that "[h]aving one profession did not at all exclude or upset having another, and in many respects having multiple professions was a necessity."[10] Thus the fact that Antonio Cornazano was a humanist, courtier, and poet, as well as an author of a dance treatise, skilled dancer, and arguably a dance teacher to Ippolita Sforza, does not debar him from being included in the men who scholars now designate by the professional title of "dance master." In this volume when the term "dance master" is used in reference to fifteenth-century figures, its meaning is confined to a "master" or expert in dance, *without necessarily implying someone who was paid for teaching or performing, and whose principal daily activities were those centered on dance.* All of these activities could be a part of the "dance master's" life, or only some of them, and he could also be involved in other activities that are not now perceived as dance-related. From the sixteenth century onward the term is used more in the modern sense of a person engaged solely in the dance profession.

Notes

1. F. W. Kent, *Lorenzo de' Medici and the Art of Magnificence* (Baltimore: Johns Hopkins University Press, 2004), p. 16.

2. Erica Veevers, *Images of Love and Religion: Queen Henrietta Maria and Court Entertainments* (Cambridge: Cambridge University Press, 1989), p. 194.

3. Thomas M. Greene, "The King's One Body in the *Balet Comique de la Royne,*" *Yale French Studies* no. 86 (1994): 75–93, especially pp. 77–81.

4. John Jeffries Martin's introduction to this collection of essays presents a valuable summary of the historiography of the Renaissance, and how each succeeding generation of scholars interpreted this period in their own way, both in reaction to what was written before them and in reaction to world political upheavals of their own time (Martin, "Introduction. The Renaissance: Between Myth and History," in *The Renaissance: Italy and Abroad*, ed. John Jeffries Martin [London: Routledge, 2003], pp. 1–23).

5. Margaret M. McGowan, "Recollections of Dancing Forms from Sixteenth-Century France," *Dance Research* 21, no. 1 (2003): 15, and McGowan, "The Art of Dance in Seventeenth-Century French *ballet de cour*: An Overview," in *Terpsichore 1450–1900: Proceedings of the International Dance Conference, Ghent, April 2000*, ed. Barbara Ravelhofer (Ghent: Institute for Historical Dance Practice, 2000), pp. 97–99.

6. For examples of dances from the sixteenth century that moved from one sphere to the other, see McGowan, "Recollections of Dancing Forms," pp. 16–17.

7. Jennifer Thorp, "Pecour's *L'Allemande*, 1702–1765: How German Was It?" *Eighteenth-Century Music* 1, no. 2 (2004): 184n7.

8. See Pamela Jones, "The Relation Between Music and Dance in Cesare Negri's *Le Gratie d'Amore*," Ph.D. diss., Kings College, London, 1988, p. 234, and Jennifer Nevile, "Cavalieri's Theatrical *Ballo* and the Social Dances of Caroso and Negri," *Dance Chronicle* 22, no. 1 (1999): 119–33.

9. Douglas Biow, "Reflections on Humanism and Professions in Renaissance Italy and the Humanities Today," *Rinascimento* 43 (2003): 334.

10. Ibid., p. 335.

I

Dance in Europe 1250–1750

Jennifer Nevile

The Dance Sources

The most obvious source of information on early dance is the dance treatises themselves. These documents vary enormously in content, scope, means of production—manuscript or printed book—reason for production, whether or not they include music, their country of origin, and the number of surviving copies. The earliest dance treatises that have survived are from fifteenth-century Italy. Dance flourished in Italy, as well as in other parts of Europe before the fifteenth century, but we have no evidence that any written treatises were produced before this time. The fifteenth-century Italian treatises are all manuscripts, and they contain a large number of choreographic descriptions, some of which have music recorded with the dance description. These works also contain a theoretical section that provides the philosophical justification for dancing, lists the principles necessary for a good dancer, and briefly describes the steps used. The next most substantial body of choreographic material from the period 1400 to 1500 are the French *basse dance* treatises. These works are mostly from the late fifteenth and early sixteenth centuries, and are in both manuscript and printed form. The French works contain choreographies, instructions on how to perform the four steps of the *basse dance* and on how to arrange these four steps in different combinations or *mesures*. But these French sources do not name any dance masters, nor do they make any attempt to place the *basse dance* practice within the contemporary intellectual framework. They make no attempt to link this dance practice with other artistic practices, not even dance practices from other countries, nor does the text of the treatises show any consciousness of the milieu in which these dances were performed. Thus the two earliest surviving groups of dance treatises illustrate the two extremes of the forms such treatises were to take right through to the eighteenth century: the French treatises which were simple compilations of choreographies, whether in the format of a beautifully decorated presentation manuscript or rough notes jotted down as an *aide-memoire* for an individual; and the Italian treatises which, in addition to describing actual dances, place the dance practice they record into an intellectual framework and social context. From the sixteenth century onward dance treatises were overwhelmingly in the form of printed books rather than manuscripts. The development of printing and engraving meant that dance treatises, and dance music, were more widely accessible and were cheaper to produce, such that by the mid-eighteenth century dance was unquestionably part of the commercial world. Eighteenth-century music publishers like Walsh & Hare and writers on dance such as John Weaver made their living from selling printed choreographies, dance treatises, and dance music, an occupation which would not have been possible in earlier centuries.

Since the surviving dance treatises from 1400 to 1750 are spread very unevenly, both in chronological and geographic terms, with Germany and Spain being particularly lacking in this regard,[1] dance historians must look to other sources for information on the dance practices. One such source is descriptions of actual dance performances from contemporary witnesses, whether in chronicles, diaries, or letters. Once again the amount of information provided by these documents varies enormously from simple statements like "and they danced until dinner," to descriptions of the dance performance and the reaction of those watching, and the inclusion of additional information such as the names of those performing, the order in which they danced, the clothes and jewels they wore, and a description of the space in which the performance took place. What information is recorded depends on the original purpose for which each description was written and the amount of knowledge each author had of the dance style he or she was describing. In sixteenth- and early seventeenth-century England many letters passed from London to the homes of the northern gentry in which the latest court masques were discussed. Yet because both the letter writers and recipients were interested in the masque as politics, these letters record "the costs, the participants, the reasons for their selection or exclusion, the masque's reception by its audience, and the sociopolitical dynamics of the occasion," while the content of the masque or comments on aesthetic matters were usually totally absent.[2] While chronicles and letters contain descriptions of actual danced events, information about dancing can also be obtained from literary descriptions of imagined danced events, from poems, plays, and romances. Writings both for and against dance are a further source of information: clerical sermons, humanistic treatises on the worldly follies and vanities by literary and philosophical figures, pedagogical treatises, such as Thomas Elyot's *The Boke Named the Governour* (1531), and courtesy manuals all contain evidence for differing attitudes to dance, and the role of dance in society.

Another important source of information on the dance practices of the time is contemporary treatises on producing danced spectacles. The work by Monsieur de Saint-Hubert (1641) on how to compose a successful ballet is a good illustration of this genre.[3] In his short essay, Saint-Hubert discusses what is necessary to produce a *ballet de cour* (court ballet), that is, the subject for the ballet, the music, the dancing, the costumes, the stage machines, and the organizational structure and management and rehearsal required to coordinate all these elements. A far longer work is the anonymous manuscript written c. 1630, probably in Florence,[4] *Il corago*, in which is described the duties of a "manager"—the *corago*—of such spectacles, and all the preparation and work required to stage a successful production, as well as the problems that could arise, and the disasters that did.[5] To avoid these was the responsibility of the *corago*.[6]

Financial records of a court can sometimes provide information on the names of the dance masters employed at a certain court, their position, how much they were paid and for what activities they were paid, as well as what dances were performed at court festivities, and the cost of costumes for dancers performing in the court spectacles. Similar payment records for dancers outside the context of the court can also be found in "town treasurer, churchwarden, and household account books."[7] In the eighteenth century the financial accounts of the theaters provide information on the working conditions and salaries of dancers employed there.[8]

Iconographic sources, although they, like every other type of source material, present their own problems of interpretation and must be used with care, also extend the picture of dance in society.[9] One well-known dance scene from the fourteenth century is found in Ambrogio Lorenzetti's fresco cycle in the Palazzo Pubblico in Siena, where nine figures dance to the sound of a tenth person singing and playing a tambourine-like drum. Over the years art historians have advanced many theories as to the identity of the dancers (female or male) and their significance within the cycle. The articles on these frescoes by Jane Bridgeman and Quentin Skinner are excellent examples of how iconographic research can add to the knowledge of a dance practice in a particular time and place. Through an analysis of the costume, appearance, and hair styles of the dancers, Bridgeman establishes that, contrary to previous beliefs, the dancing figures are male, not female.[10] Through Skinner's analysis, which points to the significance of Lorenzetti organizing an entire section of the fresco around an image of people dancing, and making the dance scene the light source for that particular fresco, much is revealed about dance and the attitude to dancing in early fourteenth-century Siena.[11]

Legal documents also provide information on dance activity during this period.[12] For example, we know of the existence of dancing schools in London in the mid-sixteenth century because of the regulations outlawing "bowling alleys and dancing schools within the city."[13] Other useful legal documents, particularly for the non-elite dance practice, are those that record ecclesiastical cases involving prosecutions for dancing on Sundays.[14] Other examples of legal sources are notarial documents that record contracts for the operation of dance schools, and regulations that tried to restrict the activities of Jewish dance masters,[15] as well as university regulations governing their students' public behavior and activities.[16]

In the seventeenth and eighteenth centuries sources for dance increase markedly, particularly the number of surviving scores for the music that accompanied the dances in operas and comedy-ballets. One major illustration of the crucial importance of examining musical scores is found in Rebecca Harris-Warrick's work on the phrase structures of Lully's dance music.[17] Through an examination of the dance music from thirteen of Lully's operas, all of which were danced to, Harris-Warrick has exploded the common misconception that all baroque dance music is metrically regular, invariably composed of four or eight bar phrases, and that an unidentified piece can be categorized as "dance music" just because it is divided into regular four or eight bar phrases. Another important source of information for the seventeenth-century *ballets de cour* is the printed program (the *livret*) which was both distributed to members of the audience prior to the performance and sent abroad to foreign courts.[18] The libretti of operas or the texts of plays in which dancing occurred also provide additional information on the dance practice in the theater.[19]

The Dance Context

The most frequent context of the dance practices examined in this volume of essays is the court, whether as private entertainment, court balls, or dancing as part of state festivities, and, at the end of the period, dancing in commercial theatrical productions. Members of the elite level in society danced because, like people from every other level of society, they enjoyed doing so.[20] It was one means of entertaining themselves in small, intimate gatherings of only a few members of the court or of one's immediate family. In his later years, Alfonso d'Aragona spent many of his afternoons relaxing in the palace gardens with his mistress. Impatient ambassadors would report home that "[h]e now spends much of the day at archery and in the garden; afterwards there is dancing . . . and so time passes."[21] Henri III of France, who was an excellent and keen dancer, would often retire to the country with the queen and only a small number of courtiers, to pass the weeks with dancing and other pursuits.[22]

Members of the elite also danced at court balls at which more than just a few participated. These evenings of dancing were often very frequent, especially during the carnival season before Lent. At Henri III's court there were some months, like January 1578, where "either ballets or balls occurred on every night."[23] Balls were also given by members of the court in their own houses. Court balls also varied in their size, scale, planning, and formality. Under Louis XIV, on two or three evenings a week, courtiers were invited to the king's apartments at Versailles for an evening of pleasure (the *jours d'appartement*) that included gambling, billiards, dancing, and musical entertainment.[24] Masked balls, often held during carnival, were less formal than the major court balls[25] which were held much less frequently and mostly to mark an important state event. The amount of dance activity engaged in by the courtiers obviously varied from year to year, but Harris-Warrick gives a picture of what a period of high dance activity would have been like.

> During the six-month period between 10 September 1684 and 3 March 1685, the beginning of Lent, there were at the court alone: 1 *grand bal*; 9 masked balls; 16 *appartements* that definitely included dancing; 42 other *appartements* that almost certainly also offered dancing; and at least 2 evenings of comedy that included dancing between the acts by courtiers. This all adds up to approximately 70 opportunities for dancing during a 175-day period, or one every two to three days.[26]

Dance was also an important part of official state events and festivities, at the celebrations of baptisms and weddings, at religious festivals, during the visits of foreign rulers or ambassadors, and at the triumphal entry of a ruler into a city. Given the frequency with which dance was part of these festivals, it is worth elaborating briefly on the nature of these ceremonies and spectacles. Ceremonies, like the entry of a ruler into a city, or the coronation of a monarch, were events which brought "power structures into being," rather than merely demonstrating "power relations in [a] symbolic fashion."[27] For example, the entry "of a monarch into a city in his or her realm . . . [is where] a legal contract between the ruler and the citizens is created. . . . Ruler and city . . . [enter] into a relationship of mutual obligation."[28] Spectacles, on the other hand, were theatrical events in which the power structures that existed in a country were acted out and presented in a symbolic fashion.[29] Spectacles included danced, multimedia performances such as the *ballet de cour,* dramatic productions, displays of military prowess, such as jousts and tournaments, horse ballets, and firework dramas. Because spectacles were a representation of the power structures of a country, and often an enactment of how those structures *should* be operating, they were not just occasions for "entertainment."

> [W]e have to be aware of regarding these kinds of festival as, in our modern sense, mere entertainment, that is, the occasion for private relaxation. Such a notion belongs more properly to the late seventeenth or the eighteenth centuries. Early modern court theatrical entertainments are either symbolic representations of the nature of power and its functioning within the society of the realm or of the court, or they present in allegorically heightened form the dynastic or civic event that they celebrate. In this way they provide the court with the tools to interpret this important occasion.[30]

Therefore, the danced component of these spectacles also fulfilled a function far beyond that of an entertaining and enjoyable diversion. Who danced with whom, the order in which they danced, the figures formed by the choreography, the allegorical personages represented by the costumed dancers, the true identity of those dancers, even the exact position of the king's chair within the performance space, all were part of the representation of power in the court, and in the wider society.

During this period rulers throughout Europe followed these principles: whatever name was given to these spectacles their political character was always present. In England, for example, the revels were spectacles that combined—in every possible permutation—"music, poetry, dance, visual spectacle, barriers, tourneys, and dialogue."[31] The revels were used by the monarch not only to "confirm [the] hierarchy at court," but also to "project an image of themselves and of their courts to foreign princes," and a method "by which diplomatic positions could be implied or stated."[32] Evidence of these danced spectacles are found across Europe, including those at Cracow in 1592;[33] the five court ballets performed in Stuttgart at the Württemberg court in 1607, 1609, 1616, 1617, and 1618;[34] in 1634 in Copenhagen the ballet that was part of the wedding celebrations of the Danish Prince Elect Christian and the Saxon Duchess Magdalena Sybille; in Brussels in 1634 where noblemen and professional dancers performed in the *Balet de Princes Indiens;*[35] and in the regular ballet performances in Stockholm from 1638 to 1654.[36]

Common Dance Practices and Attitudes

From the fifteenth century when written choreographic descriptions first appeared right up to 1750, the courts of Europe shared and participated in a common dance culture and practices. This is not to obscure the fact that during this period there were distinct "national" dance practices that were recognized at the time. Guglielmo Ebreo, dance master in fifteenth-century Italy, proudly asserts in his treatise on the art of dancing that any dance student who has diligently studied all the exercises provided by him in his treatise will be able to dance perfectly any German, Greek, or Slavonic (that is, Croat) dance, or indeed any dance from whatever country he wishes.[37] As far as Guglielmo was concerned different regions had different identifiable styles of dance. Accounts of the festivities at which dance occurred often mention dances being performed in the manner of one country or another. In 1490 the wedding of Isabella d'Aragona (the daughter of Ippolita Sforza) to the Duke of Milan, Giangaleazzo Sforza, produced a glittering array of international dance styles. Groups of four to twelve dancers from Poland, Germany, France, Spain, and Hungary, all dressed in the costume of their country, performed their own dances to honor the bridal couple. A number of Isabella's ladies-in-waiting entertained the company by dancing Neapolitan and Spanish dances, after which the Spanish contingent was invited to entertain the company with "dui balli a la spagnola." The French gentlemen and ladies then performed "dui balli a la franzosa" to the delight of Isabella.[38]

Yet at the same time as there were distinct differences between the dances from different regions of Europe, there were also choreographic elements that were common across Europe. The "single" step and the "double" step, for instance, were part of every recorded dance style in Europe in the Renaissance.[39] Dance styles from one country were regularly performed in other countries: the French *basse dance* was performed at the English court in the late fifteenth and early sixteenth centuries. The pavane and galliard were danced everywhere in Europe in the sixteenth century. Treatises from one country were translated into the language of another. This became a very common practice in the early eighteenth century when Raoul-Auger Feuillet's treatise was translated into English and German, but the same practice occurred as early as 1521, when Robert Coplande translated a French *basse dance* treatise into English. Even when no choreographic evidence from a country survives, as is the case for Germany in the fifteenth and sixteenth centuries, we have other evidence that the dance practice there was just as pervasive as elsewhere in Europe, which has extensive documentary records. From the late fourteenth century dancing greatly increased in popularity in Germany, as evidenced by the size of the dance houses built as a venue for balls for both nobles and the urban merchant classes. One example, which is still standing today, is the dance house built in Nördlingen in 1444. This building "comprises some three floors before the level of the very broad windowed roof, which contains two more floors, with attic space above the second of these."[40] The previous dance house was considered to be too small, as it had only two floors before the roof, and two floors under the eaves.[41]

Ambassadors, royal brides and accompanying courtiers, dance masters, and university students all traveled from one country to another, bringing with them the dances with which they were most familiar, and with which they had been trained.[42] One example from the fifteenth century is the German Hohenzollern and Wittelsbach families, who were related by marriage to noble families in northern Italy, France, and the Netherlands. As Keith Polk writes, "For an aspiring and ambitious young noble in the court circles of Hapsburg, Brandenburg or Bavaria, learning . . . an international repertory of dances would have been a basic requisite of the milieu."[43] Temporary political asylum also contributed to the movement of dances and dance genres across Europe. The ballet performed in Brussels in 1634 was greatly assisted by the enforced stay of the French queen mother, Marie de' Medici (who was in Brussels from 1632 to 1638), and Louis XIII's brother, Gaston d'Orléans.[44] Information about danced spectacles also traveled across Europe in letters and in written descriptions, often prompting requests for dance masters to come to a court to teach the dances seen in the spectacle. In 1584, three years after the performance at the French court of *Le Balet Comique de la Reyne*, Alfonso d'Este sent a request that Henri III send a violinist (who was also a dance teacher) to Ferrara so that this man could teach all the ballets done at the French court to him and the Ferrarese courtiers.[45]

Dance music also traveled with the musicians who played it, as dance musicians lived and worked in more than one country: many of the best wind-band players in Italy in the fifteenth century were German. In the mid-sixteenth and seventeenth centuries Italian musicians, like Jean-Baptiste Lully, and dance masters traveled to the French court to live and work. The presence of dance tunes from the repertory of one country that are recorded in manuscripts or printed books from another country is also an indication of the international nature of the dance practices during this period. One example is the keyboard tablature book compiled by the German-speaking lawyer Bonifacius Amerbach (1495–1562), which contains four French *basses dances*, all based on the *basse dance* tenor *La Spagna*. This tenor was one of the three recorded by the Italian Antonio Cornazano in his dance treatise, and remained popular throughout the sixteenth century.[46] The German Buxheimer Organ Book also includes settings of French *basses dance* tenors, such as *Une fois avant que mourir* and *Venise*. The former tenor, *Une fois*, was also known in England, as it is one of the ninety-six dance titles listed in the Gresley papers from Derbyshire, the late fifteenth-century English dance source.[47]

Not only were specific choreographies, dance steps, and dance styles common to more than one country, so too were attitudes to dancing shared across geographic areas, and over long periods of time. Two examples that illustrate this point connect late sixteenth- and seventeenth-century Spain with fifteenth-century Italy. In a comedy by Lope de Vega, *El maestro de danzar* dating from 1594, "dancing is described as 'the soul of beauty,' for 'it makes the ugly beautiful, and the beautiful even more perfect.'"[48] The attitude to dance expressed by Lope de Vega is similar to that expressed by the fifteenth-century Italian dance master Guglielmo Ebreo in his treatise, where he says that for those who have the knowledge to appreciate and understand it, dance has a virtuous effect:

> But when it is practiced by noble, virtuous and honest men, I say that this science and art is good, virtuous, and deserving of commendation and praise. And moreover not only does it turn virtuous and upright men into noble and refined persons, but it also makes those who are ill-mannered and boorish and born into a low station into a sufficiently noble person.[49]

In his treatise of 1642 Juan de Esquivel Navarro says: "The prince, the lord, the well born, the elegant and learned, steadfast and brave—in the Dance you will find brilliant adornment, since it gives any serious person graceful perfection."[50] Both the fifteenth-century Italian dance masters, Domenico da Piacenza, Guglielmo Ebreo da Pesaro, and Antonio Cornazano, and the Spanish Esquivel, stress how the dance practice they discuss is fit only for the elite in society, not those from the lower classes. Cornazano says: "We come to these *balli* and *bassadanze* which are removed from the populace, and are composed for the noble halls, and are to be danced only by the most worthy ladies, and not by the common multitude of people."[51] In his treatise Esquivel too constantly returns to the theme that dancing as taught in the dance schools is a practice of the elite.[52]

The duties of the dance master were also standard throughout the period and across Europe. Acquiring expertise in dancing meant acquiring a bodily agility, an elegance in posture and manners, and the correct and necessary presence and address. Edward Herbert, first Lord Herbert of Cherbury (1582?–1628), felt that dancing:

> doth fashion the body, gives one a good presence in and address to all companies since it disposeth the limbs to a kind of *souplesse* (as the Frenchmen call it), and agility, insomuch that they seem to have the use of their legs, arms and bodies, more than any others, who, standing stiff and stark in their postures, seem as if they were taken in their joints, or had not the perfect use of their members.[53]

In the dance treatise, *Nobiltà di dame* (1600), Fabritio Caroso discusses similar matters of deportment and etiquette: the correct behavior at a ball for both ladies and gentlemen, including how gentlemen should manage their capes and their swords; how ladies should sit on a low chair without arms; how ladies should take leave of their partners; and how they should behave if they are not invited to dance.[54] Esquivel also advocated that the dance schools teach more than just the mechanics of dancing: "Not only should one frequent the studios in order to know how to dance, but also in order to learn politeness, fine dress, modesty, fine speech, and to be competent in many subjects; because in the studios, when there is no dancing, there is talk about fencing expertise, Latin, philosophy, and all the other skills which men of good taste profess."[55]

The Dance Masters and Their Treatises

There were three men in fifteenth-century Italy each of whom wrote a dance treatise: Domenico da Piacenza, Guglielmo Ebreo da Pesaro,[56] and Antonio Cornazano, with Guglielmo and Cornazano praising Domenico as their master and teacher. In other parts of Europe—Spain, France, England, Germany, and Burgundy—we have to wait until the sixteenth century before the names of men who taught, choreographed, and performed dances emerge. Up until the fifteenth century dance instruction had presumably been an oral practice, with courtiers learning new dances directly from those most skilled. Teachers of dance seem to have been uninterested in committing their choreographies to paper, whether to produce instruction manuals outlining the basic steps and principles of the dance style or to produce treatises on dance as a gift to their patrons. Dance was seen more as a physical skill than a written one, and it was not considered necessary to be able to write about dance in anything other than general, descriptive terms. In literary works the words used to describe scenes of people dancing were those words in common usage, rather than any specialized vocabulary. However, it was in the 1440s that this mindset began to change by the appearance first of Domenico's treatise, and, within the next two decades, by the appearance of Cornazano's and Guglielmo's treatises.[57] These men were responsible for teaching the children of the leading families of Italy and performing alongside them in public at state spectacles.[58] Their working lives were spent among the elite and their own social standing was not far removed from this milieu. Cornazano was born into one of the families of the minor nobility at Piacenza, and his whole life was centered on the courts of northern Italy as a poet, humanist, ambassador, military advisor, and courtier, as well as a skilled dancer and author of a dance treatise.[59] Domenico spent most of his working life at the d'Este court at Ferrara, where he is referred to in court records by the titles "spectabilis eques" and "spectabilis miles." He was a Knight of the Golden Spur, as was Guglielmo, who was knighted by the Holy Roman Emperor in Venice in 1469.[60]

Dance teaching in Italy in the fifteenth century was not confined solely to the authors of the dance treatises. Evidence has survived of other dance teachers, who worked both at the courts and in the cities, teaching the children of the middle-ranking merchant classes. Lorenzo Lavagnolo was one *maestro di ballo* who taught the children of the Gonzaga, Sforza, and d'Este families,[61] while Giuseppe Ebreo, the brother of Guglielmo, not only ran a dancing school in Florence but also was associated with Lorenzo de' Medici.[62] As a young girl Isabella d'Este (1474–1539) was taught by Guglielmo, as well as Lavagnolo (1485) and Antonio Tamburino (1489),[63] and her interest in dancing continued throughout her life. In 1505 she requested the services of her brother, Cardinal Ippolito d'Este's dancer, Ricciardetto, in order to help her practice for the approaching wedding celebrations of their brother Alfonso d'Este and Lucrezia Borgia. In 1421 a young man in Florence, Gherardino di Gherardo, was hired to give dance lessons to the two daughters of Paliano di Falco Paliani in their own house,[64] while other dance teachers hired space in which to run dance classes, as did Mariotto di Bastiano di Francesco in 1446 in Florence.[65] In the later fifteenth century one of the dance masters in vogue in Florence was Maestro Giorgio, who, with his colleague Fede, taught dance to some of the leading Florentine families: the Strozzi, the Sassetti, and the Cresci. Giorgio and Fede were succeeded in the early years of the sixteenth century by the dance master Lanzo.[66]

In the sixteenth century the number of dance masters increased, both those who produced treatises and those who just taught and performed. It is now possible to identify "at least 134 Italian dancing masters [who were] active in the sixteenth century."[67] Unlike their fifteenth-century colleagues, these Italian dance masters traveled and worked outside of Italy at the courts of France, Spain, Germany, and England.[68] One of the most influential was Pompeo Diobono from Milan, teacher of Cesare Negri and of many other leading figures in dance in the middle decades of the sixteenth century. Diobono traveled to the French court of Henri II in 1554, and he continued to live and work in France for many years, serving both Charles IX and Henri III.[69] Henri III was served by other Italian dance masters than Diobono; for example, Jean-Pierre Gallin and Francisque de la Serre both returned to France with Henri III after the latter's progress through Italy from Poland in 1574.[70] Negri also performed in the presence of Henri III at Cremona and Monza during the festivities there and worked in France during his career.[71] The year after Diobono arrived in France another Italian, born Baldarassino da Belgioioso but better known to posterity as Balthasar de Beaujoyeulx, entered the service of the French king as a member of the violin band. His talents lay not only in music, but also in choreography and the composition and direction of court ballets: *Le Paradis d'Amour* in 1572, *Le Ballet des Polonais* in 1573, and in 1581 *Le Balet Comique de la Reyne*. His collaboration with Catherine de' Medici on the court fêtes "set him apart from his contemporaries," as did his "accuracy, proportion, knowledge and inventiveness" and his own understanding that he was the creator of new choreographic forms.[72]

Negri himself was probably about eighteen at the time of Diobono's departure for France, and he carried on Diobono's teaching activities in Milan. Dance masters who studied under Negri also worked in Spain, Poland, Germany, and Flanders.[73] In spite of, or perhaps because of, his professional activities, Negri wrote one dance treatise, *Le gratie d'amore*, published in Milan in 1602.[74] It was reissued in 1604 under the title *Nuove inventione di balli*,[75] and in 1630 it was translated into Spanish. Caroso produced two dance treatises during his lifetime, *Il ballarino* in 1581 and *Nobiltà di dame* in 1600, while Lutio Compasso, who taught in Rome and Naples, produced the *Ballo della gagliarda* (1560), a collection of variations for the *gagliarda* from the simple to the extremely complex.[76] The composing of new variations for the dance genres of the *gagliarda* and the *canario* and *passo e mezzo* must have been a common occupation for the sixteenth-century Italian dance masters, as Compasso was not the only dance master to have published a collection of such variations. Fifteen eighty-nine saw Prospero Lutij di Sulmona's work published,[77] while in 1600 Livio Lupi da Caravaggio published his book of variations.[78] Ercole Santucci's treatise[79] (finished in 1614) also contains 360 variations on the basic *gagliarda* step—the *cinque passi*—as well as 71 *gagliarda mutanze* (sequences of variations) that vary in length from two to eight *tempi*.[80]

Although the French court was a center of dance spectacle, there does not appear to have been any treatises on dance produced by the dance masters there in the second half of the sixteenth century. The only two French dance treatises known today were produced outside of the court mileu. Jean Tabourot (1520–95), who first published the dance treatise *Orchésographie* under the pseudonym of Thoinot Arbeau in 1588,[81] studied law and then made a career in the church in provincial cities, and it is not known if he was ever present at the French court. In late 1527 Antonius Arena finished a dance treatise that was part of a collection of essays addressed to his fellow students at the University of Avignon.[82] In this document Arena not only discussed dances popular at the time, the *basse dance, branles, tourdion,* and galliard, but he also commented on the behavior expected while dancing, and on the "qualities that make a gentleman," without which the "true essence of the dance" would be lacking.[83]

The movement of dance masters in the sixteenth century from one European court to another is illustrated by the personnel at the English court, which, during the course of the century included Italian, French, and English dancers. Yet by the time of the ascension of Charles I to the English throne (1625) the French influence predominated, and the dance masters at the English court were either English, Scottish, or French.[84] Just as Beaujoyleulx was both a musician and dancer, it was common for these men to teach both dance and music. Thomas Cardell, for example, who replaced the Italian Jasper Gaffoyne as court dance master in 1574, also taught the lute.[85] Why no written treatises were produced (or if any were every trace of them has disappeared) in England during the sixteenth century is a moot point. There was certainly a vibrant dance culture, similar to that in the courts of France and Italy. The French *basse dance* was widely known and performed in the early sixteenth century in England. In 1521 Robert Coplande published *The Maner of dauncynge of bace daunces,* an explanation of the French dance genre. Yet, as the twenty-six choreographic descriptions found in the Gresley family papers (c. 1500) attest, by the end of the fifteenth century there was also a distinctive English dance practice, formed from an amalgam of French, Italian, and English elements.[86]

The first three decades of the seventeenth century saw a large number of changes in the dance style that had prevailed at the French court in the previous century. It is perhaps ironic that neither of the only two works which document this changing style originate from the French court itself. One is a work on the history and practice of dancing by a French dance teacher, François de Lauze, newly arrived in England and hopeful of work. De Lauze published his treatise

Apologie de la danse in 1623 and dedicated it to George Villiers, Marquess of Buckingham, and his wife. However, before the work could be published, a colleague, another French dance master employed by Buckingham, Barthélemy de Montagut, copied a draft of de Lauze's treatise which he had been shown by the latter, changed the name to *Louange de la danse*, dedicated it to his patron Buckingham, and all the while claimed the work as his own. Both de Lauze and Montagut describe the current fashionable dances, *gaillardes, courantes,* and *branles,* as well as offer advice on deportment. Unlike the treatises of Caroso or Negri, neither version has any comprehensive or systematic description of how to execute the individual steps.[87] The second work that documents the changing style of the early seventeenth century, *Instruction pour dancer,* is a manuscript collection of sixteen French dances, mostly *branles,* but also a *gavotte, bourrée, pavanne, passepied,* a torch dance, and two dances for four couples.[88] It is anonymous and undated, but is believed to have been written at the end of the sixteenth or in the early seventeenth century, before 1612.[89] Some of the dances show similarities to dances described by de Lauze, others are versions of *branles* found in Arbeau, while the *pavanne* resembles the Italian *pavaniglia.*[90]

In Spain, the top of the professional ladder for dance masters during the sixteenth, seventeenth, and eighteenth centuries was an appointment to one of the two posts as royal dancing master, one for the household of the king, the other in the queen's household.[91] Since these appointments were usually made for life, the opportunities for the aspiring dance master were not great, in spite of the fact that sometimes assistant dance teachers were appointed.[92] Other career options existed: for example, the position of dance master to an aristocratic family, or operating one's own dance school, or to be hired by a cathedral to instruct the choirboys who danced in the Corpus Christi processions.[93] A great deal of the information we have about the Spanish dance repertory and practice comes from the treatise written by Esquivel in 1642.[94] Esquivel had studied with the king's dance master, Antonio de Almenda, and although not a professional dance master himself, he was renowned for his expertise in dancing.[95] Esquivel's work discusses dancing at the male-only dance schools and is intended mainly for middle-class readers.[96] Esquivel does not give complete choreographies in his treatise, although he mentions twenty-four different dance genres, with the most information on the *pavana, gallarda,* and the *villano.* However, Esquivel does describe the curriculum of a dance school and the behavior expected of a gentleman when dancing outside the context of a court ball in far greater detail than any other dance treatise before him.[97]

The men who performed at the courts of Louis XIII and XIV were increasingly drawn from a close, interconnected group of families, the members of whom were often specialists in both music and dance. Dance teaching and performing was becoming increasingly professionalized in the sense that sons could follow in the same position or trade as their father, just as in other professions. Claude Balon's (1671–1744) father and grandfather, for example, both taught dance. Marriage within this group was also common. The celebrated dancer Michel Blondy (1670 or 1676–1739) was not only a student of the dance master Pierre Beauchamps (1631–1705), but also his nephew, as Beauchamps's sister had married a dance master called Blondy.[98] The same sense of professionalism in the ranks of the dance masters was also seen outside of France. Italian dance masters worked at the Viennese court throughout the seventeenth century. In 1626 the Venetian Santa Ventura started work at the court, teaching dance to the sons of Ferdinand II and the other courtiers, as well as choreographing court ballets and dances in opera productions. When he died in 1677 he was succeeded as dance master by his son Domenico, who also kept the post until his death.[99] It also became increasingly possible for the successful and sought-after dance performers, teachers, and choreographers to have long careers of forty to fifty years, and to leave to their heirs a considerable estate, as did Balon, Beauchamps, and Blondy. Even after retirement men like Beauchamps were sought after by courtiers and state officials for their expertise and help in organizing private ballet entertainments.[100] These professional dancers performed not only in ballets, masquerades, and masked balls at court, but they also performed in the public sphere—in the Opéra and the theater with the leading dramatists and musicians such as Molière and Lully,[101] as well as choreographing ballets for the productions in the Jesuit colleges in Paris, as did Guillaume-Louis Pécour (1653–1729),[102] Beauchamps, and Blondy. The demand for dance instruction exploded in the seventeenth century: in the 1680s in Paris alone there were more than two hundred dance schools.[103] Consequently, the dance masters often taught private pupils in Paris, in addition to their duties in instructing members of the royal family,[104] and the children of the nobility.

The sense of professionalism was undoubtedly helped by the creation in 1661 of the Académie Royale de Danse. Louis XIV was heavily involved in the creation of this body, and in the preface to the patent letters he wrote "that the purpose of the academy was 'to restore the art of dancing to its original perfection and to improve it as much as possible,' since 'as the result of the disorders caused by the latest wars, many people were now teaching dance without qualifications.'"[105] Before the creation of the Académie the musicians' guild was responsible for the "training of dancers throughout France, [and] granting them the mastership that allowed them to teach."[106] Needless to say, the division of power between the musicians' guild and the Académie Royale de Danse was accompanied by much disputation. The second institutional change that accelerated the professionalism of the French dancers was "the creation of a permanent dance troupe for the Opéra in 1672 under the direction of Beauchamps."[107]

Just as in the second half of the sixteenth century it was the Italian dance masters who taught at the courts of Europe, one hundred years later it was the turn of the French. French dance style and French dance teachers were highly fashionable and much sought after throughout Europe. In England Anthony L'Abbé (c. 1667–c. 1756), although French, worked in London for almost forty years, and quickly became an accepted member of the English dancing masters' fraternity. He performed at Lincoln's Inn Fields and Drury Lane theaters, and in 1714 was officially appointed as dance master to the new Hanoverian royal family, replacing Mr. Isaac, who, while never holding an official position, had taught dancing to members of the previous royal family since the 1680s.[108] L'Abbé, like his predecessor, also composed ball dances in honor of the king, George I, Queen Caroline, and their children and grandchildren.[109] For the period 1700–1735, Carol Marsh has identified more than one hundred dance masters who worked in London,[110] but apart from L'Abbé there were five others who were particularly prominent—the leaders of their profession: Thomas Caverley (1648–1745), Mr. Isaac, John Weaver (1673–1760), Edmund Pemberton (c. 1670s–1733), and John Essex.[111] All were held in high regard by their contemporaries: Caverley particularly for his teaching; Isaac for the ball dances he composed;[112] Pemberton for his work as notator and publisher of L'Abbé's ball dances.[113] Weaver's contribution was principally in the form of his writings on dance, including a translation from the French of Raoul-Auger Feuillet's treatise on dance, *Chorégraphie*, which was dedicated to Mr. Isaac.[114] Weaver was not the only person to publish translations of dance treatises, or to write his own.[115] P. Siris also translated Feuillet's *Chorégraphie* into English in 1706,[116] in 1728 John Essex published his translation of Pierre Rameau's *Le maître à danser* (1725) entitled *The Dancing-Master: or, The Art of dance Explained*, while Kellom Tomlinson (c. 1693–post 1753) published his own work on dance, *The Art of Dancing*, in 1735.[117]

The French dance style was also highly fashionable in Germany and was taught by both French and German dance masters, including pupils of Beauchamps. Louis Bonin, for example, after studying with Beauchamps, taught dance at the University of Jena. His treatise was written in German[118] and included a defense of the moral nature of dance, ballroom etiquette, the current dance types, and a "set of guidelines for judging dances and dancing masters."[119] Johann Pasch was a highly respected dance master in Leipzig who, it is believed, also studied with Beauchamps.[120] Pasch published his treatise on dance in 1707,[121] while Samuel Rudolph Behr (1670–1716) published three works on dance in 1703, 1709, and 1713.[122] Gottfried Taubert's treatise, *Rechtschaffener Tantzmeister* (1717), was a monumental work of over one thousand pages. It can be divided into three parts: the history of dance, its origins and sacred position in antiquity; the current dance practices including variants of the *courante, menuet,* and *bourrée;* and dance pedagogy, the dancing and etiquette at balls and dancing in the theater. It also included a translation of parts of Feuillet's treatise on dance.[123]

The Dance Notation

Compared to its sister art of music, the art of dance has a short history of notation systems. For the majority of the period 1400 to 1750 the method used for recording dance was a written description, which gave the number of performers and their opening positions, the sequences of steps and information as to which dancer performed which steps, the direction of the steps—forward, backward, sideways, circling around, and so on. The music that accompanied each dance was either not recorded at all, notated either before or after the choreography to which it belonged, or notated together in a separate section at the end of the choreographies. All the fifteenth- and sixteenth-century Italian dance treatises, the twenty-six fifteenth-century English dances and later country dance collections, and the dances from Arena's treatise all use a written description to record the choreographies. Two major choreographic elements which are not shown by this method are the floor patterns of each dance and the exact alignment of the steps and the music, although it is possible to reconstruct the floor plan and step alignment. While Domenico and Guglielmo often commented in their treatises on how the gestures of the dancers should be in harmony with the music, the written choreographic descriptions do not include any information on what these gestures are.[124] Like any written instructions or description of physical movements, ambiguity of meaning is the greatest problem in this method of recording dance. Usually the less ambiguous the description the longer and more complex it becomes. In spite of the problems associated with this method of recording dance, its use continued into the seventeenth century with de Lauze's treatise and the anonymous French manuscript, *Instruction pour dancer,* both recording dances in this way.

The fifteenth-century French *basse dance* treatises used abbreviations to record dances, as the names of the four steps—or five if one counts the *reverence*—were abbreviated to a single letter and the letters placed under the appropriate note of the musical notation.[125] The late fifteenth-century Spanish dance manuscript from the Archives of Cervera[126] records the Castilian version of the *basse dance*, the *baixa*. In this manuscript—just two sheets of parchment—the dances are recorded with graphic symbols for each step: one horizontal line for the single step; one short, one long, and a second short horizontal line all aligned vertically for the double step; a vertical line for the branle step; a figure like a "3" for the reprise step; and a vertical then an adjoining horizontal line for the reverence.[127]

Arbeau's descriptions of the social dances current in France in the second half of the sixteenth century—the *branles,* pavans, galliards, *basses dances,* coranto, almain, gavotte, *la volta,* and a sword dance called *les Bouffons* or the *Mattachins*—are also all recorded as a written description. However, Arbeau included in his treatise small woodcuts of dancers to illustrate some of the steps, as well as writing the step names alongside the music for each dance. This allows the reader to match each step (or movement) with the appropriate note of the music. Information on the spatial patterns of the dance, however, is still missing from Arbeau's treatise.

The choreographic record of dancing at the French court in the sixteenth and early seventeenth centuries is very slim, in spite of the fact that it was a frequent occurrence—the twenty-one years between 1597 and 1618 ninety-six ballets were performed at the French court—as even the written description method of recording the choreographies was not used for this repertoire. In both the English masque and the *ballets de cour* performed at the French and Württemberg courts, the choreographies consisted of geometrical figures, letters of the alphabet, and other figures or shapes formed by the dancers. The dances were long and complex; for example, the final dance from *Le Balet Comique de la Reyne* (1581) consisted of forty different geometrical figures. Only isolated examples of what these figures looked like still exist.[128] Moreover, even when the figures are recorded, they only reveal the spatial relationships of the dancers at one fixed moment. We are not able to tell how the dancers moved from one figure to another, what steps were used for these maneuvers, and how long each figure was held.[129]

The major source of dance figures from this period is the notebook of a French dance master who worked in Belgium circa 1614–19.[130] Of the 122 folios of this manuscript, 27 folios contain just over 450 drawings of figures for five to sixteen dancers, many of which are named. These figures are arranged in a systematic way. First, the same figure is recorded for differing numbers of dancers.

Second, both forward-facing and reverse images of the same figures were recorded. Third, composite figures were recorded, figures which were built up out of smaller (and often named) figures, to create more complex geometric shapes. Thus this dance manuscript represents a "canon" of widely used figures that existed at the time and was available to those dance masters working at the French and English courts. Such a resource was essential for a dance master, as in order to choreograph a dance that lasted for an hour with such a level of variety, the French and English dance masters would have had to have had knowledge of, and access to, a large number of figures or patterns which they could use in their compositions.

By the 1680s, however, the situation had changed, as there were at least four notation systems being developed in France.[131] Around 1674 Louis XIV requested Beauchamps to develop a system of dance notation. By 1684 Beauchamps was able to use the system he had developed "to record the chaconne from Lully's *Phaeton*."[132] However, Beauchamps did not publish his work, nor take out a privilege that would allow him to prevent others from publishing it. His system was published by the younger dance master Feuillet (1659/60–1710) in 1700 in a treatise entitled *Chorégraphie*.[133] This system of notation (now usually referred to as the Beauchamps-Feuillet system) became very popular and was used to notate dances in both published and manuscript form, of which around 350 have survived from France, England, Germany, Spain, and Portugal. One of the reasons for the popularity of this system of notation was that dance masters outside Paris and other major centers were able to quickly learn new dances and then to teach them to their students, satisfying the latter's desire to be abreast of the latest trends in French dance.[134] Thus for the first time there was a system of dance notation that was far more comprehensive and concise than those of the past, and which showed the steps, floor patterns, and the music. The information on the floor plan and step sequences are easy to follow, with the notation showing the steps in relation to a line representing the floor plan of the dance. Bar lines in the music that run across the top of the page, correlated to bar lines in the floor plan, indicate more precisely the timing of the steps. The components of each step are shown far more clearly than in previous notation systems, such as bending the knees, rising on the half-toe, jumps and springs, as well as movements of the hands and arms (although in practice these are rarely notated). The relationship of the dancers to each other is also generally clear, although relative positions are shown much more clearly in Favier notation.[135]

The publication in 1716 by Gregorio Lambranzi, *Neue und curieuse theatralische Tantz-Schul* (The New and Curious School of Theatrical Dancing), can be seen as a pictorial form of "notation," comprising as it does of 101 engravings of popular theatrical dances, or dances in the grotesque style performed by both men and women.[136] Each engraving shows costumed dancers on stage, along with instructions in German and Italian, and the music at the top of each engraving.[137] As Lambranzi himself says in his preface to the reader, his book provides suggestions for improvising, rather than an encyclopedic method of study.

> My aim is not to describe in detail the choreography of these dances or any particular *pas* [step], still less to depict all their possible variations; this would be too ambitious a work and, moreover, would necessitate a large volume. But, by means of the illustration and its accompanying air, . . . I shall portray a principal character in appropriate costume, the style of his dance and the manner of its execution. I shall also explain the essential matters in such illustrations and indicate what *pas* should be employed. However, it is not my intention to restrict anyone to my method but to leave each dancer free to adapt it as he pleases.[138]

As I have briefly described in this section, the early decades of the eighteenth century witnessed a remarkable flowering of dance manuals in three different languages—French, English, and German. This intense interest, accompanied by writing and publication, in both practical and theoretical aspects of the dance practice continued until the mid-eighteenth century with the work of Auguste Ferrère, who worked on a method to notate theatrical dances by a combination of a modified Beauchamps-Feuillet notation, verbal description, and diagrams.[139]

The Dance Music

The music that was recorded in the fifteenth-century Italian dance treatises from Italy, France, and England was all notated in the same way—as one line of music, the tenor.[140] However, the music provided by the instrumental ensembles which accompanied the dancing was polyphonic. While almost any instrument could be used to accompany dancing in the thirteenth and fourteenth centuries, the two most frequent were the vielle (a bowed string instrument) and singing by the dancers themselves.[141] In the fifteenth century the shawm band (the *pifferi*) became the predominant instrumental ensemble used to accompany dances. In the early fifteenth century this ensemble consisted of three shawms, a soprano instrument, and two tenor shawms. By the mid-fifteenth century a brass instrument with a slide mechanism (some version of the trombone) had

Figure 1.1. Outdoor dance scene from fifteenth-century Italy. Detail from *Continence of Scipio*, cassone panel from workshop of Apollonio di Giovanni. Victoria and Albert Museum, London / Art Resource, New York.

become the standard third member of the shawm band.[142] It is this ensemble which is often depicted in contemporary illustrations that show dancing at a ball, or during a banquet, or outside in a city piazza, as shown in Figure 1.1. Even though it was increasingly common as the fifteenth century progressed for the instrumentalists who played in the shawm bands to be able to read notated music, they did not do so while performing: they improvised around the single line of music, one part above and one part below the tenor.[143] The instrumental ensembles that accompanied dancing often had to do so for hours at a time— balls are often described as lasting all night—and "the only really efficient way to do this . . . was through the use of various kinds of improvisations."[144]

Because much of the musical accompaniment to dancing was improvised, not a great deal of fifteenth-century dance music has survived. The situation was to change in the sixteenth century, as dance music, and instrumental music in general, became part of music publishers' output.[145] Collections of dances were published in lute tablature (particularly in Italy), keyboard tablature (particularly in Germany), and guitar tablature (particularly in Spain). Collections of *branles, basses dances,* pavanes, and galliards were published in instrumental arrangements by French publishers such as Pierre Attaingnant (c. 1494–1551/52),[146] the 1551 collection by Tielman Susato in Antwerp, and the collection of over 300 French dance pieces by the German composer Michael Praetorius, *Terpsichore* (1612).[147] When music was recorded in the sixteenth-century dance treatises it was either in lute tablature or, as in the treatises of Caroso and Negri, with the melody in staff notation accompanied by lute tablature that provided both the melody and the lower parts.

Even though published dance music was only in four, five, or six parts, or in tablature, this did not mean that the musical accompaniment for actual performances was limited to a small number of instruments. The musical forces which accompanied the sixteenth-century danced spectacles were correspondingly on a lavish scale. The six *intermedi* that were performed between the acts of the comedy *La Pellegrina* in Florence in 1589 involved at least twenty-five instrumentalists, sixty singers, as well as twenty-seven dancers.[148] The music for the dance that concluded the sixth *intermedio* alternates between sections for five parts and sections for three parts. The five-part sections were accompanied by all the available instrumental forces,[149] that is, two *chitarroni*, two *lire*, four lutes, two bass viols, four viols, one violin, four trombones, two *cornetti*, one cittern, one psaltery, one *mandola*, and one *arciviolata lira*,[150] as well as all the singers.[151] Similar forces were used for *Le Balet Comique de la Reyne* performed at the French court on 15 October 1581, where the instrumentalists and singers numbered forty in each group. Sometimes all eighty played and sang together, while at other times accompanied vocal solos alternated with music for larger ensembles of six to twelve voices.[152]

The instrumentation for balls were not on such a grand scale as that used in the theatrical productions. For the balls at the court of Henri III in the 1580s, not only was the order in which the dances were performed fixed, but so too was the choice of instruments to accompany each type of dance. The first two dances, a pavan and then an almain, were danced to pipes and tabors, while violins accompanied the *branles*, correntes, and *la volta*. The final dance, a galliard, was performed to an ensemble of violins and *cornetti*.[153] A performance of the *volta* at Henri III's court can be seen in Figure 1.2.

The musical forces available for performances of the *ballet de cour* in seventeenth-century France were formally organized into three administrative units: the singers of the royal chapel, the musicians of the king's chamber, and the musicians of the king's stables (the *grande écurie*).[154] The wind instrumentalists were usually attached to the *grande écurie*, and they included trumpets, oboes, crumhorns, fifes, and drums. The musicians of the king's chamber were primarily string players and were divided into two ensembles, the "24 violins of the king" (*vingt-quatre violons du roi*) and a smaller group of string players, the *petits violons*, or *violons du cabinet*. Both string ensembles were divided into five parts, and it was this five-part framework that "became the model for the orchestra Lully created at the Paris Opéra in 1672."[155]

Figure 1.2. The dance *la volta* performed during a ball at the Valois court, c. 1580. Musée des Beaux-Arts, Rennes. Réunion des Musées Nationaux / Art Resource, New York.

The music that accompanied the dancing during the balls, danced spectacles, and other state celebrations was both composed especially for the dance and also adapted from pre-existing music. Domenico states in his dance treatise that he composed all the tunes recorded for the *balli* except for the dance *La fia guilmina,* for which he adapted the chanson of the same name.[156] The adaptation of popular songs by the dance masters for a new choreography continued in the sixteenth century. The music for Negri's *balletto So ben mi che ha bon tempo* is Orazio Vecchi's chanson of the same name, while many *basse dance* tenors came from popular songs. The music for the anonymous *balletto La battaglia,*[157] a dance for three couples that represents a joust between the men and the women, has passages reminiscent of Clément Janequin's (c. 1485–1558) famous and influential chanson *La guerre* (published in 1528 by Attaingnant), as well as a whole section that is almost identical to the original chanson.[158] Not only is the melody identical in both pieces, but so are the melodic "echoes" repeated down the octave.[159] The sequence of pre-existing music turned into dance music also operated in the reverse order. Newly composed dance music also sometimes captured the imagination of the musical public, and composers used it as the basis for their non-dance compositions. One of the most celebrated examples of borrowing in this direction is Emilio de' Cavalieri's music for the final *ballo* of the 1589 marriage celebrations. In the one hundred years after the publication of the music and choreography, around 240 compositions were written, all of which used the chordal-bass pattern of Cavalieri's *ballo*.[160]

When music was required for the extensive choreographies of an Italian *intermedio* or a French fête, it was especially composed for the occasion. The choreography was composed first, then when this task had been completed, the music was composed so that it fitted with the choreography. If necessary, text was then added as the final stage in the compositional process. This process was followed for the final *ballo* of the 1589 *intermedi*: Cavalieri wrote both the choreography and the music, then Laura Guidiccioni composed the text for the *ballo*. This order of composition was the most common practice,[161] and the addition of the choreography first and the text last certainly allowed for the creation of more complex dance patterns and sequences than would have been the case if everything had to be accommodated to the demands of a pre-existing text or pre-existing music.[162]

The Dance Genres

While it is very clear that dancing was a common activity across all levels of society during the thirteenth and fourteenth centuries, the absence of specific choreographic sources from this period makes the identification and characterization of specific dance genres difficult.[163] It is possible, however, to identify a few general characteristics that were consistently associated with specific dance terms. The term *carole* first appears in the early twelfth century and was the most popular social dance from 1200 to 1350.[164] It was danced in a line or a circle, with the dancers holding hands and moving to the left.[165] *Caroles* were usually described as being accompanied by the singing of the dancers rather than instruments.[166] In the poems of Jean Froissart the term *danse* is used "to indicate dancing accompanied by instrumental music."[167] From descriptions of court balls (c. 1350–1400) which Froissart gives in his poems, the *danse* appears to have been a new, contrasting choreographic genre from the *carole*. Froissart describes the court balls as beginning with *danses* accompanied by wind instruments. Then the musicians stop playing, and *caroles* are danced to voices alone.[168]

In the dance treatises of fifteenth-century Italy there were two dance genres recorded: the *ballo* and the *bassadanza*. Each dance in both these genres was individually choreographed with its own unique sequence of steps and floor patterns, and each was individually named, and, in the case of a *ballo*, had its own music that was constructed of sections of differing meters and speeds.[169] The Italian style of dance genres that were constructed with sections of changing meters and speeds continued into the sixteenth century. The dance genres found in Caroso's and Negri's treatises included the *balletto*,[170] *brando*,[171] *cascarda*,[172] *bassa*, and *alta*, all of which have sections in different meters and speeds to a greater or lesser extent,[173] and the *pavaniglia, gagliarda, tordiglione, canario,* and *passo e mezzo*. The last five genres were all characterized by sequences of variations, hundreds of which may be found in the surviving treatises.

The other fifteenth-century genre which is frequently mentioned in descriptions of spectacles is the *moresca*, although no choreographic descriptions of this genre seem to have been recorded. *Moresche* were frequently performed during formal state occasions, such as banquets, triumphal entries, jousts and tournaments, marriage celebrations, and dramatic performances: they were more than private entertainments. In this genre the dancers were often masked or had their faces blackened and wore exotic costumes. Characteristics of the *moresche* included danced combat and other pantomimic dancing, including the depiction of agricultural work, exotic characters such as wild men, mythological figures such as Hercules, and allegorical figures such as vices and virtues. In spite of the implications of its name, there are actually very few recorded examples of moorish participants in *moresche*.[174] The idea that the *moresca* was originally a "moorish" dance from Spain originates in the seventeenth century and was derived solely from the etymology of the term.[175]

The French *basse dance* and the Castilian *baixa* and Aragonese *baja* were also individual arrangements of the four available steps, and each dance also had its own name.[176] Every *basse dance* always began with a *reverence* or bow. Unlike the Italian *ballo* or *bassadanza* each French *basse dance* had the same floor track, as in each *basse dance* the couple processed up and down the center of the dance space. In spite of the similarity of the name, the French *basse dance* and the Italian *bassadanza* were not the same genre; one performed north of the Alps, the other in the south. They were distinct genres, and when the Italian dance masters wished to compose a French style *basse dance*, as they did for the *bassadanze Bassa Franzesse* and *Borges Francese*, the result was quite different from that of their other *bassadanze*, both in the choice of steps and in the combination and arrangement of those steps into the choreographic sequence.

From the sixteenth century onward there is increasing evidence that the dance genres of western Europe can be divided into two broad categories: those genres that were "international," that is, they were performed throughout the courts of Europe, and those genres that were particular to one country alone, such as the Spanish *villano*.[177] As described in Esquivel's dance treatise of 1642, the *villano* was a solo dance in which the dancer was permitted to improvise in order to display his technique and skill.[178] In contrast, the *basse dance* was performed not only in France and Burgundy, but also in England and northern Spain, as was also the case for the French *branles*.[179] The two genres that best exemplified this international dance practice were the pavane and galliard, as both dances were extremely popular all over Europe in the sixteenth century.[180] For example, a *gallarda* and *pavana* were performed at an evening of dancing held as part of the marriage celebrations in 1560 for Philip II of Spain and Isabel de Valois of France, at which were present members of the Spanish, French, and Italian courts.[181] The movement of members of the elite from one court to another, whether for marriage or as part of an embassy, was a major factor in the spread of dance genres across Europe, while another contributing factor was the movement of the dance masters themselves. Even when a dance genre like the galliard was known and performed across Europe, there were different variations and steps and step sequences popular in different places. Negri states this quite explicitly at the beginning of his description of the dance *La nizzarda*: "*Nizzarda* is a joyful dance to which one is not able to give precise rules, as one can for the other dances, because each person in his own country dances it in his own manner."[182]

The English country dances were first recorded and published by John Playford in 1651,[183] although references to dances with the same name as those in Playford's collection are found in the sixteenth century, and in his treatise of 1623 de Lauze refers to the English "*contredanses*." Furthermore, there are several manuscript collections of country dances which preserve different versions of dances from those published by Playford, an indication of the oral transmission of these dances among the gentry before Playford's publications.[184] The dances themselves are group dances for couples, either standing in a line one behind the other for as many couples as there were dancing (called a "longways" formation), or for two, three, or four couples in a circle or a square. The dances were extremely popular, with eleven editions of Playford's collection appearing between 1651 and 1701, and another six between the years 1701 and 1728.[185] One hundred and five dances were recorded by Playford in his first edition, but by 1728 this number had increased to about 900. It was the visual patterns formed by the dancers rather than the steps used that created the most interest in these dances,[186] as well as the opportunities for social interaction among the dancers as the various figures of the dance progressed, and as the couples moved down and then back up the set again repeating the same patterns but with a new second (or third) couple. These dances were introduced to France from England in 1684 when Mr. Isaac visited the French court to teach its members the English dances. In the following year the French dance master André Lorin traveled to England specifically to learn these dances. Lorin's first collection of *contredanses* contains nine dances (out of a total of thirteen) that are concordant with English country dances from the 1686 seventh edition of Playford's *The Dancing Master*.[187] The genre soon became very popular at the French court, as it provided the opportunity for larger groups to dance together, a characteristic that was not a common feature of the other French dance genres of the time.

In spite of the migration of the English country dances, the dance style that was ubiquitous in Europe circa 1650 to 1750 was French.[188] The dance genre that opened the seventeenth-century formal court ball was a suite of *branles*. These dances were danced in a single line, alternating men and women, led by the king whose partner was the queen, and then members of the royal family in order of rank. Other dance genres that were primarily performed as couple dances at court balls were the *courante, menuet, passepied, bourrée, gavotte,* and *rigaudon,* whereas the *sarabande, gigue, forlana, loure, canarie, chaconne, passacaille,* and *entrée* were primarily theatrical dances.[189] The division between the theatrical dances and the ballroom dances was not absolute, as specific choreographies from the theatrical genres did establish themselves in the repertoire of social dances and were danced at balls, in particular the *sarabande, gigue, forlana,* and *loure.*

The Dance Performers

Throughout the period covered by this book the major category of performers of the dances discussed were members of the elite. Aristocratic men and women, courtiers, ambassadors, princes of the church, all were both participants and spectators on an almost daily basis. Dance was an acceptable pastime, a part of aristocratic life and civilized behavior for centuries. The Burgundian knight Geoffroi de Charny, who lived in the first half of the fourteenth century, wrote in his treatise on chivalry that dancing was one of the pastimes that men of knightly rank should pursue if they wished to safeguard their reputation and honor.

> Yet is should be apparent that the finest games and pastimes that people who seek such honor should never tire of engaging in would be in the pastimes of jousting, conversation, dancing, and singing in the company of ladies and dam-

sels as honorably as is possible and fitting, while maintaining in word and deed and in all places their honor and status. All good men-at-arms ought rightly to behave thus.[190]

Christine de Pisan's *The Treasure of the City of Ladies* from 1405 was above all a practical book, a guide for women—mostly those with power and authority—in their everyday lives. As far as Christine was concerned dancing was a normal part of court life, and an activity that was entirely suitable for aristocratic women. This attitude continued right through to the eighteenth century, even when professional dancers both male and female were forging careers in the public theaters of Europe. In the early eighteenth century the highest accolade given to a professional dancer was when he or she danced like a high-ranking person, that is, with a "noble" air.

Members of the elite started learning to dance at an early age, and the children of a ruler often performed in public before they reached adolescence. Ippolita Sforza was only ten when she danced at Tristano Sforza's wedding in Milan in 1455, while one of the daughters of Louis XIV, Madame de Duchesse de Bourbon, appeared in the court ballet *Le triomphe de l'amour* at the age of seven and a half.[191] Dance lessons started at an early age for children of the elite. Louis XIV, for example, started dance lessons in 1644 when he was six years old.[192] The lessons, which lasted for two to three hours every day, continued for the next twenty-five years. Louis XIV made his stage debut in 1651 when he was thirteen, dancing in the court ballet *Cassandre*.[193] Sixteen seventy saw his last appearance in the court ballet *Les amants magnifiques*. Over almost two decades Louis XIV danced in forty major court ballets in about eighty different roles. The Princesse de Conti, one of Louis XIV's illegitimate daughters, was also a superb dancer and had danced leading roles in every court ballet and at every court ball for fifteen years before she announced her retirement in 1701, at the age of thirty-six.[194]

Courtiers performed at both informal dances in private rooms, in formal public balls that were part of state events, as well as in what now might be termed "theatrical" productions: the *moresche* and *intermedi* from fifteenth- and sixteenth-century Italy; the dances choreographed by Negri for the visits of the Habsburg rulers; the French fêtes, English masques, and Spanish court entertainments; and the seventeenth-century French court ballets (*ballet de cour*). The presence of members of the aristocracy on these occasions does not mean that the dances performed—the *moresche* or *entrées*—were simple, easy dances. Quite the reverse. Lynn Matluck Brooks summarizes the aristocratic style of dancing in seventeenth-century Spain as "restrained virtuosity and carefully modulated display. . . . The leg- and footwork is complicated and challenging both physically and mentally, with the great detail in each step and figure demanding concentration and precision."[195] During this period the dance practice of the elite was complex, sophisticated, and difficult: it needed rigorous and regular training, an expert memory, and, above all, every movement, step, and gesture had to appear to be entirely natural. If this was not the case, then the aristocratic dancer laid himself or herself open to public ridicule and laughter. For Castiglione, writing during the second decade of the sixteenth century, it was already a necessity for a courtier to be skilled in the art of dance. The ability to perform gracefully, seemingly without any effort, was one of the distinguishing marks of a courtier, and its absence exposed a courtier to derision from colleagues. In his memoirs of the court at Versailles, Saint-Simon describes the fate of a courtier when he appeared at the two balls in honor of the marriage of the Duc de Chartes in 1692.

> I cannot pass over in silence a very ridiculous adventure which occurred at both of these balls. A son of Montbron . . . was among the company. He had been asked if he danced well: and he had replied with a confidence which made every one hope that the contrary was the case. Every one was satisfied. From the first bow he became confused, and he lost step at once. He tried to divert attention from his mistake by affected attitudes, and carrying his arms high; but this made him only more ridiculous, and excited bursts of laughter, which . . . degenerated at length into regular hooting. On the morrow, instead of flying the court or holding his tongue, he excused himself by saying that the presence of the King had disconcerted him, and promised marvels for the ball which was to follow. He was one of my friends, and I felt for him. . . . As soon as he began to dance at the second ball, those who were near stood up, those who were far off climbed wherever they could to get a sight; and the shouts of laughter were mingled with clapping of hands. Every one, even the King himself, laughed heartily. . . . Montbron disappeared immediately afterwards, and did not show himself again for a long time. It was a pity he exposed himself to this defeat, for he was an honourable and brave man.[196]

Part of the reason for the laughter of the King and the rest of the court was that dancing was seen as essential to the education of a nobleman, and figured highly in the evaluation of a person's worth, not only in sixteenth- and seventeenth-century France but throughout Europe during the Renaissance and baroque. In Germany, for example, dance was regarded by the aristocracy as a traditional knightly accomplishment, along with fencing, riding, and music. Dance taught self-control, which was itself a sign of noble virtue, and a graceful bearing, both prerequisites for those of the elite.[197] Saint-Hubert made the same point in his treatise: "Everyone knows that, for a young nobleman to be polished, he must learn how to ride, to fence, and to dance. The first skill increases his dexterity, the second his courage, the last his grace and disposition. Each of these exercises being useful at an appropriate time, one can say that they are of equal value."[198] Thus through the dancing lessons and performances "good co-ordination of movement, agility, balance, concentration, memory, sense of orientation, as well as civility, ethics and ease of manner" were instilled into the aristocratic pupils.[199] The dances which they performed with "their steps 'in' and 'off' balance, their sudden changes of focus and rhythm, their numerous beats and bounds [and] their ornate . . . patterns" all gave to the students an acute awareness and control over their body that extended to all social situations and encounters.[200]

Dancing alongside the members of the elite for much of the period were the dance masters. We know that Domenico da Piacenza not only choreographed dances for weddings and important state functions at the d'Este court and other leading centers in Italy, but he also performed in public as a partner with the women from the leading families. In 1455 Francesco Sforza asked Domenico to come to Milan to organize the dances for the wedding of Tristano Sforza, Francesco's illegitimate son, and Beatrice d'Este, the illegitimate daughter of Niccolo III d'Este. On this occasion Domenico not only choreographed and directed several large "ballets," but also participated in the dancing himself.[201] In one of the dances Domenico danced with Bianca Maria Sforza, while the other performers were Galeazzo Maria and Ippolita Sforza, the children of Bianca Maria and Duke Francesco Sforza, the Marchioness Barbara of Mantua, and the Marquess Guglielmo of Monferrato, and Beatrice d'Este who danced with Alessandro Sforza.[202] In 1481 when Isabella d'Este was only six, a letter records the fact that Isabella had twice danced with Guglielmo.[203]

Information on dancing and dance masters from early sixteenth-century Venice is found in the diary of Marin Sanudo.[204] From Sanudo's descriptions of the allegorical pantomimes, the *momaria*, it is clear that dance masters were engaged to choreograph and teach new dances to the members of the *compagnie della calza*.[205] The members of the *compagnie*—young noblemen—then performed these dances usually together with a few professional dancers.[206] Just as in the previous century, these Venetian dance masters also appeared in public at balls, dancing as the partner of an aristocratic woman. For example, on 18 March 1533 the Infanta Margherita was welcomed into Verona and honored with a banquet and a ball, as well as further balls on the following two days. At the ball on the 18 March the Infanta danced one dance with the dance master Pelegrin.[207]

Dance masters also performed alongside children of the elite and the well-to-do in the ballets produced in the Jesuit colleges; for example, in the 1715 production at the college of Louis-Le-Grand in Paris there were thirty professional dancers and nineteen students who danced with them, while in the 1749 production these numbers had increased to forty-nine professionals and twenty-five students.[208] These ballets, or danced interludes, occurred between the acts of a play,[209] usually written by the professor of rhetoric and performed by his students, and the dances were intended to explain the allegorical message of the play (as well as provide relief from the rather turgid drama for the several thousand spectators).[210] The dance masters who taught and performed at Louis-Le-Grand from the 1670s onward were the leading dancers of their day,[211] and the productions were spectacular, with complex scenery, stage machines and lavish costumes.[212] The interest and enthusiasm of the Jesuits for dance as a legitimate and worthy part of their teaching program caused the production of these danced spectacles to spread to other teaching institutions, including convents, such as the Abbaye au Bois in Paris, that taught girls from upper-class families.[213]

At the end of the sixteenth century Negri provides a long list of the occasions at which he danced before leading members of the Milanese and Habsburg rulers and dignitaries, as well as at other Italian courts.[214] In 1561 Negri performed at the wedding of Guglielmo, duke of Mantua to Leonora, the daughter of the Holy Roman Emperor, to, according to Negri, much acclaim.[215] Unfortunately, Negri does not say whether he danced with the bride or with any of the noble ladies at these celebrations, or at any of the other similar events at which he performed. The dancing activities of the members of the elite did not falter as the sixteenth century drew to a close. Negri himself lists the noted dancers—both male and female—in Milan from 1554 onward, almost all of whom were members of the elite.[216] The courtiers continued to dance in "theatrical" entertainments, as is illustrated by the names of the dancers for the 1599 festivities in Milan. The torch-bearing dancers were divided into five groups of noble ladies and four groups of gentlemen.[217]

The interest and participation in dancing among the elite did not end even when they entered enclosed religious orders. For example, dancing occurred in the fifty or so convents in Venice, especially during the carnival season, as many of the three thousand plus nuns were from the elite of Venetian society.[218] In the sixteenth and seventeenth centuries many Venetian noblewomen entered a convent because their parents could only afford to give a large dowry to one or two of their daughters, rather than because the girls themselves had a spiritual vocation. Thus these women were reluctant to relinquish completely the enjoyments from their previous, uncloistered lives. Even though the church authorities condemned the "abuses and excesses" that occurred, the "eating and drinking, playing, singing and dancing,"[219] the nuns themselves continued to enjoy both dancing themselves and providing a place for public entertainments, including the offering of wine, refreshments, and dancing to masked revelers who arrived at the convent expecting such fare.[220]

In Ferrara soon after her marriage to the Duke, Alfonso II d'Este, in 1579, Margherita Gonzaga encouraged and led a group of ladies who performed elaborate dances for the entertainment of the court. In 1581 the Florentine ambassador wrote of one such dance he saw: "The Duke [Alfonso II d'Este] wanted his Eminence [Cardinal Farnese, the most recently arrived of the guests], to see a very highly worked-out dance [*ballo molto artificioso*] performed by the Duchess, Donna Marfisa, and ten or twelve of the other ladies."[221] In the following year it was reported: "Yesterday, during the usual small party, the Duchess, Donna Marfisa, Signora Bradamante, and some other ladies (there were eight of them altogether), did a large new *ballo* . . . the dance was done twice, with costumes, and without, to the accompaniment of a substantial piece of music for voices and instruments."[222] These dances, choreographed and performed by the Duchess and her ladies, continued to be a regular feature of Ferrarese court life, "particularly during the carnival season and in honor of distinguished visitors."[223] As Iain Fenlon points out, it was the Duchess Margherita who "was responsible for training the ladies of their court to perform elaborate dances of their own devising."[224] Noble ladies and gentlemen choreographing dances were not new, Ippolita Sforza and Lorenzo de' Medici are two examples from the fifteenth century, but one assumes that Margherita must have been trained in dance technique by the dance master at the Mantuan court in her childhood and adolescence. As well as performing in the *ballets de cour*, Louis XIII also had an interest in choreographic composition. For the 1635 *Ballet de la merlaison* Louis is credited with creating the steps, the musical airs, and the costume designs.[225] Certainly aristocratic and royal women were influential in danced court entertainments. Catherine de' Medici and Marie de' Medici in France, Margherita Gonzaga in Ferrara, and Queen Anna in England all had significant input into the plot, or conceit, of the spectacle, the appropriate costumes, the performance of the dances, and, in the case of Margherita, the creation of the choreography.[226]

In the English court masques the masquers were all noble, often led by the queen herself, as in the *Masque of Blackness* (1605) and the *Masque of Queens* (1609), or Prince Henry in *Oberon* (1611), as were the dancers in the Spanish *máscaras*, staged spectacles to honor members of the royal family.[227] The sixteenth-century French court fêtes were also performed by members of the court. As Margaret McGowan discusses in her essay in this volume, Henri III was "obsessed" with dancing and was himself an expert performer. Beaujoyeulx certainly choreographed the complicated dances for the 1573 and 1581 fêtes, but the dancers were all courtiers.[228] Louis XIII continued the tradition by dancing in the *ballets de cour*, as did Louis XIV and his children, the Dauphin, the Princesse de Conti, and Madame la Duchesse de Bourbon. In the *ballets de cour* the danced *entreés* were sometimes solely performed by nobles—both men and women—and sometimes by both nobles and professionals, as was the case in *Le triomphe de l'amour* where the Comte de Brionne danced as Bacchus, and his six followers were evenly divided between noble and professional dancers.[229] In England in the later seventeenth century the standard of dancing by members of the court was much reduced from that before the Puritan Interregnum,[230] but when masques were produced at court, as in 1675, both courtiers and members of the royal family performed, as well as professional dancers from France and England.[231] Just as in fifteenth-century Italy, seventeenth-century dance masters also partnered aristocratic women at court balls, as, for example, during a masked ball held during the 1683 carnival celebrations, when Pécour and Létang *le cadet* danced a chaconne with the Princesse de Conti and Mademoiselle de Laval.[232]

The dances of the elite did not, of course, remain solely within that restricted circle. The wealthy middle class, merchants and lawyers, were just as interested in dance as those in the upper level of society, and just as keen to learn the dances performed by the elite. Thus dances first choreographed for court balls were later learned and performed by members of the middle class. In 1517 in Bologna dances recorded fifty to sixty years earlier in Guglielmo's treatise were still being performed at balls for members of the urban merchant and university communities. The "poet, soldier, bon vivant and judge," Antonius Arena, is the best illustration of the middle-class dancer.[233] Arena's time at the University of Avignon (c. 1518–1527), where he studied law, was also the period in which he developed his passion for dancing, and where he attended many balls and feasts.[234]

Arena was not the only lawyer interested in dance in sixteenth-century France. Apart from learning the fashionable dances, lawyers also copied the elite by producing ballets. In 1600, for example, the lawyer Bernard presented a ballet in his home as part of his wedding celebrations.[235] The interest of members of the legal profession in dance is not surprising, as "[l]awyers and magistrates enjoyed high social status and the power such high-robe families wielded encouraged them to cultivate the same diversions as nobles."[236] The association of law and dance was not confined to continental Europe. In England in the sixteenth and seventeenth centuries the Inns of Court had a vigorous dance tradition, which included the presentation of masques for court festivities.[237] Their reputation for dancing was such that John Playford, in the introduction to the 1651 first edition of *The English Dancing Master*, commented upon it: "The Gentlemen of the Innes of Court, whose sweet and ayry Activity has crowned their Grand Solemnities with Admiration to all Spectators."[238]

The intersection between the dance practice of the elite and the middle classes is seen not only in the gradual movement of the dances enjoyed by the court into the balls of the merchant and university communities. In the 1620s and 1630s Louis XIII and his nobles also staged performances of the *ballets de cour* for members of the bourgeois in public theaters, especially in the *Hôtel de ville*, the City Hall.[239] The reasons for the decision by Louis XIII to perform himself outside a court setting were most likely a mixture of political expediency (a desire "to cement court/city relations"), the need for self-display by the members of the court, and the desire by the "noble inventors of ballets . . . [to have] their ingenuity . . . more widely appreciated."[240] Almost a century later, from 1715 to the end of the *ancien régime*, rather than performing in front of the wealthy bourgeoise, members of the aristocracy were dancing with them in the public balls held in the theater in the Palais-Royal in Paris. At these balls there was none of the formality and observance of the social order that characterized the formal court balls. There were no formal invitations, and admission was dependent only on a payment of six pounds. Spectators were also permitted to watch those dancing, the latter of whom normally wore masks. The dances that were performed at these balls were usually group dances, rather than the couple dances favored in the formal court balls.[241]

The Dance Performance Spaces

In fourteenth- and fifteenth-century Italy dancing took place both indoors and outdoors, both in the major piazzas as well as in the gardens of the elite. The indoor dance spaces were not rooms specifically designated as ballrooms. The great halls in which dances were usually held were also the places in which banquets and receptions were conducted. When balls were held the dancing took place in the middle of the room, which was left empty, while tiers of seats were erected along the sides of the space to accommodate the members of the court. Normally those ladies and gentlemen who were intending to participate in the dancing were seated in separate areas, while a third section of the seating was allocated to the women who were not involved in the dancing. This area was the least accessible from the dance floor. The benches or seats and the walls of the hall were often covered with precious fabrics such as velvets and cloth of gold, or tapestries, in order to increase the aura of luxury, and to impress upon participants the wealth of the host. At one end of the hall it was very common to have a *credenza* (dresser) set out with costly dishes and plates of gold and silver. If the host family did not own enough precious tapestries or plate to produce the required effect of splendor, then these had to be borrowed, as happened in 1491 for the marriage celebrations of Alfonso I d'Este (heir to the Duchy of Ferrara) and Anna Sforza, daughter of the late duke of Milan, Galeazzo Maria Sforza. The duke of Ferrara, Ercole d'Este, faced with a depleted and indebted treasury, raided all his residences throughout the duchy for "tapestries, plate, works of art and any other luxury items which could be put to use."[242]

When the dancing took place outdoors in an urban space a stage was often constructed in the middle of the main piazza on which the dancing took place, and on which the king or prince, his court and honored guests were seated, while around the sides of the piazza stands were built to accommodate the spectators. The stage and seats were also covered with carpets, and expensive fabrics formed a canopy over the stage. Sometimes wooden architectural structures which resembled the indoor spaces were erected and were decorated with tapestries, precious fabrics, leaves and flowers, and gauze veils that formed a temporary ceiling. Dancing also occurred outdoors in gardens as is illustrated in one of the series of frescoes from the d'Este country villa Belfiore.[243] Here Alberto and his court are shown hunting, then feasting, then dancing by a fountain.[244] On other occasions a large tent was erected in which the dancing could take place.[245]

The practice of building temporary dance halls in outdoor spaces continued in the sixteenth and seventeenth century. One example is the 1573 ballet performed on 19 August for the visit of the Polish ambassadors to Henri III, king of France. For this production a wooden theater was especially built in the gardens of the Tuileries palace.[246] Perhaps the culmination of outdoor danced spectacles can be seen in the fêtes held at Versailles in the 1660s and 1670s.[247] The first fête, *Les Plaisirs de l'Isle Enchantée*, was held in 1664, and the entertainments included an opening procession followed by a tournament, a feast with music and dancing, a comedy-ballet by Molière and Lully, and a final court ballet.[248] The opening procession started in the gardens behind the hunting lodge and continued down the central walkway (the *Grand* or *Royale Allée*) on the second day of the festivities, with the performance of the comedy ballet, and concluded at the end of the walkway with the *Ballet du palais d'Alcine*, that took place on three islands in the Basin of Apollo, a large lake at the end of the garden.[249] Six hundred guests attended the festivities which continued for a few days after the latter *ballet* with further performances in the gardens. In 1668 a second fête was held in the gardens at Versailles, where the guests walked through the gardens to reach the place in which each event was held: a theatrical presentation, a banquet, and then a ball. Temporary structures were built in the garden in clearings formed by the crossing of the various paths.[250]

In Venice dancing outdoors included dancing on the ceremonial state barge, the *bucintoro*. For example, 1525 saw the wedding celebrations of Vienna, a granddaughter of the doge Andrea Gritti to the son of another patrician family. Therefore, no expense was spared. After the wedding ceremony at the Basilica, and a meal at the doge's palace, the bride and members of the party boarded the *bucintoro* to sail to the groom's house, during which time the guests danced on board the boat to the accompaniment of trumpets and fifes.[251]

Dancing as part of official events also occurred outdoors when it formed part of royal entries into a city. On these occasions dance performances took place at designated places along the route of the procession. A spectacular example is from Henri II's entry into Lyons in 1548, where, in the middle of reviewing a long procession of citizens, the king was honored with a dance by twelve "soldiers," who danced a pyrrhic dance in front of him that lasted for thirty minutes.[252] Dancing in public streets as part of a royal entry had a long history in Europe, although documentation is scarce prior to the fifteenth century.[253] Roman writers, such as Seneca, recalled the public dancing of the *tripudium*,[254] a dance that expressed the joyfulness of a peace imposed by the just rule of law.[255] Echoing this stance, thirteenth-century Italian writers continued to advocate that dancing was an acceptable and natural response to news of a victory that ends a war and ushers in peace.[256] That such advice was acted upon is confirmed by the peace celebrations in Padua in 1310, where the "'letters of peace brought immense *gaudia* [joyfulness] to our hearts and led to the festive dancing of the *tripudium* with high exultation among the whole populace of Padua.'"[257] Dancing was an important part of the Spanish royal entries and religious festivals, particularly the Corpus Christi processions, where dancing took place by specially trained choirboys during the procession through the streets and inside the Cathedral itself.[258]

The spaces in which dancing took place influenced the patterns formed by the dancers during the course of a choreography. In fifteenth-century Italy, the *balli* and *bassadanze* created patterns that were predominately rectilinear rather than circular; that is, the overall movement of these dances was in straight lines. While many dances do contain sections of circular patterns,[259] in the majority of the dances the overall effect is linear, with movement forward and backward along one axis. For practical reasons the size and shape of the halls in which these dances were performed was a major determining factor on the predominance of linear movement in these choreographies. Many of these halls were long, thin, rectangles. In his description of the d'Este country villa, Belriguardo, Giovanni Sabadino degli Arienti notes that the largest room is eighty-three *passi* long and twenty-one *passi* wide,[260] a ratio of length to width of almost 4:1. Since this room was used for the *feste* and other grand occasions, of which dancing would normally be a part, then much of the court dance would have been performed in it. The patterns which best fit this type of space are those whose length is far greater than their width, that is, rectangular patterns rather than circular ones. These are the patterns we find in the choreographies. Similar proportions are found in the hall of the Sforza castle in Milan, in which the spectacle *La festa del paradiso* took place on 13 January 1490. This hall is 203 feet long by only 33 feet wide.[261] The long, narrow rectangular shape was one that existed throughout the period, as illustrated by the *Palazzo della Ragione* in Padua. This building was constructed between 1172 and 1219 and was used for banquets and dances, with the space measuring 300 feet in length by 90 feet wide.[262] The site of the 1581 French court ballet, *Le Balet Comique de la Reyne*, was the great hall of the Hôtel du Petit Bourbon. This space was also a long, narrow rectangle, being 115 feet long by 49 feet wide.[263]

From the end of the fifteenth century, right through the sixteenth, seventeenth, and eighteenth centuries, dance increasingly formed part of theatrical entertainments, whether as *intermedi* (interludes) between the acts of plays, danced multi-media spectacles such as the French court fêtes and English Jacobean masques, or later in the seventeenth and eighteenth centuries as one element in a fully sung opera, as well as in comic pantomimes and plays. We first find descriptions of pantomimic dances performed as *intermedi* between the acts of plays in Ferrara in 1487. These dances of wild men, knights and damsels, and pastoral scenes with shepherds and shepherdesses were all performed on the same stage as the accompanying dramatic production. Throughout the sixteenth century theatrical dances continued to be performed both on a stage and also on the floor of a hall. In Florence in 1539 at the wedding celebrations of Cosimo de' Medici, four satyrs and four ladies dance a torch dance on the stage,[264] while the dances that concluded the third and sixth *intermedi* in Florence in the 1589 celebrations were also performed on the stage built in the *sala grande* (great hall) in the Uffizi. In 1608 the wedding celebrations were held in a hall of the Pitti Palace, and dancing occurred both on the stage itself and on the floor of the hall. In 1617 twelve men (including the Grand Duke) danced on the stage, then they were joined by twelve ladies (including the Grand Duchess) for a dance performed in the middle of the floor. The final dance was choreographed for forty couples, and it too was performed in the center of the hall floor. On other occasions the dancers remained on the hall floor throughout. For example, in 1611 for a *mascherata* in the Pitti Palace during carnival the centerpiece of the spectacle was a complex dance performed by members of the court (both men and women) that ended with the dancers forming the letters of the names of Cosimo and Magdalena. In the English court masques, the "central activity was the dancing in two or three specially choreographed entries by the most accomplished dancers, followed by the long episode of social dancing between the masquers and a select number of the audience, called the revels."[265] Both the specially choreographed dances by the courtiers and the revels' dances were performed on the floor of the hall. The masquers entered into the performance space via the stage, but processed down from the stage to perform on the floor of the hall.

The size of the stage on which the dances occurred, and indeed the decision whether to perform on a stage or on the floor of the hall, also affected the choreography. In 1599 Negri choreographed a *brando* for eight couples that concluded the comedy and accompanying *intermedi*. This event was held in the ducal palace in Milan in honor of the visit by the Infanta, Isabella Clara Eugenia (daughter of Philip II of Spain) and her husband, Albert, the Archduke of Austria. The theater itself measured 149 feet by 93 feet.[266] As Yvonne Kendall points out, "[t]he practical considerations inherent in trying to fit a relatively large number of dancers into the tight dimensions of the dance floor resulted in the creative use of many floor patterns that required little movement outside a proscribed space."[267]

By comparison, the *sala grande* in the Uffizi, the theater in which the 1589 *intermedi* were performed, was slightly larger, being 180 feet long by 67 feet wide.[268] The stage was built at one end of the hall and was as wide as the hall—67 feet—and in 1589 was 48 feet deep, and at the edge adjoining the audience was nine and a half feet high.[269] As well as allowing space for any dance performance, the stage would also have to provide the necessary space for the flats, for scene changes, the technician galleries, the hoists for the machines, and space (somewhere) for the musicians and singers.[270] Thus space was limited especially for dances with more than twelve performers.[271] Long, expansive, linear patterns would obviously not fit, and the theatrical choreographies would have had to have been compact. The amount of available space on the stage would have a direct impact on the patterns created by the dancers, as well as on the total number of dancers used. In the 1617 wedding celebrations in the Pitti Palace only the dance for twelve men was performed on the stage. The dances for more participants— the dance for twenty-four and the final dance for eighty—were performed on the floor of the hall, not the stage.

It is instructive to note that Cavalieri's final *ballo* for the 1589 *intermedi*, which was performed on the stage, was choreographed for twenty-seven dancers. Only the seven principal dancers, however, are involved in the first four parts of the dance, that is, 205 bars out of a total of 253 bars. It is not until four-fifths of the dance has been completed that the remaining twenty dancers join with the seven principals in the choreographic action.[272] When they do join in, the twenty dancers are in a large arc facing the audience, behind the smaller arc of the seven principal dancers, and are divided into four groups of five dancers each. The twenty-three bars of Part V of the choreography where all twenty-seven are dancing is taken up with five concurrent hays, one hay among the seven principals, and the other four within each group of five dancers. Dividing the twenty-seven dancers into five groups and then choreographing interaction only within each group of five (or seven) dancers drastically reduces the amount of space required. Even in the final twenty-five bars of the dance (Part VI), the majority of the step sequences are performed by the three principal male dancers.[273] The four groups of five dancers just perform the step sequence of a *riverenza*, two *seguiti*, and two *seguiti scorsi*, before remaining motionless again while the three principal men do a hay among themselves with eight *fioretti* and eight *mezze capriole*.

Apart from restrictions on space, a second major effect of the dances being performed on a stage located at one end of the hall was that instead of being surrounded on all sides by those watching, there was now a definite "front" to the performance space. This had the greatest impact on the focus of the dancers and the patterns that they created. Circular, square, or rectangular patterns in which the focus and interaction among the dancers are inward-looking would lose their effectiveness on a stage. Cavalieri resolved this problem in his final *ballo* by choreographing almost all the action in a flat plane in front of the arc of the seven principal dancers, with the focus always outward in one direction.[274]

The formal court balls held at Versailles during the reign of Louis XIV were held in the apartments of the host, as there was no official ballroom in the palace at Versailles. If Louis XIV was hosting the ball, it took place in the *Salle de Mars*, the *Salle d'Apollon*, or in the *Galerie de Glace* (the Hall of Mirrors) for important occasions.[275] Yet the actual space dedicated to dancing was only a fraction of the total space in these rooms. Scholars have estimated that for a ball held in the *Galerie de Glace* in 1697, the dance space used was only 58 feet by 20 feet, yet the hall itself has a length of 250 feet. Tiered rows of benches were assembled to divide the long hall and to delineate the dance space.[276] The *Salle de Mars*, one of the largest rooms in Louis XIV's apartments, measures 55 feet by 30 feet. In February 1692 two balls were held in this room to celebrate the wedding of Louis XIV's nephew, the Duc de Chartes to one of Louis's illegitimate daughters. Three hundred and sixteen people attended and the space of the dance floor was only 20 feet by 12 feet.[277] As Harris-Warrick has noted, the shape of the dance space was a "long, narrow rectangle" (just as it was in the fifteenth-century Italian halls) and it was also the same shape as many of the stages in the French theaters of the latter seventeenth century.[278] The seating at a court ball was arranged with the king seated on an armchair in the center of one of the short sides of the rectangle. This was designated as the "head" of the room. On either side of the king sat close family members, with other family members occupying the front row on each of the long sides of the rectangle, together with the high-ranking ladies who were participating in the dancing. The male courtiers who were also dancing sat at the foot of the room, opposite the king. The rest of the tiered benches held the non-dancing guests.[279] Thus only a small number of those attending a ball actually danced, and these were chosen in advance. At the 1692 ball in the *Salle de Mars*, for example, only 23 couples danced out of a guest list of 316 individuals.[280]

When masques were presented at the English court in the early seventeenth century, the spaces had to be prepared afresh for each production, as the rooms and halls were used for state occasions other than just masques.[281] A large dais had to be installed with seats for the king, James I, and for Queen Anna. Along the sides of the hall several tiers of benches for seating had to be constructed, along with boxes for the important courtiers. From 1605 onward, a stage, raised by six to seven feet, was constructed at one end of the hall, usually measuring 40 feet wide by 27 to 40 feet deep.[282] Also steps from the stage to the hall floor had to be built, and sometimes the floor of the hall itself was built up for the masque dances and the revels.[283]

Just as there was no permanent ballroom at Versailles, so too were the spaces for theatrical productions that included dance often temporary.[284] In seventeenth-century France court ballets appeared in halls in the Louvre, as well as in other royal palaces, including Saint-Germain-en-laye, Fontainbleau, and Versailles.[285] Other court productions took place in more permanent theaters that had proscenium stages and far more facilities for scenery and effects, such as the *Salle de Machines* in the Tuileries palace and the theater in the Palais Royal, both in Paris.[286]

Notes

1. For a listing of dance treatises and modern editions and translations, see the section at the end of this volume.

2. Barbara D. Palmer, "Court and Country: The Masque as Sociopolitical Subtext," *Medieval and Renaissance Drama in England* 7 (1995): 350.

3. M. de Saint-Hubert, *La manière de composer et faire réussir les ballets* (Paris, 1641), trans. Andrée Bergen, "How to Compose a Successful Ballet," *Dance Perspectives* No. 20 (1964): 26–33. Two other French treatises from the second half of the seventeenth century which also discuss the court ballets are Michel de Pure's *Idée des spectacles anciens et nouveaux* (1668) and the Jesuit Father, Claude-François Menestrier's *Des ballets anciens et modernes selon les règles du théâtre* (1682). Both authors advocated new aesthetic principles for the composition of ballets.

4. Roger Savage, "The Staging of Courtly Theatre: 1560s to 1640s," in *Europa Triumphans: Court and Civic Festivals in Early Modern Europe*, 2 vols., ed. J. R. Mulryne, Helen Watanabe-O'Kelly, and Margaret Shewring (Aldershot: Ashgate, 2004), 1: 58.

5. *Il corago, o vero alcune osservazioni per metter bene in scena le composizioni drammatiche*, ed. P. Fabbri and A. Pompilio (Florence: Leo S. Olschki, 1983).

6. See Savage, "The Staging of Courtly Theatre," pp. 57–74, for further discussion of this manuscript and similar documents from c. 1560–c. 1640.

7. E. F. Winerock, "Dance References in the Records of Early English Drama: Alternative Sources for Non-Courtly Dancing, 1500–1650," *Proceedings of the Society Dance History Scholars 27th and 28th Annual Conferences* (n.p.: SDHS, 2005), p. 37.

8. See Judith Milhous, "The Economics of Theatrical Dance in Eighteenth-Century London," *Theatre Journal* 55, no. 3 (2003): 481–508.

9. For an example of how even financial records present problems and "cannot be taken at their face value" (p. 17), see Sybil M. Jack, "The Revels Accounts: This Insubstantial Pageant Faded Leaves not a Wrack Behind?" *Renaissance Studies* 9, no. 1 (1995): 1–17. For a lengthy discussion on the pitfalls awaiting scholars who rely on pictorial evidence without the support of other sources of information, see Timothy J. McGee, "Misleading Iconography: The Case of the 'Adimari Wedding Cassone,'" *Imago Musicae* 11–12 (1992–95): 139–57.

10. Jane Bridgeman, "Ambrogio Lorenzetti's 'Dancing Maidens': A Case of Mistaken Identity," *Apollo* 133, no. 350 (1991): 245–51.

11. Quentin Skinner, "Ambrogio Lorenzetti's *Buon Governo* Frescoes: Two Old Questions, Two New Answers," *Journal of the Warburg and Courtauld Institutes* 62 (1999): 1–28.

12. For a discussion on the relationship between dance and the law from the medieval period to 1730, see Alessandro Arcangeli, "Dance and Law," in *Terpsichore 1450–1900: Proceedings of the International Dance Conference, Ghent, April 2000*, ed. Barbara Ravelhofer (Ghent: Institute for Historical Dance Practice, 2000), pp. 51–64.

13. Ian W. Archer, *The Pursuit of Stability: Social Relations in Elizabethan London* (Cambridge: Cambridge University Press, 1991), p. 243.

14. Winerock, "Dance References in the Records of Early English Drama," p. 37.

15. For examples of legislation regarding Jewish dance masters in Italy, see Katherine Tucker McGinnis, "Moving in High Circles: Courts, Dance, and Dancing Masters in Italy in the Long Sixteenth Century," Ph.D. diss., University of North Carolina, Chapel Hill, 2001, pp. 337–46.

16. See chapter 2 in this volume for information on the University of Paris's regulations regarding dancing.

17. Rebecca Harris-Warrick, "The Phrase Structures of Lully's Dance Music," in *Lully Studies*, ed. John Hajdu Heyer (Cambridge: Cambridge University Press, 2000), pp. 32–56.

18. See chapter 11 in this volume for further discussion on these printed programs.

19. See chapter 6 in this volume for examples of what information opera libretti provide.

20. Although this collection concentrates on the dance practice of the elite, since that is where the vast majority of the sources have survived, it is not to deny that dancing was enjoyed by all levels of society.

21. Alan Ryder, *Alfonso the Magnanimous: King of Aragon, Naples, and Sicily, 1396–1485* (Oxford: Claredon Press, 1990), p. 358. Ryder's quotation is from a letter sent to Barcelona on 23 June 1457 and is printed in the book by J. M. Madurell Marimón, *Mensajeros barceloneses en la corte de Nápoles de Alfonso V de Aragon, 1435–1458* (Barcelona, 1963), p. 590.

22. Margaret M. McGowan, "Festivals and the Arts in Henri III's Journey From Poland to France (1574)," in Mulryne, Watanabe-O'Kelly, and Shewring, *Europa Triumphans*, 1: 122–23.

23. Ibid., p. 123.

24. Rebecca Harris-Warrick, "Ballroom Dancing at the Court of Louis XIV," *Early Music* 14, no. 1 (1986): 42.

25. The most formal court balls were known as *grand bals, bal parés,* or *bals réglés.*

26. Harris-Warrick, "Ballroom Dancing," p. 42.

27. Helen Watanabe-O'Kelly, "Early Modern European Festivals—Politics and Performance, Event and Record," in *Court Festivals of the European Renaissance: Art, Politics and Performance,* ed. J. R. Mulryne and Elizabeth Goldring (Aldershot: Ashgate, 2002), p. 15. See also Helen Watanabe-O'Kelly, "The Early Modern Festival Book: Function and Form," in Mulryne, Watanabe-O'Kelly, and Shewring, *Europa Triumphans*, 1: 3–17.

28. Watanabe-O'Kelly, "The Early Modern Festival Book," p. 5.

29. Ibid., p. 16.

30. Ibid., p. 6.

31. W. R. Streitberger, *Court Revels, 1485–1559* (Toronto: University of Toronto Press, 1994), p. 4.

32. Ibid., p. 6.

33. For this event the dances were choreographed by the Polish Chancellor, Jan Zamoysky, who, in his youth, had studied in Padua (Savage, "The Staging of Courtly Theatre," p. 66).

34. See Sara Smart, "The Württemberg Court and the Introduction of Ballet into the Empire," in Mulryne, Watanabe-O'Kelly, and Shewring, *Europa Triumphans*, 2: 35–45. Smart also discusses the similarities between the later three ballets and specific contemporary court dance spectacles in England and France.

35. Stijn Bussels, "*Le Balet de Princes Indiens* (1634)," *Terpsichore 1450–1900: Proceedings of the International Dance Conference, Ghent, April 2000,* ed. Barbara Ravelhofer (Ghent: Institute for Historical Dance Practice, 2000), pp. 105–14. For further information on dance in the Netherlands, see, in the same volume, Ingeborg de Cooman, "Dances and Ballet in Seventeenth-Century Theatre of the Southern Netherlands," pp. 115–29.

36. Savage, "The Staging of Courtly Theatre," p. 66.

37. Guglielmo Ebreo da Pesaro, *Guilielmi Hebraei pisauriensis de practica seu arte tripudii vulgare opusculum, incipit,* 1463, Paris, Bibliothèque Nationale, MS fonds it. 973, f. 22r (hereafter cited as Pg).

38. Maurizio Padovan, "Da Dante a Leonardo: La danza italiana attraverso le fonti storiche," *Danza italiana* 3 (1985): 33. Padovan is quoting from E. Solmi, "La festa del Paradiso di Leonardo da Vinci e Bernardo Bellincione," *Archivio storico lombardo,* 1 (1904): 86.

39. For example, a single step on the left foot was one pace or step forward, either leaving the left foot in front or bringing the right foot forward to join the left, that is, "closing" the feet. The double step was three paces forward, with the feet either "closed" or left open at the end of the double. For more on the double step in general, and the various different ways of performing it throughout Europe, see Anne Daye, "Taking the Measure of Dance Steps 1650–1700, through the Publications of John Playford," in *On Common Ground 3: John Playford and The English Dancing Master 1651, Proceedings of the 3rd DHDS Conference March 2001*, ed. David Parsons (Stock, Essex: Dolmetsch Historical Dance Society, 2001), pp. 13–20. For information on the single and double step as found in the French *basse dance* repertory, see chapter 8 in this volume.

40. Keith Polk, *German Instrumental Music of the Late Middle Ages: Players, Patrons and Performance Practice* (Cambridge: Cambridge University Press, 1992), p. 118.

41. Ibid., p. 118. Other important dance houses are found in Cologne, Leipzig, and Nuremberg. (Keith Polk, "Review of *Medieval Instrumental Dances*," *Journal of the American Musicological Society* 44, no. 2 [1991], p. 325n1). Polk also mentions that illustrations and a discussion of German dance houses are found in Walter Salmen's *Tanz im 17. und 18. Jahrhundert*, Musikgeschichte in Bildern, vol. 4 (Liepzig: VEB Deutscher Verlag für Musik, 1988).

42. See chapter 2 in this volume for a discussion of thirteenth-century university students in Paris and the transmission of dances.

43. Polk, *German Instrumental Music*, p. 119; for more details of these marriage alliances and the travel and social contact they brought, including the exchange of dance styles, see pp. 119–20.

44. Bussels, "*Le Balet de Princes Indiens*," p. 109.

45. McGowan, "Festival and the Arts," p. 123.

46. See Frederick Crane, *Materials for the Study of the Fifteenth Century Basse Danse*, (New York: Institute of Mediæval Music, 1968), pp. 46 and 72–75.

47. David Fallows, "The Gresley Dance Collection, c. 1500," *RMA Research Chronicle* 29 (1996), p. 2. Other titles in this list also suggest connections with the French *basse dance* repertory.

48. Maurice Esses, *Dance and Instrumental Diferencias in Spain during the 17th and early 18th Centuries*, 3 vols. (Stuyvesant, N.Y.: Pendragon Press, 1992), 1: 518.

49. Pg, f. 19r-19v. "Ma quando è exercitata da huomini gentili, virtuosi, & honesti, dico essa scienza & arte essere buona et virtuosa et di commendatione & laude digna. Et più [19v] che non solamente gli huomini virtuosi & honesti fa tornare gentili & pellegrini: ma anchora quegli sonno male acostumati & di vil conditione nati, fa divenir gentili & d'assai."

50. Lynn Matluck Brooks, *The Art of Dancing in Seventeenth-Century Spain: Juan de Esquivel Navarro and His World* (Lewisburg, Pa.: Bucknell University Press; London: Associated University Press, 2003), p. 269, (chapter 1, f. 6v of Esquivel's treatise).

51. "Vegniromo a quelli balli et bassedanze che son fora del vulgo fabricati per sale signorile e da esser sol dançati per dignissime Madonne et non plebeie" (Antonio Cornazano, *Libro dell'arte del danzare*, Rome: Biblioteca Apostolica Vaticana, Codex Capponiano, 203, f. 12v; hereafter cited as V).

52. Esses, *Dance and Instrumental Diferencias in Spain*, 1: 505–6 and 523.

53. Quotation from Aileen Ribeiro, *Fashion and Fiction: Dress in Art and Literature in Stuart England* (New Haven: Yale University Press, 2005), p. 179, from Herbert's autobiography. Herbert would have been well aware of the advantages of a good education in dance. He served as ambassador to France from c. 1619 to 1624 and was friends with Ben

Jonson and Thomas Carew (who were authors of court masques). One of his younger brothers, Sir Henry Herbert, was Master of the Revels from 1623.

54. Fabritio Caroso, *Nobiltà di dame*, Venice 1600. Facsimile ed. (Bologna: Forni, 1980), pp. 65–88. For a translation see Julia Sutton, trans. and ed., *Nobiltà di dame. Fabritio Caroso* (Oxford: Oxford University Press, 1986), pp. 134–50.

55. Esses, *Dance and Instrumental Diferencias in Spain*, 1: 523 (Esquivel's treatise chapter 5 f. 34v-35r; the same passage is found on page 293 of Brooks' translation).

56. Around 1463–65 Guglielmo Ebreo converted to Christianity and took the name Giovanni Ambrosio. Although some of the redactions of his treatise use the Christian version of his name, in this volume he will be referred to as Guglielmo.

57. One version of Guglielmo's treatise is dated 1463, while the first version of Cornazano's treatise, now lost, dedicated to his pupil Ippolita Sforza, was written in 1455 and the second version, dedicated to Ippolita's half-brother, Secondo Sforza, in 1465.

58. In two versions of his treatise Guglielmo recorded an autobiographical section in which he mentions the occasions at which he was present and/or performed and choreographed dances. See Pg f. 22r-23r and Guglielmo Ebreo da Pesaro, *Domini Iohannis Ambrosii pisauriensis de pratica seu arte tripudii vulgare opusculum faeliciter incipit*, Paris, Bibliothèque Nationale, MS fonds it. 476, f. 72r-80v (hereafter cited as Pa), and F. Alberto Gallo, "L'autobiografia artistica di Giovanni Ambrosio (Guglielmo Ebreo) da Pesaro," *Studi musicali* 12, no. 2 (1983): 189–202, for a discussion of the autobiography and a transcription of the text from Pa. For an English translation of the text from Pg and Pa, see Guglielmo Ebreo da Pesaro, *De practica seu arte tripudii: On the Practice or Art of Dancing*, ed. and trans. Barbara Sparti (Oxford: Oxford University Press, 1993), pp. 121 and 248–54.

59. For more information on Cornazano's life, see the articles on him in the *International Encyclopedia of Dance* (New York: Oxford University Press, 1998), and *Dizionario biografico degli Italiani*, vol. 29 (Rome: Istituto della Enciclopedia Italiana, 1983).

60. The date Domenico was knighted is not known, but in his treatise Cornazano refers to Domenico as "cavaliere aurato" (V, f. 28v). The Order of the Golden Spur was not a military order. For more information on Domenico's life see articles on him in the *International Encyclopedia of Dance* (New York: Oxford University Press, 1998) and the *Dizionario biografico degli Italiani*, vol. 40 (Rome: Istituto della Enciclopedia Italiana, 1991), and Barbara Sparti, introduction to *De practica seu arte tripudii: On the Practice or Art of Dancing*, by Guglielmo Ebreo, ed. and trans. Barbara Sparti (Oxford: Oxford University Press, 1993), pp. 23–45, for Guglielmo's life and dance activities.

61. For more details on Lavagnolo's career, see McGinnis, "Moving in High Circles," pp. 250–52.

62. For more details on Giuseppe's activities, see Timothy J. McGee, "Dancing Masters and the Medici Court in the 15th Century," *Studi musicali* 17, no. 2 (1988), pp. 201–24, and Alessandra Veronese, "Una *societas* ebraico-cristiano *in docendo tripudiare sonare ac cantare* nella Firenze del quattrocento," in *Guglielmo Ebreo da Pesaro e la danza nelle corti italiane del xv secolo*, ed. Maurizio Padovan (Pisa: Pacini, 1990), pp. 51–57.

63. A. William Smith, "Dance at Mantua and in Northern Italy: The Tradition Inherited by Leone de' Sommi and His Generation," in *Leone de' Sommi and the Performing Arts*, ed. Ahuva Belkin (Tel Aviv: Tel Aviv University, 1997), p. 84.

64. Robert Black, "École et société à Florence aux XIVᵉ et XVᵉ siècles: Le témoignage des *ricordanze*," *Annales: Histoire, Sciences sociales* 59, no. 4 (2004): 839.

65. Frank A. D'Accone, "Lorenzo the Magnificent and Music," in *Lorenzo il Magnifico e il suo mondo*, ed. Gian Carlo Garfagnini (Florence: Leo S. Olschki, 1994), p. 263n8.

66. Black, "École et société à Florence," pp. 845–46. "M^oGiorgio" is the same name that appears at the beginning of a redaction of Guglielmo's treatise, a copy of which was in the possession of the Medici family from the mid-sixteenth century. In 1990 Andrea Francalanci hypothesized that the manuscript was a dancing master's notebook, and that "M^oGiorgio" could be "a dancing master, someone practiced in the art of the dance whose responsibility it was to put together this manuscript" (Andrea Francalanci, "The '*Copia* di M^oGiorgio e del guideo di ballare basse danze e balletti' as found in the New York Public Library," *Basler Jahrbuch für Historiche Musikpraxis* 14 [1990], pp. 93–95). Based on the Florentine records examined by Black, I would suggest that the "Giorgio" manuscript was indeed a copy of Guglielmo's treatise which belonged to the dance master Maestro Giorgio, and which he used in his teaching activities in Florence. The early sixteenth-century dance master Lanzo could well be the same person identified as "Il Lanzino," author of some of the dances found in the "Il Papa" manuscript, a collection of choreographies from the early sixteenth century (Il Papa, New York Public Library, Dance Collection, [S] *MGZMBZ-Res. 72–255). This manuscript has no date, and while the dates that have been suggested by dance historians vary from 1500 to c. 1560, the consensus assigns the manuscript to the early sixteenth century. David Wilson suggests the first quarter of the sixteenth century (*The Steps Used in Court Dancing in Fifteenth-Century Italy*, 3rd rev. ed. [Cambridge: David R. Wilson, 2003], p. 7), while Barbara Sparti suggests 1515–20 ("Would You Like to Dance This Frottola? Choreographic Concordances in Two Early Sixteenth-Century Tuscan Sources," *Musica Disciplina* 50 [1996]: 138–40).

67. McGinnis, "Moving in High Circles," pp. 176–77. McGinnis lists these names in Appendix B, pp. 400–408.

68. From 1600 to 1676 the dance masters in Graz were all Italian, but post-1676 they were Viennese who had been trained in France. See Gudrun Rottensteiner, "Vom 'Ballarino' zum 'Maitre à danser': Grazer Tanzmeister des 17. Jahrhunderts," in *Morgenröte des Barock. Tanz im 17. Jahrhundert*, ed. Uwe Scholttermüller and Maria Richter (Freiburg: Fa-gisis, 2004), pp. 181–88.

69. For further discussion on the influence of Italian dance in France in the sixteenth century, see chapter 4 in this volume.

70. McGowan, "Festivals and the Arts," p. 123.

71. See chapter 10 in this volume on Negri's time in France.

72. Margaret M. McGowan, "Beaujoyeulx, Balthazar de," *International Encyclopedia of Dance* (Oxford: Oxford University Press, 1998), I: 398.

73. McGinnis, "Moving in High Circles," pp. 355–56; p. 388.

74. Cesare Negri, *Le gratie d'amore*, Milan 1602. Facsimile ed. (New York: Broude Brothers, 1969).

75. For a comparison of the two editions of Negri's treatise, see Pamela Jones, "The Editions of Cesare Negri's *Le Gratie D'Amore*: Choreographic Revisions in Printed Copies," *Studi musicali* 21, no. 1 (1992): 21–33.

76. Fabritio Caroso, *Il ballarino*, Venice 1581. Facsimile ed. (New York: Broude Brothers, 1967); *Nobiltà di dame*, Venice 1600. Facsimile ed. (Bologna: Forni, 1980); Lutio Compasso, *Ballo della gagliarda*, Florence 1560. Facsimile ed. (Freiburg: Fa-gisis, 1995).

77. Prospero Lutij di Sulmona, *Opera bellissima nella quale si contengono molte partite, et passeggi di gagliarda* (Perugia: Pietropaolo Orlando, 1589).

78. Livio Lupi da Caravaggio, *Mutanze di gagliarda, tordiglione, passo è mezzo, canari* (Palermo: Carrara, 1600).

79. Ercole Santucci, *Mastro da ballo*, 1614. Facsimile ed. (Hildesheim: Georg Olms, 2004).

80. For a discussion on Santucci's variations see Barbara Sparti, "Introduction" to Santucci, *Mastro da ballo*, pp. 60–69.

81. Thoinot Arbeau, *Orchesography* (Langres, 1588), trans. Mary Stewart Evans (1948; reprint, New York: Dover Publications, 1967).

82. The work was first printed in February or March 1528 (W. Thomas Marrocco and Marie-Laure Merveille, "Antonius Arena: Master of Law and Dance of the Renaissance," *Studi musicali* 18, no. 1 [1989]: 23). The first edition proved extremely popular, and it continued to be reprinted until 1770. See Robert Mullally, "The Editions of Antonius Arena's *Ad Suos Compagnones Studiantes*," *Gutenburg-Jahrbuch* (1979): 146–57, for information on the many editions of Arena's work, and John Guthrie and Marino Zorzi, trans., "Rules of Dancing: Antonius Arena," *Dance Research* 4, no. 2 (1986): 3–53, for an English translation of Arena's dance treatise.

83. Marrocco and Merveille, "Antonius Arena," p. 31.

84. Barbara Ravelhofer, "Introduction," to B. de Montagut, *Louange de la Danse: In Praise of Dance*, ed. Barbara Ravelhofer (Cambridge: Renaissance Texts from Manuscripts, 2000), p. 40n38.

85. Andrew Ashbee and David Lasocki et al. (comp.) *A Biographical Dictionary of English Court Musicians 1485–1714*, 2 vols. (Aldershot: Ashgate, 1998), 1: 230.

86. See Fallows, "The Gresley Dance Collection," pp. 1–20; Jennifer Nevile, "Dance in Early Tudor England: An Italian Connection?" *Early Music* 26, no. 2 (1998): 230–44; Jennifer Nevile, "Dance Steps and Music in the Gresley Manuscript," *Historical Dance* 3, no. 6 (1999): 2–19; David R. Wilson, "Performing Gresley Dances: the View from the Floor," *Historical Dance* 3, no. 6 (1999): 20–22.

87. For an account of the whole affair, discussion on the lives of de Lauze and Montagut, including the social context of their work, as well as the plagiarised text of de Lauze's treatise in parallel with the text of Montagut's work and a translation and commentary on the latter, see B. de Montagut, *Louange de la Danse*, ed. Barbara Ravelhofer (Cambridge: Renaissance Texts from Manuscripts, 2000).

88. Instruction pour dancer: *An Anonymous Manuscript*, ed. and introduced by Angene Feves et al. (Freiburg: Fa-gisis, 2000).

89. Angene Feves, "Introduction," in Instruction pour dancer: *An Anonymous Manuscript*, p. 36. For further details on this manuscript see pp. 13–37.

90. Ibid., p. 14. See also Barbara Ravelhofer, *The Early Stuart Masque: Dance, Costume, and Music* (Oxford: Oxford University Press, 2006), p. 53.

91. Similarly, during the seventeenth century the court in The Hague usually employed a dance master (often a Frenchman) to teach the pages and young princes there (Lynn Matluck Brooks, "Court, Church, and Province: Dancing in the Netherlands, Seventeenth and Eighteenth Centuries," *Dance Research Journal* 20, no. 1 [1988]: 19).

92. Esses, *Dance and Instrumental Diferencias in Spain*, 1: 489–94. See p. 489 for a list of royal dance masters from 1589 to 1692.

93. This was the case in the seventeenth century when Toledo Cathedral hired professional dance masters (ibid., 1: 514–16). For more information on the dancing choirboys, see Lynn Matluck Brooks, "Cosmic Imagery in the Religious Dances of Seville's Golden Age," *Proceedings of the 14th Annual Conference of the Society of Dance History Scholars* (Riverside: SDHS, 1991), pp. 82–94, and Lynn Matluck Brooks, *The Dances of the Processions of Seville in Spain's Golden Age* (Kassel: Reichenberger, 1988).

94. Brooks, *The Art of Dancing*. This book includes a translation of Esquivel's treatise and a commentary on the text.

95. Esses, *Dance and Instrumental* Diferencias *in Spain*, 1: 423.

96. Brooks, *The Art of Dancing*, p. 78.

97. Ibid.

98. Through the families of both his father and mother Beauchamps was related to "families who supplied more than 40 violinists to the King's chamber" (Régine Astier, "Pierre Beauchamps and the Ballets de Collège," *Dance Chronicle* 6, no. 2 [1983]: 143).

99. Gunhild Oberzaucher-Schüller, "L'Austria," *Musica in scena: Storia dello spettacolo musicale Vol. V, L'Arte della danza e del balletto*, ed. Alberto Basso (Turin: Unione Tipografico-Editrice Torinese, 1995), p. 550.

100. John S. Powell, "Pierre Beauchamps, Choreographer to Molière's Troupe du Roy," *Music and Letters* 76, no. 2 (1995): 186.

101. See chapter 5 in this volume for information on Beauchamps's work with Molière. For Lully's role in court ballet, see Barbara Coeyman, "Lully's Influence on the Organization and Performance of the 'Ballet de Cour' after 1672," in *Jean-Baptiste Lully*, ed. Jérôme la Gorce and Herbert Schneider (Heidelburg: Laaber, 1990), pp. 517–28.

102. Pécour was one of the most famous dance masters of his day, and part of his reputation, especially for modern scholars, lies in the fact that 120 dances by Pécour have survived in notation, a number far greater than for any other of his contemporaries (Moira Goff, "'The Art of Dancing, Demonstrated by Characters and Figures': French and English Sources for Court and Theatre Dance, 1700–1750," *The British Library Journal* 21, no. 2 [1995]: 207–208 and 228n23). For more on Pécour's life, see Jérôme la Gorce, "Guillaume-Louis Pecour: A Biographical Essay," trans. Margaret M. McGowan, *Dance Research* 8, no. 2 (1990): 3–26, and for further discussion of the dance masters' activities at the Jesuit colleges, see Régine Astier, "Pierre Beauchamps and the Ballets de Collège," pp. 138–63. The latter article includes a list of the ballets performed at the two Jesuit colleges from 1669 to 1749, and a list of the surviving ballet scores for the Jesuit ballets composed by Beauchamps from 1680 to 1687.

103. Régine Astier, "Louis XIV, 'Premier Danseur,'" in *The Sun King: The Ascendancy of French Culture during the Reign of Louis XIV*, ed. David Lee Rubin (Washington/Toronto: Folger Shakespeare Library/Associated University Presses, 1992), p. 95.

104. Beauchamps became Louis XIV's teacher in 1650, two years after Beauchamps's name first appeared as a dancer in a court ballet (Powell, "Pierre Beauchamps," p. 169).

105. Astier, "Académie Royale de Danse," in *International Encyclopedia of Dance* (Oxford: Oxford University Press, 1998), 1: 3. See also Maureen Needham, "Louis XIV and the Académie Royale de Danse, 1661—A Commentary and Translation," *Dance Chronicle* 20, no. 2 (1997): 173–90, and Rose A. Pruiksma, "Generational Conflict and the Foundation of the *Académie Royale de Danse*: A Reexamination," *Dance Chronicle* 26, no. 2 (2003): 169–87.

106. Astier, "Académie Royale de Danse," p. 3.

107. Rebecca Harris-Warrick and Carol G. Marsh, *Musical Theatre at the Court of Louis XIV: Le Mariage de la Grosse Cathos* (Cambridge: Cambridge University Press, 1994), p. 9.

108. Jennifer Thorp, "Your Honor'd and Obedient Servant: Patronage and Dance in London c. 1700–1735," *Dance Research* 15, no. 2 (1997): 86.

109. Moira Goff, "Dancing-Masters in Early Eighteenth-Century London," *Historical Dance* 3, no. 3 (1994): 19. See also Thorp, "Your Honor'd and Obedient Servant," pp. 86–88.

110. See Carol G. Marsh, "French Court Dance in England, 1700–1740: A Study of Sources," Ph.D. diss., City University of New York, 1985, pp. 289–99.

111. For information on all these men, see Goff, "Dancing-Masters," pp. 17–23.

112. See chapter 12 in this volume for a detailed analysis of one of Isaac's ballroom dances, *The Pastorall*.

113. For information on Pemberton's work as notator, see Goff, "'The Art of Dancing, Demonstrated by Characters and Figures,'" p. 210, and Moira Goff, "Edmund Pemberton, Dancing-Master and Publisher," *Dance Research* 11, no. 1 (1993): 52–81.

114. For an annotated facsimile edition of all of Weaver's publications, plus an account of his life and an evaluation of his contribution to the field of dance, see Richard Ralph, *The Life and Works of John Weaver* (London: Dance Books, 1985).

115. See Moira Goff and Jennifer Thorp, "Dance Notations Published in England *c.* 1700–1740 and Related Manuscript Material," *Dance Research* 9, no. 2 (1991): 32–50.

116. See Jennifer Thorp, "P. Siris: An Early Eighteenth-Century Dancing-Master," *Dance Research* 10, no. 2 (1992): 71–92, and Thorp, "Your Honor'd and Obedient Servant," pp. 95–96.

117. For more information on Essex's and Tomlinson's publications, see Goff, "'The Art of Dancing, Demonstrated by Characters and Figures,'" pp. 213–15, and Thorp, "Your Honor'd and Obedient Servant," pp. 92–94, for information on Tomlinson's *Art of Dancing*.

118. Louis Bonin, *Die neuste Art zur galanten und theatralischen Tantz-Kunst* (Frankfurt: Joh. Christoff Lochner, 1711).

119. Judith L. Schwartz and Christena L. Schlundt, *French Court Dance and Dance Music: A Guide to Primary Source Writings 1643–1789* (Stuyvesant, N.Y.: Pendragon Press, 1987), p. 18.

120. Fiona Garlick, "A Measure of Decorum: Social Order and the Dance Suite in the Reign of Louis XIV," Ph.D. diss., University of New South Wales, 1992, p. 107.

121. Johann Pasch, *Beschreibung wahrer Tanz-Kunst* (Frankfurt: Wolffgang Michahelles & Johann Adolph, 1707). See Schwartz and Schlundt, *French Court Dance and Dance Music*, pp. 55–56, for a brief description of the contents.

122. See Schwartz and Schlundt, *French Court Dance and Dance Music*, pp. 11–16, for a brief description of the contents and examples of illustrations from these works.

123. See ibid., pp. 68–69, for a further brief description of the contents, and Angelika R. Gerbes, "Eighteenth Century [*sic*] Dance Instruction: The Course of Study Advocated by Gottfried Taubert," *Dance Research* 10, no. 1 (1992): 40–52, for a discussion on Taubert's life and his method of teaching dance.

124. The sixteenth-century Italian dance style also included gestures. (See G. Yvonne Kendall, "Ornamentation and Improvisation in Sixteenth-Century Dance," in *Improvisation in the Arts of the Middle Ages and Renaissance*, ed. Timothy J. McGee [Kalamazoo: Medieval Institute Publications, 2003], pp. 176–78.) Sometimes the gestures found in one dance practice did not translate well when performed in a different regional or societal setting. One example is the sixteenth-century Venetian regulations that prohibited the *ballo del capello* (dance of the hat) and "some other French dances full of lascivious and damnable gestures," yet when the *ballo del capello* was performed at a ball in Verona in 1533 in honor of the Infanta Margherita, it was regarded only as a "great game" (*gran gioco*). (Patricia Fortini-Brown, *Private Lives in Renaissance Venice: Art, Architecture, and the Family* [New Haven: Yale University Press, 2004], p. 152. Fortini-Brown is quoting from the Archivio di Stato, Venice, Senato, Terra, Register 18, c. 14. The information on the 1533 performance is from Marin Sanudo, *I diarii di Marin Sanuto (1496–1533)* [reprint ed., Bologna: Forni, 1969–79], 57: 651.)

125. For an illustration of this method of recording dance see Figure 8.4 in chapter 8 in this volume.

126. Cervera, Arxiu historic, Comarcal, unnumbered ms.

127. Nine of the eleven choreographies are notated solely with these graphic symbols, the remaining two dances with a combination of symbols and descriptive verbal directions. For examples of this notation see Alan Stark, "What Steps did the Spaniards Take in the Dance?" in *Proceedings of the 14th Annual Conference of Society of Dance History Scholars* (Riverside: SDHS, 1991), pp. 61–62, and Carles Mas i Garcia, "Baixa Dansa in the Kingdom of Catalonia and Aragon in the 15th Century," *Historical Dance* 3, no. 1 (1992): 18–21.

128. For an illustration of some of the figures in a ballet at the court of Württemberg in 1618, see Ravelhofer, *The Early Stuart Masque*, pp. 79 and 93.

129. For a discussion on the possible length of these dance figures and the complete ballets, see ibid., pp. 80–81.

130. Stockholm, Kungliga Biblioteket, Cod. Holm S. 253. For a detailed analysis of this manuscript, and a comparison with the figures from the 1610 ballet, see Jennifer Nevile, "Dance Patterns of the Early Seventeenth Century: The Stockholm Manuscript and *Le Ballet de Monseigneur de Vendosme*," *Dance Research* 18, no. 2 (2000): 186–203.

131. Notation systems were being developed by Beauchamps, André Lorin, Jean Favier the elder, and Sieur de la Haise. The latter three never achieved the widespread popularity that Beauchamps's system did. For more information, see Ken Pierce, "Dance Notation Systems in Late 17th-Century France," *Early Music* 26, no. 2 (1998): 286–99. For a detailed discussion of Favier's system and a facsimile of the masquerade that was notated using this system, see Harris-Warrick and Marsh, *Musical Theatre*. Lorin used his system of notation to record *contredanses* in two manuscripts dated 1685 and 1688.

132. Pierce, "Dance Notation Systems," p. 287.

133. Raoul-Auger Feuillet, *Chorégraphie ou l'art de décrire la dance* (Paris: Michel Brunet, 1700). See Schwartz and Schlundt, *French Court Dance and Dance Music*, pp. 29–31, for a brief description of the contents of this treatise. For details on the legal disputes that followed between Beauchamps and Feuillet, see Pierce, "Dance Notation Systems," p. 287. For further information on the control exercised over the printing of notated dances by Feuillet and Pécour, and then by Dezais and Gaudrau, see Goff, "'The Art of Dancing, Demonstrated by Characters and Figures,'" pp. 207–8.

134. For a comparison between the dance treatises and choreographies published in Beauchamps-Feuillet notation in France and those published in England in the first fifty years of the eighteenth century, see Goff, "'The Art of Dancing,'" pp. 202–31; for a chronological listing of these works, see pp. 217–27.

135. However, it should be noted that the Lorin, Favier, and Beauchamps-Feuillet notation systems were developed for, and tied to, one particular style of dance, unlike the system of dance notation developed by Rudolf Laban, which can theoretically notate any movement of the human body. Therefore, there were types of movements that they could not depict or were very bad at notating.

136. Gregorio Lambranzi, *Neue und curieuse theatralische Tantz-Schul* (1716), ed. Kurt Petermann (Leipzig: Peters, 1975).

137. For further information on Lambranzi and his treatise, see Klaus Abromeit, "Lambranzi's *Theatralische Tantz-Schul*: Commedia dell'arte and French Noble Style," *Studi musicali* 25, nos. 1–2 (1996): 317–28; Daniel Heartz, "A Venetian Dancing Master Teaches the Forlana: Lambranzi's *Balli Teatrali*," *Journal of Musicology* 17, no. 1 (1999): 136–51;

Marianovella Fama, "Gregorio Lambranzi: un 'maestro di ballo' da Venezia a Norimberga," *Biblioteca teatrale nuova serie* no. 8 (1987): 61–82.

138. The translation is from Gregorio Lambranzi, *New and Curious School of Theatrical Dancing,* trans. Derra de Moroda (London, 1928; facsimile ed., New York: Dover, 2002), p. 15.

139. See Rebecca Harris-Warrick and Bruce Alan Brown, eds., *The Grotesque Dancer on the Eighteenth-Century Stage: Gennaro Magri and His World* (Madison: University of Wisconsin Press, 2005), especially pp. 173–278.

140. The music in Playford's collection of English country dances, almost all of the music in Arbeau's treatise, as well as the music recorded for the choreographies in the Beauchamps-Feuillet notation were also just one line, but in these cases it was the melody that was recorded rather than the tenor part. The reason only the melody was recorded with the dance notation in the Beauchamps-Feuillet system was that the music was present on the page as an aide-memoire to accompany the steps, or as a tune to be played by the dance master on his pochette (a small violin) while his pupil executed the dance steps. For a modern edition of the country dance tunes, see Jeremy Barlow, ed., *The Complete Country Dance Tunes from Playford's Dancing Master (1651–ca. 1728)* (London: Faber Music, 1985).

141. See Timothy J. McGee, *Medieval Instrumental Dances* (Bloomington: Indiana University Press, 1989), pp. 23–26, and Robert Mullally, "Dance Terminology in the Works of Machaut and Froissart," in *Medium ævum* 59, no. 2 (1990): 252.

142. For more on the shawm band, its composition and development, see Polk, *German Instrumental Music,* pp. 46–86.

143. For skilled musicians improvising two parts around a tenor was not too difficult, since in "a texture based on the tenor voice much is firmly established from the outset. Cadence points can be predetermined along with phrase lengths and much of the harmonic outline." Also in a three-part texture, "skilled improvising performers could negotiate around harmonic clashes with reasonable success." (Keith Polk, "Instrumentalists and Performance Practices in Dance Music, c. 1500," in *Improvisation in the Arts of the Middle Ages and Renaissance,* ed. Timothy J. McGee, [Kalamazoo, Mich.: Medieval Institute, 2003], pp. 100–101).

144. Polk, "Instrumentalists and Performance Practices," p. 101. The length of time instrumentalists were expected to play might also provide a clue to the discrepancy between the contemporary illustrations of a wind band with three players and archival documents that often list five players in a band. As Polk has suggested, one method of avoiding player fatigue would be to perform according to a rotation scheme, so that every player received a break while a minimum of three parts were maintained at all times (Polk, *German Instrumental Music,* p. 81).

145. See Howard Mayer Brown, *Instrumental Music Printed Before 1600. A Bibliography* (Cambridge, Mass.: Harvard University Press, 1965).

146. For a list of the contents of all of Attaingnant's music publications and modern editions, see Daniel Heartz, *Pierre Attaingnant, Royal Printer of Music: A Historical Study and Bibliographical Catalogue* (Berkeley: University of California Press, 1969).

147. For further information on Praetorius's *Terpsichore,* see Ravelhofer, *Early Stuart Masque,* pp. 51–52.

148. Nino Pirrotta and Elena Povoledo, *Music and Theatre from Poliziano to Monteverdi,* trans. Karen Eales (Cambridge University Press, 1982), p. 233.

149. "Questo ballo fù cantato da tutte le voci e sonato da tutti gli Strumenti sudetti"

(Cristofano Malvezzi, *Intermedii et concerti fatti per la commedia rappresentata in Firenze nelle nozze del serenissimo don Ferdinando Medici, e madama Christina di Loreno, gran duchi di Toscana* [Venice: G. Vincenti, 1591], ninth partbook, p. 19).

150. Ibid., p. 16.

151. For further discussion of the instrumental forces used in the Italian danced spectacles, see Iain Fenlon, "Guarini de' Sommi and the Pre-History of the Italian Danced Spectacle," in Belkin, *Leone de' Sommi and the Performing Arts*, pp. 49–65.

152. Ultimately, as common sense would suggest and the contemporary documents advise, the final number of instruments used in danced spectacles like the *intermedi* or French *ballets* was determined by the proportions of the hall and the stage (Massimo Ossi, "*Dalle macchine . . . la maraviglia*: Bernardo Buontalenti's *Il rapimento di Cefalo* at the Medici Theater in 1600," in *Opera and Context: Essays on Historical Staging from the Late Renaissance to the Time of Puccini*, ed. Mark A. Radice [Portland: Amadeus Press, 1998], p. 23).

153. David Potter and P. R. Roberts, "An Englishman's View of the Court of Henri III, 1584–1585: Richard Cook's 'Description of the Court of France,'" *French History* 2, no. 3 (1988): 341.

154. For a summary of these three groups see Harris-Warrick and Marsh, *Musical Theatre*, pp. 4–8.

155. Ibid., p. 7.

156. Domenico da Piacenza, *De arte saltandj & choreas ducendj De la arte di ballare et danzare*, Paris, Bibliothèque Nationale, MS fonds it. 972, f. 7r.

157. Florence, Biblioteca Nazionale, MS Magl. XIX, 31, f. 2r–5r.

158. Clément Janequin, *La guerre*, in *Chansons Polyphoniques*, vol. 1, ed. A. Tillman Merritt and François Lesure (Monaco: L'Oiseau-Lyre, 1983), pp. 23–53.

159. The common passage is the second section of the dance and bars 20–29 of the chanson. The sections, which are not identical but still very similar, include repeated notes on the same pitch to sound like drums, and long elaborations of the tonic sonority (F A C) that resemble trumpet calls.

160. See Warren Kirkendale, *L'aria di Fiorenza, id est Il ballo del Gran Duca* (Florence: Leo S. Olschki, 1972).

161. Fenlon, "Guarini de' Sommi," pp. 59–61.

162. Kirkendale, *L'aria di Fiorenza*, pp. 46–47.

163. For a discussion of the various terms used by thirteenth- and fourteenth-century French writers to refer to dance, or dancing, and the changes that occurred in the terminology in the fourteenth century and the confusion that can arise, see Robert Mullally, "Dance Terminology," pp. 248–49. See also Timothy J. McGee, *Medieval Instrumental Dances*, and Timothy J. McGee, "Medieval Dances: Matching the Repertory With Grecheio's Descriptions," *Journal of Musicology* 7, no. 4 (1989): 489–517, for a discussion on medieval dance "types" starting from a musical viewpoint: the surviving music, and the information contained in Johannes de Grocheio's theoretical music treatise, *De musica* (c. 1300).

164. Robert Mullally, "Reconstructing the *Carole*," in *On Common Ground 4: Reconstruction and Re-creation in Dance before 1850*, Proceedings of the 4th DHDS Conference, March 2003, ed. David Parsons (Stock, Essex: Dolmetsch Historical Dance Society, 2003), p. 79.

165. See ibid., pp. 79–82, for a different interpretation, that is, that the *carole* was always danced in a circle, as it was "the circular form that defined the dance" (p. 80).

166. For further discussion on the *carole*, see chapter 2 in this volume.

167. Mullally, "Dance Terminology," p. 252.

168. Ibid., p. 252.

169. See chapter 7 in this volume for an examination of the music for the *balli* and the relationship of the music to the choreography.

170. In the sixteenth century the word *"balletto"* was also used in the general sense to refer to a dance.

171. A *brando* was a longer, more complex choreography than a *balletto*, with a larger number of performers (G. Yvonne Kendall, "Theatre, Dance and Music in Late Cinquecento Milan," *Early Music* 32, no. 1 [2004], p. 95n29).

172. See Marcus Lehner, "The *Cascarda*: An Italian Dance Form of the Sixteenth Century," in *Terpsichore 1450–1900: Proceedings of the International Dance Conference, Ghent, April 2000*, ed. Barbara Ravelhofer (Ghent: Institute for Historical Dance Practice, 2000), pp. 11–20, for an analysis of the structure of the *cascarda* genre.

173. A *cascarda* was usually in triple meter, but there are a few examples, like *Fulgente Stella* from *Il ballarino*, that contain sections of triple and duple meter. The *basse* were mostly in duple meter, but, like the *cascarde*, there were dances with sections where the meter changed. In one of Negri's *basse*, the *Bassa Imperiale*, the Italian love of rhythmic variety was richly indulged, as the second musical section is constructed of "bars" of triple *minima* and then duple *minima* (Negri, *Le gratie d'amore*, pp. 206–207).

174. John Forrest, *The History of Morris Dancing, 1458–1750* (Toronto: University of Toronto Press, 1999), p. 89.

175. For the reasons behind the enduring popularity of this theory of origin, see ibid., pp. 5–7.

176. See chapter 8 in this volume for a detailed discussion on the arrangement and grouping of steps in the *basse dance*, and how this structure changed over the period c. 1450–1550.

177. Brooks, *The Art of Dancing*, p. 148.

178. Ibid., pp. 148–151.

179. *Branles* were group dances, with the dancers often arranged in couples in a circle and moving to the left and to the right with sequences of stepped and jumped single and double steps, and kicks. Some *branles* were pantomimic, like the Washerwomen's *branle*, which Arbeau says was given its name by the sound the dancers make by clapping their hands, which is like the noise of women beating their washing on the banks of the Seine (Arbeau, *Orchesography*, p. 155).

180. The pavane was a processional dance for couples, consisting of repetitions of the step sequence "single, single, double." A galliard was a lively, energetic dance. The basic "step" (the *cinque passi*) consisted of five movements, four kicks alternating feet in the air, then a large jump that ends with a *cadenza* or posture. There were literally hundreds of step variations, and long sequences of steps, that the man and woman could perform during a galliard. The structure of a galliard often involved first one partner parading in front of the other while dancing complex step sequences, then the other partner followed with his or her own variations. For further description of the galliard, its steps and variations, and its performance across Europe, see Barbara Sparti, "Introduction," to *Ballo della gagliarda*, by Lutio Compasso, Florence 1560. Facsimile ed. (Freiburg: Fa-gisis, 1995), pp. 5–19.

181. Esses, *Dance and Instrumental Diferencias in Spain*, 1: 427.

182. "La Nizzarda e un ballo allegro, alquale se non si può dar regola certa, come à gli altri balli, perche ogn'uno nel suo paese la balla à suo modo." Cesare Negri, *Le gratie*

d'amore, (Milan, 1602), p. 268. See also the essay by Federica Calvino Prina, "Nizarda! Qué danza es esa?" in *L'arte della danza ai tempi di Claudio Monteverdi, Atti del convegno internazionale, Torino, 6–7 settembre 1993*, ed. Angelo Chiarle (Turin: Istitutio per i Beni Musicali in Piemonte, 1996), pp. 17–32.

183. John Playford, *The English Dancing Master or, Plaine and easie Rules for the Dancing of Country Dances, with the Tune to each Dance* (London, 1651).

184. See Carol G. Marsh, "The Lovelace Manuscript: A Preliminary Study," in *Morgenröte des Barock. Tanz im 17. Jahrhundert*, ed. Uwe Scholttermüller and Maria Richter (Freiburg: Fa-gisis, 2004), pp. 81–90.

185. For a discussion on the changes in the English country dances during this period, and on the evidence for the influence of the contemporary French dance style on the English practice, see Daye, "Taking the Measure of Dance Steps 1650–1700," pp. 16–19.

186. For a detailed examination of the country dance patterns found in the dances by Thomas Bray, who was a dancer and dance master at the Drury Lane, Dorset Garden (from 1689), and then Lincoln's Inn Fields theaters, see Cruickshank, "Circling the Square," in *On Common Ground 3*, pp. 35–42.

187. Sutton, "Lorin and Playford: Connections and Disparities," in *On Common Ground 3*, p. 135.

188. However, in spite of the ubiquitous nature of the French style, the Italian dance style continued to be practiced and cannot be overlooked in any consideration of dance in the seventeenth and eighteenth century. For works that examine the Italian dance practice c. 1600–1800, see Harris-Warrick and Brown, *The Grotesque Dancer on the Eighteenth-Century Stage*; Irene Alm, "Winged Feet and Mute Eloquence: Dance in Seventeenth-Century Venetian Opera," ed. Wendy Heller and Rebecca Harris-Warrick, *Cambridge Opera Journal* 15, no. 3 (2003): 216–80; Barbara Sparti, "La 'danza barocca' è soltanto francese?" *Studi musicali* 25, nos. 1–2 (1996): 283–302.

189. For a visual demonstration as well as a summary of the main characteristics of these genres, see the DVD by Paige Whitley-Bauguess, *Introduction to Baroque Dance*, 1999 and 2005 (www.baroquedance.com). See also Francine Lancelot, *La belle dance: catalogue raisonné* (Paris: Van Dieren, 1996), pp. xxxviii–lviii.

190. Richard W. Kaeuper and Elspeth Kennedy, *The Book of Chivalry of Geoffroi de Charny: Text, Context, and Translation* (Philadelphia: University of Pennsylvania Press, 1996), p. 113. The original text is given on p. 112: "Et toutevoies devroit il sembler que li plus beaux gieux et li plus beaux esbatemens que telles gens qui tel honnour veulent querre devroient faire seroient qu'il ne se doivent point lasser de jouer, de jouster, de parler, de dancer et de chanter en compaignie de dames et de damoiseles ainsi honorablement comme il puet et doit appartenir et en gardant en fait et dit et en tous lieux leur honneur et leurs estas, que toutes bonnes gens d'armes le doivent ainsi faire de droit."

191. Harris-Warrick and Marsh, *Musical Theatre*, p. 10n27.

192. Astier, "Louis XIV, 'Premier Danseur,'" p. 74.

193. Ibid., p. 80. Louis danced at his first formal court ball on 27 February 1645. See ibid, p. 77, for a description of this event.

194. Lisa C. Devero, "The Court Dance of Louis XIV as Exemplified by Feuillet's *Chorégraphie* (1700) and How the Court Dance and Ceremonial Ball Were Used as Forms of Political and Socialization," Ph.D. diss., New York University, 1991, p. 41.

195. Brooks, *The Art of Dancing*, p. 119.

196. M. le duc de Saint-Simon, *Memoirs of Louis XIV and the Regency*, trans. Bayle St. John, 3 vols. (London: Allen & Unwin, 1926), 1: 19–20, quoted in Wendy Hilton, *Dance of*

Court and Theatre: The French Noble Style, 1690–1725 (London: Dance Books, 1981), pp. 15–16.

197. Karin J. MacHardy, "Cultural Capital, Family Strategies and Noble Identity in Early Modern Habsburg Austria 1579–1620," *Past and Present* 163 (1999): 55–56.

198. M. de Saint-Hubert, "How to Compose a Successful Ballet," p. 26.

199. Astier, "Louis XIV," p. 76.

200. Ibid.

201. Artur Michel, "The Earliest Dance Manuals," *Medievalia et Humanistica* 3 (1945): 119–20.

202. While the presence and technical skill of a dance master undoubtedly assisted in the smooth running of dance performances, the elite did have a choice in whether to include them or not. If the social stigma of their participation and partnering of the women of the elite was too great, then they would not have been included no matter how skilled they were, and the dance performances would have been supervised from the side-lines.

203. A. William Smith, trans., Introduction to *Fifteenth-Century Dance and Music: Twelve Transcribed Italian Treatises and Collections in the Tradition of Domencio da Piacenza* (Stuyvesant, N.Y.: Pendragon Press, 1995), p. xxi.

204. Marin Sanudo, *I diarii di Marin Sanuto (1496–1533)*, 58 vols., ed. Rinaldo Fulin et al. (Venice: 1879–1903; reprint, Bologna: Forni, 1969–79).

205. The *compagnie della calza* were companies of young noblemen that were formed for the purposes of organizing aristocratic carnival activities: planning parties, sponsoring pageants, masquerades, dances, banquets and fireworks, comedies—usually lascivious— and *momaria* (Edward Muir, *Civic Ritual in Renaissance Venice* [Princeton: Princeton University Press, 1981], pp. 167, 170–71). For more information on the activities of the *compagnie* during carnival, including their dancing activities, see Muir, *Civic Ritual*, pp. 166–75, and Maria Teresa Muraro, "La festa a Venezia e le sue manifestazione rappresentative: Le compagnie della calza e le *momarie*," in *Storia della cultura veneta*, vol. 3 (Vicenza: N. Pozza, 1976), pp. 315–41. For descriptions of the danced parts of the *momarie*, see A. William Smith, "Dance in Early Sixteenth-Century Venice: The *Mumaria* and Some of Its Choreographers," in *Proceedings of the 12th Annual Conference of Society of Dance History Scholars* (Riverside: SDHS, 1989), pp. 126–38.

206. McGinnis, "Moving in High Circles," p. 325.

207. Sanudo, *I diarii*, 57: 650.

208. Judith Rock, *Terpsichore at Louis-Le-Grand: Baroque Dance on the Jesuit Stage in Paris* (St. Louis: Institute of Jesuit Sources, 1996), pp. 54, 60–61.

209. In Rome dramatic productions were held every year from 1565 to 1647, but only for some years is dance mentioned in the records as part of the spectacle (Alessandra Sardoni, "'Ut in voce sic in gestu'. Danza e cultura barocca nei collegi gesuitici tra Roma e la Francia," *Studi musicali* 25, nos. 1–2 [1996]: 311). For example, dance was included with the plays performed in 1597 and 1598, while in 1622 in Rome there were "dances by Indians, by centaurs, and by ocean waves" (Louis J. Oldani, S.J. and Victor R. Yanitelli, S.J., "Jesuit Theater in Italy: Its Entrances and Exit," *Italica* 76, no. 1 [1999]: 22). Dance teachers were employed at the French Jesuit colleges on an ad hoc basis from 1604 to 1638. From 1638 they appear in college records as regular employees (Rock, *Terpsichore at Louis-Le-Grand*, pp. 55–56).

210. For more information on the different types of Jesuit drama and the themes of the plays performed in various Italian cities, as well as connections between the Italian colleges and colleges in Germany, France, England, and Spain, see Oldani and Yanitelli, "Jesuit Theater in Italy," pp. 18–32.

211. See Rock, *Terpsichore at Louis-Le-Grand*, p. 56, for a list of the dance masters at Louis-Le-Grand from the late 1660s to 1760. Unfortunately, the Roman Jesuit records do not mention the name of a single dance master (Sardoni, "'*Ut in voce sic in gestu*,'" p. 311).

212. Estimates of the rehearsal time devoted to the annual play and ballet range from three months to one year (Rock, *Terpsichore at Louis-Le-Grand*, p. 52).

213. Jeannine Dorvane, "Ballet de Collège," in *International Encyclopedia of Dance* (New York: Oxford University Press, 1998), 1: 284.

214. Negri, *Le gratie d'amore*, pp. 7–16, and for a translation see G. Yvonne Kendall, "'Le Gratie d'Amore' 1602 by Cesare Negri: Translation and Commentary," D.M.A. thesis, Stanford University, 1985, pp. 34–52. See also chapter 10 in this volume for a narrative account of Negri's career.

215. Negri, *Le gratie d'amore*, p. 7, and Kendall, "'Le Gratie d'Amore' 1602," p. 34.

216. Negri, *Le gratie d'amore*, pp. 17–30, and Kendall, "'Le Gratie d'Amore' 1602," pp. 52a–80a.

217. Kendall, "Theatre, Dance and Music," pp. 83–84.

218. Mary Laven, *Virgins of Venice: Enclosed Lives and Broken Vows in the Renaissance Convent* (London: Viking, 2002), pp. xxii and 4.

219. Ibid., p. 134.

220. Ibid., p. 138.

221. Iain Fenlon, "The Claims of Choreography—Women Courtiers and Danced Spectacle in Late Sixteenth-Century Paris and Ferrara," in *Frauen und Musik im Europa des 16 Jahrhunderts: Infrastrukturen-Aktivitaten-Motivationem*, ed. Nicole Schwindt (Kassel: Barenreiter, 2005), p. 76.

222. Ibid., p. 77.

223. Ibid., p. 78.

224. Ibid., p. 87.

225. Savage, "The Staging of Courtly Theatre," p. 67.

226. In 1610 Marie de' Medici, the mother of Louis XIII, also "collaborated in the composition of her own ballet." See Karen Britland, "An Under-Stated Mother-in-Law: Marie de Médicis and the Last Caroline Court Masque," in *Women and Culture at the Courts of the Stuart Queens*, ed. Clare McManus (Houndsmills: Palgrave Macmillan, 2003), pp. 204–23, especially pp. 206–7.

227. Esses, *Dance and Instrumental Diferencias in Spain*, 1: 356. See also Louise K. Stein, "The Musicians of the Spanish Royal Chapel and Court Entertainments, 1590–1648," in *The Royal Chapel in the Time of the Hapsburgs: Music and Court Ceremony in Early Modern Europe*, trans. Yolanda Acker, English version ed. Tess Knighton (Woodbridge: Boydell Press, 2005), pp. 173–78.

228. See chapter 4 in this volume for extensive discussion on these court fêtes, the courtiers who danced in them, and the roles they took.

229. Harris-Warrick and Marsh, *Musical Theatre*, p. 10. The names of all the dancers, both noble and professional and their roles, were included in the *livrets* of Louis XIV's *ballets de cour*. These *livrets* are published in the two-volume work edited by Marie-Claude Canova-Green, *Benserade: Ballets pour Louis XIV* (Toulouze: Societé de Littératures Classiques, 1997). In the court ballets at Stuttgart in the first two decades of the seventeenth century, all the noble dancers were male, and these gentlemen portrayed both male and female roles. However, the non-participation of ladies in the court ballets was not a universal phenomenon at German courts: at Dessau in 1614 the dancers included ladies of the court (Smart, "The Württemberg Court and the Introduction of Ballet into the Empire," pp. 36 and 45).

230. Anne Daye, "Theatre Dance in the Private and Public Domains of Stuart and Commonwealth London, 1625–1685," in *The Restoration of Charles II: Public Order, Theatre and Dance, Proceedings of a Conference, London February 2002*, ed. David R. Wilson (Cambridge: Early Dance Circle, 2002), p. 13.

231. Andrew Walkling, "Masque and Politics at the Restoration Court: John Crowne's *Calisto," Early Music* 24, no. 1 (1996): 32–42.

232. Harris-Warrick and Marsh, *Musical Theatre*, p. 10.

233. Marrocco and Merveille, "Antonius Arena," p. 19.

234. Ibid., pp. 21–22.

235. Margaret M. McGowan, "Ballets for the Bourgeois," *Dance Research* 19, no. 2 (2001): 108.

236. Ibid.

237. For a transcription of the dance manuscripts associated with the Inns of Court that record the choreographies of the dances commonly performed, see David R. Wilson, "Dancing in the Inns of Court," *Historical Dance* 2, no. 5 (1986–87): 3–16, and Ian Payne, *The Almain in Britain, c.1549–c.1675: A Dance Manual from Manuscript Sources* (Aldershot: Ashgate, 2003). The manuscripts date from c. 1570 to c. 1672. For further information on the Inns of Court's masques and their dancing activities, see Peter Walls, *Music in the English Courtly Masque, 1604–1640* (Oxford: Clarendon Press, 1995), pp. 260–67.

238. John Playford, *The English Dancing Master*, 1651. Reprint of the 1933 edition ed. Hugh Mellor and Leslie Bridgewater (London: Dance Books, 1984).

239. For a detailed examination of five ballets performed in the *Hôtel de ville*, as well as the ball given there by Louis XIV in 1649 for courtiers and invited citizens, and an examination of the reasons for Louis—father and son—to voluntarily perform before such an audience, see McGowan, "Ballets for the Bourgeois," pp. 106–24.

240. Ibid., pp. 120–21.

241. For a detailed examination of these balls, see Richard Semmens, *The bals publics at the Paris Opéra in the Eighteenth Century* (Hillsdale, N.Y.: Pendragon Press, 2004). It is from pp. 1–22 of this work that the information in this paragraph is taken.

242. Richard Brown, "The Reception of Anna Sforza in Ferrara, February 1491," *Renaissance Studies* 2, no. 2 (1988): 234.

243. Belfiore was built as a hunting retreat by Alberto d'Este around 1390–92.

244. Werner L. Gundersheimer, ed., *Art and Life at the Court of Ercole I d'Este: The De triumphis religionis of Giovanni Sabadino degli Arienti* (Geneva: Librairie Droz, 1972), p. 68.

245. As illustrated in another series of frescoes from Belfiore, this time depicting the duke and duchess, Ercole d'Este and Eleonora d'Aragona and their court. After hunting the court moves to the seashore to fish, and then to dance and to play chess in a pavilion to the accompaniment of pipes and a drum (Gundersheimer, *Art and Life*, p. 71).

246. Fenlon, "The Claims of Choreography," p. 84. See also Barbara Coeyman, "Opera and Ballet in Seventeenth-Century French Theaters: Case Studies of the Salle des Machines and the Palais Royal Theater," in Radice, *Opera and Context*, pp. 43 and 308n23.

247. For an examination of these events, and their connection to the sixteenth-century Valois court fêtes, see Orest Ranum, "Islands and the Self in a Ludovician Fête," in Rubin, *The Sun King*, pp. 17–27.

248. Sarah R. Cohen, *Art, Dance, and the Body in French Culture of the Ancien Régime* (Cambridge: Cambridge University Press, 2000), p. 70.

249. Ibid., pp. 71–72. See also John S. Powell, *Music and Theatre in France 1600–1680* (Oxford: Oxford University Press, 2000), pp. 337–50.

250. For a contemporary engraving of the ballroom built in the garden for this occasion, see Cohen, *Art, Dance, and the Body*, p. 76 fig. 32. It looks very much like a permanent indoor dance space. For more information on the garden ballroom and the location of the various events in the gardens, see Barbara Coeyman, "Social Dance in the 1688 *Feste de Versailles*: Architecture and Performance Context," *Early Music* 26, no. 2 (1998): 264–82.

251. Patricia H. Labalme and Laura Sanguinetti White, "How to (and How Not to) Get Married in Sixteenth-Century Venice (Selections from the Diaries of Marin Sanudo)," trans. Linda Carroll, *Renaissance Quarterly*, 52, no. 1 (1999): 54–60, and especially 58.

252. Margaret M. McGowan, "A Renaissance War Dance: The Pyrrhic," *Dance Research* 3, no. 1 (1984): 29–38.

253. See chapter 2 in this volume for an example of dance as part of a royal entry from the early fourteenth century.

254. Seneca described the *tripudium* as a "'manly style in which the heroes of olden times used to dance at the time of the games and festive celebrations'" (Skinner, "Ambrogio Lorenzetti's *Buon Governo* Frescoes," p. 24. Skinner is quoting Seneca, *De tranquillitate animi*, in *Moral Essays*, ed. and trans. J. W. Basore, 3 vols. [London, 1928–35], 2: 280: "ut antiqui illi viri solebant inter lusum ac festa tempora virilem in modum tripudiare").

255. Skinner, "Ambrogio Lorenzetti's *Buon Governo* Frescoes," p. 22.

256. Ibid., p. 24.

257. Ibid., p. 25 (Skinner is quoting from the contemporary document, *Gradulatio Patavini potestatis*, in *Antiquitates Itaticae*, ed. Lodovico Muratori, Milan 1741, 4: 131–32).

258. Esses, *Dance and Instrumental Diferencias in Spain*, 1: 411–16. For dancing as part of Spanish royal entries, see David Sanchez Cano, "Dances for the Royal Festivities in Madrid in the Sixteenth and Seventeenth Centuries," *Dance Research* 23, no. 2 (2005): 123–52.

259. Circular patterns were often created by one partner circling around the other, or where two dancers change places while circling around a third.

260. Gundersheimer, *Art and Life*, p. 65.

261. Pirrotta and Povoledo, *Music and Theatre From Poliziano*, p. 293.

262. Ingrid Brainard, "Medieval Dance," in *International Encyclopaedia of Dance* (Oxford: Oxford University Press, 1998), 4: 349.

263. Barbara Coeyman, "Opera and Ballet," pp. 308–309n26.

264. Andrew C. Minor and Bonner Mitchell, *A Renaissance Entertainment: Festivities for the Marriage of Cosimo, Duke of Florence in 1539* (Columbia: University of Missouri Press, 1968), pp. 349–50.

265. Daye, "Theatre Dance in the Private and Public Domains," p. 11.

266. Kendall, "Theatre, Dance and Music," p. 91.

267. Ibid.

268. Massimo Ossi, "*Dalle macchine . . . la maraviglia*," p. 18. See pp. 299–300n18 for the differing estimates of the size of this room by modern scholars, and the reason for these differences.

269. Ibid., p. 18.

270. Ossi cites the example of the space that would be required behind the stage to deliver "a cloud toward the front of the stage" as six meters (ibid., p. 22). Machines required space on the sides, above and underneath the stage, as well as behind.

271. In an earlier article I estimated that the average space needed to perform a dance for six to twelve performers would be 50 feet by 21 feet. But as Barbara Ravelhofer has correctly pointed out, this estimate was based on modern performers who take large steps

and are generally much taller than sixteenth- and seventeenth-century performers (Ravelhofer, *Early Stuart Masque*, p. 89).

272. For a discussion of this *ballo* and a reconstruction of the choreography, including a correlation of the steps and the music, and a reconstruction of the floor plan together with the music, see Jennifer Nevile, "Cavalieri's Theatrical *Ballo* 'O che nuovo miracolo': A Reconstruction," *Dance Chronicle* 21, no. 3 (1998): 353–88.

273. For evidence supporting my division of the seven principal dancers into four women and three men, see Nevile, "Cavalieri's Theatrical *Ballo*: A Reconstruction," pp. 361–63.

274. See also on this point Pamela Jones, "Spectacle in Milan: Cesare Negri's Torch Dances," *Early Music* 14, no. 2 (1986): 182–96. For a discussion on the changes (or lack of changes) between Cavalieri's theatrical *ballo*, and Caroso's and Negri's dances recorded in their treatises, see Jennifer Nevile, "Cavalieri's Theatrical *Ballo* and the Social Dances of Caroso and Negri," *Dance Chronicle* 22, no. 1 (1999): 119–33.

275. Harris-Warrick, "Ballroom Dancing," p. 43.

276. Ibid., pp. 44–45. On p. 45 is a plan of the dance space for this ball.

277. Ibid., p. 44.

278. Ibid.

279. Ibid., pp. 43–44. See also Garlick, "A Measure of Decorum," pp. 164–65, for details on the seating arrangements at court balls.

280. Harris-Warrick, "Ballroom Dancing," p. 44.

281. For a detailed examination of the Banqueting House in Whitehall as a dance space, see Anne Daye, "The Banqueting House, Whitehall: A Site Specific to Dance," *Historical Dance* 4, no. 1 (2004): 3–22.

282. The *Masque of Blackness* in 1605 was the first to use a raised stage. Before then masques were performed entirely on the floor of the hall, and on moveable pageant cars that could enter and exit the performance space.

283. For a detailed examination of the theatrical use of space in the masque, and the significance and meaning of this division of space, see Jerzy Limon, "The Masque of Stuart Culture," in *The Mental World of the Jacobean Court*, ed. Linda Levy Peck (Cambridge: Cambridge University Press, 1991), pp. 209–29.

284. For a description of the temporary theaters at Versailles, see Barbara Coeyman, "Sites of Indoor Musical-Theatrical Production at Versailles," *Eighteenth-Century Life* 17 (1993): 59–64.

285. Barbara Coeyman, "Opera and Ballet," p. 46.

286. For detailed descriptions of these theaters and the productions that were held in them, see ibid., pp. 37–71.

Part 2

Dance at Court and in the City

Pre-fifteenth-century dance is the least documented of any of the dance practices covered by the label "early dance," both in terms of dance-specific primary source material and also in the depth of modern scholarship and reconstruction. Karen Silen's essay on dance in Paris at the end of the thirteenth century focuses on the dance activities of students at the University of Paris, leading into a discussion of medieval dance, what is known about it, what is not, and where the information we do have comes from. Her chapter is an introduction to medieval dance and its social setting, and is especially valuable when read in conjunction with chapter 14 by Alessandro Arcangeli. Here in chapter 2 we are also introduced to themes that recur in the next two chapters: how ability in dance was an important social skill for both men and women; and the part dance played in official ceremonies, court entertainments and public, city–wide festivities. In the thirteenth century an expertise in dance would increase the social standing of aristocratic performers and of those who worked in the papal and secular aristocratic courts. Three hundred years later, by the end of the sixteenth century, as discussed in chapter 4 by Margaret M. McGowan, it was a necessity for anyone seeking to obtain a position at court, particularly an administrative position, to be able to dance well. Furthermore, the high level of ability and interest in dance exhibited by the French monarchs, Charles IX, Henri III, and Louis XIII, has been documented in detail, and at this period the court dance performances had an important function in upholding and exhibiting the king's personal authority. McGowan discusses how early in the sixteenth century dance contributed greatly to the presentation of an image of magnificence by François I, but by the second half of the century court dance performances were an integral part of national and international politics, a thread that is explored further by Julia Prest in chapter 11 when she discusses Louis XIV's dance performances. Chapter 3 on dance in fifteenth-century Italy similarly examines dance as part of court ceremonies and festivities, exploring how dance was an important part of ritual events and the ordered, formal behavior demanded by these rituals. Throughout the late medieval period and the Renaissance, movements of the body were viewed as the outward, physical manifestations of movements of the soul. In fifteenth-century Italy, therefore, dance was seen as a sign of civilized behavior and a way to expressing virtuous emotions, teaching as it did control over one's bodily movements, gestures and one's emotions. Dance was also a form of ritualized courtship, expressing as it did the daily interactions of women and men at court.

From the fifteenth century dance becomes a written art as well as a set of physical skills. Not only dance masters, but also humanists, philosophers, and poets argued for dance to have a place alongside other art forms, utilizing in their arguments the works of classical authors such as Aristotle, Plato, and Lucian to support their opinion, and to remind their readers of the long traditions of dance. The relationship between dance and the other arts, and the connection between the classical traditions of dance and contemporary practices in fifteenth-century Italy and sixteenth-century France are discussed in chapters 3 and 4, as well as in chapters 14 and 15 in part 6. Chapters 3 and 4 (and chapter 15) emphasize that the court-danced spectacles were multi-media events that required close collaboration between various artists, musicians, designers, engineers, and architects, as well as choreographers. The interdisciplinary nature of these theatrical spectacles take center stage in part 3.

2

Dance in Late Thirteenth-Century Paris

Karen Silen

In the sixth decade of the thirteenth century Henri Bate was enjoying life as a student at the University of Paris.[1] Writing about his time there (in the third person) Bate recounted:

> Besides every kind of musical song was known to him . . . and various species of popular songs in various languages, and he sang most willingly, and was also a trouvère [lit. "composer"] of verse and songs, a lively, agreeable, and courteous leader of round dances and a conductor of the dances, striving for games, entertainments, and pastimes to be prepared in gardens, also mingling the diversion of dancing with others. These activities, moreover, and similar things are not especially injurious to studies among the young.[2]

In this passage Henri is making two main points: he could sing and dance so well that he could invent dance songs and lead dances, and also that dancing was not harmful to students. Henri's dance skills were not unusual at the time: they appeared quite frequently in stories and reports about noble characters, and were a mark of courtliness. In the late twelfth-century and early thirteenth-century romances of Jean Renart, for example, *caroles* were danced at the court of the emperor, as well as in the nursery for the imperial children, while in the romances of Gerbert de Montreuil aristocratic girls and women (and occasionally knights and squires) are described as dancing at tournaments, weddings, and other cele- bratory occasions.[3] Henri himself came from a good family, and after his time at the University of Paris he became a high-ranking church official, a cantor of St. Lambert Cathedral in Liège, and a distinguished astronomer and theologian.[4]

Most of the thirteenth-century texts describing medieval dance were writ- ten by "clerics," a term that by the thirteenth century had widened its original meaning of a person in ecclesiastical orders, to also include scholars, that is, those who were educated and learned, even if these men were not in ecclesiasti- cal orders.[5] This is especially true for those who wrote in Latin rather than the vernacular languages. Henri's comments shed light on the prestige enjoyed by dance, at the same time raising questions about the role of dance in clerical edu- cation and professional life, about how and where students learned to dance, and whether this knowledge was useful in their professional careers. Like many documents written before the fifteenth century, Henri's biography assumes that its readers already knew how dances were performed, who created them, and how they were taught. Dancing's popularity may in fact be part of the problem: there was no need to write down what everyone already knew.

For the dance historian it is both tantalizing and frustrating to confront depictions of dance without details of the way they were performed or transmit- ted. The earliest known dance treatises, which include step descriptions, chore- ographies, and in some cases the accompanying music, did not appear until the fifteenth century. But the challenge in reconstructing earlier dance practices comes not from an absence of sources but from a variety of sources new to dance history, sources in which dancing is not the primary focus but appears in discus- sions of other topics. Assembling the many fragments that describe dance makes it possible to form a picture of dancing in the medieval period, especially when limited to a particular location and period of time. An investigation of questions raised by Henri Bate's autobiography offers just such an opportunity.

Whether Henri Bate or other university students carried their love of dancing with them when they left Paris is a question that can only be a matter of conjecture in the absence of any further documentary evidence of their activi- ties. What we do know is that Paris played a pivotal role in the production and dissemination of many aspects of medieval culture, especially of music and mu- sical notation, and of books and ideas. Students came from across Europe to study with some of the best masters of their day, and when they left they sought and received jobs in papal, episcopal, and noble courts across Europe. Although we cannot know whether clerics taught dancing, it is certain they participated in, and contributed to, the cultural life of which dancing was a part.

Dancing and the Church

The Church in the thirteenth century was an association of individuals and groups with sometimes widely different beliefs about life, religion, and dance. It is not surprising, then, that writers expressed a range of views and perspectives about dance.[6] In terms of sheer numbers, negative comments appear to outweigh moderate or positive views of dance, but this is largely due to the kinds of documents that were widely produced and copied at the time, such as preaching aids, in which negative opinions of dance were expressed. While the abundance of preaching materials represents their importance to preachers and members of the mendicant orders (for example, the Franciscans and the Dominicans), they do not reflect the position *vis-à-vis* dance of all members of the clergy. Even within the mendicant orders opinions on dance differed. For example, some of the official accounts of the life of St. Francis, written by Franciscans, depict St. Francis dancing as part of his spiritual discipline, as well as the pope and the inhabitants of heaven dancing.[7]

Two important aspects of the mendicants' work were preaching and at times hearing confession, and to aid both these tasks a large body of reference manuals were created, copied, and widely distributed. These reference manuals included books on vices and virtues that were useful in determining which activities were considered sinful, as well as confession manuals that included detailed questions confessors could ask penitents to determine whether they had sinned. Under the section on "lust," for example, questions sometimes appeared asking whether a man had attended or participated in public dances, since these were a likely place for him to meet women, which might lead to confessions of sinful behavior.[8] Collections of *exempla* and sermon collections containing notes and ideas for sermons on various topics were also produced in large numbers.[9] One noteworthy example from this type of literature was the *Summa de vitiis et de virtutibus* (before 1249/50)[10] of the Dominican prior, Guillaume Peyraut, which contained a lengthy attack on dancing, and whose circulation was phenomenal.[11]

The large numbers of anti-dance comments in preaching materials reflected a strategy used by many mendicants to attempt to convince or frighten listeners into living more Christian lives. Although dancing was not the focus of such texts, it was frequently presented as a potentially dangerous activity supervised by demons and best avoided, as the following *exempla* shows. In this story from a work by John Bromyard, a group of mendicants approached a town, planning to preach to the citizens, but when they came close to the gates of the town they

> saw a demon sitting upon the ramparts of the city, and when he was asked why he sat there alone he replied: "I do not need the help of anyone, because all the city is obediently subject to us [the forces of the Devil]." Entering the city they found the population in a state of the greatest dissoluteness, that is to say dancing *caroles* and occupied with diverse other entertainments. Terrified, they left that city.[12]

Stories like this were gathered into collections to be used by preachers in their sermons, adapted if necessary to emphasize a point.[13] The stories were not expected to be strictly realistic, as the preacher often included "fabulous" elements in his tales to capture and hold the attention of his listeners. As Alessandro Arcangeli has pointed out, *exempla* were not vehicles for the transmission of subtle arguments and distinctions.

> Oppositions are dramatic, lives change suddenly, rewards and punishments are distributed openly, allowing no doubt about God's judgement. As an oratorical device the *exemplum* relies on such structural simplicity in order to realize its principal functions: impressing listeners and providing memorable teaching. The desired effect of providing a moral warning is achieved as the story is remembered.[14]

Thus, the negative view of dancing, so often expressed in *exempla*, does not, by the very nature of the vehicle in which it was expressed, represent the nuanced views of dance held across all sections of the Church.

The tale above starkly contrasts with the opinion of another famous Dominican and a master at the University of Paris from 1245, Albertus Magnus, who discussed the social benefits of various forms of play and entertainment, including dance:

> It is true, moreover, that amusements as singing, fiddling, dancing, leaping, tragedies, and comedies, and things of this kind are necessary for the prudent man to organize adequately, so that every delighted inhabitant among the citizens might be found in amusements worthy of a free man. . . . Leaping,[15] moreover, prepares the motive powers, and makes a citizen fleet.[16]

Albertus Magnus's view was that it was either the circumstances and manner of performance, or the people who were dancing, that made dance sinful or worthy of praise, rather than the activity itself.[17] Records show that students and their masters at the University of Paris were happy to follow his views in this matter, as both enjoyed participating in dancing as members of a university community, as clerics, and as residents of Paris.

Public Dancing in Paris

During the second half of the thirteenth century residents of Paris could participate in at least two major types of public dancing events that we know about: large, official, city-wide celebrations, such as the ones described by Albertus Magnus and John Bromyard, and smaller, more casual public dances. Not surprisingly, official records tell us more about the former than the latter. One event in particular took place soon after Henri's arrival in 1267: King Louis IX held a knighting ceremony for his eldest son, Philip, and sixty-eight other young men. It was one of the largest civic festivals of the century and was attended by important nobility and prelates from all over France. As part of the festivities honored guests were greeted, feasted, and entertained by the royal court and the inhabitants of city of Paris. Unfortunately, the chronicles from this period did not elaborate on the entertainments involved; the best descriptions of this type of event come from another Parisian knighting ceremony that took place in 1313, almost fifty years later. In this later festival, four separate dance events were recorded: performances by noble women, bourgeoisie women, men who were not in guilds, and fifty-four professional dancers who performed nude before the visiting king, Edward II of England.[18] The chronicles describe the dance performances that were special to this occasion, but other types of dancing also typically attended knighting ceremonies or royal entries: the private "balls" of the nobility; welcoming dances performed by young men and women for visiting royalty or nobility as they entered into the city; and the more spontaneous outbursts of public street dancing performed at times of celebration.[19]

The *carole*

By far the most popular type of dance mentioned for both public and courtly dances was the *carole* (English "carol," Latin "*chorea*"). An exact definition of the *carole* has evaded scholars, most of whom conclude that the word refers to a general rather than specific type of dance.[20] In contemporary writings it was characterized as an aspect of festive entertainment in which dancers accompanied themselves by singing. A leader sang the verses of a song and the rest of the group responded with the chorus, also known as a refrain or "burden." Only rarely were *caroles* described as being accompanied by instrumentalists. Part of the *carole's* appeal may have stemmed from its adaptability and portability: it could be performed almost anywhere, indoors or out. They were performed in circles, lines, or processions, in streets and town squares, church yards and cemeteries, in meadows and courtly halls. But despite the many references to *caroles*, few medieval sources described how the dancers moved. Some sources refer to clapping or hand gestures, beating one foot against another, or moving quickly and lightly. In Peyraut's treatise dancers are described as holding hands while moving in a circular motion. The movement of the *carole* always started by moving to the left, but could also move back to the right before returning to the left. This could possibly happen several times.[21] It is most likely that the steps of *caroles* were as well known, and as easy to learn and to remember, as the music and lyrics that accompanied them.[22] In many dances it appears that performers needed only to know the one or two lines of the refrain, as long as a leader knew—or could improvise—the words to the verse.[23]

More is known about the lyrics that accompanied dancing than perhaps any other aspect of the *carole*. Secular dance song music and dance movements were recorded only rarely, but lyrics were gathered into collections, inserted into stories, discussed in sermons, and jotted into the margins of manuscripts. The following lyric (from about 1210 to 1228) describes aspects of the dance event as well as providing accompaniment for dancing: "The girl from Oissery never neglects to go to festivities; she's so wonderful that she makes the game under the elm-tree even better. On her head she wore a garland of fresh new roses; she had a face fresh and blushing, sparkling eyes, a bright, sweet, lovely face. To make the others envious she wore many fine jewels."[24]

Dance song lyrics like this appear to have been extremely popular, but were also a source of complaint by moralists who objected to women's attention to their appearance or the "amorous" nature of some songs. Some preachers even claimed that anyone who heard a dance song and forgot to declare it in confession would be punished by eighteen days in Purgatory.[25] But various means were found to avoid the censure attached to secular dance songs. Some clerics, for example, simply created new, more acceptable lyrics in Latin. In the *Red Book of Ossory* from the second half of the fourteenth century, a bishop in Ireland wrote new words for clerics to sing on holy days, "so that their throats and ears, consecrated to God, might not be sullied by dramatic, lewd and secular songs."[26] Another collection of dance songs with Latin lyrics was written in Paris in the late twelfth century at Notre-Dame; although the original was destroyed, a copy of it (with an illustration of dancing clerics) is now in Florence.[27] These collections suggest that many clerics enjoyed dancing, a fact confirmed by several sources. Clerics danced in churches, cemeteries, and processions; at Christmas and Easter and especially on certain saints and holy days. Some of this information comes from synod reports, like that held in Paris in 1208, which forbade priests to dance *caroles* in the church, in cemeteries, and in processions. But many other sources express no hostility toward dance; they simply refer to it as a customary part of the church calendar or as the natural expression of religious enthusiasm.[28]

Given that at least some clerics enjoyed dancing and that vernacular dance songs were sometimes condemned, it is not surprising that some enterprising clerics—possibly students—invented Latin lyrics to dance to. Although Henri Bate claimed to be an inventor of dance songs, he does not tell us where he acquired this skill, nor in which language he composed his songs.[29] We must consider that he and other students learned or developed this ability at the university because evidence survives of at least one master of music who taught at the Sorbonne and wrote a music treatise on the different types of music practiced in Paris in the late thirteenth century: Johannes de Grocheio.[30]

Dancing at the University

Johannes de Grocheio, in his treatise from the end of the thirteenth century entitled *De musica* (*Concerning Music*), distinguished between several different types of popular song, including dance songs. He provided essential information on the number and placement of verses and refrains and the use or otherwise of the same melodies for the verses and refrains, all of which would allow students to invent their own melodies and lyrics to accompany specific types of dances.[31] If Henri Bate studied with Grocheio, or other music teachers like him, he would have had the perfect opportunity to learn how to invent dance songs, and perhaps the movements that went with them. Certainly Grocheio did not condemn dancing but rather took a more balanced view, as is illustrated by his description of the vocal dance song, the *ductia*: "The [vocal] carol (*ductia*) is a song that is light and rapid in its ascent and descent, and which is sung in a *carole* by young men and women. . . . This song, indeed, guides the hearts of young women and men and keeps them from vanity, and it is said to be effective against that passion which is called erotic love."[32]

Even though students had opportunities to dance, it does not automatically follow that they took advantage of them. However, sources show that they did dance, at least in their free time. One text describes dancing at Saint Germain des Prés, where students congregated in their free time. In a medieval translation and adaptation of Ovid's *Ars Amatoria*, written as a guide on how to get, keep, and get rid of a lover, young men were advised that the public dances (*caroles*) were the best place to meet lovers, and that these public dances took place in Saint Germain des Prés: "If you have been in Paris you will find it hard to go anywhere else to love women or girls. . . . 'To what part shall I go?' 'Towards St Germain des Prés. . . . It is there that the girls dance their *caroles*, [the girls] who willingly speak of love.'"[33]

The most concrete evidence of dance by students are the rules and regulations prohibiting this activity. While none were issued during Henri's years at the university, regulations did appear in 1252, 1275, 1276, and 1280. They were aimed at preventing students and their masters from dancing on feast days and at graduation "parties" that processed through the streets; that is, they were concerned solely with dancing in public, where non-university people could see and hear them. The rules were especially concerned with keeping the peace and seem to coincide with periods of extreme tension between town dwellers and members of the university. The first rule to forbid public dancing was recorded following the violence caused when the Pastoreaux, a religious sect that incited violence against clerics, entered Paris; the rule appears to have been part of an effort by masters at the university to reduce tensions between students and masters of the university and the townspeople.[34]

Student regulations provide limited and conflicting information: clearly students and their teachers danced or there would not have been regulations against it, but at certain times at least, they were not allowed to do so in public. We have no evidence whether the rules against dancing were obeyed or broken, although the constant repetition of dress codes suggests that at least some rules were frequently overlooked by students. Frustratingly, the rules regulating student behavior reveal nothing about whether students and masters danced in Church, in the rooms where classes were held or where students lived, or on the field near Saint Germain des Prés, as they were only concerned with the students' behavior in public. But records show that students could and did practice dancing in their free time; that they could learn the musical distinctions between different types of dances; that they could hear arguments on the benefits of dancing; and that collections of Latin dance song lyrics were composed by and for clerics. Henri Bate certainly could have learned the dancing skills he claimed as a student in Paris: for those who wished to learn and practice dancing, the University at Paris seems to have been an ideal training ground—as long as one did not disturb the neighbors' peace.

Conclusion

Medieval texts, when examined in their social and historical context, reveal a vision of dance in late thirteenth-century Paris, albeit a fragmented one. But they also raise a number of questions. Did Henri or other students pass along their ability to lead dances, to invent dance songs, or to argue for or against the performing of dances? On this the sources are silent in two regards. Little is known about the dancing activity of university students once they left the university, and at the same time, we have little evidence of how dances were transmitted: we can only suppose from the lack of written instruction that dances were not learned from texts but by observation and participation.

But if the role of students and clerics in the transmission of dances and dance techniques is undocumented, we do know that that clerics were responsible for the creation and dissemination of texts that documented some dance practices and attitudes toward dance. For it is through the analysis of their writings—preaching materials, chronicles, religious and scholarly treatises, and romances—that much of our picture of dance in this period emerges. Although rarely focusing on dance, these texts provide snippets and songs, commentaries and condemnations that, when pieced together, are suggestive of a vivid portrait of dance in Paris in the second half of the thirteenth century.

Notes

1. This chapter draws on material from a paper given at the annual conference for the Society of Dance History Scholars, 21 June 2002, as well as my dissertation on dance theory and practice in late thirteenth-century France and French Flanders. I would like to thank members of SDHS, as well as Steven Justice and James Whitta, for comments on some sections or passages.

2. "Amplius omne genus musici cantus sibi notum est . . . et diverse species cantionum vulgarium in diversis linguis ipseque cantans libentius, rithmorum quoque inventor et cantionum, hylaris, iocundus amatiuus corearum ductor et dux tripudiorum in virgultis ludos conuiuia et iocos parari affectans, ludum quoque saltationis aliis interponens. Hec autem et huiusmodi non sunt operationibus studiosis inimica maxime in iuuenibus." Henri Bate, *Nativitas magistri Henrici Mechliniensis*, Paris, Bibliothèque Nationale, ms. lat. 7324, fol. 32v; the passage quoted above is from Nicole Goldine, "Henri Bate, chanoine et chantre de la cathédrale Saint Lambert à Liège et théoricien de la musique (1246-après 1310)," *Revue Belge de Musicologie* 18 (1964): 10–27; at p. 14n6, and it is cited by Christopher Page, *Voices and Instruments of the Middle Ages: Instrumental practice and songs in France 1100–1300* (Berkeley: University of California Press, 1986), pp. 59–60. The translation is by Randall Rosenfeld.

3. John Baldwin, *Aristocratic Life in Medieval France: The Romances of Jean Renart and Gerbert de Montreuil, 1190–1230* (Baltimore: Johns Hopkins University Press, 2000), p. 170.

4. For further information on Henri Bate see Nicole Goldine, "Henri Bate," and Carlos Steel, "Introduction," in *Speculum divinorum et quorundam naturalium/Henricus Bate*, vol. 12, edited Helmut Boese (Leuven: Leuven University Press, 1990), pp. ix–xxxiii.

5. In the thirteenth century the Holy Roman Emperor, Frederick II, for example, "could be said, without any sense of anomaly to be [a] great 'clerk.'" Alexander Murray, *Reason and Society in the Middle Ages* (Oxford: Clarendon Press, 2002), pp. 263–64.

6. See the chapter by Alessandro Arcangeli for further discussion on the attitude of the Church, both Catholic and Protestant, on dancing.

7. For example, see *Compilatio Assisiensis. Verba sancti Francisci*, section 38, sentences 1–5; *Sacrum commercium. Sancti Francisci cum domina Paupertate*, chapter 31, sentence 22; *Speculum perfectionis*, chapter 93, sentences 1–6; *Vita prima s. Francisci. Opusculum tertium*, section 121, sentence 4, section 124, sentences 2–4, section 125, sentence 11.

8. Christopher Page, *The Owl and the Nightingale: Musical Life and Ideas in France 1100–1300* (London: J. M. Dent & Sons, 1989), p. 120. Arcangeli also discusses how dancing is addressed in confession manuals in "Dance Under Trial: The Moral Debate 1200–1600," *Dance Research* 12, no. 2 (1994): 127–55.

9. *Exempla* are stories that preachers used to make a point in their sermons; though said to be "true," preachers could use or change the stories to fit the point they wished to make. The use of *exempla* as a source for historical research is discussed by Jacques Berlioz and Marie-Anne Polo de Beaulieu in *Les exempla médiévaux: Nouvelles perspectives* (Paris: Honoré Champion Éditeur, 1998); also Jacques Berlioz, "Exempla as a Source for the History of Women," in *Medieval Women and the Sources of Medieval History*, ed. Joel T. Rosenthal (Athens: University of Georgia Press, 1990), pp. 37–50; and Claude Bremond, Jacques Le Goff, and Jean-Claude Schmitt, *L' "exemplum"* (Turnhout: Brepols, 1982).

10. Page, *The Owl and the Nightingale*, p. 115.

11. David L. d'Avray, *The Preaching of the Friars: Sermons Diffused from Paris before 1300* (Oxford: Clarendon Press, 1985), p 148. Christopher Page provides a partial translation of Peyraut's text which exists only in manuscript and early printed versions, but not in an edited publication; see *The Owl and the Nightingale*, pp. 126–29, for the English translation and pp. 196–98 for the Latin text of the translated passage.

12. "viderunt daemonum in muro civitatis, et interrogantibus cur solus ibi sederet, respondit non indigeo alicuius auxilii, qui tota civitas nobis obedienter est subiecta, et intrantes civitatem invenerunt homines in maxima dissolutione, videlicet choreizantes, aliis diversis ludis occupatos. Ipsi vero timentes exierunt de civitate illa" (quoted and translated in Christopher Page, *The Owl and the Nightingale*, p. 113, from John Bromyard, *Summa predicantium*, I. f. 153v). Although Bromyard was an English preacher, Page argues that it is typical of French sources from the period.

13. For a collection of *exempla* about dance with full text access, see http://gahom .ehess.fr/thema/index.php?recueil=%&rep=%&mc=Danse.

14. Alessandro Arcangeli, "Dance and Punishment," *Dance Research* 10, no. 2 (1992): 31–32; see pp. 30–42 for further discussion and examples of *exempla* about dance.

15. Even though in this passage Albertus Magnus has used the word *saltatoria* ("leaping") to describe the movements that keep the citizen agile and well exercised, in this context it seems reasonable to hypothesize that "leaping" does describe a type of dancing.

16. "Delectationes autem quidem sicut cantoria, viellatoria, tripudia, saltatoria, tra-

goedia, et comoedia, et hujusmodi, quas oportet politicum sufficienter praeordinare, ut omnis civis jucundus apud civ[itat]em in delectabilibus liberalibus inveniatur. . . . Saltatoria autem virtutes motivas preparans, civem facit velocem." Quoted in Christopher Page, *The Owl and the Nightingale*, pp. 172–73, from Albertus Magnus, (Commentary on Aristotle's Politics and Ethics) *Beati Alberti Magni . . . Opera Omnia*, ed. A. Borgnet, 38 vols. (Paris, 1890–99), 7: 30, trans. Randall Rosenfeld.

17. Page, *The Owl and the Nightingale*, p. 131.

18. Elizabeth A. R. Brown and Nancy Freeman Regalado, "*La grant feste*: Philip the Fair's Celebration at the Knighting of His Sons in Paris at Pentecost of 1313," in *City and Spectacle in Medieval Europe*, ed. by Barbara A. Hanawalt and Kathryn L. Ryerson (Minneapolis: University of Minnesota Press, 1994), pp. 71–72.

19. For dancing as an important aspect of civic celebrations and royal entries, see Brown and Regalado, "*La grant feste*: Philip the Fair's Celebration"; Page, *The Owl and the Nightingale*, pp. 89–92; and Margit R. Sahlin, *Étude sur la carole médiévale: L'origine du mot et ses rapports avec l'église* (Uppsala: Almqvist & Wiksells, 1940), pp. 186–88.

20. For differing definitions of the word *carole* see, Sahlin, *Étude sur la carole médiévale*, pp. 17, 36, and 212; Christopher Page, *The Owl and the Nightingale*, pp. 116–17; John Stevens et al., "The English Carol," in *Report of the Tenth Congress of International Musicological Society, Ljubljana, 1967*, ed. Dragotin Cvetko, pp. 284–309 (Kassel: Bärenreiter, 1970); Richard L. Greene, "Introduction," in *The Early English Carols*, ed. Richard L. Greene (Oxford: Clarendon Press, 1977), pp. xxi–clxxii at page xlv; and Robert Mullally, "Reconstructing the Carole," in *On Common Ground 4: Reconstruction and Re-creation in Dance before 1850*, Proceedings of the 4th DHDS Conference, March 2003, ed. David Parsons (Stock, Essex: Dolmetsch Historical Dance Society, 2003), pp. 79–82.

21. Page, *The Owl and the Nightingale*, p. 115.

22. Although one should always take into consideration that just as much medieval musical notation was a minimal record of the things notated rather than a maximal record, this state of affairs could also apply to dance descriptions in medieval manuscripts as well.

23. Analyzing several types of dance songs from this period, John Stevens describes them as simple, "'catchy', easily memorable—which is what a dance-song needs to be." John Stevens, *Words and Music in the Middle Ages: Song, Narrative, Dance and Drama, 1050–1350* (Cambridge: Cambridge University Press, 1986), p. 190.

24. "C ele doisseri.ne met en oubli.q[ue] naille / au cembrel. tant abien enli.q[ue] m[out] embeli / legieu soz lormel.En son chief otchapel / de roses fres novel.face et fresche coloree / vairs oils.cler vis.simple et bel.p[or] les au / tres fere envie.i porta mai[n]t belioel." Jean Renart, *The Romance of the Rose or of Guillaume de Dole*, ed. Regina Psaki (New York: Garland Publishing, 1995), pp. 156–59.

25. Page, *The Owl and the Nightingale*, p. 126.

26. Joan Rimmer, "Carole, Rondeau and Branle in Ireland 1300–1800: Part 1 The Walling of New Ross and Dance Texts in the Red Book of Ossory," *Dance Research* 7, no. 1 (1989): 22–23.

27. The collection is known as the *Magnus liber organi* and the text is discussed in Jacques Chailley, "La danse religieuse au Moyen Age," in *Arts Liberaux et Philosophie au Moyen Age: Actes du IVe Congrès International de Philosophie Médiévale, Montreal, 1967* (Montreal: Institut d'Études Médiévales, 1969) pp. 357–80; Sahlin, *Étude sur la carole médiévale*, p. 153; and in far greater detail in Y. Rokesth, "Danses cléricales du XIIIe siècle," *Publications de la Faculte des Lettres de l'Université de Strasbourg*, 106 (1947): 93–126.

For an edition of the surviving vocal dance repertoire from the *Magnus liber organi* in modern notation, see Gordon Athol Anderson, ed., *Notre-Dame and Related Conductus: Opera Omnia. Pars octava: 1pt—The Latin Rondeau Répertoire* (Henryville, Pa.: Institute of Mediaeval Music, 1979). See also Craig M. Wright, *Music and Ceremony at Notre Dame of Paris, 500–1550* (Cambridge: Cambridge University Press, 1989).

28. On clerical dancing see Chailley, "La danse religieuse"; Pierre Riché, "Danses profanes et religieuses dans le haut Moyen Age," in *Histoire sociale, sensibilités collectives et mentalités: Mélanges Robert Mandrou* (Paris: Presses Universitaires de France, 1985), pp. 159–67; Craig M. Wright, *The Maze and the Warrior: Symbols in Architecture, Theology, and Music* (Cambridge, Mass.: Harvard University Press, 2001); L. Gougaud, "La danse dans les églises," *Revue Historique Ecclésiastique* 15 (1914): 5–22, 229–45; and Sahlin, *Étude sur la carole médiévale.*

29. Page has suggested Flemish, French, and Latin (*Voices and Instruments,* p. 60).

30. Given the contents of Grocheio's treatise, it seems very likely that his intended audience was the students at the university for whom he was providing a summary of both sacred and secular music as currently performed (Timothy J. McGee, "Medieval Dances: Matching the Repertory with Grocheio's Descriptions," *Journal of Musicology* 7, no. 4 [1989]: 516)—though, as Robert Mullally has pointed out, the musical forms discussed by Grocheio were not performed exclusively in Paris, but were found elsewhere (Robert Mullally, "Johannes de Grocheo's 'Musical Vulgaris,'" *Music & Letters* 79, no. 1 [1998]: 25).

31. Johannes de Grocheio, *Concerning Music: De musica,* trans. Albert Seay (Colorado Springs: Colorado College Music Press, 1967).

32. "Ductia vero est cantus levis et velox in ascensu et descensu, quae in choreis a iuvenibus et puellis decantatur, . . . Haec enim ducit corda puellarum et iuvenum et a vanitate removet, et contra passionem, quae dicitur amor vel eros, valere dicitur." Cited in Christopher Page, *The Owl and The Nightingale,* p. 133, from E. Rohloff, ed., *Die Quellenhandschriften zum Musiktraktat des Johannes de Grocheio* (Leipzig: Deutscher Verlag f. Musik, 1972), p. 132, trans. Randall Rosenfeld.

33. "Ja se tu estais a Paris, / Mar iras en autre païs, / Por amer dames ne puceles . . . / 'Quel part?' Vers s. Germain des prez. . . . / Illue(c) les puceles quarolent / Qui uolentiers d'amors parolent." Cited and translated in Page, *The Owl and the Nightingale,* p. 123, from H. Kühne and E. Stengel, eds., *Maître Elie's Überarbeitung der ältesten französischen Übertragung von Ovid's Ars Amatoria,* Ausgaben und Abhandlungen aus dem Gebiete der Romanischen Philologie, 47 (1882), ll. 101–7 and 133–38.

34. For much of the thirteenth century the university was disturbed by tensions between city dwellers and members of the university, as well as internal university conflicts between the new mendicant orders (both the Franciscans and Dominicans set up schools in the second half of the century) and the secular masters. This tension inadvertently resulted in records of activities and rules that provide us with information about dance. The rules appear in Heinrich Denifle and Émile Chatelain, eds., *Chartularium Universitatis Parisiensis,* 4 vols. (Paris: Delalain, 1889–97). For further discussion on the tensions between the members of the town and the university and the interaction of these tensions with university regulations, see Pearl Kibre, *Scholarly Privileges in the Middle Ages: The Rights, Privileges, and Immunities, of Scholars and Universities at Bologna, Padua, Paris, and Oxford* (Cambridge, Mass.: Medieval Academy of America, 1962), p. 102, and Olaf Pedersen, *The First Universities: Studium Generale and the Origins of University Education in Europe* (Cambridge: Cambridge University Press, 1997), p. 238.

Recommended Reading

Alexander, Jonathan J. G. "Dancing in the Streets." *Journal of the Walters Art Gallery* 54 (1996): 147–62.

Earp, Lawrence. "Genre in the Fourteenth-Century French Chanson: The Virelai and the Dance Song." *Musica Disciplina* 45 (1991): 123–41.

Harding, Ann. *An Investigation into the Use and Meaning of Medieval German Dancing Terms.* Göppingen: Alfred Kümmerle, 1973.

McGee, Timothy. *Medieval Instrumental Dances.* Bloomington: Indiana University Press, 1989.

Miller, James L. *Measures of Wisdom. The Cosmic Dance in Classical and Christian Antiquity.* Toronto: University of Toronto Press, 1986.

Mullally, Robert. "Dance Terminology in the Works of Machaut and Froissart." *Medium ævum* 59, no. 2 (1990): 248–59.

Page, Christopher. *The Owl and the Nightingale: Musical Life and Ideas in France 1100–1300.* London: J. M. Dent and Sons, 1989.

———. *Voices and Instruments of the Middle Ages: Instrumental Practice and Songs in France 1100–1300.* Berkeley: University of California Press, 1986.

Silen, Karen. "Elizabeth of Spalbeek: Dancing the Passion." In *Women's Work: Making Dance in Europe before 1800,* ed. Lynn Matluck Brooks, pp. 207–27. Madison: University of Wisconsin Press, 2007.

Wright, Craig. *The Maze and the Warrior: Symbols in Architecture, Theology, and Music.* Cambridge, Mass.: Harvard University Press, 2001, especially chap. 5, pp. 129–58.

3

Dance and Society in Quattrocento Italy

Jennifer Nevile

For members of the elite in fifteenth-century Italy dance was an ever-present part of their daily lives. It was an activity in which both men and women participated, both on public occasions in front of hundreds of spectators and in private surrounded only by family members, guests, or close friends. Public performances of dances were frequently part of official state occasions, such as betrothals or wedding ceremonies, state visits by foreign ambassadors or princes, and victory celebrations. Therefore, the performers at these events were always members of the leading families. In fifteenth-century Italy dance was a symbol of civilized, educated behavior. Knowledge and skill in dance was a sign of a person's level of education and intellectual ability, as dance was increasingly seen as one of the liberal arts, by virtue of its association with music.[1] A public dance performance was also one way in which the social order was demonstrated. Thus those who were the highest in rank, or who were the most honored guests, initiated the dancing, or led a line of couples who were also arranged in order of rank.

Furthermore, dance functioned as a social marker, since the rules and postural codes of courtly dance were part of the mechanisms by which those in the elite made themselves appear superior and inaccessible to the rest of society. The courtiers believed that their superiority was demonstrated to the rest of society by the different way in which they moved, walked, danced, and even stood in repose. Dancing taught people control over their body and all their actions, and a public dance performance was visible evidence that they were capable of appearing in public without making an exhibition of themselves.

The balls which were such an important part of the festivals and celebrations in fifteenth-century Italy often lasted for hours. The dances that were performed there (and also recorded in the dance treatises) were for both men and women, and provided a rare opportunity for social interaction between noble women and their male peers. Thus dance also functioned as ritualized courtship, a social function that is reflected in the recorded choreographies with their dramatic presentation of the interaction between the sexes. Dance as an expression of power, dance as a social marker and a sign of civilized behavior, dance as an expression of the social order and dance as ritualized courtship, all of these functions operated in fifteenth-century Italy and are discussed in this chapter.

Dance as an Expression of Power and Social Order

In fifteenth-century Europe identity, both the larger communal identity and the personal identity of a ruler was expressed in rituals, myths, and material culture. *Quattrocento* Italy was a society in which rituals, ceremonies, and deference patterns mattered. In late fifteenth-century Florence, for example, state ceremonial rules listed twenty-three different forms of address for people of differing rank from a pope to a knight, while for ambassadors there were seven additional forms of address.[2] Sometimes hotly contested disputes over precedence would erupt between members of visiting delegations as to their exact placement in processions, thus causing embarrassment to the host city.[3] As Ercole d'Este, the duke of Ferrara, "candidly admitted" in a letter to his wife, Eleonora, "the reputation of his state depended as much on *ceremonia* [social order and protocol] as it did upon the splendour of the decoration or the lavishness of the expenditure."[4] One of the reasons for Ercole d'Este's concern was that the precise but correct gradations of position was a clear sign that a court "reflected not only a traditional social and political order but also a higher, sacred order, of which the duke and his servants were the agents."[5]

Dance was an important part of ritual events at this time and was part of the ordered formal behavior demanded by these rituals and state events. A good example of this ordered, formal behavior, and the importance attached to it by members of the elite, is vividly illustrated in a letter from Eleonora d'Aragona to her husband, Ercole d'Este, written while she was in Milan during the 1491 Carnival season for the wedding celebrations of their daughter, Beatrice d'Este, to Ludovico Sforza.[6] Eleonora describes an evening of dancing held in the *sala grande* (great hall) of the *palazzo* in which she was staying. In her letter Eleonora stresses the "order" of the *festa*: the manner in which all aspects were controlled by social protocol. When the invited guests were ready to enter the hall they did so in order of rank, carefully watched by ceremonial officials who knew the social rankings and would not allow anyone to deviate from them. The guests then seated themselves, once again in order of rank. The dancing then began, also following "the formal conventions."[7] When the dancing began to the sound of the *pifferi* (shawm band) and the *tamburini* (small drums), the appearance in order of rank continued, with the first to dance being the Duchess of Milan. The duchess was then followed by Isabella and Beatrice d'Este, the daughters of Eleonora and Ercole, and Bianca Maria Sforza and Anna Sforza, the sisters of Gian Galeazzo Sforza.[8] It was not until these women who were closely connected to the ruling family had danced that the other ladies of the court descended from the tribunal on which they were sitting to participate in the dancing. When the evening's dancing had concluded Eleonora again mentioned in her letter that Ludovico Sforza initiated the break-up of the party, with all the ladies departing as they had arrived, "*cum grande ordine*" ("with great order," that is, in the correct, hierarchical ranking).

The concern over "order" and the correct protocols was so strong in fifteenth-century Italy that it was not ignored even during supposedly spontaneous acts of merry-making during Carnival. For example, it was the custom in Ferrara during Carnival for the Duke and the members of his family to unexpectedly arrive at a private house and to join in the festivities there. "The duke and his courtiers customarily rode through the city streets after dark, accompanied by *piffari* and *tamburini,* the specially decorated court *carette* [carts], and members of the signorial household to enter private homes and join in the carnival merriment."[9] But such occasions were carefully planned and ordered, as is admitted by Francesco Bagnacavallo in a letter to Isabelle d'Este, where he "records the careful planning of Jacamino Compagno for his *festa* in honour of the signorial family," and how before dinner the "formal rules of dancing were observed," and upon the banquet commencing, the guests were all seated "according to precedence."[10]

The order in which people danced also reflected their position in the social hierarchy. This is illustrated by an incident at the court of Naples, toward the end of the reign of Alfonso, in the middle of the century. At this time Alfonso was enamored of Lucrezia d'Alagnos, who became his mistress. Lucrezia maneuvered herself to Naples, and took up residence at the court. During a visit of the Holy Roman Emperor and his wife, Lucrezia's status was publicly acknowledged by her position in the dancing; that is, in third place behind the empress and the Duchess of Calabria.[11] At balls associated with wedding celebrations it was often the bride who began the dancing. Thus in Naples in 1473 at the festivities associated with the engagement of Eleonora d'Aragona to Ercole d'Este it was Eleonora herself who opened the dancing on a stage especially erected in the main piazza in front of thousands of spectators. On other occasions it was the guest in whose honor the celebrations were held who initiated the proceedings. This was certainly the case in 1459 at the ball held in the *Mercato Nuovo* in Florence, as part of the celebrations for the visit of the pope and Galeazzo Maria Sforza, heir to the Duchy of Milan. It was not until Galeazzo had danced several dances that the other Florentine and Milanese courtiers were permitted to join the dancing.

Obviously other elements in the rituals associated with state events also functioned as a measure of the power relationships between the ruler and his court and that of the visitors. The clothes and jewels that were worn, the gifts that were given to the guests, the exact meeting place of the visiting party and its distance from the city, the forms of address and the gestures associated with meeting others, along with the dances performed, all were indications of subtle differences of position in the social hierarchy of the participants, and were commented upon and noted down. In 1461, for example, the chancellor of the Florentine embassy to France recorded how the French king had "honored the Florentines by his gait and by the movement of his cap."[12] Small matters by today's standards, perhaps, yet five hundred years ago they were invested with significant meaning.

The dances that occurred as part of the official state events were mostly performed outdoors in front of members of the court, but also in front of hundreds if not thousands of spectators from the lower levels of society. Therefore, when a duke or prince and the leading members of his court danced in public in the main piazza, he was displaying his magnificence,[13] and in doing so he was displaying his power.[14] Not only was the ruler sumptuously dressed, his clothes loaded with pearls and precious stones, but he would also be moving in a manner that was unfamiliar and strange to many of those watching. The vast bulk of society did not learn these dances, nor did they even know how to move in the manner they saw displayed before them. Thus the dances performed by the ruler was one clear signal of the gulf that existed between the dancers and those who were watching.

Another way in which dance performances were used by the ruler to enhance his position and power was through an association with mythological heroes and gods in allegorical enactments of mythological scenes. To cite just one example: in 1473 Eleonora d'Aragona journeyed north from Naples to Ferrara to marry Ercole d'Este, duke of Ferrara. When Eleonora stopped in Rome, the Cardinal Pietro Riario organized a stupendous banquet in her honor. The banquet concluded with a dance performed by eight couples dressed as mythological characters, including Jason and Medea. These sixteen performers danced among themselves until they were interrupted by the arrival of dancing centaurs. The mythological figures, led by Hercules, then made a "beautiful battle" with the centaurs, defeating them. Thus Eleonora's husband-to-be, Ercole, was honored by the identification with the mythological hero Hercules, who in this case was also the leader of the group who vanquished the centaurs.

The dance genre most frequently associated with such danced scenes was the *moresca*. Danced by courtiers as well as by "professional" dancers, *moresche* were elaborate stage shows with sumptuous costumes and masks, elaborate scenery, and special effects. They were intrinsically a public spectacle used for political purposes: the aggrandizement of the ruler and increasing the honor and reputation of the state.[15] Often the *moresche* and danced scenes commented directly upon political events of the time, as was the case in Venice in May 1493. On this occasion Beatrice d'Este was sent to Venice to represent her husband Ludovico Sforza and Milan at the celebrations for the newly formed alliance between Venice, Milan, the Papal States, Mantua, and Ferrara. One danced scene occurred on boats and was based on the contest between Neptune (symbolizing Venice) and Minerva (symbolizing Beatrice and Milan). In the myth Minerva was declared the winner of the contest as she gave the most useful gift to the world: an olive tree, symbol of peace and abundance. In Venice Neptune was the first to dance, then Minerva, then they danced together, before Minerva fired an arrow into a mountain from which sprang an olive tree, thus "winning" the contest and emphasizing the current political need for union and peace, and the necessity of the League, as well as honoring the Milanese guests. A few days later at a *festa* in honor of Beatrice in the ducal palace the allegorical dance performances again praised Milan, particularly the duke Ludovico Sforza, as well as alluding to the other partners in the League.[16]

Dance as a Social Marker and a Sign of Civilized Behavior

The dance masters who taught the *balli* and *bassadanze* to the members of the elite in fifteenth-century Italy were always careful to differentiate their dance practice from that of the lower levels of society. Part of the reason for this was obvious; that is, their desire to increase their status and to raise the dance to the level of a liberal art, as well as to distance themselves from the continuing moral criticisms of dancing. But part of their claim was true. In *quattrocento* Italy dance had become a social marker; it was one way by which the elite level of society distanced itself from the rest of society. The dances they performed were symbols of their superiority, and a mechanism by which others were excluded from the group that held the power. Skill in dancing was regarded as an accomplishment for which its practitioners could be praised, along with their abilities in music, knowledge of Latin and Greek, and their skills in the military and gymnastic arts.

One of the reasons why dance was able to function as a social marker was that it was an ever-present symbol in a visual age of the difference between those in the elite level of society and those who were not. In external comportment the courtiers' claim to difference (if not to superiority) was true. Through their dance training they moved and danced in a manner completely separate from the rest of society. Their dance training usually began at an early age, and the style itself was not easy. It needed constant practice before a potential dancer was able to master the many necessary skills before he or she would be able to perform in public, gracefully and without error. All these skills, including learning the correct carriage of the body and coping with the speed and meter changes in the choreographies, needed years of regular practice if any performance was to be carried out with an air of ease and self-assurance. The way of moving on the dance floor had to become completely natural, as the manner in which a member of the elite moved had to remain the same whether walking, standing in repose, or dancing.

Under the influence of the humanists' promotion of the necessity of a classical education for those in the elite level of society, dance increasingly came to be seen as one of the signs of such an education; that is, a sign of civilized, educated behavior. Women especially received praise for their skill and expertise in dancing, as is illustrated by the lines from a poem by Angelo Galli from the mid-1440s, in which he praises the ability of the wife of Federico da Montefeltro in the dance, an ability that produces such a picture of virtue that by watching her he is inspired to contemplate similar virtues: "In her dancing her noble carriage—magnanimous, magnificent and aristocratic—inspires my mind to higher matters."[17] Guglielmo Ebreo had close ties to Federico and his court of

Urbino, recording as he does in his dance treatise a number of occasions he was present at Urbino for various *feste*, for many of which he choreographed dances.[18] Ippolita Sforza, a pupil of Antonio Cornazano, received praise when she danced and sang new *balli*. Ippolita's example is an interesting one, as on this occasion she had also composed the two new dances herself.[19] Thus not only was it acceptable to be an expert performer, but composing new dances was also considered an honorable occupation for those at the top of society.

One of the functions of the dance practice for members of the elite was that the dance training they received taught them control over their bodily movements and gestures, and also control over their emotions. This function became increasingly important as the century developed and continued in the sixteenth century, as the conduct demanded of courtiers became increasingly intricate, both in terms of spoken courtesies and bodily movement.[20] It was the training provided by the dance masters that enabled the courtier to meet these new standards: to move with grace and eloquence, to be aware of her or his surroundings and fellow courtiers, and at all times to be in control of his or her movements and gestures. As Giuliano de' Medici (the youngest son of Lorenzo de' Medici and Clarice Orsini) says in the debate over the power of music: "I believe that music is not only an ornament but a necessity for the courtier."[21]

According to Guglielmo, in order to dance perfectly a noble man or lady must follow the rules that he sets out in the theoretical section of his treatise. Thus perfection in the art of dance is achieved by controlling and regulating the dancer's body, performing all movements with moderation, and always being aware of the external circumstances, so that his or her steps are adapted to the music, the size of the room in which one is dancing, one's partner, and the clothes that are being worn while dancing.[22] Moderation in movement was a central component in the dance masters' understanding of what constituted eloquent movement. The concept of moderation adopted by the dance masters and the humanists came from the teachings of Aristotle (384–323 B.C.), as well as from rhetorical texts. The exhortation to avoid extremes of movement appears throughout the dance treatises, particularly Domenico's: "This *misura el tereno* is a light *misura*, and this is the one that keeps the whole of your body within the mean of the movement. And this movement is neither too much nor too little. And you must avoid the extremes of movement according to what has been said here above."[23] As Kolsky concludes: "Dance is the asethetic ordering of gesture in order to represent in a stylized manner the basic values of court society. Harmonious movement confirms the ordered power of the court."[24]

The dance masters also advocated that the dance practice which they taught was capable of teaching ethical behavior. Their insistence that their art inculcated elegant and graceful movements is partly explained by their belief that movements of the body were an outward manifestation of the movements of a person's soul. This belief was not unique to the dance masters: it was widely shared by the humanists. For example, in his treatise on painting, Leon Battista Alberti also repeats this belief several times. The belief that movements of the soul were revealed by movements of the body was also found in medieval theories of gesture and deportment, such as the work *De institutione novitiorum*, a training manual for regular canons.[25] This belief is stated explicitly by Guglielmo in the preface to his treatise:

> This virtue of the dance is none other than an external action reflecting interior spiritual movements (or movements of the soul). These movements must agree with the measured and perfect consonances of a harmony that descends with delight through our hearing to our intellect and to our welcoming senses, where it then generates certain sweet emotions. These sweet emotions, just as if they are constrained against their nature, try as much as possible to escape and make themselves visible in active movement.[26]

The emotions of the dancers—sorrow, anger or happiness for instance—were made visible through the movements of their body, thus giving them both a tremendous power and responsibility: a power to affect the emotions of those who watched, and the responsibility only to represent morally edifying emotions. A person watching a dance performance could learn to recognize virtues by observing their physical representations. Since a virtuous person when dancing would be imitating in his or her movements various positive ethical states, these would then be recognized by the spectators, who could then learn to imitate these virtues in their own lives. This is indeed the same sentiments expressed by Galli in his poem praising the dancing of Gentile Brancaleoni, the first wife of Federico da Montefeltro. Galli says that by watching the dancing of Gentile, dancing that is so noble, and is such a moving example of gracious and princely values, he is inspired to reflect on "higher things."

Naturally the reverse position was also true; that is, a dancer's movements could represent negative emotional states. Guglielmo did not seek to deny that the art of dance could be abused and used for immoral or improper purposes. But he also argued that when used by upstanding individuals, it could have a positive ethical effect on its practitioners and on those who observed it.

> But when it is practised by noble, virtuous, and honest men, I say that this science and art is good, virtuous, and worthy of commendation and praise. And moreover not only does it turn virtuous and upright men into noble and refined persons, but it also makes those men who are ill-mannered and boorish and

born into a low station into a sufficiently noble person. The character of everyone is made known by the dance.[27]

Dance as Ritualized Courtship

The dances that were recorded in the fifteenth-century Italian dance treatises were all for small groups of both men and women, from one couple to six couples, with the majority of the *balli* and *bassadanze* choreographed for two, three, or four performers. Thus in their choreographies the dance masters were interested in portraying the relationships between small groups of men and women. We know from other sources such as letters and descriptions of the dancing at *feste* that members of the court also performed more "theatrical" dances in which the dancers represented figures from Greek mythology, fabulous animals such as centaurs, or famous people from history. Unfortunately, none of these choreographies were recorded in the treatises. Those dances that were recorded were all "social" dances, in that the choreographies, the step sequences, and floor patterns, all expressed different aspects of the relationships and interactions between men and women, and contributed to creating opportunities for ritualized courtship.

When viewed in these terms the dances are revealed as a series of social events, most of which provide opportunities for interaction with one's partner, or with all the members of the opposite sex in the dance. A detailed study of the *balli* reveal seven major categories of social events: "formal greeting," "inspection," "social progress," "confrontation," "chase," "imitation," and "opening sequence." The category of "formal greeting" includes the acknowledgment of one's partner, and those watching the dancing, when a couple meet or leave each other. The *riverenza* and *continenza* steps are commonly used in this category.[28] The category of "inspection" occurs where a man or woman (or one half of a line of couples) circles around their partner(s), while the category of "social progress" mirrors the situation of meeting others, acknowledging their presence and then passing on to greet another dancer. The movement pattern associated with this situation is that of a long spiral path among and around lines of dancers. "Confrontation" represents the battle between the sexes, with advances and retreats by both sexes. The common movement pattern associated with this social event is where a woman faces two men. The three then move forward to meet each other, then cross over and move away from each other, then turn 180 degrees, and move toward each other again. The category of "chase" is simply where one gender chases the other. For example, where the man goes forward, then he stands still while the woman follows him, or vice-versa. In the "imitation" category, each couple (or each dancer) simply repeats the actions of those in front of them. The category "opening sequence" is so called because it often occurs at the beginning of the dance. It is a sequence of movements in which all the dancers perform the same steps. There is no definite path stated in the choreography for this category.

The opportunities that balls afforded for dalliance with the opposite sex were clearly recognized and appreciated in a society in which men's and women's lives were far more segregated and controlled than is the case today. This contemporary recognition of one of the functions of dance as ritualized courtship is clearly illustrated in the long and detailed account of the festivities associated with the visit of Galeazzo Maria Sforza to Florence in 1459. In the section of the poem that describes the ball held outdoors in the *Mercato Nuovo*, the anonymous author describes the ladies and young girls, all sitting in their allotted seats close to the dance space, and all of them doing their best to attract the interest of the male courtiers and to draw this attention to themselves: "That day was when one could satisfy one's hunger for the sight of beautiful women and lovely things, and examine in detail all their guiles. In this form the coquettish ladies were all sitting in the first rank: a lovely mixture of unmarried and married women."[29] The whole occasion was one for making love with one's eyes, for sending and receiving desiring glances, for inciting passion in the courtiers so that there was "no breast in which the heart did not burn with a fierce flame."[30] There is nothing ambiguous here about the actions of the dancers and their response to each other. The ball was an opportunity for flirtation and coquetry, for inciting desire, and for pursuing the object of one's own desires.

Conclusion

As we have seen, dance in *quattrocento* Italian society operated on several different levels, from an entertainment that gave pleasure, amusement, and exercise, to the level of a political commentary on current events. Dancing was an activity that occurred indoors and out, on land or water, at small intimate gatherings or at large, public events, before and after banquets, or between the acts of a play. Dancing was a common part of the lives of the elite and an activity that mirrored their life at court, not only in the area of courtship, but in other aspects of court life as well. For example, one of the choreographies of Domenico da Piacenza is the *ballo Gelosia*, a dance for three couples that portrays the theme of jealousy. In his poem on the jealousy of the ladies at court, the Sforza courtier and poet, Andrea Baiardo, has the Duke of Milan ordering his musicians to play the music of the *ballo Gelosia*. Thus the fact that the dances composed by Domenico and his colleagues and performed by the courtiers were engaged with the realities of court life was widely recognized at the time and was used in other artistic commentaries on court life.

Dance was one means by which courtiers could learn control over their bodily movements and gestures. In fifteenth-century Italy it became a social marker, one way in which the elite distanced themselves from the rest of society. Participation in dance performances by a ruler and the members of the court was a visual reminder of each person's position in the social hierarchy. It was also part of the expression of power on the part of the ruler. Through its association with music, dance was seen as one of the liberal arts and as a sign of a person's humanistic education. Dance was a sign of civilized behavior in that it was capable of teaching ethical behavior. Since movements of a person's body were outward manifestations of their emotional states, the emotions of those dancing were made visible and recognizable to those watching a dance performance. Thus dancers had the responsibility to represent only edifying emotions, so that those watching could recognize these virtues and imitate them in their own lives.

Notes

1. For further information on the liberal arts, see chapter 13 in this volume, and David L. Wagner ed., *The Seven Liberal Arts in the Middle Ages* (Bloomington: Indiana University Press, 1983).

2. Richard C. Trexler, *Public Life in Renaissance Florence* (Ithaca: Cornell University Press, 1991), p. 309.

3. Richard Brown, "The Reception of Anna Sforza in Ferrara, February 1491," *Renaissance Studies* 2, no. 2 (1988): 236.

4. Ibid., pp. 231–32.

5. Gregory Lubkin, *A Renaissance Court: Milan under Galeazzo Maria Sforza* (Berkeley: University of California Press, 1994), p. 67.

6. While Ludovico Sforza was only the uncle of Gian Galeazzo, the young Duke of Milan, he was the de facto ruler of the city. The information in this paragraph is taken from Richard Brown, "The Politics of Magnificence in Ferrara 1450–1505: A Study in the Socio-political Implications of Renaissance Spectacle," Ph.D. diss., University of Edinburgh, 1982, pp. 314–16.

7. Ibid., p. 315.

8. Anna Sforza was betrothed to Alfonso d'Este, the eldest son of Eleonora and Ercole d'Este. Their wedding celebrations would take place in Ferrara in a few weeks time (11–15 February), just before the start of Lent, hence Eleonora's intense interest in the cere-

monial procedure and management of the Sforza spectacles. For more details on the celebrations in Ferrara, and the duke's and duchess's concern over the proper ceremonial procedures, see Brown, "The Reception of Anna Sforza," pp. 231–39.

9. Brown, "The Politics of Magnificence," p. 308.

10. Ibid., pp. 313–14.

11. Alan Ryder, *Alfonso the Magnanimous: King of Aragon, Naples, and Sicily, 1396–
1458* (Oxford: Clarendon Press, 1990), p. 397.

12. Trexler, *Public Life in Renaissance Florence*, p. 295.

13. In the fifteenth century "magnificence" was increasingly seen as a princely virtue.
The concept came from Book 4 of Aristotle's *Nicomachean Ethics*, where he discusses "magnificence" as the mean between vulgarity or bad taste, and meanness or stinginess. Magnificence is a virtue concerned with grand expenditure for the common good, on such things as
large-scale public buildings, religious services, theatrical productions, or banquets for an entire city (Aristotle, *The Ethics of Aristotle: The Nicomachean Ethics*, trans. J. A. K. Thomson,
rev. Hugh Tredennick [Harmondsworth: Penguin, 1976], pp. 149–52). Already in the fourteenth century magnificence "appears to have helped the *signore* emphasize his power and legitimacy," while by the end of the fifteenth century it was clear that "the judicious application of magnificence" demonstrated the moral suitability of the ruler to govern the state, as
well as being a display of his power (Rupert Shepherd, "Giovanni Sabadino degli Arienti,
Ercole I d'Este and the Decoration of the Italian Renaissance Court," *Renaissance Studies 9*,
no. 1 [1995]: 20–21). In the first half of the fifteenth century "magnificence" was mainly associated with large expenditure on buildings, but by the latter part of the century the expenditure included banquets, lavish and rich wedding celebrations, extensive hospitality for visitors, jousts, tournaments, funerals, and even hunts (Guido Guerzoni, "*Liberalitas,
Magnificentia*, Splendor: The Classic Origins of Italian Renaissance Lifestyles," in *Economic
Engagements with Art*, Annual Supplement to Volume 31 of *History of Political Economy*, ed.
Neil De Marchi and Craufurd D. W. Goodwin [Durham, N.C.: Duke University Press,
1999], p. 359). Magnificence was a concept that was deeply embedded in European conscious-
ness, and for a thorough discussion on how this concept came to be so influential in western
European society from Aristotle to the humanist writers of the Renaissance, see Guerzoni,
"*Liberalitas, Magnificentia*, Splendor," pp. 332–78.

14. For an essay that elaborates how music and dancing were "critical components of
the Italian Renaissance court's political and social structures," and how they "epitomize[d]
the role of the courtier" (p. 1), see Stephen Kolsky, "Graceful Performances: The Social
and Political Context of Music and Dance in the *Cortegiano*," *Italian Studies 53* (1998): 1–19.

15. For further discussion of the *moresca* in Renaissance Italy, see Barbara Sparti, "La
danza come politica al tempo di Machiavelli," in *La lingua e le lingue di Machiavelli: atti del
convegno internazionale di studi, Torino, 2–4 dicembre 1999*, ed. Alessandro Pontremoli
(Florence: Leo S. Olschki, 2001), pp. 295–313, and Alessandro Pontremoli and Patrizia La
Rocca, *Il ballare lombardo: Teoria e prassi coreutica nella festa di corte del xv secolo* (Milan:
Vita e Pensiero, 1987), pp. 216–31. For a wider study of this genre across Europe but partic-
ularly in England, see John Forrest, *The History of Morris Dancing, 1458–1750* (Toronto:
University of Toronto Press, 1999).

16. For an extensive discussion of the spectacles in Venice in 1493 and their significance, see Pontremoli and La Rocca, *Il ballare lombardo*, pp. 210–17.

17. "Nel suo danzar el portamento altero / magnanimo superbo et signorile / subleva
la mia mente ad alte cose." From Nicoletta Guidobaldi, *La musica di Federico: Immagine e
suoni alla corte di Urbino* (Florence: Leo S. Olschki, 1995), p. 86.

18. For more details on the life of Guglielmo Ebreo and his ties to Urbino, see Barbara Sparti, introduction to *De practica seu arte tripudii: On the Practice or Art of Dancing*, by Guglielmo Ebreo, ed. and trans. Barbara Sparti (Oxford: Clarendon Press, 1993), pp. 23–45.

19. Eileen Southern, "A Prima Ballerina of the Fifteenth Century," in *Music and Context: Essays for John M. Ward*, ed. Anne Dhu Shapiro (Cambridge, Mass.: Department of Music, Harvard University, 1985), p. 192.

20. Katherine Tucker McGinnis, "Moving in High Circles: Courts, Dance, and Dancing Masters in Italy in the Long Sixteenth Century," Ph.D. diss., University of North Carolina, Chapel Hill, 2001, p. 3.

21. Baldesar Castiglione, *The Book of the Courtier*, trans. George Bull (Harmondsworth: Penguin, 1981), p. 96.

22. For further discussion on this point, see Jennifer Nevile, *The Eloquent Body: Dance and Humanist Culture in Fifteenth-Century Italy* (Bloomington: Indiana University Press, 2004), pp. 99–102.

23. Domenico da Piacenza, *De arte saltandj & choreas ducendj De la arte di ballare et danzare*, Paris, Bibliothèque Nationale, MS fonds it. 972, f. 2r (hereafter cited as Pd). "Questa mexura el tereno è mexura legiera e questa è quella che fa tenire el mezo del tuo motto dal capo a li piedi el quale non è ní tropo ní poco e fate fugire li extremi segondo ha dicto lui qui di sopra."

24. Kolsky, "Graceful Performances," p. 14.

25. The treatise is thought to have been written c. 1100–1125 by Hugh of St. Victor (ibid., pp. 14–16).

26. Guglielmo Ebreo da Pesaro, *Guilielmi Hebraei pisauriensis de practica seu arte tripudii vulgare opusculum, incipit*, 1463, Paris, Bibliothèque Nationale, MS fonds it. 973, f. 5v (hereafter cited as Pg). "La qual virtute del danzare non è altro che una actione demonstrativa di fuori di movimenti spirituali: Li quali si hanno a concordare colle misurate et perfette consonanze d'essa harmonia: che per lo nostro audito alle parti intellective & ai sensi cordiali con diletto descende: dove poi si genera certi dolci commovimenti: i quali chome contra sua natura richiusi si sforzano quanto possano di uscire fuori: & farsi in atto manifesti."

27. Pg, f. 19r–19v. "Ma quando è exercitata da huomini ge[n]tili, virtuosi, & honesti, dico essa scienza & arte essere buona et virtuosa et di commendatione & laude digna. Et più [19v] che non solamente gli huomini virtuosi & honesti fa tornare gentili & pellegrini: ma anchora quegli sonno male acostumati & di vil conditione nati, fa divenir gentili & d'assai: La qual da apertamente a cognoscere la qualità di tutti."

28. A *riverenza* was an "honor" or "reverence," a gesture of respect with which most Renaissance dances began and ended, while a *continenza* involved a small step to the side. For detailed description and analysis of all fifteenth-century Italian dance steps, see David R. Wilson, *The Steps Used in Court Dancing in Fifteenth-Century Italy*, 3rd rev. ed. (Cambridge: David R. Wilson, 2003), and pp. 12–15 and 41–44 for the *continenza* and *riverenza*. See Figure 1.1 for an illustration of one type of *riverenza* being performed by the half-kneeling man in the center-right foreground.

29. Translation by Giovanni Carsaniga, from Florence, Biblioteca Nazionale, Magl. VII 1121, f. 66r. ll. 6–11. "Quel giorno fu da cchavarsi la fame / di veder belle donne & belle chose / & bene examinar tutte lor trame. / In questa forma le donne vezzose / si stavan tutte dinanzi a ssedere: / in bel meschuglio di fanclulle & spose." For a complete transcription and translation of folios 63r–69v in this poem that describe the ball see Appendix 1 in Nevile, *The Eloquent Body*, pp. 141–57.

30. Magl. VII 1121, f. 67v. ll. 9–10.

Recommended Reading

Brainard, Ingrid. "The Role of the Dancing Master in Fifteenth-Century Courtly Society." *Fifteenth-Century Studies* 2 (1979): 21–44.

Bryce, Judith. "Performing for Strangers: Women, Dance, and Music in Quattrocento Florence." *Renaissance Quarterly* 54, no. 4.1 (2001): 1074–1107.

Padovan, Maurizio, ed. *Guglielmo Ebreo da Pesaro e la danza nelle corti italiane del xv secolo.* Pisa: Pacini, 1990.

Sparti, Barbara. Introduction to *De pratica seu arte tripudii: On the Practice or Art of Dancing,* by Guglielmo Ebreo da Pesaro. Ed. and trans. Barbara Sparti. Oxford: Clarendon Press, 1993, pp. 3–72.

———. "Dancing Couples Behind the Scenes: Recently Discovered Italian Illustrations, 1470–1550." *Imago Musicae* 13 (1996): 9–38.

4

Dance in Sixteenth- and Early Seventeenth-Century France

Margaret M. McGowan

❧

The Magnificence of the French Court

The French court in the Renaissance enjoyed a reputation for splendor, extravagance, and conspicuous consumption. This was especially marked in the time of François I, when foreign visitors regularly commented on the constant round of divertissements as, for example, when the Mantuan ambassador reported in 1541: "At this court they only think of giving themselves a good time, all day long, with tournaments and festivities with exceptionally beautiful masquerades which are always different."[1] The scale of the court, the beauty of the noble rooms it inhabited, the handsome demeanor of courtiers, and the ostentatious attire of their ladies provided a context within which the choreographic art could flourish and seduce everyone. In its turn, dancing contributed enormously to the image of magnificence.

The court increased in size throughout the sixteenth century and needed better and larger accommodation. Royal palaces were built, refurbished, and made splendid with galleries and large halls designed for public spectacle. The king enjoyed showing important visitors around, leading the English ambassador through his newly completed gallery at Fontainebleau and showing off its famous frescoes to emperor Charles V when he came to France in 1539. When exceptionally large structures were required for the celebration of significant dynastic occasions, such as the formal entry of King Henri II into his capital in 1549 or the double marriages in 1559 between France and Spain and France and Savoy, then vast temporary structures were erected in Paris by the king's architect Philibert de L'Orme. These were magnificent buildings, decorated *à l'antique* with doric columns, and with their interior walls covered with royal devices—and they provided the ample space demanded by banquets, balls, and danced spectacles of the most elaborate kind.[2]

However, already by about 1530, François I had recognized that such temporary arrangements were unsatisfactory for a court that wanted to indulge in festivities on a daily basis. He therefore ordered work to begin on a ballroom at his palace of Saint Germain-en-Laye, and ten years later he commissioned Sebastiano Serlio to transform the loggia at Fontainebleau into the magnificent ballroom that can still be admired today. Later, under Henri II, work began on transforming the Louvre, creating the banqueting hall and *salle de fêtes*, which were later praised and described by Felix Platter when he journeyed to the French capital in 1599.[3]

Enhancing every spectacle was the rich apparel of the ladies and gentlemen of the court, the sumptuousness of which may still be gauged from the surviving (but fragmentary) accounts of the king's treasury, showing the enormous expenditure incurred under François I, Charles IX, and Henri III for cloth of gold and figured velvets for the queen and her ladies. The sieur de Vieilleville described a typical scene at court in 1556 after the wedding of Monsieur de Vaudemont with Mademoiselle de Nemours. Here the ladies were adorned in their most sumptuous garments with many jewels shimmering in the torch lights. So dazzling was the effect that the memorialist could find no better way of conveying their glamour than by conjuring up goddesses and nymphs of times past as celebrated by the poets. Those fabulous, poetical creatures could not compare (Vieilleville argued) with the beauty and grace of the French ladies ready to begin their ballet in brilliant attire, and with their jewels expertly placed to catch the light.[4]

Training for the Dance and Connoisseurship

Anyone striving for a position at court had to dance well. Even the pragmatic Italian historian Francesco Guicciardini—who disliked what he called "frivolities" such as music and dancing—admitted that these accomplishments opened "the way to the favour of princes, and for those who abound in them it may be the beginning or cause of immense profit and promotion."[5] Many Renaissance writers believed likewise. In thus acknowledging that skill in music and dancing were at the very core of a culture of display which defined the French court at this time, Guicciardini was rehearsing sentiments that had been advanced previously by Balthasar Castiglione. These views had quickly filtered into France through early translations of *Il Cortegiano* and influenced generations of ambitious courtiers.

Similarly, dancing masters had underlined the advantages of their art. In their prefaces to treatises on dancing, they argued that their skills were especially appropriate to noble men and women, for they insisted that the art of choreography was aligned to other arts and sciences, to music, geometry, architecture, and philosophy. Long ago, Guglielmo had argued that the dance was both a liberal art and a virtuous science, "of the most extraordinary efficacy, and most auspicious and sustaining to the human race."[6] These were lofty claims, but uttered in all seriousness. Fabritio Caroso, in his address to the Reader at the beginning of his *Nobiltà di dame* (1600), oriented his remarks to a more specifically court context, claiming that dancing was essential to good breeding, bringing together "grace, beauty and decorum in the eyes of the beholder."[7] Such views had resonated powerfully in France, where advocates of dancing had made even more substantial claims, using ancient authorities to bolster their image and significance, citing freely from Plato and Lucian, Aristotle and Plutarch, to signal the powerful traditions to which they belonged. The prose works of Pontus de Tyard or the *Louenge du bal* of Béranger de la Tour are but two examples.[8] In this approach, dancing masters, poets, and philosophers sought to place the art of dancing in the broader context of other art forms, to attribute to the choreographer powers of persuasion similar to those of the orator, and achievement of beauty and proportion like the harmonies built by architects or painters.[9]

Memoirs and personal diaries, although often written in old age whence the glories of youth seemed so attractive, emphasized how individuals learned dancing while still very young. Some, like Charles IX, Marguerite de Valois, and Henri III loved dancing all their lives and excelled at it, while others—mostly military men like the duc de Bouillon or Gaspart de Saulx, seigneur de

Tavannes—were impatient with their dancing lessons. Members of the administrative class recognized that their careers necessitated skillful performance on the dance floor. So Villeroy, secretary of state to several kings of France, sent his son Charles to Italy in 1588 to learn to dance and to fence at Padua; and the great Sully—powerful minister to Henri IV—adored dancing and took every opportunity to observe it, to perform himself, and to promote lavish productions.

Knowing how to dance, and having the ability to judge good dancing from bad, imposed rules on the performer who, in this context of connoisseurship, was obliged to dance with the utmost circumspection and self-criticism. There were many satires at the time that ridiculed the individual who overreached himself, or attempted to master the vast variety of dances that had become available. Philibert de Vienne may be cited as one who provided a subtle analysis of the situation where dancing was so popular that it constantly spawned new steps, novel forms, and complex figures. In his *Philosophe de court* (1547), he maintained that it was impossible to master all the skills needed to dance with ease and nonchalance as Castiglione and his many followers had advocated. Nonetheless, there were superb performers: Marguerite de Valois, extolled by both Brantôme and the prince of poets Pierre de Ronsard; the comte de Brissac and La Motte who danced with extraordinary speed and grace; and the Grand Prieur de France who so impressed Elizabeth I by his terpsichorean skills.[10]

Italian Influence on French Dancing

It has been demonstrated that, although there are a few isolated choreographies which survive for Northern France and Burgundy, the first significant treatises on dancing were written in Italy. These texts make clear the intensity of activity in North Italian courts and the rivalry among dancing masters. It seems evident also that dancing was popular in many of the major Italian cities if we are to judge from the indications found in the archives for Siena.[11] It was in this atmosphere of immense attention to the dance that kings of France, Louis XII and François I, learned to appreciate dancing in the Italian manner. Louis XII, in fact, brought back to France a magnificent copy of Guglielmo Ebreo's *De pratica seu arte tripudii*,[12] while François I enjoyed dancing every evening while he was in Milan and on his return journey home in 1516/17.[13] Moreover, the popularity of Italian dancing can be measured by the vast number of books of dance music arranged for lute, guitar, or spinet that poured forth from printing presses in

Paris and Lyon throughout the sixteenth century. Pierre Attaingnant, the king's printer, published at least one such book every year from 1529, while the lute books of Milanese composers, like Jean Paulo Paladino, introduced French audiences to dances such as *la volta* which showed great advances in technique.[14] (See Figure 1.2 for a picture of *la volta* being performed at the Valois Court.)

It was mainly through the Italian dancing masters that princes and their courtiers throughout Europe learned to dance. Cesare Negri, in the opening pages of his book *Le gratie d'amore*, demonstrates how his school in Milan spread its influence and its students right across Europe. Bernardino de Giusti worked in Savoy; Beccaria at the court of Emperor Rudolf; Giulio Cesare Lampugnano in Spain at the court of Philip II; and Virgilio Bracesco who, having accompanied Princess Elizabeth to Spain in 1559, returned once more to the French court at the behest of Henri III in 1574.

The habit of employing Italian dancing masters in France was supplemented by the presence of Italian instrumentalists at the French court. Charles IX in particular augmented their number, spending large sums on the best violins from Milan and Cremona, and encouraging violin players and lutenists to come to his court in order to satisfy his great love of music and dancing.[15] The Italian influence had, of course, been encouraged by his mother Catherine de' Medici, who enticed many musicians and choreographers into France. A major role was played, for instance, by the comte de Brissac, who came in 1555 with his band of violins. He was himself a famous performer, but more celebrated still was a member of his company—the violinist and choreographer Balthazar de Beaujoyeulx, who was to invent some of the most startling *ballets de cour* for the French court. By the reign of Henri III, seventy-six percent of violin players were Italian, and of professional dancers one hundred percent.

Designs for Ballets and Masquerades

Any attempt to convey the development of dance through the sixteenth and the early seventeenth centuries must recognize that the scale of performances was infinitely fluid, dictated by circumstance, by the private or public nature of the occasion, by the time for preparation, and by the funds available. In France, there was no straight evolution from ball to masquerade to ballet. All forms developed concurrently and invaded each other. Court balls, for instance, could be completely taken over by masquerades that had been prepared in advance. This was the case at the marriage in 1541 of the king's niece, the princesse de

Navarre, to the duc de Clèves, where there were nine masquerades which inter-acted with the ballroom dancing.[16]

Such performances demanded rich surroundings; but almost more impor-tant were the contributions of artists who spent hours designing machines: ex-traordinary floats to bring on the dancers, clouds that brought down gods to earth and returned them to heaven, magical fountains and rocks that moved to display dancers playing musical instruments, gardens of paradise, and sights of hell. Al-though the principal architects in France at this time were French[17]—Philibert de L'Orme, Jean Bullant and Androuet Du Cerceau, and although French sculptors like Jean Goujon were inspired by examples from the antique—the Italian influ-ence continued to be paramount in the sphere of decorative arts with Rosso, Pri-maticcio, Nicolò and Camillo dell'Abate, and Nicolò da Modena.

The most prolific artist at the French court for four decades, 1530–70, was Francesco Primaticcio, who carried his inspiration from the frescoes he created for the *salle de bal* (ballroom) and the *galerie d'Ulysse* at Fontainebleau (painted by Nicolò dell'Abate) into the invention of décor and costumes for masquerades and ballets.[18] We know the nature of his designs not only from surviving draw-ings but also from the letters of the many foreign agents attached to the French court, who were fascinated by the detail of costumes. In January 1541, Gian-Bat-tista Gambara commented on the wonderful variety of costumes of the mas-querades, displaying figures as diverse as Roman emperors, arquebusiers, Janus with two faces, Acteon, or peasants.[19] The dancers were always dressed in cloth of gold, often bizarre in design or inspired by classical models, suggesting on the one hand that dancing was imitative and grotesque, and on the other that stately dances were also performed to capture the statuesque beauty of forms *à l'antique*. In February 1541, for instance, François I and the cardinal de Lorraine danced into the ballroom disguised as trees, while the Dauphin simulated Diana; and Primaticcio's drawings show designs for such trees and goddesses as well as dignified inventions for the king as a Turkish nobleman. The following year, at Blois, Hymen was played by the Dauphin, while Perseverance was represented by Charles d'Angoulême in the guise of a lady spinning, slowly making his way into the hall on a tortoise.

The splendor of the designs and their setting can be viewed in the Valois Tapestries now hanging in the Uffizi Gallery in Florence. These were commis-sioned by Catherine de' Medici to persuade the rest of Europe of the greatness of France and, in particular, of the magnificence of the French court. The tap-estries, woven in Flanders, from drawings provided by Antoine Caron, depicted the major court festivities held in France from the reign of Charles IX. They in-cluded water fêtes at Fontainebleau (1564) and Bayonne (1565), showing, in *The*

Whale, the rustic dances performed to entertain the queen of Spain and, in the *Polish Ambassadors*, an elegant court ball danced to music performed by ladies seated on a mobile rock similar to that which had brought in the dancers for the *Ballet des Polonais* (1573).[20]

For further evidence of such designs and records of conspicuous consumption we have to wait until the reign of Louis XIII, whose court enjoyed regular performances of ballets and other spectacles for which we have complete accounts of expenses—as for the *Ballet de Tancrède* (1619) and the *Ballet des Fées de Saint Germain* (1625).[21] These describe in detail the work of Italian scene designers (Tommaso Francini), the inventions of choreographers (Jacques de Belleville), of musicians (Pierre Guédron), and of costume designers (Daniel Rabel). The album of Rabel's drawings, which relate to a series of ballets performed at court between 1615 and 1633, reveals how elegant were the conceptions for the melodramatic choreographies created to extol the power of the monarch and how imaginative and vigorous were the grotesque designs for the many acrobatic and burlesque performances which the king so often favored.[22]

Dancing as National and International Policy

Dancing played a key role in national and international politics. When François I wanted to dazzle the international community, as when his son (the future Henri II) married Catherine de' Medici in Marseille in 1533, he put on balls, ballets, and masquerades. His daughter-in-law took his example to heart, and when she sought to give advice to her son Charles IX in 1563, she wrote him a formal letter reminding him of his grandfather's strategy: keep the court busy with festivals and with balls twice a week.[23]

The extravagance loved by François I may be exemplified by two festivals. The first, from the beginning of his reign, is generally known as the fête at the Bastille (1518), a lavish event put on to celebrate the treaty between France and England, and the engagement between the Dauphin (ten months old) to Princess Mary of England (aged three years). The second, from the end of his monarchy, comprised the celebrations at Fontainebleau in 1546 for the baptism of his granddaughter Elizabeth, future queen of Spain. The first fête required that a temporary structure be made in the courtyard of the Bastille—a space that could accommodate banquets, balls, and masquerades with large numbers of performers. A contemporary account by Bernardino Rincio—a Milanese in the entourage of Galeazzo Visconti who had charge of all the arrangements—provides details of every aspect of the occasion.[24] Not only does he evoke the rich clothes of the performers and their dancing, he also describes the size, decoration, and layout of the hall. At one end, erected above the level of the dancing area, was a tribune so that the king, his family, and his most important guests might be seen, while on the two sides were graded steps and wooden balustrades providing good viewing for the spectators who did not dance.

As soon as the guests were assembled at 4:30 P.M. trumpets, flutes, and Milanese brass instruments played music for pavanes that the king and other princes danced for some two hours. After the banquet, a series of masked dancers entered the hall: richly dressed Spaniards and Frenchmen; prophets and Sibyls, Greeks and others with headdresses made like cardinals' miters. After a while they began to dance, first in circles and later in lines, performing moresques which brought much applause. Immediately, trumpets and flutes sounded again, and forty masked and disguised couples invaded the dancing area where they performed *à la mode milanaise* until midnight. The numbers and scale of the performance are noteworthy, as is the Italian influence pervading all the choreography—as might be expected when the master of ceremonies was an Italian who had frequently impressed François I with his inventions in Milan.

The 1546 ballets and masquerades had an altogether different and more exotic flavor. At the end of his life, François I was still concerned to publish his grandeur to the world, and (according to the Ferrarese ambassador) he still danced as though he were a young man of twenty. For the fêtes, the king chose the palace and domain of Fontainebleau, which he had filled with beautiful things: casts of the most famous antique statues in Rome, paintings by the most renowned Italian artists, galleries and rooms festooned with frescoes peopled with gods and goddesses, and decorated with all the paraphernalia of festivity. The oval courtyard was covered in to accommodate a wooden pavilion, fashioned *à l'antique* and decorated with inscriptions, devices, and heraldic images. The structure resembled an enormous marquee as canvas was stretched across the roof and down the sides, held up by a stout mast below which had been erected a buffet, its nine levels laden with the royal plate that François I had ordered to be sent from Paris so that it might astonish all who saw it. So beautiful and gilded were the many vases and vessels that observers reflected that the king must have gathered there the pick of the collections of all European princes.[25] In this extraordinary place whose floor had been covered with cloth for the dancing, musicians occupied two galleries and played continuously. The dancing began as soon as the king and his princes arrived and continued "in good measure and excellent grace" until they were interrupted by strange masquerades: men with outsize faces, wild beasts, and birds of prey so well made that they frightened many.[26]

Such disguises, which encouraged all kinds of choreographic antics, were common at François I's court. The king himself often assumed such guises, as a bear or centaur, as we know from Primaticcio's drawings.

Catherine de' Medici's use of dancing for the purposes of policy was more specific. In order to encourage peace at a time of civil war and to bring Protestants and Catholics together, she invited them to dance out their quarrels and differences in performing ballets and tournaments, thus—she hoped—releasing tension and creating harmony among rivals.[27] In the fêtes enjoyed at Fontainebleau in the spring of 1564, the court spent forty-three consecutive days participating in masquerades, concerts, balls, and fighting at the barrier. A seventeenth-century historian of Fontainebleau recalled "bals, les balets, les festins et autres semblables divertissemens; ce fut ainsy à quoy la Cour passa icy le temps"[28] ("balls, ballets, banquets and similar entertainments; in this way, the Court passed away the time"). Participants, like the future French ambassador in England, Michel de Castelnau, sieur de Mauvissière, specifically recalled that the fêtes were conceived as a process of reconciliation, a process—according to him—that did not work, as the Catholic Guise still hated in their hearts the Protestant admiral de Coligny. Whether the ballets danced for peace failed in that purpose or not, nevertheless, it remains significant that choreography was at the center of policy.[29]

Dancing was an even more crucially persuasive agent during the month-long series of "Magnificences" that celebrated the encounter between Spain and France at Bayonne in 1565. French observers were only too happy to record the astonishment of their Spanish guests who had never seen such displays of riches and of skills—especially in the dancing. Balls were a regular evening event in the vast new ballroom that had been built for the occasion and, as her particular contribution, Catherine had organized rustic dances to greet visitors as they stepped out of the boats which had taken them along the river Adour to the island where a banquet awaited them. Then in the octagonal hall that had been contrived in a large clearing, they witnessed a *ballet des nymphes*, harmonious dancing "dont les espagnols s'emerveilloyent et y prindrent sy grand plaisir" ("which the Spanish marvelled at, and found there enormous pleasure").[30]

Personal Taste Dominates the Ballet

The king, Charles IX, was at the center of all the activity, for on him depended the future stability of the realm; his purse met the costs of the entertainments;

and his tastes dictated their form and themes.[31] Contemporary writers, Papire Masson and Archange Tuccaro, report that he excelled in dancing and music and all the knightly arts.[32] When the king and his court moved from Paris, ballets and masquerades followed them. Moreover, in his tour of the country (1564–66), Charles IX was greeted by local dances everywhere he went: the *volta* at Brignolles, the *treille* at Montpellier, the *Martingale* at Castelnaudry, or basque dances and branles at St. Jean de Luz, and branles again at Nantes.[33]

The king was anxious that his court should be admired for its culture and splendor, and took pains to entertain important visitors with lavish spectacles. He even approved Pierre de Ronsard's dedication of the *Mascarades* to Queen Elizabeth in 1565, recognizing the international attention it would bring.[34] He also supported other ventures such as the establishment of the Academy of Poetry and Music (*Académie de Poésie et de Musique*) in 1571, where the poet Antoine de Baïf, the composer Thibault de Courville, and other artists experimented with poetry, music, and dance in the expectation of reviving the powerful moral "effects" on participants' emotions which they believed had been achieved by the Greeks.[35] Baïf wrote to Charles (1 February 1571) how they were planning in the *Académie* to put on a ballet where all the arts were combined together. Having—he explained—already blended together verse and music, they proposed to bring to life again the ancient art of choreography:

> After, I recounted how I had renewed
> Not only the graceful blending
> Of verses and music in ancient style,
> But also, I have renewed their style of dancing.[36]

Henri III intended his court to be well regulated, and with this in mind he created a *maître de cérémonies* (master of ceremonies) in 1585 and issued a series of *règlements* (guidelines or ceremonial protocols) that dictated the rhythm of fêtes. Dancing was to occupy two or three evenings a week, for which the great hall of the Louvre had to be made ready and musicians prepared. Nobles had to dress in suitable garments and were frequently responsible for mounting a ballet or masquerade at their own expense. From a memorandum that Richard Cook prepared for Lord Derby in 1584, we learn that there was a well-established hierarchy for dancing at court.[37] The king danced with the queen, followed by nobles of the highest rank and their ladies; the monarch then chose to dance with the bride of a great marriage or with any lady he favored. The queen danced with no one except the king, or possibly her brother—the duc de Mercoeur—or with another prince, but only at the express command of the king. Everyone understood the ritual and any deviation from the expected order aroused comment and speculation.

Figure 4.1. Court ball on occasion of the wedding of Duc de Joyeuse, 1581. Louvre, Paris. Erich Lessing / Art Resource, New York.

The dances, too, were performed in a traditional pattern. First came the slow and stately pavane; then the allemandes, still relatively sedate in character. The ensuing branles were usually danced in a circle and were followed by the courantes, and finally the *volta* in which (Cook reports) "the king taketh his greatest pleasure." (See Figure 1.2 for the *volta*.) The ball usually ended with galliards where the most nimble performers could show off their skills. The most immediate vision of a ball at court is provided in a series of contemporary depictions of dancing during the reign of Henri III. The painting, commonly called the *Bal du duc de Joyeuse* (housed in the Louvre) shows the duke with his bride Marguerite performing a pavane in the presence of the court, and provides a sense of the noble style of dancing necessitated by the grand clothes that ladies wore. The great hall of the Louvre is shown foreshortened and crowded with many spectators who, oddly, are looking out of the picture seemingly indifferent to the dancing couple. (See Figure 4.1 for a black and white reproduction of this painting. Henri III is seated under the canopy next to his mother, Catherine de' Medici, at the back left of the painting.)

Henri III was himself a notable dancer, graceful and dexterous, and able to execute fast steps and strong leaps. He had adored dancing from an early age and, well trained by Pompeo Diabono and Ludovico Palvallo, he was attracted by new steps and bold inventions.[38] His performances were frequently commented upon by resident ambassadors at the French court—his dancing described by Lord Cobham, for example, in 1580 as "strange and difficult."[39] His increasing obsession with the dance was adversely referred to by observers who thought that the money lavished on court extravagances might more profitably be used for better purposes. Pierre de L'Estoile, in his journal, repeatedly lamented "ballets et forces mascarades," which Jacques-Auguste de Thou also criticized. The historian admonished the king for his lack of concern for political and military affairs, and condemned Henri III's absorption in his "pleasures" [ballets] which, de Thou maintained, were used to dissimulate and hide his true policies.[40]

The lavish style of ballets performed during Henri III's reign may be illustrated by two examples. The first, the *Balet Comique de la Reyne* (1581), was commissioned by the queen as her contribution to the marriage celebrations of the king's favorite—the duc de Joyeuse and her sister, but dedicated by its author, Balthazar de Beaujoyeulx, to the king.[41] The second was conceived for the king himself, who was the principal performer in an ambitious work invented to impress the English Embassy which came to Paris in 1585 to present Henri III with the Order of the Garter.[42]

The *Balet Comique de la Reyne* carried further the geometrical pattern of dancing that aroused such favorable comment when the *Ballet des Polonais* had entertained the Polish ambassadors in 1573, although the ballet in 1581 supported a drama of more universal importance. The *Balet Comique* was concerned with matters of order representing allegorically the current political situation in France where the forces of evil and disorder continually threatened to disrupt the stability invested in the monarchy and in the proper institutions of the state. In this ballet, choreographed by Beaujoyeulx and set to music by musicians who had attended Baïf's *Académie*, Circé represented the principle of disorder whose power was only finally overcome by the combined forces of the king and the gods. Despite her defeat, which constituted the action of the ballet, and despite the fact that she is led ignominiously round the hall and presented to the king as "entirely vanquished and bereft of all her powers," Circé survives. That survival signals the fragile state of the order that had been established during the performance. The spectacle lasted five hours; and not only did it employ performers, musicians, singers, and dancers, but it also required the contribution of scene and machine designers, costume makers, composers, poets, and choreographer. If we concentrate on the final dance of the ballet, it is possible to gain a good sense of the scale of the performance, the variety and complexity of the dancing, and the control exercised overall by the choreographer.

The final dance exemplifies the system of pause and renewal that characterized geometrical dancing in France at this period. It had seemed that Circé had been vanquished. Yet the fragility of the order restored is made plain in the first ballet of the final act. The dancers adopt a triangular formation as they snake forward until they are in front of the king's dais. There, to the sprightly music of the violins, they perform a joyous dance to the well-known tune *La Clochette*. The gaiety of their dance arouses Circé, who rushes down the length of the hall to immobilize the dancers with her wand. The violins are also silenced. This violent interruption destroys harmony in full flow and makes manifest the power of evil. The stunned silence is only shattered by the sound of a cloud machine bringing Mercury down to earth. The god anoints the performers with the virtuous juice of his herb, Moly, and they resume their music and dancing, only to be rendered senseless a second time by an enraged enchantress who forces them all into her domain.

Various forces rush to the rescue: the powers of land and sea. Minerva and the four cardinal virtues make their appearance on mobile machines showing in their music and song, as they circled the hall, their determination to defend order. Finally Jupiter appears, and with all the good powers assembled under the king's influence they march on Circé, whose defiance delays their triumph. It is after the fall of Circé that the sixteen reanimated nymphs (twelve naiads and four dryads) come to resume their interrupted dancing and—through their figurations—to display the order that had been reestablished. They came forward toward Henri III in an initial fifteen passages of dancing. These were followed by the final ballet made up of forty *figures géometriques* ["geometric figures"] (as Beaujoyeulx called them)—a continuous structuring of forms by the twelve naiads "tantost en quarré, et aussitost en triangle, accompagné de quelque petit quarré et autres petites figures" ("now in square formation, then in triangular fashion, linked in with tiny square steps and other little figures"). The geometrical patterns were no sooner made than they were dissolved by the interactive dancing of the dryads; and out of their disappearance, new forms emerged. Halfway through this series of interrupted patterns, when the nymphs' movements were regularly stilled by the dryads, all the dancers together formed a chain of elaborate design as if they were in a kind of battle formation. Their strict pattern, their movement faultlessly performed to a variety of rhythms and sounds, constituted the ultimate moment of the work when harmony restored was made visible to all.

The divertissements designed to entertain the large English Garter of 1585 were unusually costly and magnificent,[43] and from the moment the delegation arrived in Paris and settled in the Hôtel de Longueville, housed entirely at Henri III's expense, they enjoyed banquets, ballets, concerts, and comedies. The high point of their visit came on the Sunday after the ceremony of the Garter when the king put on his ballet in the Louvre with 120 dancers. Each company of dancers was introduced by an extended concert of instruments and, throughout the entertainment, dancing alternated with music culminating in a vocal performance by forty musicians, which lasted half an hour. The ballet was unusual. The 120 dancers, richly dressed, interpreted complex choreographic figures at which the English visitors marveled, hardly finding words to describe "so strange a manner of dancing" before ending with a dance spelling out the names of the king and his spouse on the floor of the hall. Then came the royal ball, where twenty-four couples danced courantes and the *volta*, displaying the skills and ingenuity of French dancing which, by this time, had become internationally renowned. Only a year earlier, the duke of Ferrara had written to enquire whether some French instrumentalists might be sent so that his courtiers could learn French modes of dancing; and soon French choreographers were to settle in London, Brussels, and elsewhere, receiving high salaries and much consideration. Indeed it is likely that the final choreography of the famous fête *La Pellegrina* (1589), performed in Florence to welcome their new duchess from Lorraine, was, in part, inspired by French practice.

Exploitation of the Ballet by Bourbon Monarchs

Henri IV had participated in the court festivities from 1563, and he had danced with alacrity at all of them. When he became king, however, preoccupied with constant military hostilities against stubborn Catholic factions, he relied on his courtiers and (later) on his wife, Marie de' Medici, to organize ballets and masquerades, although he—too—recognized their value as propaganda tools. For example, he celebrated the Peace of Vervins (1598) with elaborate ballets to impress his Spanish rivals, while two years later he entertained the duc de Savoie in similar style exploiting the choreographic skills of his courtiers in order to seduce the duke who was easily influenced by outward display. The character of the ballets and masquerades changed very little at this time. Masquerades were built on a series of danced entries designed to show off exotic and often grotesque costumes and to display the skills of individual dancers.[44] Elaborate ballets were also occasionally attempted, such as the *Ballet de Monseigneur de Vendosme* (1610) with the well-tried theme of French knights under the eye of the monarch overcoming the wicked wiles of an enchantress. The Dauphin, yet too young to play a role in this ballet inspired from Torquato Tasso's work, had developed his own interest in dance and music, trying out his first steps (according to his doctor Héroard) at the age of four.[45] When he succeeded as Louis XIII, ballet (while continuing to favor forms which concentrated on individual entries and on burlesque themes) was transformed.

Royal ministers had understood that *ballets de cour* provided unique opportunities to bolster the king's personal authority, by demonstrating allegorically and through the dance his ability not only to demolish manifestations of evil or disorder but also to control the activities of his nobles as they fought and danced under his command. The eye of the king had released knights from their enchantment in the *Ballet de Monseigneur de Vendosme* (1610). In the *Délivrance de Renaud* (1617), the presence of the king dancing before his court and performing like a second Godefroy de Bouillon stamped his personal authority on the occasion. His supremacy is projected in the Grand Ballet at the apex of the choreographic structure,[46] when dressed as the *démon du feu* (a fire spirit), he led out his troops (the foremost nobles of the court) in a final ballet whose harmonious figures secured peace and control. His choreographic skills were evident and were supported and enhanced by the spectacular setting created by Francini. Mountains turned, rocks shook their heads, fountains emerged and disappeared, forests rose from the floor of the stage, and—at the climax of the spectacle—the whole scene was transformed to show Louis XIII "comme un autre Godefroy sur un trosne dans ce pavillon de toille d'or" ("like another Godefroy seated on a throne in this pavilion of golden silk"). The pavilion turned on its axis, and the king and his companions stepped down to perform the last ballet with figures that lasted an hour.

With the spectacular scenes that stage designers were now able to achieve came even greater exploitation of dance for the needs of the monarchy. The *Ballet de Tancrède* (1619) extended the power of astonishing an audience with the sight of a king triumphing in magnificent settings that were appropriate to his status and seemed somehow to have been contrived by him.[47] This ballet ended in a remarkable apotheosis: a hundred figures hanging in the sky, a similar number dancing on the stage, and yet more showing off their skills on the dancing space in the *orchestra* of the hall.

Richelieu turned all of this into a veritable propaganda machine. As Louis XIII's victories over the Protestants accumulated, so the need to celebrate such achievement became more compelling. Under Richelieu's patronage, choreographers, poets, musicians, artists, and stage designers were encouraged to extol the king and the greatness of France in a series of ballets. In 1635, the *Ballet de la Marine* exhibited the qualities and successes of the French fleet; the *Ballet de la Félicité* (1639) presented the wonderful order of the State and reminded a captive audience of past ills that had been banished; and in 1641, to crown his career, Richelieu commissioned the *Ballet de la Prospérité des armes de la France*, whose title made his intentions plain. Performed in the new theater which had been constructed in the Palais Cardinal, where the ability to astonish spectators had been enhanced by stage machinery of the latest design, the ballet—formally divided into five acts—provided a sequence of triumphs, visually of such miraculous splendor that machines seemed to have taken over part of the role hitherto performed by music and dancing. It is worth looking at this transformation of the *ballet de cour* in some detail.[48]

The curtain, on which was depicted a palace, opens revealing a forest scene above which hovered Harmony amid soft, billowing clouds. Her song tells of the remarkable harmony that now controlled the State of France through the efforts of Louis XIII and Richelieu. Yet the ballet has to show their struggle and achievement, so Harmony's song is interrupted by a sudden change of scene, depicting this time a view of Hell, with demons and evil creatures, representing disorder in the State and tyranny. These are then vanquished before our eyes through the deeds of a new Gallic Hercules (Louis XIII) who, victorious over the powers of darkness, reestablishes order and peace. Act II, however, brings further tumult: the spectacle of battles against Protestants and Spaniards, Casal and Arras, won by the French and represented in nine danced entries. A seascape opens Act III with Pallas, high in the heavens, watching over the triumphs which are extolled by Sirens as French vessels sink a crowd of Spanish galleons. It is now time for all the gods to appear to praise heroes whose deeds match their own. The nine Muses, Venus and the three Graces, Mercury, Bacchus, Apollo, and Minerva all make their entrances on triumphal cars, while Jupiter seated on a luminous throne begs Hercules (Louis XIII) to be content.

The final scene was overloaded with manifestations of joy. Allegories—Concord and Abundance, Peace, and Victory—from their chariots of triumph preside over an extraordinary display of good things: games, acrobatics, professional dancers exhibiting their prowess with leaps and jumps that took one's breath away, and dancers who pirouetted round the stage with delight at the success of French armies and at the glory of their king. It seemed as though the extravagant ballet was over. But after the curtain fell, it opened again almost immediately onto a glorious sight, a vast room all gold, lit up by a quantity of crystal chandeliers that revealed two thrones, for the king and queen. Then, imperceptibly, a bridge appeared from beneath the theater; it stretched forth over the heads of the audience until it touched the royal dais at the end of the hall, providing the way for the monarch and his spouse to pass onto the stage/ballroom. Allegorical congratulations now became reality. Louis XIII and Anne of Austria opened the court ball in these glittering surroundings. The elevated stage transformed the nature of the dancing and how it was perceived. It no longer made sense to inscribe complex geometrical figures on the floor of the dancing area to be viewed and interpreted from above. Now the whole body of the dancer became the focus of attention.

Conclusion

Through the sixteenth and the early seventeenth centuries, we witness the rising power of the choreographer, a better understanding of the techniques of the dance, and the increasing complexities of its inventions. Dance evolved and projected its role on the international scene, with enhanced participation in political maneuvering. Whereas under François I dancing simply signaled skill and magnificence, under later Valois kings ballet played a significant role in political argument. The *Ballet des Polonais* (1573), conceived by Jean Dorat and Beaujoyeulx, set forth a vision of social and political harmony in France where provinces, rich and plentiful, danced together, while the *Balet Comique* (1581) placed the king at the center of the action attributing to him the power to overcome evil and to establish order. French choreography was in demand everywhere. French style even penetrated the entourage of dance-loving Philip III of Spain; and French dancing masters and instrumentalists dominated the production of masques at the English court, giving form to the inventions of Ben Jonson and Inigo Jones and preparing the way for Queen Henrietta's ballets.

It had been the aspects of personal and political aggrandizement which had attracted Richelieu. He saw *ballet de cour* as an instrument of power and policy, useful to the State; a form that brought nobles into submission, playing out in the ballet the orders of the monarch. He developed the form so that it became the visual expression of political achievement and French hegemony. Thus, by the end of Louis XIII's reign, the *ballet de cour* was ripe for exploitation by Louis XIV and his ministers. When, after the civil wars of the Fronde in 1653, in the *Ballet de Cassandre*, Louis XIV appeared as *le Roi Soleil* (the Sun King) he was—in his person—bringing to a climax the trends that had begun in the 1570s.

Notes

1. "Dans cette cour on ne s'occupe qu'à se donner du bon temps tout le jour avec des joutes, des fêtes avec de très belles mascarades toujours différentes." Reports from visiting ambassadors are found in Armand Baschet, *La diplomatie vénitienne* (Paris: H. Plon,

1862); and in Carmelo Occhipinti, ed., *Carteggio d'arte degli ambasciatori estensi in Francia, 1536–1553* (Pisa: Scuola normale superiore, 2001).

2. The temporary palaces built in 1549 and 1559 have been brought to life by Catherine Grodecki, *Les travaux de Philibert Delorme pour Henri II et son entourage* (Paris: Librairie des Arts et Métiers-Éditions Jacques Laget, 2000), and by Jean-Marie Pérouse de Montclos, "Philibert de l'Orme à Paris. Le Palais de la Cité et les fêtes de 1549 et 1559," *Revue de l'art*, no. 114 (1996): 13–15.

3. See Monique Chatenet, *La cour de France au XVIe siècle: vie sociale et architecture* (Paris: Picard, 2000); and Felix Platter, *Beloved Son Felix. The Journal of Felix Platter: A Medical Student in Montpellier in the Sixteenth Century*, trans. Sean Jeannett (London: F. Muller, 1961).

4. Léon de Laborde, *Les comptes des bâtiments du roi, 1528–71*, 2 vols. (Paris: J. Baur, 1887–80); for this description, François de Scépeaux, sire de Vieilleville, *Mémoires de la vie*, ed. J. Michaud et J. J. F. Poujoulat (Paris, 1838), vol. 9.

5. Francesco Guicciardini, *Ricordi* [1530]. Cecil Grayson, ed., and Margaret Grayson, trans., *Francesco Guicciardini: Selected Writings* (Oxford: Oxford University Press, 1965), p. 45.

6. Guglielmo Ebreo, *De pratica seu arte tripudii: On the Practice or Art of Dancing*, ed. and trans. Barbara Sparti (Oxford: Oxford University Press, 1993), p. 89.

7. Fabritio Caroso, *Nobiltà di dame* (Venice, 1600). Facsimile ed. (Bologna: Forni, 1980), p. 2.

8. Pontus de Tyard, *Le Solitaire second, ou prose de la musique* (Lyon, 1555); and Béranger de la Tour d'Albenas, *Choréide, autrement, louenge du bal* (Lyon, 1556).

9. For this tradition, Jennifer Nevile, *The Eloquent Body: Dance and Humanist Culture in Fifteenth-Century Italy* (Bloomington: Indiana University Press, 2004); and Mark Franko, *The Dancing Body in Renaissance Choreography (c. 1416–1589)* (Birmingham, Ala.: Summa Publications, 1986).

10. Philibert de Vienne, *Le philosophe de court* (Lyon, 1547), Ed. P. M. Smith (Geneva: Droz, 1990); Pierre de Bourdeille, seigneur de Brantôme, *Oeuvres complètes*, 8 vols., ed. Louis Jean Nicolas Monmerqué (Paris, 1822), 4: 88; and Pierre de Ronsard, *Oeuvres complètes*, ed. Paul Laumonier (Paris: Didier, 1946), vol. 13, *Elegies, Mascarades et la Bergerie*.

11. Frank A. D'Accone, *The Civic Muse: Music and Musicians in Siena during the Middle Ages and the Renaissance* (Chicago: University of Chicago Press, 1997).

12. Guglielmo, *De pratica seu arte tripudii: On the Practice or Art of Dancing*, p. 7.

13. Raffaele Tamalio, *Federico Gonzaga alla corte di Francesco I de Francia nel carteggio privato con Mantoua, 1515–1540* (Paris: Champion, 1994).

14. On the profusion of dance tunes, see Howard M. Brown, *Instrumental Music before 1600. A Bibliography* (Cambridge, Mass.: Harvard University Press, 1965); Daniel Heartz, *Pierre Attaingnant, Royal Printer of Music: A Historical Study and Bibliographical Catalogue* (Berkeley: University of California Press, 1969); and Jeanice Brooks, *Courtly Song in Late Sixteenth-Century France* (Chicago: University of Chicago Press, 2000).

15. Brooks, *Courtly Song*, appendix.

16. *Cronique de François Ier de ce nom*, ed. Georges Guiffrey (Paris: J. Renouard, 1860), pp. 366–67.

17. Catalogues: *Le Colloque de Fontainebleau* (Paris, 1972); and *L'Ecole de Fontainebleau: Grand Palais* (Paris, 1972).

18. For Primaticcio's work at Fontainebleau, Catalogue: *Primatice. Maître de Fon-*

tainebleau, Musée du Louvre, 22 septembre 2004–3 janvier 2005; and Sylvie Béguin, *Le château de Fontainebleau* (Paris, 1960).

19. Occhipinti, ed., *Carteggio d'arte degli ambasciatori estensi*, pp. 56–57.

20. Frances A. Yates, *The Valois Tapestries* (London: Warburg Institute, 1959); and Jean Ehrmann, *Antoine Caron: peintre des fêtes et des massacres* (Paris: Flammarion, 1986).

21. See my *L'art du Ballet de cour en France, 1581–1643* (Paris, 1963), for details from the Bibliothèque Nationale de France, ms. Clairambault 808.

22. See my *The Court Ballet of Louis XIII: A Collection of Working Designs for Costumes 1615–33* (London: Victoria & Albert Museum in association with Hobhouse & Morton Morris, 1986), for a discussion of Rabel's album; on burlesque ballet, Mark Franko, *Dance as Text: Ideologies of the Baroque Body* (Cambridge: Cambridge University Press, 1993).

23. For the political and philosophical context of ballet, see Frances A. Yates, *The French Academies of the Sixteenth Century* (London: Warburg Institute, 1947); the introduction to my edition of the *Balet Comique de la Reyne, 1581* (Binghamton, N.Y.: Center for Medieval and Early Renaissance Studies, 1982); and J. R. Mulryne and Elizabeth Goldring, eds., *Court Festivals of the European Renaissance* (Aldershot: Ashgate, 2002).

24. Bernardino Riccio, *Le Livre de la Forest . . . contenant et explicant briefvement L'appareil: les Jeux: et le Festin de la Bastille* (Paris, 1518); for an analysis of this fête, Anne-Marie LeCoq, "Une fête à la Bastille en 1518," in *Il se rendit à Rome. Etudes offertes à André Chastel* (Paris: Flammarion, 1987), pp. 149–68.

25. An account of the occasion is given in D. Godefroy, *Le Cérémonial françois*, 2 vols. (Paris, 1649), 2: 146–48.

26. The strangeness of the dancing is emphasized by Guillaume Paradin, *Histoire de nostre temps* (Lyon, 1550), pp. 144–46.

27. Frances A. Yates first discussed the strategies used by Catherine in fêtes, *French Academies*, chapter 11, pp. 236–74.

28. Père P. Dan, *Le Trésor des merveilles de la maison royale de Fontainebleau* (Paris, 1642), p. 223.

29. Michel de Castelnau, sieur de Mauvissière, *Mémoires*, ed. J. Michaud et J. J. F. Poujoulat (Paris: Adolphe Everat, 1838), 9: 500.

30. The diverse accounts of the fêtes at Bayonne (1565) were printed in Victor E. Graham and W. McAllister Johnson, *The Royal Tour of France by Charles IX and Catherine de' Medici, Festivals and Entries, 1564–66* (Toronto: Toronto University Press, 1979).

31. For a discussion of Charles IX's role, see my article "Fêtes: religious and political conflict dramatized. The role of Charles IX," *Writers in Conflict in Sixteenth-Century France. Essays offered in honour of Malcolm Quainton*, eds. Elizabeth Vinestock and David Foster (Durham: Durham University Press, 2007).

32. Papire Masson's *Histoire de Charles IX* is printed in L. Cimber, *Archives curieuses de l'histoire de France* (Paris: Beauvais, 1836), 8: 333–51; Archange Tuccaro, *Trois dialogues de l'exercice de sauter, et voltiger en l'air* (Paris, 1599).

33. Graham and McAllister Johnson, *The Royal Tour of France*.

34. Pierre de Ronsard, *Elégies, Mascarades*.

35. Yates, *French Academies*, pp. 319–20.

36. "Après je vous disoy comment je renouvelle / Non seulement des vieux la gentillesse belle / Au[x] chansons et aux vers; mais que je remettoys / En usage leur dance." Antoine de Baïf, *Euvres en rime*, 5 vols. (Paris: A. Lemerre, 1881–90), 2: 230.

37. Published in David Potter and P. R. Roberts, "An Englishman's view of the Court

of Henri III, 1584–1585: Richard Cook's 'Description of the Court of France,'" *French History* 2, no. 3 (1988): 312–44.

38. For Henri III's obsession with dancing, see my article "L'Essor du ballet à la cour de Henri III," in *Henri III, Mécène. Les lettres, les sciences, et les arts sous le règne du dernier Valois*, eds. Isabel Conihout, Jean-François Maillard, and Guy Poirier (Paris: Presses de l'Université de Paris–Sorbonne, 2006), pp. 81–91.

39. *Calendar of State Papers, Elizabeth*, 1580–81, February, Lord Cobham to the Queen.

40. Pierre de L'Estoile, *Mémoires-Journaux, 1574–1611*, 11 vols., ed. G. Brunet et al. (Paris: Librairie des bibliophiles, 1875–83), 5 March 1581, and 12 February 1588; and Jacques-Auguste de Thou, *Histoire universelle*, 16 vols. (London, 1734), book lxxiv [1581], p. 531.

41. See my facsimile edition of the *Balet comique*.

42. For a discussion of this festival see McGowan, "l'Essor du ballet," and Roy Strong, "Festivals for the Garter Embassy at the Court of Henri III," *Journal of the Warburg and Courtauld Institutes* 22 (1959): 60–70.

43. *Calendar of State Papers, Elizabeth*, 1581, Cobham to the Queen.

44. McGowan, *L'art du Ballet de cour*.

45. Jean Héroard, *Journal sur l'enfance et la jeunesse de Louis XIII, 1601–1628*, 2 vols., ed. E. Soulié and E. de Barthélemy (Paris: Librairie de Firmin Didot, 1868).

46. For a discussion of this evolution, see my *L'art du Ballet de cour*, and the arguments of Kate van Orden, *Music, Discipline, and Arms in Early Modern France* (Chicago: University of Chicago Press, 2005).

47. See chapter 8 of my *L'art du Ballet de cour*, pp. 133–53.

48. For these transformations see my *L'art du Ballet de cour*, chapter 10, pp. 169–90.

Recommended Reading

Franko, Mark. *Dance as Text: Ideologies of the Baroque Body*. Cambridge: Cambridge University Press, 1993.

McGowan, Margaret M. "The Arts Conjoined: A Context for the Study of Music." *Early Music History* 13 (1994): 171–98.

———. *Ideal Forms in the Age of Ronsard*. Berkeley: University of California Press, 1985.

———. "Recollections of Dancing Forms from Sixteenth-Century France." *Dance Research* 21, no. 1 (2003): 10–26.

Ravelhofer, Barbara. *The Early Stuart Masque: Dance, Costume, and Music*. Oxford: Oxford University Press, 2006.

Strong, Roy. *Art and Power: Renaissance Festivals, 1450–1650*. Woodbridge: Boydell Press, 1984.

Van Orden, Kate. *Music, Discipline, and Arms in Early Modern France*. Chicago: University of Chicago Press, 2005.

Part 3

Dance and the Public Theater

It is not until the final century of the period dealt with in this volume that dance entered the realm of the public, commercial theater. The dancer, choreographer, dance teacher, musician, and composer Pierre Beauchamps is firmly center-stage in chapter 5 by John S. Powell. In this chapter Powell explores Beauchamps's long and varied career in French theatrical circles, both in court productions and in public commercial ventures, and his collaboration with the leading theatrical and musical figures, such as Molière, Lully, and Charpentier. The French theatrical seasons of the 1660s and 1670s produced multi-media spectacles that combined dance, music, scenery and stage design, and stage machines in "richly inventive ways." For example, the *Académie Royale des Opéra* from the winter of 1671 were so popular that "the Parisian public was literally beating down the doors to see it." Beauchamps personified both the multi-media aspect of the 1671 productions and their incredible success, in his own life with his amazing abilities in dance performance that continued at least to his seventieth birthday, as well as in the large number of roles he fulfilled in the *ballet de cour*, court productions of the *comedies-ballets*, productions in the Jesuit colleges, and, of course, productions in the public theater. The picture Powell presents of Beauchamps's activities that stretched over five decades provides insight into the extraordinarily vital role dance had in French theatrical productions in the second half of the seventeenth century, the interconnectedness between court productions and those in the public theater, and the way the spheres of music, dance, and the spoken dramatic arts were so tightly interwoven that one cannot speak of one without invoking the other.

In chapter 6 Jennifer Thorp provides a vibrant picture of dance in the London theater scene in the first half of the eighteenth century. These fifty years represented a period of entrepreneurial vigor and opportunity in theatrical life, and dance was now fully enmeshed into this commercial world, with its experiments in form, overnight successes, and sudden bankruptcies, the importation of foreign "stars" (many of whom were French and trained at the Paris Opera), and the growing pool of local choreographic and performing talent. As Thorp emphasizes, in London at that time, "there were only a few days in the year . . . when one could not attend a theatrical performance with dancing somewhere in its programme." Thorp discusses the wide spectrum of dance performances that were seen at the time: whether as part of an opera or masque, dancing in pantomimes, as one-off entr'acte dances, or as longer suites of dances performed between the acts of a play or between the main play and the afterpiece. (The latter was an important innovation that arose in English theaters from the 1710s onward.) She also discusses the wide range of dance types and styles that were performed, from the "serious" type, such as those by Anthony L'Abbe, to the "grotesque" type, as illustrated by François le Roussau's comic *Entry for Two French Country Men*, which deliberately undermines the "normal" baroque dance conventions.

5

Pierre Beauchamps and the Public Theater

John S. Powell

Pierre Beauchamps came on the scene at a seminal time in the development of French musical theater. His first recorded appearance as a dancer in the *Ballet du dérèglement des passions* (performed in the Palais-Cardinal on 23 January 1648) followed in the wake of Cardinal Mazarin's early attempts at importing Italian opera to France (with *Orfeo* of Rossi and Buti). The year 1648 began the golden age of the mythological machine play, an important forerunner of French opera, when the Théâtre du Marais performed their grandest *pièce en machines* on the Orpheus myth: Chapoton's *La Grand Journée des Machines, ou le Mariage d'Orphée et Euridice* (with sets and machines by Denis Buffequin and music by Charles Coypeau, *dit* Dassoucy). Pierre Corneille would set a new standard of spectacular musical theater with his 1650 production of *Andromède* (with sets and machines by Giacomo Torelli).

This was also a time of fomenting civil unrest in France. The Parisian populace rose up against Cardinal Jules Mazarin in the summer of 1648, and the royal family fled Paris and took refuge in the château of Reuil for nearly a year. A power struggle between the nobility and the monarchy ensued, and the Fronde (as this civil war was called) would last until 1652. During these years Beauchamps became unofficial dancing teacher to the young Louis XIV.[1] In 1653 Beauchamps danced alongside his royal pupil in the *Ballet de la nuit*, a work that also marked the court début of Jean-Baptiste Lully. Beauchamps would hitch his wagon to the younger Lully's star during the 1650s and 1660s, when the two appeared together in a succession of court ballets—including the dance *entrées* intercalated in the Caproli/Buti opera *Le Nozze di Peleo e di Theti*, performed at the Petit Bourbon in April of 1654.[2] Beauchamps's reputation as a virtuoso dancer quickly grew. For his agile movements, precision, and high, bold leaps he executed in the *Ballet des plaisirs troubles* (1657), Beauchamps was praised by Loret as the best dancer in France. In the Benserade-Lully *Ballet d'Alcidiane* of the following year, according to Loret, Beauchamps "surpassed all the other dancers."[3] Beauchamps's career as a dance choreographer began around 1656. According to Loret, Beauchamps composed some of the dances for an unnamed masquerade by Lully, given in Mazarin's apartments in the Louvre on 3 February 1656.[4] As Beauchamps's reputation grew, he was called upon to choreograph and perform in ballets given for important state occasions, and he choreographed many of the major court ballets of the 1660s.

Beauchamps, Molière, and Lully

Beauchamps's professional association with Molière was strengthened through family ties. For two generations, municipal and court orchestras included musicians from two related families: the Beauchamps (Christophe, Denis, Louis, Nicolas, Vincent, and Pierre) and the Mazuels (Adrian, Guillaume, Jehan, Jehan II, Jean, Michel, and Pierre). Guillaume Mazuel, who played in Louis XIII's *grande bande* along with the elder Pierre and Louis Beauchamps, was our Pierre Beauchamps's great-uncle and Molière's great-grandfather.[5] No doubt Beauchamps's career profited from his relation to the soon-to-be-famous actor and playwright.

Pierre Beauchamps danced in the court premières of nine of the Molière-Lully *comédies-ballets*. His name often heads professional *baladins* listed in the livret, where he portrayed a variety of colorful and exotic characters. These range from the elegant (a "galant") to the comic (a buffoon, a jester, a dog keeper, a solicitor, a pantomime, and Scaramouche), from deities and mythological figures (a sea-god, a Cyclops, and a fury) to pastoral characters (a shepherd, a faun, and a follower of Bacchus), along with exotic figures (a gypsy, a Moor, a Biscayan, a Turk, and a Spaniard). Beauchamps danced alongside the king in *Le Mariage forcé* (1664), in *Le Sicilien* (1667), and in *Les Amants magnifiques* (1670). In the *Ballet d'Alcine* that concluded the third day of *Les Plaisirs de l'Île enchantée* (1664), Beauchamps danced the role of Roger (Ruggiero)—thereby standing in for the king, who had portrayed the Christian knight during the previous days of the fête.

Whereas Beauchamps is credited with composing the dances for the court premières of the Molière-Lully *comédies-ballets*, modern scholars disagree with regard to which works.[6] Be that as it may, the careers of Beauchamps and Molière would become closely intertwined throughout the 1660s. Their first collaboration was *Les Fâcheux*, Molière's first *comédie-ballet* that was commissioned by Nicolas Fouquet, then Minister of Finance. Fouquet had wished to entertain Louis XIV with a *ballet à entrées*, the king's favorite form of entertainment. In this type of ballet, each dance *entrée* was related thematically to the chosen subject: the one chosen for Fouquet's ballet was the various species of "nuisances" (*fâcheux*) that plagued the court and annoyed the king. Like other professional acting companies of the time, Molière's troupe was no stranger to *ballet de cour* and its conventions.[7] For the performance of *Les Fâcheux* at the château of Vaux-le-Vicomte, Molière replaced the *récits* (solo vocal commenting on the ensuing action) that traditionally introduced each ballet *entrée* with comic episodes that presented still more varieties of *fâcheux*. The dramatic continuity provided by a play transformed a *ballet à entrées* into what Molière enthusiastically announced to be "un mélange qui est nouveau pour nos théâtres" (a mixture that is new for our stages; "Avertissement" to *Les Fâcheux*).[8]

Having but two weeks to write the play and rehearse the dancing actors, Molière left other aspects of the production to his colleagues. The poet Paul Pellisson (Fouquet's secretary) wrote the verse prologue, Beauchamps composed the ballet and its music, Charles Le Brun painted the scenic embellishments, and Giacomo Torelli designed the sets and stage machines. Even Lully, whom the king had appointed to the post *Surintendant de la musique et compositeur de la musique de la chambre* the previous May, provided a sung *courante* for the entertainment. Indeed, Molière's play hints that Lully may well have had a larger hand in the ballet. When in Act I, scene 3 the dancing nuisance leaves to show "Baptiste le très cher" his courante and to entreat him to "compose the parts," perhaps Molière is slyly letting us in on a secret: that Lully similarly helped Beauchamps with the scoring of his ballet.[9]

What, then, was the extent of Beauchamps's participation in the Vaux-le-Vicomte première of *Les Fâcheux*? A marginal inscription at the beginning of the sole surviving manuscript (by the king's music librarian, André Danican Philidor), states that "this ballet was composed, the airs and the dances, by Mr. Beauchamps."[10] From this it seems clear that Beauchamps composed both the dance music and the choreography. We might further speculate that he took on some of the traditional duties of the organizer of ballets', as described in Saint-Hubert's 1641 ballet treatise, *La Manière de composer et faire réussir les ballets.*[11] These duties include overseeing the rehearsals of the dancers, selecting masks and props for the different *entrées*, guiding the entrances and exits of the dancers, conducting the orchestra (or perhaps just signaling the players when to begin), marking the dancers' positions on the dance floor, and indicating when the *entrées* should start. Certainly, Beauchamps had his hands full with these duties, and he appears to have had some help with the choreography: according to the gazetteer Jean Loret, Hilaire d'Olivet "composed several pleasant *entrées.*"[12] D'Olivet was a *maître de danse particulier,* that is, a private dance teacher, and one of the original thirteen members of the Académie Royale de Danse. Beauchamps and d'Olivet had jointly choreographed the *Ballet de l'impatience* earlier that year, so it stands to reason that d'Olivet probably contributed some choreography to this performance of *Les Fâcheux.*[13]

Molière and his company were invited to Fontainebleau on 25 and 27 August 1661 to repeat *Les Fâcheux* on a double-bill with the playwright's new comedy, *L'École des maris*—for which the king paid them the princely sum of 15,428 *livres* for "decorations, baladins, danseurs, nourriture et recompense des comédiens" (decorations, professional dancers, [other] dancers, meals and compensation for the actors).[14] No doubt Molière used Beauchamps's music and choreography when he presented *Les Fâcheux* for a highly acclaimed run of forty-four performances at the Théâtre du Palais-Royal in Paris, beginning in November 1661. Loret, in his letter of 19 November 1661, proclaimed: "*Les Fâcheux,* this new play which, by its extreme cleverness, so greatly enchanted these past days the most judicious at Court, is now being performed in Paris: and, certainly, everyone attests that among all plays until now, one sees nothing funnier."[15] Whereas it is not known whether or not Beauchamps collaborated in these 1661 performances of *Les Fâcheux,* we know that in the years following Beauchamps would serve Molière and his Troupe du Roy in several capacities—as *maître de ballet,* as choreographer, and even as conductor of the theater orchestra.

Beauchamps's next collaboration with Molière and Lully was *Le Mariage forcé* (1664), a *comédie-ballet* written upon royal command for performance in the Louvre apartments of the Queen Mother. In his capacity as the newly appointed Superintendant of the King's Music, Lully composed the dance airs and the vocal numbers. Some of the dances were conceived for performance by professional *baladins* (d'Olivet, Saint-André, des Brosses, de Lorge, Le Chantre, Beauchamps, the des-Airs brothers, Raynal, Noblet, La Pierre, d'Heureux, and Le Mercier), whereas others featured the king and his courtiers (the Comte d'Armagnac, the Marquises de Villeroy and de Rassan, and Messieurs de Tartas de La Lanne, du Pille, and Le Duc). The professionals danced ballet-pantomimes for Jealousy, Chagrins, and Suspicions (*Première entrée*), for the magician and four demons (*Quatrième entrée*), and for the dancing master (*Cinquième entrée*), while the noble amateurs joined them in the dances for four "jokers" (*Deuxième entrée*), gypsy men and women (*Troisième entrée*), Spanish ladies and gentlemen (*Sixième entrée*), and four gallants (*Dernière entrée*).

For the public performances of *Le Mariage forcé* at the Théâtre du Palais-Royal beginning 15 February 1664, Beauchamps was paid 550 *livres* "pour faire le ballet" (for composing the ballet). According to the company's financial register, the play was performed with "le ballet et les ornemens" ("ornemens" referring presumably to the instrumental and vocal music). Indeed, it appears that Molière attempted to offer the Parisian public a spectacle on the same scale as the court première—for the accounts kept by the actor La Grange list a daily expense of 109 *livres* for music and dance in excess of the ordinary operating expenses.[16] By comparing these expenses with those recorded in a second register kept by the actor La Thorillière,[17] we can deduce that Molière's company employed twelve strings, a singer, around four oboes, and two *tambours de basques* (tambourines) for the *intermèdes*. Nine professional dancers were also hired for these twelve performances—an unprecedented number for the public theater. Although the *comédie-ballet* was a popular success, the financial drain substantially reduced the company's profit margin and impacted upon each actor's share of the house receipts. For example, after production expenses were deducted from the 200 *livres* taken in for the tenth performance, each actor's earnings amounted to a meager 2 *livres* 5 *sous*.

Molière and Lully collaborated in nine more *comédies-ballets* during the years 1664–1670, and Beauchamps's name regularly appears listed among the professional dancers who performed in them at court. As with *Le Mariage forcé*, after their court premières Molière capitalized on his success by producing the majority of his *comédies-ballets* before the general public at the Théâtre du Palais-Royal. The daily financial registers of theatrical seasons from 1665 to 1671 have not survived, and so there is no evidence to indicate that Beauchamps assisted in adapting these *comédies-ballets* to the public stage during this period. Indeed, there is evidence to the contrary—that after *Le Mariage forcé* Molière's company engaged a new *maître de ballet*. For *La Princesse d'Élide*, which played at the Palais-Royal from 9 November 1664 until 4 January 1665, 220 *livres* were paid to a "Mr des Brosses."[18] This must be Anthoine des Brosses, the dancer who performed the role of "un Chagrin" in the *premier intermède* of *Le Mariage forcé* at court. In the three-day fête at Versailles (*Les Plaisirs de l'Île enchantée*) during which *La Princesse d'Élide* was first given, des Brosses danced as one of the signs of the zodiac, as a monster, and as a knight. Thereafter Molière evidently engaged des Brosses as ballet master for his Paris performances of *La Princesse d'Élide*—even if in the following year des Brosses was in the service of the Théâtre du Marais, where he was ballet master for its production of Boyer's machine-play *Les Amours de Jupiter et de Sémélé*.[19]

While there is no record of Beauchamps's association with the public theater during the years 1664–1670, he and Molière may have collaborated on a ballet some time in 1667 or 1668. An "Air de Ballet de M. de Beauchamp," with poetry ascribed to Molière, appears in the *Recueil des plus beaux vers qui ont été mis en chant* (1668).[20] According to Georges Couton, Molière's verses seem to be addressed to Mlle du Parc (Marquise Thérèse de Gorla), one of the leading actresses of Molière's company who was often praised for her singing and dancing. The gazetteer Loret singled out her performance in *Les Fâcheux* for acclaim, and another author recalled, with more than a hint of fetishism, that she used to perform "certain remarkable cabrioles—for one could see her legs and part of her thighs through the slit in her skirt, as well as her silk hose attached to her tights."[21] In *Le Mariage forcé* Mlle du Parc played the flirtatious Dorimène, who dances with four gallants at her own wedding.[22] The height of her recognition at court came in 1664, when she performed the role of Alcina, the enchantress of *Les Plaisirs de l'Île enchantée*. In the final *Ballet du Palais d'Alcine*, she danced opposite Beauchamps (who danced the role of Ruggiero, or Roger).

Beauchamps and the Académie Royale des Opéra

It appears that Beauchamps did not work again for the Théâtre du Palais-Royal until the 1671–72 season. But in the meantime, he became involved in *Pomone*, the inaugural production of Pierre Perrin's Académie Royale des Opéra, which opened on 3 March 1671 in a rented theater (the Jeu de Paume de la Bouteille) and ran for 146 performances. Beauchamps and other veteran *baladins* of court ballets—including Saint-André, Favier, and La Pierre—performed the dances,[23] and Jean de Tralage also credits Beauchamps with the choreography.[24] A document of around 1672, preserved in the archives of the Comédie-Française, further clarifies Beauchamps's involvement in this production:

And as for the opera *Les Peines et les plaisirs de l'Amour* (that is, the second production of Perrin's Académie Royale des Opéra), he stated that all of the music
was ready before *Pomone* closed, since Monsieur de Beauchamps, who danced
for about two months in *Pomone*, heard the rehearsal of the aforesaid second
opera on the first day that he joined the opera, and that Monsieur des Brosses
had all of the dance airs of this second opera before he relinquished his position
to the aforesaid Beauchamps.[25]

This intriguing document reveals that des Brosses initially served as *maître de
ballet* for Perrin's Académie Royale des Opéra, and that Beauchamps took over
des Brosses's position for the last two months of the seven- or eight-month run
of *Pomone*. Meanwhile, des Brosses evidently left to take a position as *maître de
ballet* for the elaborate production of Donneau de Visé's musical machine-play,
Le Mariage de Bacchus et d'Ariane, which was to be given at the rival Théâtre du
Marais during the winter of 1671–72.

Beauchamps, Psyché, and collaboration with Molière and Charpentier

The winter of 1671 was an exciting theatrical season—one that was exploding
with multi-generic spectacles that combined music, dance, décor, and machines
in richly inventive ways. The operas of *Pomone* (text by Perrin, music by Cambert) and *Les Peines et les Plaisirs de l'Amour* (text by Gilbert, music by Cambert)
at the Académie Royale des Opéra were wildly successful, to the extent that the
Parisian public was literally beating down the doors to see it. Molière's latest
comédie-ballet Le Bourgeois Gentilhomme (text by Molière, music by Lully) had
enjoyed an unprecedented run of performances at the Théâtre du Palais-Royal.
And the Théâtre du Marais premièred *Le Mariage de Bacchus et d'Ariane*, the
first in a trilogy of machine-plays by Jean Donneau de Visé, with visually stun-
ning sets and complex aerial machine-effects designed by Denis Buffequin, in
an extended three-month run. The rush was on to create works of musical theater on an ever grander scale.

Beauchamps was one of several *maîtres de ballet* who were involved in the
court production of *Psyché*, a *tragicomédie et ballet* by Molière, Pierre Corneille,
and Philippe Quinault, with music by Lully and sets and machines by Carlo
Vigarani. The première took place on 17 January 1671 in the Grande Salle des
Machines, the spectacular playhouse within the Tuileries Palace built ten years

earlier. The theater had not been used since Cavalli's opera *Ercole amante* (1662) had played there, and in its *garde-meubles* were the sets and stage machines which had been designed for use in future production. Lully's dances for *Psyché* included (in addition to "danses ordinaires") colorful dance-pantomimes for a variety of characters: dryads, sylvan deities, demigods of the streams (*Prologue*); afflicted men wandering in the desert (*Premier intermède*); fairies and Cyclops who forge silver vases (*Second intermède*); cupids and zephyrs (*Troisième intermède*); furies and leaping goblins (*Quatrième intermède*); the entourages of Apollo (gallant shepherds), of Bacchus (maenads and gypsies), of Momus (Punchinellos and buffoons), and of Mars (enseign-, spear-, mace- and shield-bearers) in the final *intermède*. In all, some eighty-two dancers performed in the ballet episodes. From the royal accounts, we know that Beauchamps received 300 *livres* "pour ses peines et recompenses d'avoir servy audit ballet" (for his trouble and compensation for having served in the aforesaid ballet), and was assisted by two other *maîtres de danse*: Anthoine des Brosses (who received 200 *livres*) and Nicolas Delorge (150 *livres*). It seems likely that these three were in charge of choreographing the dances to Lully's music (undoubtedly with Lully's input) and supervising their execution.[26]

Molière subsequently engaged Beauchamps for his somewhat reduced production of *Psyché* at the Théâtre du Palais-Royal. But before they could stage this *pièce à grand spectacle,* the company voted to remodel the stage to accommodate the elaborate scene changes (so essential to the play) and the technically demanding machine effects and aerial flights. By the end of the Lenten break upgrading on the stage and auditorium was completed, and on 15 April 1671 work began on "the machines, decorations, music, ballet, and generally all of the ornaments necessary for this grand spectacle."[27] For the ballet numbers Beauchamps had at his disposal twelve dancers and four *petits danseurs*; two graces and six little cupids and zephyrs to perform the aerial flights; and two acrobats. The number of dancing characters were pared down to roughly half that of the court production, and no doubt there was much doubling of roles.[28] We do not know the names of the dancers who appeared in these performances, but it is probable that some were among the eighty-two dancers who had danced in the court première.

Performances of *Psyché* began on 24 July 1671 and lasted until October. The financial register kept by La Grange provides details of Beauchamps's duties and the amounts he was paid: 1,100 livres "for having composed the ballets [*pour avoir faict les ballets*] and for leading [*conduire*] the music," together with an additional payment of 11 *livres* per performance "for beating time to the music [*pour batter la mesure à la musique*] as well as for supervising [*entretenir*] the ballets."[29] From these *précisions* it appears that Beauchamps choreographed the dances, coordinated the movements with Lully's music, oversaw the execution of the ballets, and conducted the orchestra for the Palais-Royal performances.

The first run of *Psyché* lasted for thirty-eight performances, from 24 July until 25 October of 1671; the second for thirty performances, from 15 January to 6 March 1672. Meanwhile, Perrin's Académie Royale des Opéra fell into financial trouble owing to mismanagement. The theater was closed by royal decree on 1 April 1672, whereupon Lully stepped in to take over and obtain a new opera *privilège* from the king. At about the same time, Lully and Molière fell out— probably over the former's acquisition of this royal *privilège*, which amounted to a monopoly on opera. An early draft of the document contained a clause, aimed primarily at the Palais-Royal, prohibiting theater companies from performing works "with more than two airs and two instruments"; Molière and his company petitioned the king to have these restrictions struck from the final version.[30]

Possibly in retaliation, Molière revived several of his nonmusical comedies (*L'Avare, L'École des maris, Le Cocu imaginaire, L'Étourdi, Amphitryon, Les Femmes savants*, and *Le Misanthrope*) during the spring and summer of 1672 and supplied them with orchestral music. Moreover, the company's financial registers show that Beauchamps assisted with the revival of several of Molière's earlier *comédies-ballets*, presumably with Lully's original music.[31] *Le Bourgeois Gentilhomme*, revived on 24 May 1672 for a run of ten performances, featured "strings, dancers, and vocal music"—for which Beauchamps received 11 *livres* per performance. Next, Molière revived *Monsieur de Pourceaugnac* for five performances, beginning on 7 June 1672, with "violons et danceurs"; again, Beauchamps received 11 *livres* daily. Then on 8 July 1672, the company began a run of fourteen performances of *Le Mariage forcé*, which was given on a double bill with Molière's 1671 comedy *La Comtesse d'Escarbagnas* (this was the Paris première). La Grange's financial register documents this production as follows:[32] "Note further that *Le Mariage forcé*, which has been performed with La Comtesse d'Escarbagnas, has been accompanied with ornaments, for which Monsieur Charpentier has composed the music and Monsieur Beauchamps the ballets, Monsieur Baraillon the costumes, and Monsieur de Villiers was used in the musique of the interludes." Beauchamps designed the dance choreography to music newly composed by Marc-Antoine Charpentier, and another financial register notes that "M[rs] De B. et C[er]" (that is, Monsieurs Beauchamps and Charpentier) together received 269 livres "pour reconnaissance" (in gratitude).[33] These new dances included a minuet, a gavotte, three dance-pantomimes entitled *Les maris* (The Husbands), *Le songe* (The Dream), and *Les grotesques* (Grotesque Characters), and a sung saraband entitled *Les boemienes* (The Gypsies). Evidently, Molière's company presented the *comédie-ballet* as an interior entertainment given for the characters of *La Comtesse d'Escarbagnas*.[34] Later that autumn (7 and 9 October 1672), Molière replaced *Le Mariage forcé* with his *comédie-ballet L'Amour médecin* (1665), and performed it in context with *La Comtesse d'Escarbagnas* with "vocal music, dance, and symphony." Again, Beauchamps received 11 *livres* daily for his services.[35] The Molière-Charpentier-Beauchamps collaboration continued with a late summer revival of *Les Fâcheux,* for which Charpentier and Beauchamps each received 11 *livres* daily.[36] Given the cool relations between Lully and Molière at this time, one wonders whether Molière might have changed the clever references to "Baptiste le très cher" and whether Charpentier might have replaced the sung courante for the dancing nuisance Lysandre with his own music.

Beauchamps and the Comédie italienne

Taking the lead from Molière's musical revivals during the summer of 1672, Fiorilli's company of Italian actors (which shared the Théâtre du Palais-Royal with Molière's company on alternate days) presented their own Italianate farces with music and dance. Joseph Girardin's *Le Collier de perles* was the first of these, for which Charles Robinet praised its "bonne musique, et de tres beaux pas de ballet" (fine music, and very lovely dance numbers).[37] Based on an incident reported by Donneau de Visé in the first issue of the *Mercure galant, Le Collier de perles* told of a young man who, having stolen a pearl necklace, swallowed its thirty-two pearls in order to conceal his crime; later, he was caught and forced (by means of enemas) to surrender his ill-gotten goods.[38] In the Italians' production, Arlecchino frenchified his character's name to "Arlequin Sbrofadel, Marquis François" to portray the hapless young man in question. Not only did the work resemble Molière's shorter *comédies-ballets* (such as *L'Amour médecin* and *Monsieur de Pourceaugnac*), but some of its comic material parodies Molière's *Le Bourgeois Gentilhomme*.[39] While the composer is not mentioned by name, the play's preface states:

> Moreover it is futile to name the one who has taken the trouble to compose the airs and the ballet *entrées* which embellish it; whereas this illustrious person had used only the few spare moments left to him from the entertainments that he prepares for the King, one cannot help but recognize right away his admirable genius, and to judge that it could only be from him that such things so surprising and effortless could issue.[40]

Many scholars (myself included) initially misunderstood this as a reference to Lully—which attests to Beauchamps's stature in the early 1670s. Beauchamps's score (for which only the dance numbers are preserved) is found in the Paris Bibliothèque Nationale (headed by the title "Le Collier de perlle Comedie Italliene Represente au palais Royalle faict par Monsieur de Bauchamps"),[41] and consists of an *Ouverture* followed by seventeen dance numbers: *Les satires, Deuziesme satires, Entré, Laquais, Les escoliers, Gavotte, Scaramouche, Entré, Entré, Entré, Les facheuz, Les advocats, Entré, Entré, Sarabande, Entré,* and *Chaconne*.[42]

Beauchamps and Le Malade imaginaire

Even if by the summer of 1672 it was increasingly apparent that Beauchamps's continued association with Molière would put him at odds with Lully, Beauchamps still signed a contract (now lost) in July committing his services to Molière and his company. A few weeks later, the August issue of the *Mercure galant* announced a revival of *Psyché* for the winter of 1672–73 and a new work for the coming Carnival season that would once more feature ballets by Beauchamps:[43] "We will see at the beginning of winter the grand spectacle of *Psyché* triumph again on the stage of the Palais-Royal; and, for Carnaval, a new spectacular play, entirely comic, will be performed; and as this play will be by the famous Molière and the ballets for it will be composed by Monsieur de Beauchamps, we may expect nothing but the best."

On 15 November 1672, Lully inaugurated his Académie Royale de Musique with an opera-pastiche, *Les Festes de l'Amour et de Bacchus,* for which Lully engaged Anthoine des Brosses as his *maître de ballet*.[44] A new ordinance dated 12 August 1672 prohibited theaters from hiring either singers and instrumentalists retained by Lully's Académie Royale de Musique or dancers currently on the royal payroll. This forced Molière and Beauchamps to replace all of the professional singers and court dancers who had performed in the first run of *Psyché,* and it further deprived Beauchamps of the best dancers available.[45] But despite this setback, the third run of *Psyché* began on 11 November 1672 (four days before the inauguration of Lully's Académie Royale de Musique) and ran for twenty-one performances until 22 January 1673—two weeks before the première of *Le Malade imaginaire.*

According to La Grange's register, this was a lavish and expensive production "filled with dances, vocal music, and stage properties."[46] General preparations began on 22 November 1672,[47] while dance rehearsals began on 19 December; these latter were scheduled nearly every day of the week and lasted for several hours from eight in the morning into the early afternoon.[48] Altogether, there were a total of eighteen rehearsals for the actors, which started on Monday, 16 January 1672. After thirty-three dance rehearsals, the ballet was combined with the spoken comedy on 23 January for the "grandes répétitions"—in all, fifty-three rehearsals of the ballet, fifteen with the comedy.[49] Even after *Le Malade imaginaire* opened on 10 February 1673, dance rehearsals continued.

The extra amount of attention devoted to the ballet might well testify to the complexity and elaborateness of Beauchamps's choreography. However, it could also suggest the inexperience of the dancers with whom he had to work. Since Lully had appropriated the best dancers around for his Académie Royale de Musique, Beauchamps's *corps de ballet* was composed largely of actors and supernumeraries who no doubt required additional training and attention. In fact, it has been suggested that Molière and Beauchamps had in mind to establish an academy of singing and dance to prepare the way for future musical productions at the Théâtre du Palais-Royal. These two months of rehearsals for *Le Malade imaginaire* had served to train a new generation of singers and dancers, for which classes continued under the direction of Beauchamps after the production was under way.[50]

Moreover, until 22 January performances of *Psyché* continued on Tuesday, Friday, and Sunday afternoons—following the morning rehearsals of *Le Malade imaginaire*. No doubt some of the dancers who rehearsed the latter also appeared in *Psyché*. And, during these months, Beauchamps was responsible not only for daily rehearsals of the ballets for *Le Malade imaginaire*, but for conducting *Psyché* thrice weekly. As the première of *Le Malade imaginaire* approached, Molière scheduled nonmusical plays (Donneau de Visé's *Les Maris infidèles*, Molière's *Les Femmes savantes*) "so as to allow the dancers and singers, tired by the rehearsals, to rest," according to Thierry.[51] On Tuesday, 7 February, the theater was closed for the final dress rehearsal.

Molière's unexpected and tragic death after the fourth performance on 17 February brought a temporary halt to performances. During this critical period, Beauchamps stayed on to assist with the production. Perhaps family loyalty influenced Beauchamps's decision to remain, albeit temporarily, with Molière's former company. But this situation would not last for long, for one month after Molière's death the king granted Lully exclusive use of Molière's former playhouse. Rather than leave with the evicted company (actually companies, as the Italian actors were dislodged as well), Beauchamps chose to remain at the Théâtre du Palais-Royal—which now became home to Lully's Académie Royale de Musique—to become Lully's principal choreographer.[52] By 1674, Beauchamps's former position in the company (now relocated to the Hôtel de Guénégaud) had been taken over by the dancer-violinist Pierre de La Montagne, who remained with the actors (soon to become the Comédie-Française) until 1689.

Beauchamps and the Académie Royale de Musique

During the 1670s and 1680s, Beauchamps served as *maître de ballet* (along with Anthoine des Brosses and Hilaire d'Olivet) to Lully's Académie Royale de Musique. His name appears among the dancers for the following Lully operas: *Cadmus et Hermione* (1673), *Alceste* (1674), *Thésée* (1675), *Atys* (1676), *Isis* (1677), *Bellérophon* (1679), and *Amadis* (1684).[53] The abbé Dubos tells us that Lully gave Beauchamps and des Brosses the responsibility of composing the *ballets ordinaires*, and drew upon the special talents of d'Olivet for ballet-pantomime:[54] "Lully paid such great attention to the ballets mentioned here that he engaged for their choreography a private dancing teacher named d'Olivet. It was he, and not des Brosses or Beauchamps (whom Lully engaged for the "ballets ordinaires"), who composed the ballets of the infernal scenes of *Psyché* and *Alceste*." Raguenet, however, gave high praise to the Beauchamps-Lully collaborations, when he stated that "[t]hey have carried these works to a higher degree of perfection than anyone, be it in Italy or in any other place of the world, has ever attained or will ever attain."[55]

Beauchamps's Retirement

In her memoirs, Elizabeth Charlotte (second wife to Louis XIV's brother, Philippe d'Orléans) recalled, "When I came to France, I saw a gathering of men of talent such as will not be seen again in many centuries. It was Lully for music, Beauchamps for ballets; Corneille and Racine for tragedy; Molière for comedy."[56] Beauchamps retired as *maître de dance* to the Académie Royale de Musique upon Lully's death in 1687, and was succeeded by his pupil Guillaume-Louis Pécour.[57] During his years at the Académie Royale de Musique and after his retirement, Beauchamps also worked as a composer and choreographer for numerous ballet productions presented at the Jesuit colleges in Paris.[58] A manuscript compiled in 1690 by André Danican Philidor, the royal music librarian, preserves Beauchamps's music for three of these Jesuit ballets.[59]

After his retirement from the Académie Royale de Musique, Beauchamps remained in demand by nobles and state officials to organize private ballet entertainments. His name heads the list of private dancing masters in du Pradel's *Livre commode* of 1692 (a kind of White Pages), where he is described as "le premier homme de l'Europe pour la composition [de ballet]" (the top man in Europe for the composition [of ballet]).[60] His surprising vigor permitted Beauchamps to prolong his dancing career into his later years: La Bruyère was amazed by his skill at performing high leaps after the age of sixty.[61] In a 1692 court revival of the 1664 *comédie-ballet La Princesse d'Élide*, Beauchamps (aged sixty-one) danced the final *chaconne* as a solo; then on the eve of his seventieth birthday, he danced in honor of the Spanish ambassador in December of 1701—to the latter's surprise and admiration.[62] Beauchamps seems to have remained active professionally as a *maître de danse* up until his death in February 1705: in a letter dated 12 January of that year, the Comte de Pontchartrain advised, "Vous ne pouvez mieux faire que de vous server de B[eauchamps] pour les danses" (You cannot do better than to make use of B[eauchamps] for the dances).[63]

Notes

1. According to Pierre Rameau, the king took daily lessons from Beauchamps for 20–22 years; see *Le Maître à danser* (Paris, 1725), p. III.

2. For a contemporary colored image of Beauchamps as "La Chirurgie" from the final *entrée* of *Le Nozze di Peleo e di Theti*, as well as other illustrative material relating to Beauchamps's theatrical activities, see the website http://www.personal.utulsa.edu/~john-powell/Beauchamps_images/La_Chirurgie_Beauchamps.jpg.

3. Charles-Louis Livet, *La Muze historique* (Paris, 1877), vol. 2, p. 445 (letter of 16 February 1658).

4. Livet, *La Muze historique*, vol. 2, p. 157 (letter of 5 February 1656).

5. See Régine Astier [Kunzle], "Pierre Beauchamp: the Illustrious Unknown Choreographer, Part I," *Dance Scope* 8, no. 2 (1974): 36 and Part 2 in *Dance Scope* 9, no. 1 (1975): 31–44. The Mazuel family tree is given in Elizabeth Maxfield-Miller, "Louis de Mollier, musician et son homonyme Molière," *Recherches sur la musique française classique* 3 (1963): 25–38 [at 35], and in *Cent ans de recherches sur Molière*, ed. Madeleine Jurgens and Elizabeth Maxfield-Miller (Paris: Imprimerie Nationale, 1963), pp. 732–33.

6. See Marie-Françoise Christout, *Le Ballet de cour de Louis XIV, 1643–1672: mises en scène* (Paris: Picard, 1967), pp. 264–67; Louis Auld, "The Unity of Molière's Comedy-Ballets: A Study of Their Structure, Meanings, and Values," Ph.D. diss., Bryn Mawr College, 1968, pp. 187–209; Nathalie Lecomte, "Beauchamps, Pierre," in *Dictionnaire de la musique en France aux XVIe et XVIIe siècles*, ed. Marcelle Benoit (Paris: Fayard, 1992), pp. 61–62; Françoise Dartois-Lapeyre, "Comédie-ballet," in *Dictionnaire de la musique*, p. 166.

7. In fact, Molière's first acting company (called the "Illustre Théâtre") retained four "maîtres joueurs d'instruments" and a professional dancer to perform "tant en comédie que ballets." See Jurgens and Maxfield-Miller, *Cent ans de recherches*, pp. 232–34 ("Engagement de Claude Godart, Michel Tisse, Adrien Lefebvre et Laurent Gaburet, joueurs d'instruments, pour servir les comédiens de l'Illustre Théâtre pendant trois ans," 31 October 1643) and pp. 241–42 ("Engagement de Daniel Mallet, danseur, avec les comédiens de l'Illustre Théâtre," 28 June 1644).

8. A facsimile of the *livret* and my transcription of Beauchamps's musical score may be consulted online on my website, "Music and Theater in 17th-Century France." http://www.personal.utulsa.edu/~john-powell/theater/index.htm.

9. Ironically, in later life Lully himself would notate the melody and bass line for his instrumental works, and then have his secretaries compose the inner parts.

10. Philidor's 1681 ms. copy of Beauchamps's score is available online through http://gallica.bnf.fr, Notice no. FRBNF39749767.

11. Facsimile ed. Geneva: Minkoff, 1993, with introduction and notes by Marie-Françoise Christout, and an English translation by Andrée Bergens ("How to Compose a Successful Ballet") in *Dance Perspectives* 20 (1964): 26–37.

12. Livet, *La Muze historique*, vol. 3, p. 431 (letter of 19 November 1661).

13. Christout, *Le Ballet de cour*, p. 200.

14. Paris, Bibliothèque Nationale, Mélanges Colbert 264, f. 11; given in Georges Mongrédien, *Recueil des textes et des documents du XVIIe siècle relatifs à Molière*, 2 vols. (Paris: CNRS, 1965), 1: 152.

15. "Les Fâcheux, ce nouveau Poëme, / qui par sa gentillesse extréme / charma si fort, ces jours passez, / à la Cour tous les mieux sensez, / dans Paris, maintenant se joüe: / et, certes, tout le monde avoüe / qu'entre les Piéces d'à-présent, / on ne void rien de si plaizant."

16. Bert Edward Young and Grace Philputt Young, eds., *Le registre de La Grange, 1659–1685, reproduit en fac-similé avec un index et une notice sur La Grange et sa part dans le théâtre de Molière*, 2 vols. (Paris: Droz, 1947), 1: 142–43.

17. Archives, Bibliothèque-Musée de la Comédie-Française.

18. Recorded in the second Registre de La Thorilliere for the 1664–65 theatrical season (Archives of the Comédie-Française); this payment was made on 11 November 1664.

19. See S. Wilma Deierkauf-Holsboer, *Le Théâtre du Marais*, 2 vols. (Paris: Nizet, 1954), 2: 159.

20. Given in Mongrédien, *Recueil des texts et des documents*, 2: 310, and in Georges Couton, ed., *Œuvres complètes de Molière*, 2 vols. (Paris: NRF/Gallimard, 1971), 2: 1183–84.

21. From a "Lettre sur les comédiens" in the *Mercure de France*, May 1740; given in Frédéric Hillemacher, *Galerie historique des portraits des comédiens de la troupe de Molière* (Lyon, 1869), pp. 44–45.

22. In his letter of 2 February 1664, Loret commented on her feminine allure as well as her dancing: "Of La du Parc, nothing more can I say, that makes men joyful than by her appeal, by her bearing, and by her lovely steps and her dancing" ("De la du Parc rien je ne dis, / qui rendoit les gens ébaudis / par ses appas, par sa prestance, / et par ses beaux pas et sa danse." See Livet, *La Muze historique*, 3: 159).

23. See Jacques-Bernard Durey de Noinville, *Histoire du théâtre de l'Académie Royale de Musique en France*, 2nd ed. (Paris, 1757; reprint, Geneva: Minkoff, 1972), 2: 26 and 74.

24. See the "Recueil de Tralage" (c. 1697), Paris, Bibliothèque de l'Arsenal, MS 6544, IV, f. 223v (=243v).

25. "Et pour l'opera des peines et des plaisirs d'Amour il constant que toute la musique estoit preste auparavant que Pomone cessat puisque Mr de beauchamps qui a dansé environ deux mois a Pomone a entendu la repetition dudit second opera le premier jour qu'il entra a l'opera et que Mr des brosses avoit tous les airs des ballets de ce second opera auparavant qu'il cedat sa place audit beauchamps."

26. See the "État officiel de la dépense faite pour représenter Psyché au théâtre des Tuileries in 1671," dated 23 November 1671; reprinted in Jurgens and Maxfield-Miller, *Cent ans de recherches*, p. 501.

27. Young and Young, *Le Registre de La Grange*, I: 124–26.

28. Comparison of the two *livrets*—that of the January 1671 court première and that of the June 1671 Palais-Royal production—illustrates how the choreographic forces were systematically reduced by half.

29. Young and Young, *Le Registre de La Grange*, I: 126.

30. "Plainte de Molière et des comédiens contre Lully" (29 March 1672), reprinted in Jurgens and Maxfield-Miller, *Cent ans de recherches*, pp. 509–10.

31. These performances are documented in the financial register kept by the actor André Hubert; see Sylvie Chevalley, "Le 'Registre d'Hubert' 1672–1673: Étude critique," *Revue d'histoire du théâtre* 25 (1973): 12–67. See also William Leonard Schwartz, "Molière's Theater in 1672–1673: Light from *Le Registre d'Hubert*," *Publications of the Modern Language Association* 56 (1941): 395–427.

32. Young and Young, *Le Registre de La Grange*, I: 137. "Nᵃ encores que le mariage forcé qui a esté joué avec la Comtesse d'Escarbagnas a esté accompagné d'ornemens dont Monsʳ Charpentier a faict la Musique et Monsʳ de Beauchamps les ballets, Mʳ Baraillon les habits et Mʳ de Villiers avoit employ dans la musique des intermedes."

33. Chevalley, "Le 'Registre d'Hubert,'" p. 31.

34. My edition of this music, *Marc-Antoine Charpentier: Music for Molière's Comedies* (Madison: A-R Editions, 1990), includes a preface that discusses the manner in which Charpentier's numbers might have been distributed among the spoken comedy and its internal *comédie-ballet*. A reconstruction of the entire entertainment (including facsimiles of both plays and my transcription of Charpentier's musical score—inserted where the musical numbers plausibly might have been performed) may be consulted online on my website, "Music and Theater in 17th-Century France" (see note 8).

35. Chevalley, "Le 'Registre d'Hubert,'" pp. 66–67.

36. According to "Le 'Registre d'Hubert,'" performances were given on 30 August, 2 and 4 September, and 4 October.

37. See Robinet, letters of 30 July and 13 August 1672 ; given in William Brooks, ed., *Le Théâtre et l'opéra vus par les gazetiers Robinet et Laurent, 1670–1678* (Paris: Papers on French Seventeenth-Century Literature, 1993), pp. 117–18.

38. *Le Mercure galant* (1673), I: 7–17; reprinted in Claude and François Parfaict, *Histoire de l'ancien Théâtre italien* (Paris, 1767; reprint, New York: AMS Press, 1978), pp. 388–405.

39. For instance, the scene where Arlequin's tailor, hatmaker, and apprentice wigmaker argue over the relative importance of their professions derives from the altercation between the Maître de Musique, the Maître à Danser, and the Maître d'Armes in Act II, scene 2 of *Le Bourgeois Gentilhomme*. Patricia Ranum and Catherine Cessac believe that in good-natured revenge, Molière and Charpentier invented some new incidental music for

Le Mariage forcé "in which commedia dell'arte characters mock Harlequin's braying and Beauchamps' harmony." See Patricia M. Ranum and Catherine Cessac, "Trois favoris d'ut ré mi fa sol la': août 1672, les Comédiens français taquinent leurs confrères italiens," in *Marc-Antoine Charpentier: un musicien retrouvé*, ed. Catherine Cessac, pp. 209–23 (Paris, 2005), and Patricia M. Ranum, *Portraits around Marc-Antoine Charpentier* (Baltimore: Dux Femina Facti, 2004), pp. 145–46 [from which this quote is taken].

40. "Au reste il est inutile de nommer celui qui a pris la peine de composer les airs, & les entrées de ballet qui en sont tout l'ornement ; quoique cet illustre n'y ait employé que le peu de momens que lui laissent les divertissemens qu'il prépare pour le Roi, on ne laisse pas de reconnoître d'abord son admirable génie, & de juger que ce n'est que de lui seul que peuvent partir des choses si surprenantes, & si peu forcées." See *Sujet de la comédie italienne intitulée le Collier de perles, mêlée de ballets et de musique* (Paris, 1672), 2; available online at http://gallica.bnf.fr, Notice no. FRBNF33616342.

41. Fonds du Conservatoire, Rés. F. 516. See Régine Astier [Kunzle], "Pierre Beauchamps and the Ballets de Collège," *Dance Chronicle* 6, no. 2 (1983): 162–63, and Jérôme de la Gorce, "*Le Collier de perles* et la musique de Pierre Beauchamps," in *Histoire, Humanisme et Hymnologie, Mélanges offerts au Professeur Edith Weber*, ed. Pierre Guillot and Louis Jambou (Paris: University of Paris-Sorbonne Press, 1997), pp. 99–107.

42. *Les Ballets Des Iesuistes Composé par Messieurs Beauchant Desmatins et Collasse Recueillie par Philidor Laisné en 1690.* Philidor's 1690 ms. copy of Beauchamps's score is available online through http://gallica.bnf.fr, Notice no. FRBNF39748343.

43. *Mercure galant*, 6 August 1672; given in Mongrédien, *Recueil des texts et des documents*, 2: 420. "On verra au commencement de l'hiver le grand spectacle de Psyché triompher encore sur le théâtre du Palais-Royal; et, dans le carnaval, en représentera une pièce de spectacle nouvelle, toute comique et comme cette pièce sera du fameux Molière; et que les ballets en seront faits par M. de Beauchamp, on n'en doit rien attendre que de beau."

44. Lecerf de la Viéville makes it clear that Lully and des Brosses shared in choreographing the dances: "Une partie du Ballet des fêtes de l'Amour & de Bachus avoit été composée par lui [Lully], l'autre par Desbrosses" (One part of the ballet of *Les Festes de l'Amour et de Bacchus* had been composed by him, the other by des Brosses). See *Comparaison de la musique italienne et de la musique françoise* (Paris, 1704; reprint, Geneva: Minkoff, 1972), 2: 228.

45. The "Ordonnance portent defenses a toutes les troupes de comediens francois et estrangers de louer la sale qui a servy aux representations des ouvrages de theatre en musique" is reprinted in Marcelle Benoit, *Musiques de cour: Chapelle, Chambre, Écurie (1661–1733)* (Paris: Picard, 1971), pp. 38–39.

46. Young and Young, *Le Registre de La Grange*, 1: 144.

47. "On a icy commancé la preparation du malade Imaginaire" (next to entry dated 22 November 1672; ibid., 1: 140).

48. "Mémoire pour les danseur[s] du palais Royal," transcribed in Edouard Thierry, *Documents sur le 'Malade imaginaire': Estat de la recette et despence* (Paris: Berger-Levrault, 1880), pp. 159–61.

49. The bill submitted by Jeanne Magoullet, the candlemaker, shows that she furnished candles for eighteen rehearsals. At first rehearsals were held on days when there were no performances at the Palais-Royal, but daily rehearsals were scheduled beginning 3 February. These practices took place in dim light (2 lbs. of candles), except for the dress rehearsals (32 lbs. of candles); performances required 53 lbs. of candles. See Thierry, *Documents sur le 'Malade imaginaire'*, pp. 145–58.

50. Ibid., 164–65.

51. Ibid., 94.

52. André Levinson, "Notes sur le ballet du XVIIe siècle: les danseurs de Lully," *La Revue musicale* 4, no. 5 (1925): 44–55 (at 51–52). According to the Parfaict brothers' manuscript, "Histoire de l'Académie Royale de Musique" (Paris, Bibliothèque Nationale, MS. n. a. 6532, 14n), "it was only beginning with the opera *Cadmus* that Lully put him [Beauchamps] in charge of the Ballets for his Academy."

53. These *livrets* are cited in Claude and François Parfaict, *Dictionnaire des théâtres de Paris*, 7 vols. (Paris, 1756; reprint of 1767–70 ed., Geneva, 1971). Maureen Needham ("Beauchamps, Pierre," in *The New Grove Dictionary of Opera*, ed. Stanley Sadie [London: Macmillan, 1992], 1: 364) states that Beauchamps also choreographed dances for the premières of *Les Fêtes de l'Amour et de Bacchus* (1672), *Cadmus et Hermione* (1673), *Thésée* (1675), *Atys* (1676), and *Le Triomphe de l'Amour* (1681).

54. "Lulli faisoit une si grande attention sur les ballets dont il s'agit ici, qu'il se servoit pour les composer, d'un maître de danse particulier, nommé d'Olivet. Ce fut lui, & non pas des Brosses ou Beauchamps, dont Lulli se servoit pour les ballets ordinaires, qui composa les ballets de la pompe funèbre de Psyché & de celle d'Alceste." *Réflexions critiques sur la poésie et sur la peinture* (Paris, 1719; reprint, Geneva: Slatkine, 1967), p. 357.

55. "Ils ont porté ces pieces à une si haut degree de perfection que personne, ny en Italie, ny en aucun autre endroit du monde n'y a sceu atteindre depuis, et n'y atteindra jamais." François Raguenet, *Parallèle des Italiens et des Français en ce qui regarde la musique et les opéras; Défense du Parallèle des Italiens et des Français en ce qui regarde la musique et les opéras* (Paris, 1702; reprint, Geneva: Minkoff, 1976), p. 20.

56. "Quand je suis venue en France, j'y ai vu une reunion d'hommes de talent, comme on n'en trouvera plus dans beaucoup de siècles. C'étaient Lulli pour la musique, Beauchamp pour les ballets; Corneille et Racine pour la tragédie; Molière pour la comédie." Cited in Mongrédien, *Recueil des texts et des documents*, 1: 401.

57. According to Nathalie Lecomte, Beauchamps "taught an entire generation of professional dancers who went on to have brilliant careers, such as Lestang, Faure, Pécour and Blondy." The *Mercure galant* adds that "de pareils Écoliers à qui Mr. De Beauchamps a donné & donne encore tous les jours des Leçons, quoy qu'ils soient déjà grands Maistres, font voir qu'il est dans son Art des plus habiles Hommes du monde" (such pupils to whom Monsieur de Beauchamps has given and still gives lessons daily, even though they are already great dancing masters, shows that in his art he stands among the most skilled men in the world). (See Lecomte, "Beauchamps," pp. 61–62).

58. See Astier, "Pierre Beauchamps and the Ballets de Collège," pp. 152–63, for a list of the ballets worked on with the Jesuits. Beauchamps's association with Parisian educational establishments was of long standing. Nuitter and Thoinan mention that "en 1673 . . . le sieur Filz, qui tenait une institution pour les jeunes gens de bonne famille . . . faisait jouer à ses élèves des tragédies avec intermèdes de danse et de musique. Le Seur, le maître de danse de la maison, réglait les danses, assisté de Beauchamps, qui de plus composait la musique de ses intermèdes" (in 1673 . . . sieur Filz, who ran a school for young people from good families . . . had his pupils perform tragedies with interludes of dance and music. Le Seur, the dancing teacher of the school, directed the dances assisted by Beauchamps, who moreover composed the music of his interludes"). See Charles Nuitter and Ernest Thoinan, *Les origines de l'Opéra français; d'après les minutes des notaires, les registres de la Conciergerie et les documents originaux conservés aux Archives nationales, à la Comédie, français*

et dans diverses collections publiques et particulières (Paris, 1886; reprint, New York: Da Capo Press, 1977).

59. "Les Ballets Des Jesuistes Composé par Messieurs Beauchant Desmatins et Collasse Recueillie par Philidor L'aisné en 1690." This manuscript may be consulted online at http://gallica.bnf.fr, Notice no. FRBNF39748343.

60. Abraham du Pradel, *Le Livre commode contenant les adresses de la ville de Paris, et le tresor des almanachs pour l'année Bissextile 1692* (Paris, 1692; reprint, Geneva: Minkoff, 1973), p. 73.

61. Jean de La Bruyère, *Les Caractères de Théophraste, traduits du grec, avec Les Caractères ou les mœurs de ce siècle*, ed. Robert Pignarre (Paris, 1692; reprint, Paris: Garnier-Flammarion, 1965), 3: 33.

62. See Lecomte, "Beauchamps," pp. 61–62.

63. Cited in Pierre Mélèse, *Répertoire analytique des documents contemporains d'information et de critique concernant le théâtre à Paris sous Louis XIV, 1659–1715* (Paris: Droz, 1934), p. 105.

Recommended Reading

Astier, Régine [Kunzle]. "Pierre Beauchamps and the Ballets de Collège." *Dance Chronicle* 6, no. 2 (1983): 138–63.

———. "Pierre Beauchamp: The Illustrious Unknown Choreographer." *Dance Scope* 8, no. 2 (1974): 32–45 (Part 1) and *Dance Scope* 9, no. 1 (1975): 31–44 (Part 2).

Ferguson, Ian. "Some Notes on the Beauchamps Family." *Dancing Times* 72, no. 854 (November 1981): 107.

Houle, George ed., *Le Ballet des Fâcheux: Beauchamp's Music for Moliere's Comedy*. Bloomington: Indiana University Press, 1991.

Lecomte, Nathalie. "Beauchamps, Pierre." In *Dictionnaire de la musique en France aux XVIe et XVIIe siècles*, ed. Marcelle Benoit. Paris: Fayard, 1992, pp. 61–62.

Powell, John S. "Pierre Beauchamps, choreographer to Molière's Troupe du Roy." *Music and Letters* 76, no. 2 (1995): 168–86.

Richardson, Philip J. S. "The Beauchamp Mystery: Some Fresh Light on an Old Problem." *Dancing Times* 37 (1946): 299–302.

6

Dance in the London Theaters c. 1700–1750

Jennifer Thorp

❧

Dance in the London theaters during the first half of the eighteenth century encompassed a wide range of activity and provides a fascinating insight to the entrepreneurial spirit and sheer vigor of theatrical life in London at that time. The apparent continuity of three theaters operating by royal patent in 1705 (Drury Lane, Lincoln's Inn Fields, and the Queen's Theatre Haymarket) and after the Licensing Act of 1737 (Drury Lane, Covent Garden [opened in 1733 as the new home of the Lincoln's Inn Fields company], and the now King's Theatre Haymarket) belies a very complex history of rival houses supplemented at different times by a plethora of small unlicensed theaters: Goodman's Fields, the Little Theatre Haymarket, and Sadler's Wells, to name a few.[1] And there were only a few days in the year—on Sundays, on Fridays during Lent, at Easter and Christmas, at times of court celebrations or of national mourning, and during those summer weeks when the London fairs took over—when one could not attend a theatrical performance with dancing somewhere in its program.

The types of dancing to be seen in the theaters varied according to who was performing. At one end of the spectrum were the social dances seen within plays, often to celebrate weddings or other on-stage festivities. Then there were dances which formed an intrinsic part of the plot, such as the scene in *The Gentleman Dancing-Master* in which Mr. Gerrard courts Hippolita Formal under the guise of teaching her a dance.[2] Most of these dances were performed by the actors themselves, many of whom had a wide range of skills which included general dancing. At the other end of the spectrum were the fairground skills of rope-dancers and contortionists, who also appeared now and again in the commercial theaters, or the highly specialized routines by tumblers and acrobats (and even some dancers) who could work in flying harness, leap out from trapdoors, or work inside bizarre costumes to perform special effects dances as monsters, flying witches, and the like, in operas and pantomimes. Both of these extremes, however, are outside the scope of this chapter, which is concerned only with dance by those who undertook lengthy formal training in the highly sophisticated style and technique of the day known as "la belle danse" or "la danse noble": two terms borrowed from French dance theorists of the late seventeenth century. Often these dancers supplemented their income by teaching, and so passed on their own skills in that way.[3]

Even within "la belle danse," however, there were several different types of theatrical dance. These were categorized by the dancing-master John Weaver in his *Essay towards an History of Dancing*, published in 1712,[4] as "serious" (very similar to the formal dancing taught in academies and seen at Court, but with more complex steps), "grotesque" (the representation of the passions, both serious and comic, by the use of gesture and body language to supplement steps and movements), and "scenical" (the representation of whole stories by actions, that is, by steps, movement and gesture). His ideas derived from a study of ancient classical authors, whom he quoted repeatedly in his own writings. By 1728, however, when he published his *History of the Mimes and Pantomimes*, his ideas had undergone an interesting change: he now thought, for instance, that "serious" dancing was also capable of expressing the passions, and that "grotesque" dancing should be confined to *commedia dell'arte* characters such as Harlequin, Scaramouche, and Pierrot. In short, he was forming new definitions of expressive dance which almost certainly reflected the changes in theatrical dance since 1712; they were very likely rooted in his own work at Drury Lane with leading expressive dancers like Hester Santlow (Mrs. Barton Booth—see Figure 6.1), and in his creation of a new genre of dramatic dance based on the pantomimes of classical antiquity.[5]

Weaver claimed that the French excelled at "serious" dancing, and fashionable London audiences at the beginning of the century had certainly flocked to the theater to see dancers imported from Paris. This initiative was due to Thomas

Figure 6.1. Hester Santlow Booth as a female harlequin: portrait by John Ellys, c. 1725. Most unusually for a portrayal of harlequin, she is depicted without the usual face mask, but otherwise is in a characteristic pose. Victoria and Albert Museum, London / Art Resource, New York.

Betterton, manager of the Lincoln's Inn Fields theater, who was constantly on the lookout for new wonders which would give his theater the edge over its rival at Drury Lane. He went to Paris in the late 1690s and invited some of the stars of the Paris Opera back to London to dance in his theater, but the very high fees he paid them had the commentators of the day in ferment. In his survey of the London theatrical world, John Downes was particularly critical of Betterton's activities: "In the space of Ten years past," he wrote, "Mr Betterton to gratify the desires and Fancies of the Nobility and Gentry, procur'd from Abroad the best Dance[r]s ... as, Monsieur L'Abbé, Madam Sublini, Monsieur Balon ... who being Exorbitantly Expensive, produce'd small profit to him and his Company"; and his voice was only one of several.[6] The exorbitant expenses included 400 guineas to Claude Balon, for a very few performances in 1699, and a similar sum to Marie-Thérèse de Subligny in January 1702, which all but bankrupted Betterton's company. The third dancer however, Anthony L'Abbé, made London his home and stayed on to become the main theatrical choreographer of his day and a teacher of great renown.

We can still catch a glimpse of what these three stars danced during their visits to London, for a duet later described as "Loure or Faune, perform'd before His Majesty King William ye 3d by Monsr. Balon and Mr. L'Abbé" in 1699 was written down in Beauchamps-Feuillet dance notation[7] and published during the 1720s.[8] It records a very beautiful and technically difficult duet, set to music from Lully's *Acis et Galatée*, and takes the form of an entrée grave, one of the most demanding theatrical dance forms for men in the "serious" style of its day. One of Subligny's solos survives in a collection of French theatrical dances published in 1704, where it is described as "Gigue pour une femme, dancée par Mlle Subligny en Angleterre"[9] ("Gigue for a woman, danced by Miss Subligny in England") and its music is a lively gigue from Gatti's recent opera *Scylla*.

The appearance of such skilled French dancers in London, and the gradual adoption of the French academy's codification of dance steps and methods of training in "la belle danse," encouraged many English dancers also to make a name for themselves. The theater bills and advertisements of the time record some of their repertoire, working conditions, benefit nights, and royal command performances, and a little of the repertoire itself still survives in notated form.

Mainpieces: Dance in Opera

Dance had formed an integral part of the staging of many operas and masques in London since the seventeenth century, and the tradition continued in some of the works staged at Vanbrugh's new theater, which opened in 1705 as the Queen's Theatre in the Haymarket. In December Vanbrugh persuaded the Lord Chamberlain to grant him a monopoly of producing both English and Italian operas, and a month later the Queen's Theatre had its own opera company headed by leading Italian and English singers but also including a small corps of dancers.

One production which hardly figures at all in the advertisements of the day, so far as dancers were concerned, though information about them is known from other sources, was *Love's Triumph*, which ran at the Queen's Theatre from late February to late April 1708.[10] Set in Arcadia, this three-act opera set to a text by Peter Motteux concerns the tangled love lives of three sets of shepherds and shepherdesses. In general the dancing occurs at the end of each act, within scenes of reconciliation and pastoral happiness in which arias, two-part songs, and choruses alternate with or lead into dances. The opera's Playbook indicates that both Acts I and II end with a song, repeated as a chorus in which dancing takes place at the same time as the singing,[11] and that Act III ends with a Grand Dance followed by a Grand Chorus before the entire cast leaves the stage. Much of the singing was presented in the Italian style of da capo arias, and all the dancing seems to have been in the French style of "serious" dance. Documents among Vice-Chamberlain Coke's papers note that the choreography was by René Cherrier and Monsieur Desbarques (two more French "imports" who stayed to perform and teach in London) and name the eight dancers who took part in each act.[12] As well as Cherrier and Desbarques, they included Cherrier's former student Hester Santlow, Mr. Lagarde (perhaps Charles Delagarde, who had been dancing at the Queen's Theatre since 1705), Miss Evans (who, like Hester Santlow, had been enticed away from Drury Lane to join the Queen's Theatre company), and Miss Alloway (about whom nothing further is known). The most junior dancers were John Shaw (just embarking on what was to be a short but dazzling career),[13] and his partner Miss Cadet (who is otherwise unknown), for neither were described as soloists and both received much lower wages than the other six dancers. They were, however, described as "Mr Cha en peysan" and "ma[demoise]lle Cadet paysanne" for Act II, so perhaps their chance to shine was in a peasant (*paysan*) duet in that act. No other dance characters are specified, and it has to be assumed that all eight dancers otherwise appeared as shepherds and shepherdesses mingling with the chorus: a typical stage direction for them was (in Act I) "Enter Licisca[14] attended by many Shepherds and Shepherdesses, who advance and place themselves on both sides of the Stage; the Music playing a March all the while."

Such dance activities within opera at the Queen's Theatre, however, may not have lasted much beyond the 1708/9 season, as the opera company became more and more committed to the expense of full Italian opera, and dancers like Santlow and Shaw left to pursue careers in other theaters. That there may have been a still greater gulf between Italian opera and dance by the third decade of the century is suggested by a snide attack on the former in a letter published in *The Prompter* in December 1735, in which Italian opera was derided as too long and too boring; the correspondent added that the audience would be more satisfied by "a warm scene in a well-acted Play, or the agile motions of a Roland or a Denoyer[15] than by all the Quaverings of an emasculated Wretch at the Opera."[16]

Despite such misgivings, however, there had been an attempt in 1719 to form a Royal Academy of Music for the production of opera with dance at the King's Theatre, Haymarket. In its submission to the Lord Chamberlain, the opera company undertook to maintain there "by yearly sallary and pensions a proper number of Singers with voices well Sorted"; moreover, "the necessary Performers of an Orchestre as also Dancers" were to be engaged on a similarly permanent footing.[17] The minutes of the Academy's Court of Directors' meeting on 30 November 1719 note that George Frederick Handel was appointed as "Master of the Orchester," and on 2 December Anthony L'Abbé was asked to draw up proposals and costs for a troupe of dancers within the company. L'Abbé proffered a ballpark figure first of £520 and later of £1000 for dancers. But by then the total budget had topped £12000 and the project (so far as the dancers were concerned) fell by the wayside, almost certainly because of the huge costs of maintaining such a company in which fees to leading Italian singers gobbled up most of the available budgets,[18] and dance was not destined to play a role in the Academy's short-lived existence (it was defunct by 1729). Nevertheless, the seeds had been sown by which a ballet company would be maintained as part of the Opera at the King's Theatre later in the century.

Entr'acte Dances and Danced Entertainments

The playbills and advertisements suggest that entr'acte dances and longer suites of dances, sometimes advertised as "entertainments of dancing," accounted for a very large proportion of dance on stage during the first half of the eighteenth century.[19] Surviving collections which record entr'acte dances in London are those of Kellom Tomlinson, Anthony L'Abbé, and François le Rousseau, dating from just before and during the 1720s. There are also five extant notations, dating from between 1707 and 1731, for dances created originally for performance at Court on the occasion of royal birthdays, New Year's Day or other court celebrations and subsequently performed in the theater.[20] All these dances are written in Beauchamps-Feuillet notation, and between them they provide us with over two dozen dances that audiences would have seen performed on stage as one-off entr'acte dances or as longer entertainments of dancing, either between the acts of a play or between the mainpiece and afterpiece.

Kellom Tomlinson learned his skills as an apprentice, between 1707 and c. 1713, to the revered London dancing-master Mr. Caverley and the theatrical dancer Monsieur Cherrier. It is thanks to the survival of Tomlinson's student notebook, begun in 1708 and continued after he had become a dancing-master in his own right, that we know not just who trained him and the dances which he studied as a student, but also his own creation of a suite of dances for Lincoln's Inn Fields theater in 1716 and 1721, set to music by Jean-Baptiste Loeillet.[21]

Five of the dances appear in the notebook in connection with a benefit performance at Lincoln's Inn Fields on 10 May 1716. The benefit was for the dancer Anthony Moreau, who had made his debut at that theater some eighteen months earlier, and the program offered a mainpiece (Peter Motteux's semi-opera *The Island Princess*) and dancing either interpolated into that work or following after it. Tomlinson's notebook records that the five dances comprised solos and duets performed by Mrs Schoolding and by Tomlinson's own apprentice, and the advertisement quoted in *The London Stage* for that performance confirms the performance of a danced "Entry by Kellum's Scholar and Miss Schoolding." The "Scholar" was John Topham, who was one of Tomlinson's most successful apprentices, and his partner was either Diane Schoolding, the actress-dancer who married Anthony Moreau in 1717, or her sister.[22] Tomlinson indicates several times that in 1721 he revived all five dances as *An Entertainment of Dancing for the Stage*, but his notebook is the only evidence for this: the surviving advertisements and performance rosters (which are by no means complete) make no reference to Topham, Schoolding, or Tomlinson that year.

According to his notebook, the running order of the dances was a duet (in the form of a triple time rondeau), followed by a solo rigaudon (in duple time), the music of which was repeated for Topham's more complex solo rigaudon, then a solo minuet, and ended with a duet in the form of a Canary (a lively dance in $\frac{6}{8}$ time). Despite their importance as a unique source of choreography for an entertainment of dancing in the early eighteenth century, it has to be said that these five dances are a little disappointing. For so promising a student, Topham's dances scarcely do him justice: they are simply constructed and technically not very demanding, apart from a series of *entrechats six* in his solo rigaudon. However, if in the duets he was partnering someone who was an actress first and an inexperienced dancer second, the level of choreography would of necessity be pegged to her abilities: in this case, moderately easy sequences of sometimes repetitive steps which are made interesting by the delicate floor patterns they trace.

What this suite of dances does reveal, however, which more than makes up for any choreographic diffidence, is the highly unusual way in which the group of dances ends. The first four all start and end conventionally, that is, center-stage or upstage center. The final Canary, however, ends with the dancers travel-ing far downstage and then splitting apart, one to leave stage left and the other stage right. It is a unique ending in the extant repertoire of dances, and presum-ably was intended either to frame whatever was happening next (another per-former entering upstage center) or to get out of the way of upstage flats or scenic cloths moving to reveal the next stage-set in the program.

Tomlinson's work book also reveals that Topham had a chance to shine in other performances in 1716 (although again they are not noted in any of the ex-tant advertisements or performance rosters), in a solo *Sarabande* set to music composed by Tomlinson himself. This is more what we would expect of a prom-ising male dancer: the very controlled execution of deceptively languorous steps (the music is marked "very slow"), interspersed with crisp *entrechats six*, pirou-ettes with multiple beats at the ankle, and *tours en l'air* incorporating yet more *entrechats six*. It puts Topham into quite a different league and gives us an in-sight to his huge success as a performer in the years which followed.

A slightly later theatrical dance by Tomlinson confirms his capacity for providing choreography suited to the experience or abilities of his dancers. This is *The Submission* (to music once more by Loeillet) which he created in 1717 for the two French child-prodigies François and Marie Sallé, and which they danced on four occasions between 21 and 25 February at Lincoln's Inn Fields. Tomlin-son was later to write exuberantly that they performed this dance "to very con-siderable Audiences, every Night, for a whole week together,"[23] and on the strength of that success he later published the notation of the dance "as it was perform'd at the Theatre in little Lincoln's-Inn-Fields, by Monsieur and Made-moiselle Sallé, the Two French Children."[24] Marie was ten when she danced *The Submission*, and her brother only two years older, but the dance Tomlinson made for them opens with an elegant section in triple time followed by a minuet section, and ends with a lively rigaudon section. In terms of the use of space and the step vocabulary selected, it is much more sophisticated than the *Island Prin-cess* dances of the previous year, yet still well within the capacities of gifted stu-dents, and it must have helped establish Tomlinson as a respected teacher of dancing.

Another dancing-master who commanded great respect both as a teacher and as a performer and creator of theater dances was Anthony L'Abbé, whose career in London spanned several decades.[25] Born in France and trained at the Paris Opera under the great Pécour, he came to London in 1698 to work for Betterton at Lincoln's Inn Fields theater, and also danced at Court on several occasions. In 1705 he was sufficiently settled, and sufficiently unimpressed by Betterton's chaotic business methods, to cast his net wider and started to appear at Vanbrugh's new Queen's Theatre in the Haymarket. Here he continued to strengthen his links with the dancers who had appeared with him at Court, including the leading Drury Lane dancers Cherrier and du Ruel, and at this date he was frequently partnered on stage by the English dancer Mrs. Elford. It seems likely that L'Abbé considered himself a freelance who would work wherever the work was offered; perhaps living in London as an emigré brought up in the sometimes stifling orthodoxy of the Paris Opera made him particularly appreciative of the flexible opportunities offered by the commercialism which drove the London theater world.

L'Abbé's own performing career is not well documented after 1706, due to the poor survival rate of the theater bills and advertisements, but it seems likely that it flourished. Even after he took up a post as dancing-master to three of King George I's granddaughters he continued to create dances for the theater, and thirteen of these were published for him by François le Rousseau in the mid-1720s.[26] If they are typical of English theatrical dance in the "serious" style during the first half of the eighteenth century, then it was indeed impressive for its technical complexity, musicality, and beauty. The collection consists of solos and duets created between c. 1699 and c. 1722 for dancers of the caliber of messieurs Balon and Desnoyer, and the English mesdames Elford, Santlow, Bullock, and Younger. The theatricality of the collection is also indicated by some of the dance types: four passacailles or chaconnes, and four loures or entrées graves, the music for all but one of these being taken from French opera tunes popular in London at the time. The last dance in the collection, *The Turkish Dance*, devised for Monsieur Desnoyer and Mrs. Younger in c. 1721–22, is an example of what John Weaver at that date called "grotesque" dance (and dancing-masters later called "demi-caractère" dance), but additional interest lies in its structure (three linked sections comprising male solo, female solo, duet) and highly unusual ending in which the dancers both move sideways to stage left and end abruptly on one foot, as if suddenly frozen in space. Also in the collection is a showpiece dance of technical brilliance, the *Pastoral performed by a Gentleman*, consisting of a loure and a hornpipe to music by the emigré court and theater composer Jacques Paisible.

If Anthony L'Abbé's extant theater dances represent a very high standard of "serious" dance in early eighteenth-century London, then some of the dances created by his notator François le Roussau, and preserved in his own manuscript collection of 1720, give us a rare and valuable insight to comedy in English theatrical dance at this time. Le Roussau himself twice performed a comic dance as a drunken Pierrot at the Little Theatre in the Haymarket in March 1724, and his manuscript collection of dances reveal a clear gift for comedy. In particular, his *Entry for Two French Country Men* supplements its ungainly steps, angular lines, and stomping rhythms by deliberately subverting baroque dance conventions (such as facing front and working in mirror symmetry to begin and end the dance) for humorous effect.[27] (See Figure 6.2 for an example of Le Roussau's disregard for conventions of symmetry in the closing section of his *Entry for Two French Country Men*.) Le Roussau is chiefly remembered, however, for the last dance in his collection, the *Chaconne for Arlequin*, which was later engraved and published as *Chacoon for a Harlequin*.[28] It is the only surviving dance for a *commedia* character on the English stage in the first half of the eighteenth century, although the many references to such dances among the theater advertisements testify to their great popularity.[29] Le Roussau's *Chaconne* contains similar types of steps to two other solo *Entrées d'Arlequin* which survive among early eighteenth-century French notated dances;[30] all were choreographed in the "belle danse" genre, with recognizable steps or variants of steps deriving from orthodox dance vocabulary and therefore capable of being recorded in Beauchamps-Feuillet notation. But le Roussau's dance includes more grotesque gestures and postures than the other harlequin dances, and contains preliminary pages of written descriptions of the various movements as well as small drawings against the notated steps.

Afterpieces: "Dramatick Entertainments of Dancing" and Pantomime

Important innovations to emerge in England from the second decade of the eighteenth century onward were the very popular "dramatick entertainments of dancing" and pantomimes as designed by John Weaver and his contemporaries. Presented as full length afterpieces (that is, in the second half of the program), pantomimes were influenced by, and possibly developed out of, the strong visual comedy of earlier "Night Scenes." These had been popularized by

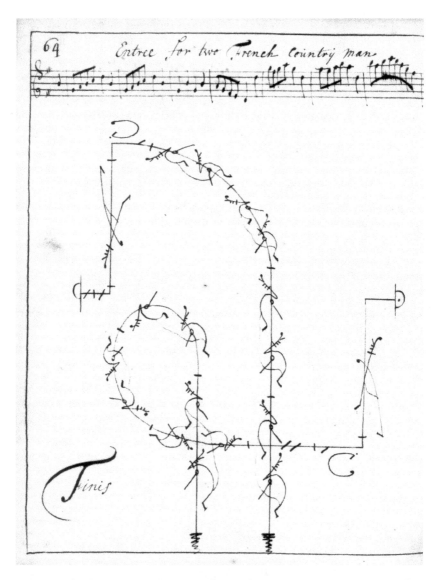

Figure 6.2. The closing section of Le Roussau's *Entry for Two French Country Men,* 1720. The notation shows the two dancers circling and skipping off side by side, with their backs to the audience and a total disregard for the conventions of symmetry. Edinburgh University Library, Special Collections, MS La.III.673 p. 64. By permission of Edinburgh University Library.

French fairground performers who appeared on the English stage in the early years of the century and performed *commedia dell'arte* scenes which followed a loose plot based on visual comedy and mime, and also included dancing.

From the point of view of expressive dance which made use of gesture and, when extended to "scenical" dancing, a narrative storyline, the most significant form of pantomime in the first half of the eighteenth century sprang from the work of John Weaver. The actor Colley Cibber stated this clearly when writing later about Weaver's *Loves of Mars and Venus* of 1717:

> To give even dancing therefore some improvement, and to make it something more than motion without meaning, the fable of *Mars and Venus* was formed into a connected presentation of dances in character, wherein the passions were so happily expressed and the whole story so intelligibly told by a mute narration of gesture only, that even thinking spectators allowed it both a pleasing and a rational entertainment.[31]

In their purest forms Weaver's "dramatick entertainments of dancing" comprised "serious" scenes of classical mythology expressed through dance, singing, and mime, interspersed with comic scenes "in grotesque characters" by *commedia dell'arte* characters, and this duality of form became the basic structure of eighteenth-century English pantomimes. Yet very little is known of the choreographies created for pantomimes. An entr'acte dance such as le Roussau's *Chaconne for Arlequin* would have been performed by a dancer rather than by an actor, and seems unlikely to represent the sort of *commedia* dancing seen in English pantomimes by actors such as Colley Cibber at Drury Lane, or the famous harlequin Lun (the stage persona of John Rich, the actor-manager of Lincoln's Inn Fields theater).[32] Indeed, all Weaver's "dramatick entertainments" seem to have employed experienced dancers and dancer-actresses from within the Drury Lane company for both the serious and grotesque scenes.[33]

Pantomimes in their fully developed form, however, of action, song, dance, and show-stopping magical transformations, both by Weaver's protegé John Thurmond at Drury Lane and by Lewis Theobald for John Rich's rival company at Lincoln's Inn Fields (often in direct competition with each other) invariably employed a mixture of dancers and actors from within their respective house companies. Take, for example, the rival productions of the *Harlequin Faustus* pantomimes, which opened during the winter of 1723/4 and continued to be performed in close rivalry for many years.[34] Thurmond's *Harlequin Dr Faustus* opened at Drury Lane on 23 November 1723 and included in its cast the following dancers who were as much respected for their "serious" dancing as for their antics in pantomime: Harlequin Dr. Faustus was played by John Shaw, Mephistophilus by Thurmond himself, and Scaramouche by John Topham, alongside established comic actors like William Penkethman as the Salesman and Mr. Harper as the Landlady, both well able to "hoof" their way through any basic dancing required of them. Yet the "serious" part of the work was represented by a "Masque of the Heathen Deities" which ended the whole work, and was danced by, among others, Thurmond, Shaw, and the very able female dancers Anne Bullock and Hester Booth. On 20 December 1723 Lincoln's Inn Fields retaliated with Theobald's *The Necromancer or Harlequin Dr Faustus*. This included songs set to music by Ernest Galliard, and a cast which included the singers Mrs. Chambers as Hero, Messrs La Guerre and Leveridge as Leander and Charon, respectively, alongside Lun as Harlequin, and dancers of the calibre of Louis Dupré, Francis Nivelon, and Henrietta Ogden, among others.

Conclusion

Despite the survival of only about two dozen notated dances from the repertoire of the London theaters, and despite the patchy survival of other primary sources, the overall picture of theatrical dance in London between 1700 and 1750 suggested by the extant music, advertisements, and contemporary comment is one of a continual, varied, and dynamic presence, an integral and essential part of the theatrical scene. Competition was lively: between the theaters, whether licensed or unlicensed, between the genres of stage performance, whether operatic, dramatic, or pantomimic, and between the different styles of dancing, whether "serious" or "grotesque." All these elements added to the vibrancy and commercial inventiveness of the theatrical scene. London never ceased to attract dancers from Paris, encouraged perhaps by the entrepreneurial opportunities in London; but there was also a large amount of native talent which both reflected and influenced what was happening on stage. Although the variety of entr'acte dances diminished in the 1740s, there was compensation in the growing number of grand ballets and pantomimes (particularly at Covent Garden) which required the theaters to support larger companies of dancers; by the mid-1740s both Drury Lane and Covent Garden boasted a resident dancing-master in charge of an average of fourteen dancers at Drury Lane (alongside fifty-nine actors and actresses, some of whom also danced) and twenty-three dancers at Covent Garden (alongside forty-eight actors and actresses).[35] Whatever the ups and downs of theater life in London by the 1750s, a strong dance element had come to stay.

Notes

1. The most useful general survey of London theaters between 1700 and 1747 is still Emmet L. Avery, ed., *The London Stage 1660–1800: A Calendar, Part 2 1700–1729* (Carbondale: Southern Illinois University Press, 1960), pp. xxii–xxxix, and Arthur H. Scouten, ed., *The London Stage 1660–1800: A Calendar, Part 3 1729–1747* (Carbondale: Southern Illinois University Press, 1965), pp. xix–xli (hereafter cited as LS).

2. William Wycherley, *The Gentleman Dancing-Master* (London, 1673, reprinted 1702), Act III, scene I.

3. Biographical details of most of the performers mentioned in this chapter may be found in *A Biographical Dictionary of Actors, Actresses, Musicians, Dancers, Managers and other Stage Personnel in London 1660–1800*, 16 vols., eds. Philip H. Highfill, Kalman A. Burnim, and Edward A. Langhans (Carbondale: South Illinois University Press, 1973–93). Additional biographical sources are cited, where appropriate, in the relevant notes.

4. Facsimiles of all Weaver's publications are reprinted in Richard Ralph, *The Life and Works of John Weaver* (London: Dance Books, 1985).

5. Discussed in Moira Goff, "Art and Nature Join'd: Hester Santlow and the Development of Dancing on the London Stage, 1700–1737" (Ph.D. diss., University of Kent at Canterbury, 2000), particularly pp. 99–103, 206–209. Santlow's roles in Weaver's pantomimes from 1717 onward are described on pp. 212–60.

6. John Downes, *Roscius Anglicanus* (London, 1708), p. 46. For similar criticisms see also *A Comparison between the Two Stages* (London, 1702), p. 30, and Colley Cibber, *An Apology for the Life of Colley Cibber, Comedian* (London: printed by John Watts for the author, 1740), p. 180.

7. The most widely used of several notation systems originally developed in France during the late seventeenth century as part of the move to codify the steps and technique of "la belle danse." It was published in the form of a manual titled *Chorégraphie* by Raoul-Auger Feuillet in 1700, translations of which appeared in England in 1706 (Ken Pierce, "Dance Notation Systems in Late 17th-century France," *Early Music* 26, no. 2 [1998]: 286–99).

8. F[rançois] le Roussau, *A New Collection of Dances . . . composed by Monsieur L'Abbé* (London, c. 1725), pp. 1–6. See also n. 25.

9. Raoul-Auger Feuillet, *Receuil de dances . . . entrées de ballet de Mr. Pecour* (Paris, 1704), pp. 41–47. A facsimile of the whole collection has been published as Raoul-Auger Feuillet, *Receuil de dances . . . entrées de ballet de Mr. Pecour 1704* (Farnborough: Gregg International, 1972).

10. The Playbook was published as Peter Motteux, *Love's Triumph, an Opera as it is perform'd at the Queen's theatre in the Hay-Market* (London, 1708); it includes a list of the six singers, and their roles, but does not list the dancers. The songs and instrumental parts were published by the firm of Walsh & Hare: see William C. Smith, *A Bibliography of the Musical Works published by John Walsh 1695–1720* (London: The Bibliographical Society, 1968), nos. 271–73.

11. The convention of simultaneous chorus and dance is also seen at the end of *The Island Princess*, in the stage direction "Cupid, with the Four Ages and the Four Seasons, mingle in a Dance while the following Grand Chorus is sung" (Peter Motteux, *The Island Princess* [London, 1699], p. 45). It also occurs in Purcell's *The Fairy Queen*, while the convention of repeating the music of the Grand Chorus as a dance occurs in his *Dioclesian*

(Michael Burden, *Henry Purcell's Operas: The Complete Texts* [Oxford: Oxford University Press, 2000], pp. 400, 247, respectively). John Weaver was later to adopt similar conventions to end two of his pantomimes, *Perseus and Andromeda* and *The Judgement of Paris* (Ralph, *Weaver*, pp. 834, 852, respectively).

12. Judith Milhous and Robert D. Hume, *Vice Chamberlain Coke's Theatrical Papers 1706–1715* (Carbondale: Southern Illinois University Press, 1982), pp. 101–2, documents 65, 66. For the salaries of the dancers, singers, and instrumentalists at the Queen's Theatre in the spring of 1708, see pp. 78–79, document 50.

13. Shaw's fellow-apprentice Kellom Tomlinson later described him as "not only one of the finest Theatrical Dancers, but one of the most beautiful performers in the Gentleman-like way" (Kellom Tomlinson, *The Art of Dancing* [London, 1735], preface). Another dancing-master, John Essex, described "the late Mr Shaw, who has so often appeared with Mrs Booth . . . he was very excellent in many characters; the last he performed was Mercury in Dr *Faustus* [Drury Lane pantomime by Thurmond] which he did with that Correctness and Truth in all its Attitudes, that those who have attempted that Character fall but short of him" (John Essex, *The Dancing Master* [London, 1728], preface, p. xiv). Shaw died in December 1725.

14. A fickle shepherdess, sung by Katherine Tofts.

15. Anne and Catherine Roland were in great demand as dancers at Drury Lane and Covent Garden at this time, specializing in both comic and serious roles. Monsieur Desnoyer had come to Drury Lane from Hanover in 1721, and by 1735 was still at the height of his powers both as a performer on stage and as dancing-master to Frederick, Prince of Wales. Three dances created by Anthony L'Abbé for Desnoyer in 1721–22 survive within the *New Collection of Dances*, pp. 72–96.

16. The letter appeared in *The Prompter*, no. 116, 19 December 1735: see Judith Milhous and Robert D. Hume, *A Register of English Theatrical Documents 1660–1737* (Carbondale: South Illinois University Press, 1991), 2: 867, no. 3961.

17. London, Public Record Office, LC/7/3, folios 46–47.

18. Ibid., folio 59. Some of the three-figure fees and salaries to be offered to the Italian singers are noted in these minutes. For a fuller account of the formation and first season of the Academy, including a transcript of the minutes and associated papers, see Judith Milhous and Robert D. Hume, "New Light on Handel and the Royal Academy of Music in 1720," *Theatre Journal* 35, no. 2 (1983): 149–67.

19. See Moira Goff, "'*Actions, Manners* and *Passions*': Entr'acte Dancing on the London stage, 1700–1737," *Early Music* 26, no. 2 (1998): 213–28.

20. Four of these dances were by Mr. Isaac: *The Union* (danced by Monsieur Desbarques and Hester Santlow at Drury Lane on 8 March and 3 April 1707), *The Saltarella* (danced by Charles Delagarde and Hester Santlow at Drury Lane on 21 February 1708), *The Friendship* and *The Morris* (danced by Charles Delagarde and Anne Russell Bullock at Lincoln's Inn Fields on 10 and 15 March 1715 and 10 January 1716, respectively). The fifth was Anthony L'Abbé's *The Prince of Wales's Sarabande* (danced by William Essex and Hester Santlow Booth at Drury Lane on 22 March 1731).

21. See Robert Petre, "Six New Dances by Kellom Tomlinson: A Recently Discovered Manuscript," *Early Music* 18, no. 3 (1990): 381–91; Jennifer Shennan, ed., *A Work Book by Kellom Tomlinson* (Stuyvesant, N.Y.: Pendragon Press, 1992). For details of Tomlinson's life and career, see the *International Encyclopaedia of Dance* (Oxford: Oxford University Press, 1998) and the *Oxford Dictionary of National Biography* (Oxford: Oxford University Press, 2004).

22. Tomlinson wrote later that John Topham "appeared upon the Stage with no small Applause . . . upon both Theatres, under the name of Mr Kellom's Scholar" (Kellom Tomlinson, *Art of Dancing*, preface). Of Miss Schoolding's identity there is less certainty, and much confusion exists in print concerning the various Schooldings performing at this date. A Mr. and Mrs. Schoolding were actor-dancers from Dublin performing at Lincoln's Inn Fields by 1715. A young actress referred to as "Miss Schoolding's sister" spoke a new prologue to *The Marriage Hater Match'd* on 18 May 1715, at Schoolding's benefit, and may be the Mrs/Miss Schoolding who danced in Tomlinson's five dances on 10 May 1716 or may be the Miss Schoolding described as "scholar to Moreau" who made her debut as a dancer (as opposed to an actress) almost a year later, having "never danc'd on the stage before" (LS, 23 April 1717). The Miss Diane Schoolding who married Anthony Moreau on 24 February 1717 (London: Westminster Archives center, parish registers of St Clement Danes, vol. 30, marriages 1716–1754) may have been either of these two Miss Schooldings. The relative simplicity of Tomlinson's dances for 1716 suggests that they were designed either for an inexperienced newcomer or for someone who was an actress first and a dancer second.

23. Tomlinson, *Art of Dancing*, preface. LS notes that the duet was performed on Thursday, 21 February 1717 (*"The Submission*, a new dance, compos'd by Kellom and perform'd by Sallé and Mlle Sallé"), Friday 22, Saturday 23, and Monday, 25 February. It may have been their presence that decided Topham to move to Drury Lane and continue his career there.

24. *Six Dances compos'd by Mr Kellom Tomlinson, being a collection of all the yearly Dances publish'd by him from the Year 1715 to the present Year* (London, 1720), no. 3. It had already been published under its own title page in 1717 as a dance for the ballroom and did not confirm its link with the Sallé children until the reissue of 1720.

25. For details of the life and career of Anthony L'Abbé see *International Encyclopaedia of Dance* and *Oxford Dictionary of National Biography*. It is not certain whether all the evidence of London activities by a dancer named Monsieur L'Abbé relate only to one person: performance advertisements between 1705 and 1713 refer to another dancer sometimes known as "Mons. l'Abbé's scholar" or as "young L'Abbé," without any indication of which of them might be Anthony L'Abbé.

26. F[rançois] le Roussau, *A New Collection of Dances . . . composed by Monsieur L'Abbé* (London, c.1725). A facsimile has been published as *Anthony L'Abbé, A New Collection of Dances, originally published by F. Le Roussau, London c.1725*, with an introduction by Carol G. Marsh, in *Music for London Entertainment 1660–1800*, Series D, volume 2 (London and New York: Stainer & Bell, 1991). Throughout this chapter I have followed Francine Lancelot's identification of le Roussau's forename as François (Francine Lancelot, *La belle danse: catalogue raisonné* [Paris: Van Dieren, 1996], p. 228).

27. Discussed in more detail in Jennifer Thorp, "Serious and comic dance in the work of F. le Roussau," in *Structures and Metaphors in Baroque Dance: Proceedings of the Conference at the University of Surrey Roehampton 2001* (Roehampton: University of Surrey, 2001), pp. 10–20. See also Jennifer Thorp, *Harlequin Dancing-Master: the Career of F. le Roussau* (forthcoming).

28. F[rançois] le Roussau, *A Collection of New Ball- and Stage Dances . . . 1720* (Edinburgh, University Library, Laing MSS, La.III.163), *Chaconne for Arlequin;* subsequently engraved and published as *Chacoon for a Harlequin* (London, n.d.). Meredith Little and Carol G. Marsh, *La Danse Noble: an Inventory of Dances and Sources* (New York: Broude Bros., 1992), pp. 124–25, assign a date of c. 1728 to the engraved version.

29. Some 228 entr'acte dances just for Harlequin and/or Scaramouche are noted in LS between 1700 and 1730, and the numbers continued to rise throughout the next twenty years. There was also a phenomenal rise in the popularity of Pierrot dances in the four years between 1726 (17 dances) and 1730 (118 dances).

30. See Little and Marsh, *La Danse Noble*, nos. 1880, 2760, and Edith Lalonger, "Les chaconnes d'Arlequin conservées en notation Feuillet," in *Arlequin danseur au tournant du XVIIIᵉ siècle: atelier rencontre et recherche, Nantes, 14–15 mai 2004* (Paris: Annales de l'Association pour un Centre de Recherche sur les Arts du Spectacle au XVIIᵉ et XVIIIᵉ siècles, no. 1, Juin 2005), pp. 13–17. The notations of all three dances are reproduced in Lalonger, pp. 38–72.

31. Colley Cibber, p. 299. However, he was aware of the way in which popular pantomime moved away from Weaver's high ideals, and bewailed the "succession of monstrous medlies . . . infesting the stage" which subsequently developed as pantomimes.

32. For a discussion of pantomime from the actor's point of view, and pantomime's capacity to embody politically subversive messages, see John O'Brien, *Harlequin Britain: Pantomime and Entertainment 1690–1760* (Baltimore: Johns Hopkins University Press, 2004).

33. See cast lists in the texts of Weaver's works reprinted in Ralph, *Weaver*, pp. 735–852. For an overview and discussion of Weaver's considerable contribution to the art of expressive and pantomimic dancing see Moira Goff, "Steps, gestures and expressive dancing: Magri, Ferrère, and John Weaver," in *The Grotesque Dancer on the Eighteenth-Century Stage: Gennaro Magri and His World*, ed. Rebecca Harris-Warrick and Bruce Alan Brown (Madison: University of Wisconsin Press, 2005), pp. 199–230.

34. Synopses and cast lists of both works were published by T. Payne as *An Exact Description of the Two Fam'd Entertainments of Doctor Faustus* (London, 1724).

35. These figures are averaged from the lists at the beginning of the 1742/3 to 1744/5 seasons in LS.

Recommended Reading

Cohen, Selma Jean, ed. *The International Encyclopaedia of Dance*. Oxford: Oxford University Press, 1998. Includes articles on several English dancers of the early eighteenth century.

Early Music 26, no. 2 (1998): issue devoted to early dance.

Goff, Moira. "Art and Nature Join'd: Hester Santlow and the Development of Dancing on the London Stage, 1700–1737." Ph.D. diss., University of Kent at Canterbury, 2000. Available from the British Thesis Service, The British Library, Boston Spa.

Marsh, Carol G. "French Court Dance in England, 1706–1740: A Study of Sources." Ph.D. diss., City University of New York, 1985. Available from University Microfilms, Inc. Dissertation Information Service.

Oxford Dictionary of National Biography. Oxford: Oxford University Press, 2004. Regularly updated online (www.oxforddnb.com) with information about some of the leading performers on the London stage as new research continues.

Ralph, Richard. *The Life and Works of John Weaver*. London: Dance Books, 1985.

Shennan, Jennifer, ed. *A Work Book by Kellom Tomlinson*. Stuyvesant, N.Y.: Pendragon Press, 1992.

Part 4

Choreographic Structure and Music

For the ancient Greeks dance and music were two parts of one art, and while this intimate pairing has loosened over the centuries, the relationship between dance and music was central in the five hundred years covered by this book. It is the relationship between dance and music that binds together the three chapters in part 4, all of which address the issue of choreographic structure: that of the fifteenth-century Italian *ballo* and *bassadanza* in chapter 7 by Jennifer Nevile; the mid-fifteenth to the mid-sixteenth-century *basse dance* in chapter 8 by David Wilson; and that of baroque dance in chapter 9 by Ken Pierce. Through all three chapters common elements are identified, which first appear in the fifteenth century and are still present in the early eighteenth century. For example, both baroque dance steps and Italian Renaissance dance steps could be, and were, performed in both duple and triple time, while the change from triple to duple time in the *basse dance* repertoire occurred in the sixteenth century. Furthermore, the dance steps from all three practices were performed in the time of either one bar or half a bar, thus meaning that the steps and music moved at the same pace, while each step, and each element of a step, had to be timed to coincide with particular beats of the bar. The necessity for precision and timing of the dance steps and music did not alter over 350 years. In both the Italian and baroque dance practices each dance was a unique choreography and had its own unique accompanying music (except for the *bassadanze* in the fifteenth century and the generic baroque dances like the ballroom menuet). Aesthetic principles were also common across the centuries. As Pierce has shown, baroque dance masters were "more interested in artfully combining existing steps in pleasing sequences and floor patterns, rather than inventing new steps." The same can also be said of the *quattrocento* Italian dance masters, and the anonymous creators of the *basse dance* repertory. Even though the size of the step vocabulary of the two Renaissance practices was tiny compared to the baroque (Feuillet lists 530 steps in this treatise), inventing new steps does not appear to have been a priority for the Italian dance masters until the mid-sixteenth century.

Through his examination of the choreographic structure of baroque dance and the relationship between the dance steps and the music, Pierce reveals how the dances were constructed, that is, what was important for the dance masters and what choices they faced when they created a new dance in terms of steps, step sequences, use of repetition, and symmetry. Pierce demonstrates how the character of a dance was defined by such structural elements as the variety of the dance figures, the frequency and rhythm of the changes from one figure to another, the relative frequency of the different types of symmetries used, and the occurrence of passages that interrupt the symmetrical structure of the dance.

Nevile addresses similar issues to Pierce in her chapter on the fifteenth-century Italian dance practice, that is, she examines how the dance masters manipulated the musical and kinetic aspects of their compositions in order to create a new choreography. In addition, Nevile shows how the music and dance of this period were linked through proportion and thereby bound to the proportions that ordered the cosmos, a subject that reappears in part 6. For the Italian dance masters the dance they taught was an outward, physical expression of the harmony of the music. Thus the music and dance were linked on both the philosophical and practical levels.

Even though the *basse dance* has hitherto not been seen as a genre that exhibited flexibility and variability in its choreographic structure, in chapter 8 Wilson discusses how this genre changed over one hundred years, and the variety exhibited by the step sequences in the surviving choreographies. Wilson also discusses the surviving sources for the *basse dance* and summarizes current thinking on performance practice of this genre. In addition he highlights the unusual features of these dances, including the fact that, unlike most other dance genres, the music and dance steps of a *basse dance* had their own structure that moved in parallel and normally only coincided at the beginning and end of the dance.

7

The Relationship between Dance and Music in Fifteenth-Century Italian Dance Practice

Jennifer Nevile

The dances that adorned the festivities of the Italian courts in the fifteenth century were a dazzling exhibition of the choreographic art, and examples of a close collaboration with the art of music. For the dance masters music was an indispensable part of dance as a creative activity, one which was a product of human ingenuity and skill. When performing, dancers had to harmonize and adjust their steps to fit the music, otherwise their performance was viewed as lacking in grace. Unless modern scholars consider both the choreographic and the musical aspects of the dance practice in their research, they will be looking at only half the picture. The purpose of this chapter is to examine the relationship between the two arts of music and dance in fifteenth-century Italy, on both a philosophical and a practical level. The first half of this chapter examines how the dance masters viewed the relationship between music and dance, that is, how dance was an outward, physical expression of the harmony of music. I then discuss the consequences of this belief for the performance of the choreographies that both music and dance were ordered by the same proportions that ordered the universe. The second half of this chapter analyzes how the dance masters of the day manipulated the musical and kinetic aspects of their compositions.

Dance as a Physical Expression of Music

It is in the prologue to Guglielmo Ebreo's treatise on dance that one finds the clearest exposition of the philosophical relationship between the liberal art of music and the art of dance. Guglielmo thought that of all the liberal arts, music was the one most suited to human nature. "[A]nd [music] is the most apt, and conforms itself to human nature almost more than do the other [arts]. Because . . . it offers through listening to it great comfort to all our senses, almost as if it were the most natural food of our souls."[1] For the fifteenth-century Italian dance masters, Domenico da Piacenza, Guglielmo Ebreo da Pesaro, and Antonio Cornazano, music and dance were inextricably linked as a creative activity, a unified skill that necessitated teaching, learning, and practice. They were of course well aware that the ability to dance was an innate ability, a gift from God distributed in uneven quantities, and that dancing itself was a natural activity which occurred when people moved with measured steps in harmony with one another. However, when music was played, and the dancers adjusted their steps to fit that music, then dancing moved from being a natural activity to being an art.[2] According to the dance masters, it was the inclusion of music in a dance performance that changed the natural activity of dancing into an art: an activity transformed by human skill and knowledge. This transformation of dancing into an art was one of the reasons why, when performing, dancers had to adjust their steps to fit the music. If this was not done, then not only was their performance seen as lacking in grace, it was also viewed by the dance masters as reducing the art they had created to merely a natural activity.

As far as Guglielmo and his colleagues were concerned, dance proceeded naturally from music; that is, dance was the outward, physical expression of the harmony of the music: an ordering of the movements of the human body that was concordant with the proportioning of the music which accompanied it. "These things show us the great excellence and supreme dignity of the science [that is, music] from which the joyful art, and the sweet effect of dancing, is naturally proceeded. This virtue of the dance is none other than an external action reflecting interior spiritual movements (or movements of the soul)."[3] The important consequence of Guglielmo's view of the relationship between dance and music is that since dance proceeds from music, it also shares the characteristics of music, that is, it too is a realization of the proportions that govern all the cosmos, and which tie human beings into the harmony of the universe.

The dance that Domenico, Guglielmo, and Cornazano were teaching, performing, composing, and promoting was, through music, one of the liberal arts. Therefore, dance had to share the numerical basis of music and the other arts of the quadrivium. The belief that numbers were the ultimate constituents of reality, that both the human world and the heavenly world consisted of, and was to be comprehended through, numbers was the central tenet of the Pythagorean and Platonic tradition, a tradition that had been transmitted to the medieval West through the work of scholars such as Boethius.[4] Through this belief that numbers were the principles and elements of all things, philosophers were able to form a unified system, with all parts of nature, including mankind, connected through number and proportion.[5] Musical harmony was seen to be an earthly imitation of the natural harmony or system of ratios that organized the cosmos. These numbers or ratios that represented the cosmos were seen as beautiful, good, and true, while other numbers were seen as bad or corrupt. Certain musical harmonies, melodies, and rhythms and certain movements of the body were invested with specific ethical values. For example, certain rhythms were held to be good as they induced virtue in mankind and drew the soul toward divine contemplation, while other rhythms induced drunkenness, laziness, and other defects of character. Music, therefore, had the property of being able to influence the moral character of human beings either for the better or for their detriment. The beautiful, good, and true proportions that governed the cosmos, and which formed the perfect consonances in music, were the ratios of 1:2 (the octave), 2:3 (the fifth), and 3:4 (the fourth). These same ratios were found in dance.

Proportion in Dance

For the fifteenth-century Italian dance masters, dance proceeded from music: it was a physical expression of the harmony of the music. Music and dance were linked through proportion (*misura*) and thereby bound to the proportions that ordered the cosmos. But how were these proportions expressed in the dance practice? In fifteenth-century Italian dance the primary way in which these ratios were expressed was through the ratios between the relative speeds of the four different combinations of meter and speed found in the *balli*. These combinations were called *misure*. The four *misure* from which the *balli* were constructed were *bassadanza misura*, the slowest in speed, *quaternaria misura*, the next fastest, *saltarello misura*, and finally the fastest, *piva misura*. In the theoretical section of their treatises, Domenico and Cornazano go to a great deal of trouble to explain the proportions between these four *misure*.[6] Domenico especially is extremely precise in his explanation, and he is most insistent that *bassadanza misura* is the basis of all the other three *misure*. The ratios between *bassadanza misura* and the other three *misure* are the same ratios that represent the cosmos: 2:1, 3:2, and 4:3.

In his treatise Domenico describes the relative speeds of the four *misure*. He is saying that *bassadanza misura* is the slowest of the four *misure* and it is the speed from which all the others are measured. *Piva misura* is the fastest *misura*, and it is three-sixths faster, or twice the speed of *bassadanza misura*. Thus every three breves (or bars) of *bassadanza misura* takes the same time to play or dance as six breves (or six bars) of *piva misura*. This creates a ratio between the speed of *bassadanza misura* and *piva misura* of 1:2. *Saltarello misura* is the second-fastest *misura*. It is two-sixths faster than *bassadanza misura*. Therefore, for every four breves of *bassadanza misura* one can perform six breves of *saltarello misura*, creating the ratio of 4:6 or 2:3. *Quaternaria misura* is one-sixth faster than *bassadanza misura*. This means that for every five breves of *bassadanza misura* one can perform six breves of *quaternaria misura*, creating the ratio 5:6. Thus the three ratios or proportions between the different speeds are 1:2 (*bassadanza* to *piva*), 2:3 (*bassadanza* to *saltarello*), and 5:6 (*bassadanza* to *quaternaria*).

Domenico also describes the relationship between the four *misure* in symbols, by using mensural terminology to indicate proportions.[7] It is by this method of describing the relative speeds of the *misure* that the ratio of *bassadanza* to *quaternaria* as 3:4 is produced.[8] (The ratio of 5:6 between *bassadanza* and *quaternaria* is derived from Domenico's written description of "one-sixth faster, two-sixths faster, three-sixths faster.") After half a millennium since the flowering of this dance practice it is unclear as to which ratio was meant by the dance masters, or indeed what was the exact relationship between the speed of *bassadanza* and *quaternaria misura*, when performed for a *ballo* in the ducal palace. Certainly Domenico's scheme of "one-sixth, two-sixths, three-sixths faster" is simple and elegant, and is one which could be easily remembered by practical dancers. On the other hand, the concept of proportion was vitally important to the dance masters. It may well have been the case that in the time of five breves worth of *bassadanza* steps a dancer did perform six breves worth of *quaternaria* steps. But in terms of mensural notation the ratio 3:4 is as close as one can come to the ratio of 5:6, since the only proportions that are possible if one is using mensuration signs to show proportions are those numbers which are divisible by two or three.

Structural Relationship between the Choreography and the Music of the Balli

The choreographies recorded in the dance treatises of Domenico, Guglielmo, and Cornazano were *balli* and *bassadanze*. The dances in these two genres were all individually choreographed, with their own unique sequence of steps and floor patterns, and each with its individual name. Each *ballo* had its own music that was especially composed by the dance masters, or adapted from an existing chanson, to fit the choreography.[9] The music for a *ballo* is dependent upon the choreography, since each *ballo* is constructed of a number of short, irregular sections of steps in the four different *misure*, that is, in the four different combinations of tempi and meters. These sections do not follow any regular pattern and are unique to each *ballo*. Thus the music has to be different for every choreography and is often provided in the dance treatises themselves. The *bassadanze* were normally in only one combination of speed and meter, *bassadanza misura*, with only a few bars of *saltarello misura* occurring occasionally. Thus any music with the right time signature and with the appropriate number of breves would fit a *bassadanza* choreography.[10]

For Domenico and his colleagues an intrinsic part of dance was variation in tempo: changes in speed from slow to fast, and the concomitant changes in the speed of the steps and gestures of the dancers. For them a *ballo* was not a building block of dance types, stuck together like bits of fabric in a patchwork quilt, but, rather, each *ballo* was a unity in which the changes in speed and meter was like the ebb and flow of the tide. Even though the *ballo* is a dance form in which the sections of the choreography are continually changing speed, the dance masters did not appear to have any set rules as regards these speed changes, as there is no discernable order in the way the sections of differing speed were used. The *balli* do not conform to any rule such as a slow start, then an increase in speed, then a decrease of speed toward the end of the dance. Each dance is unique, with the changes in speed underlying the dramatic aspects of each dance.

If the dance masters did not appear to follow any set pattern as to the ordering of the sections of different *misure* in their *balli*, they did use each *misura* in a different manner, even though all four *misure* appear with roughly the same frequency. *Piva misura*, the fastest in tempo, is the *misura* that occupies the highest number of breves, yet it only occurs in a small number of dances, with almost half the occurrences of *piva* found in only two *balli*, *Tesara* and *Pizochara*. Normally *piva misura* occurs in short sections near the end of a dance, while *saltarello misura* is used mainly at the beginning of a dance. By contrast, sections of *bassadanza* and *quaternaria misura* are used throughout the course of a dance.

The music for each *ballo* is constructed of sections of differing *misure*, sections that vary in meter and speed. Although a dance may contain any number of these sections from two to thirteen, the majority of the *ballo* tunes have either five, six, or seven musical sections. These sections are not of any set length, nor is the music consistently phrased in any particular manner, such as four or eight bar phrases.[11] The musical sections can either be played only once, or they can be repeated a specific number of times as indicated by the appropriate numeral that appears underneath the section. The *ballo Merçantia*, for example, begins with twelve breves of *saltarello misura*, followed by six breves of *quaternaria*, then twelve and a half breves of *bassadanza misura*. The sequence *saltarello*, *quaternaria*, *bassadanza* is repeated, but the length of the last three sections are not the same as the first three. In this dance there are no even groupings of four or eight bar phrases, and *Merçantia* is typical in this regard. *Verçeppe* has phrases that vary from one breve (bar) to one and three-quarters, two and a half, three, three and a quarter, three and a third, four, and four and a half breves (bars) in length. Therefore, both the musicians and the dancers had to know the music extremely well as they had to be able to change from one section of irregular length to another section of irregular length, without any pauses, hesitations, and usually no upbeats to establish the new tempo.

What, therefore, is the relationship between the musical sections and the choreographic sections? Choreographic sections in the *balli* are identified by factors such as the cessation of movement on the part of a performer, a change in direction of the performers, a change in the type of steps being performed, and the manner in which the sequence of steps was originally set down in the fifteenth century in the written description of the choreography. Are the musical sections connected in any way with the choreographic sections? Do the manipulations of the musical material correspond in any way to the manipulations of the choreographic elements? Are certain steps associated with any particular repeated melodic material?

On one level there is a very obvious answer to the question concerning the relationship between the music of a *ballo* and its choreography. Since every *ballo* is a unique arrangement of steps, and each tune was written to fit a specific dance, then the choreography and the music cannot but be connected. This matching of the choreography and the music, however, does not imply that there always had to be an identical structure between musical sections and choreographic sections. Take, for example, a dance for three performers, A, B, and C, which has in it a section of four *bassadanza doppi* in which A moves forward for four steps, then B follows with another four *bassadanza doppi*, and finally C joins A and B with a second repeat of the four *bassadanza doppi*. Thus music for this sequence of movements would have to be twelve breves (or bars) of *bassadanza misura*, but the dance master would have had a choice of writing these twelve breves as twelve breves straight, six breves repeated once, or four breves played through three times. All three options would fit the choreography, but only in the last option would the music mirror the structure of the choreography.

While it is not invariably the case, in the majority of the *balli* that possess both choreographic instructions and music, the dance masters set the repetition of a sequence of movements of one performer by another performer to a repeat of the music that was used to accompany the original execution of step sequence. One of the many *balli* that illustrate this point is *Tesara*, the music of which has thirteen separate sections. The dance is choreographed for ten performers, four couples who stand in a line behind one another, and two extra men, who stand one in front and one behind the four couples. In this dance the musical sections 2, 3, 5, 7, and 8 are repeated. In all of these five sections the musical repetitions are reflected in the choreography. The parallel structure between the repetitions of the music and choreography in sections 2, 3, 5, 7, and 8 also applies when the music of one section is used for another section. Thus in *Tesara* when the music of sections 3 and 4 occur a second time in sections 5 and 6, so too does the exact same choreography and the exact same floor pattern. In the case of *Tesara* one can speculate as to the reason Domenico da Piacenza might have had for keeping the music and choreographic sequences so closely linked. Since the dance is long when compared to many of the other *balli* and, due to the number of performers, also quite complicated, the close relationship between the music and choreographic sequences for the majority of the dance helps to unify the piece and to reinforce its structure in the eyes of the onlookers.

The connection between the music and the choreography is brought into sharper focus when one considers the relationship between the floor shapes and the musical sections. The choreographic descriptions all had a regular written structure, which clearly identified individual sequences of steps, separated by the words *et poi* ("and then"). In this context the term "floor shape" is defined as the smallest unit of shape, that is, the individual sequences of steps contained between the words "and then" in the choreographic descriptions. The combination of several floor shapes is defined as a "floor pattern," while the term "floor track" refers to the path of the entire dance from start to finish, that is, a sequence of several floor patterns. When the points at which the musical sections begin and end are compared with the floor shapes of each *ballo*, one finds that musical sections change at the beginning of a new floor shape, not in the middle of one.[12] *Ingrata* is one *ballo* where the musical and choreographic boundaries can be clearly seen, as the pauses in the choreographic sequence occur at the end of the musical sections.[13] The first musical section is entirely taken up with the opening floor shape: the *saltarello doppi* in *saltarello misura*. The second floor shape, four *sempi*[14] forward by the woman, is performed to the second musical section, with the musical repeat matching the repetition of the choreographic material by the two men. The start of the third musical section introduces a new phase in the choreography, that is, the separation of the woman and the two men to form a triangle, a shape that is maintained throughout the third and fourth musical sections. The short fifth musical section accompanies the *mezavolta* (a 180 degree turn) by the men and the women, as they turn to face one another again, preparatory to their final advance in order to meet again. The advance of two *sempi* and two *riprese*,[15] repeated twice, is performed to the sixth musical section, which is also heard three times. The final musical section accompanies the woman performing a figure-of-eight, turning as she does so to first one man and then the other, in order that the three dancers finish as they began, standing beside each other in a line.

The musical material for each *ballo* is also manipulated on a smaller level than the repetition of entire sections. Often several bars from one section will be joined to several bars from another to create a new section, or sometimes the opening bars of a *ballo* will be reused as the initial bars of another section. Unlike repetitions of whole sections, the manipulations of smaller segments of melodic material do not, in the majority of cases, bear any relationship to the choreography of the dance. The music of *Verçeppe*,[16] for example, is constructed of three basic phrases that are repeated, amalgamated, and varied slightly to form the nine different sections of the music. The choreography of the dance, however, does not reflect this detailed level of musical alteration.

We can conclude, then, that while the choreography and music of the *balli* are closely linked on the section level, the relationship is more ambivalent on a more detailed structural level: sometimes the two coincide, but mostly they do not. This lack of correspondence between dance and music at the subsectional level is also reflected in the fact that the dance masters did not associate any particular step or step sequence with any specific phrase or motif. Furthermore, when the music changes *misura* in the *balli* there is no consistent pattern of the melodic material from one *misura* being reworked in a different *misura*. Musical repetition and variation do occur in the music for the *balli*, but more often only two or three bars worth rather than whole sections. When whole sections are repeated it is usually due to the demands of the choreography, as is the case in *Pizochara*.

Enhancing the Dramatic Effect of a Dance

The total dramatic effect of a dance was created by the fusion of the music and the choreography, a fusion that was carefully controlled and arranged by the *maestri di ballo* (dance masters). One example of how the dance masters manipulated the music so that it added to the dramatic effect of the dance can be seen in the *ballo*, *Pizochara*.[17] In this dance the sixth musical section (bars 35–44) is a repeat of the fourth musical section (bars 26–33), and the choreography for these two sections is almost identical. In bars 26–33 the men are weaving around the stationary line of women, parading themselves and their mastery of the dance technique with a sequence of eleven *bassadanza doppi*.[18] Such an extended sequence of a single step required each *doppio* to be subtly varied in performance, and the slow tempo of the *bassadanza misura* would give the men time to add improvised variations to each step. The men arrive back beside their partners, taking hands while doing a *ripresa*, a step to the side. Instead of remaining beside their partners, the women suddenly depart, weaving around the line of men, but with a series of far more lively *saltarello doppi*. In its first appearance the tenor line is in the slow *bassadanza misura*, and in a clear compound duple ($\frac{6}{8}$) rhythm. When the melody returns in the sixth musical section, Domenico has increased the speed of the music by calling for *saltarello misura*, and the unambiguous $\frac{6}{8}$ rhythm has been changed to a mixture of $\frac{3}{4}$ and $\frac{6}{8}$. The rhythmic syncopation of the sixth musical section, and its faster tempo, reflect the men's surprise and confusion at the unexpected departure and teasing parade of the women at this point.

Conclusion

For the Italian dance masters music and dance were closely interwoven on both a philosophical and on a practical level. Music was an essential part of any dance performance: it was not to be ignored by those dancing, and it was far more than just an aural blanket to cover the swish of the dancers' feet on the floor. Since dance was an outward physical expression of the proportions found in the music, the two had to be in harmony with one another: dancers had to adjust their steps to fit the music. When this was done the performance was seen as graceful and virtuous. Most important for the Italian dance masters, dance shared the essential characteristics of music: in both were found the same proportions, or ratios, that governed the cosmos, and which tied human beings and the world they inhabited into the harmony of the divine world.

The dance and accompanying music were also closely connected on a practical level. In one of the main genres of dances, the *ballo*, the music for each dance was dependent upon the choreography and was either newly composed by a dance master or adapted by him from an existing chanson to fit the choreography. Thus the dramatic effect of a dance was created by a combination of the music and choreography, both of which were under the control of the dance master.

Notes

1. Guglielmo Ebreo da Pesaro, *Guilielmi Hebraei pisauriensis de practica seu arte tripudii vulgare opusculum, incipit*, 1463, Paris, Bibliothèque Nationale, MS fonds it. 973, f. 4r "et quasi al humana natura più che alchuna dell'altre aptissima & conforme: Impero che . . . porge ascoltando a tutti nostri sensi singular conforto quasi si chome ella fusse di nostri spiriti naturalissimo cibo" (hereafter cited as Pg).

2. Pg, f. 18v–19r.

3. Pg, f. 5v. "Le qual cose ci mostrano la grande excellenza & suprema dignitate d'essa scienza dalla qual l'arte giocunda e 'l dolce effetto del danzare è naturalmente proceduto. La qual virtute del danzare non è altro che una actione demostrativa di fuori di movimenti spirituali."

4. For more information on the transmission of these ideas from ancient Greece to the medieval West, see Ann E. Moyer, *Musica Scientia: Musical Scholarship in the Italian Renaissance* (Ithaca: Cornell University Press, 1992), pp. 24–35.

5. For an extended discussion on this subject see S. K. Heninger Jr., *The Touches of Sweet Harmony: Pythagorean Cosmology and Renaissance Poetics* (San Marino, Calif.: Huntington Library, 1977).

6. For a complete analysis of how the dance masters discussed these ratios in their

treatises, see Jennifer Nevile, *The Eloquent Body: Dance and Humanist Culture in Fifteenth-Century Italy* (Bloomington: Indiana University Press, 2004), pp. 110–18.

7. See ibid., pp. 158–60, for a detailed argument as to how Domenico used mensural terminology to express these ratios.

8. The ratio 3:4 (*bassadanza* to *quaternaria*) comes from the description of *quaternaria misura* as minor imperfect and *bassadanza misura* as major imperfect. The ratio of major imperfect (₵) to minor imperfect (₵) produces the ratio 3:4 on the minima level. In his symbolic explanation of the ratios between the relative speeds of the four *misure* Domenico did not notate factors of two. Thus two breves (or bars) of *quaternaria misura* as C (minor imperfect) has to equal one breve (or bar) of *bassadanza misura* (₵). Therefore the ratio of *bassadanza misura* to *quaternaria misura* is the ratio of ₵ : ₵, which is 6 minima to 8 minima, or 3:4.

9. Domenico da Piacenza, *De arte saltandj & choreas ducendj De la arte di ballare et danzare*, Paris, Bibliothèque Nationale, MS fonds it. 972, f. 7r. One example of where Domenico adapted an existing chanson to provide the music for a *ballo* is *La fia guilmina*.

10. The dance masters do not provide music for the *bassadanze* in their treatises. The only exception is Cornazano, who records three tenor lines that were often used for performances of *bassadanze*.

11. Regular four-bar phrases were also extremely rare in the written polyphony of the fifteenth century (David Fallows, *Dufay* [London: Dent, 1987], p. 96).

12. In the fifty-four choreographies that include music, a musical section ends in the middle of a floor shape only eight times.

13. For a transcription of the music for *Ingrata* and a reconstruction of its floor track, see Nevile, *The Eloquent Body*, pp. 170–75.

14. A *sempio*, or "single step" was one forward pace. See David R. Wilson, *The Steps Used in Court Dancing in Fifteenth-Century Italy*, 3rd rev. ed. (Cambridge: David R. Wilson, 2003), pp. 48–53.

15. *Riprese* were sideways steps. See ibid., pp. 37–41.

16. For a transcription of the music for *Verçeppe* and a reconstruction of its floor track, see Nevile, *The Eloquent Body*, pp. 182–88.

17. For a transcription of the music for *Pizochara* and a reconstruction of its floor track, see ibid., pp. 176–81.

18. A *doppio*, or double step, consisted of three paces forward alternating feet.

Recommended Reading

Berger, Anna Maria Busse. *Mensuration and Proportion Signs. Origins and Evolution.* Oxford: Clarendon Press, 1993.

Caldwell, John. "Some Observations on the Four *misure*." In *Terpsichore 1450–1900, Proceedings of the International Dance Conference, Ghent, April 2000*, ed. Barbara Ravelhofer, pp. 9–10. Ghent: Institute for Historical Dance Practice, 2000.

8

The Basse Dance

c. 1445—c. 1545

David R. Wilson

Up to the middle of the fifteenth century we know the names of dances that were current and have examples of their music, but we can only guess at their steps and choreographic structure. A number of manuscripts survive from the thirteenth and fourteenth centuries that preserve very danceable music for *estampie, saltarello, trotto,* and so forth (Table 8.1),[1] but, unhappily, it is not possible to reconstruct dances from their music alone.

The earliest record so far known in Europe of the actual steps used in named dances presents us with the contrary problem. The document is a personal memorandum of the sequence of steps in each of seven dances current at the French royal court, apparently made at Nancy in 1445 (Table 8.2, no. 1).[2] The corresponding tunes were not included, however, so although some of the dances were explicitly described as *basses dances,* our attempts to understand their character will need to take into account better-documented examples from later in the century. We shall return to the "Nancy dances" in due course, but first we must fast-forward to the 1490s.

A Fifteenth-Century "Teach Yourself" Booklet

We have two relevant documents for the *basse dance* in the last decade of the fifteenth century, similar to one another in content but very different in form. One is the earliest known extant printed book on dancing in Europe. It was issued c. 1495 by a Parisian printer/publisher named Michel Toulouze and is generally referred to by his name, as *Toulouze* (Table 8.2, no. 4).[3] Five small pages are devoted to "the art and instruction of dancing the *basse dance*." In modern language, this is a "Teach Yourself" booklet covering two main topics: classification of the *mesures* (measures) out of which *basses dances* are composed, and correct performance of the individual types of step involved. In addition, it explains the name *basse dance* (literally "low dance")—from this it appears that "low" is not to be understood in a purely literal sense as "not rising above the floor"; rather, it means "grave and serene." Another nineteen pages give worked-out examples of forty-eight different dances, giving both their tunes and appropriate step sequences for them. Although this booklet was a commercial publication, only one copy of it is known to have survived into modern times. The second document was not printed, but handwritten with gold and silver inks on black-dyed parchment, a very handsome and expensive present for the library of Marguerite of Austria, probably made in the period from 1497 to 1501. It nevertheless contained virtually the same introductory text, followed by details of fifty-eight dances, of which forty-four are also present in *Toulouze*. This manuscript is in the Royal Library in Brussels and is known to students of *basse dance* as the "Brussels MS," or simply *Brussels* (Table 8.2, no. 6).[4]

It is clear that both Toulouze and Brussels are derived from the same original compilation, presumably through other handwritten copies that have not survived. Where they give the same text, each can be used to correct errors present in the other; but each of them also contains details of dances that are unique to itself, added at a relatively late stage in the sequence of transmission. Indeed, even if we suppose that all the dances listed must have still been current at the end of the fifteenth century, there is reason to suggest that this list accrued over a period of time that may have gone back thirty years or more.[5]

Steps Used in the Basse Dance

According to both sources, only four types of step were used in the *basse dance*. These were the *pas simple* (single), always found in pairs and therefore always represented by the doubled abbreviation *ss*; the *pas double* (double), represented by the abbreviation *d*; the *desmarche* or *reprise*, represented by *r*, seeing that *d* was already required for *pas double*; and *branle*, represented by the abbreviation *b*. Singles and doubles were the common currency of all known dances in England, France, Italy, and Spain in the fifteenth century. A *pas simple* was literally a single step, made in the time of what we should today call one bar of music (two or three counts according to whether it was in duple or triple time). A *pas double* involved three constituent steps, with the free foot either passing through or else making a close on the final count. The time taken by a *pas double* was twice that of a *pas simple*. In the *basse dance* these steps are said to have been begun by "raising the body" (probably going onto the half toe) and then stepping forward; we should expect that their end was marked by lowering the heel of the supporting foot in readiness for a new step.

Desmarche and *branle* are less clearly described. The *desmarche* served both as a reverence at the beginning of each dance and as a step within the dance that could also be called *reprise*. When it was a reverence, the left foot was taken back at an angle such that partners could regard one another while "inclining the body"; then they presumably recovered to their previous position (though this is not explicitly stated). When it was a *reprise*, the *desmarche* became a true traveling step (in the time of a *pas double*), made directly to the rear in the first or third of a set of three, but angled like the reverence in the second one. The exchange of courtesies implicit in the treatment of the second *desmarche* (conceivably a Burgundian innovation) makes it very probable that in the late fifteenth century the two dancers were stepping on opposite feet. As for the *branle*, there is reason to think it comprised two symmetrical movements by which the dancers turned first toward their left and then toward their right, without lifting their feet from the ground.

These steps were grouped into a number of *mesures* in accordance with conventions that changed over time and probably also from one region to another. *Toulouze* and *Brussels* set out the conventions current in the later fifteenth century, almost certainly as practiced in Burgundy and in other regions under Burgundian influence. The dance as a whole started with a *révérence* (R) and a *branle* (b). Then each of a series of *mesures* was composed of the following steps, always in the same order: two *pas simples*; an odd number of *pas doubles* (1, 3 or 5); an optional further pair of *pas simples*; an odd number of *desmarches* (1 or 3); and a *branle* to mark the end of the *mesure*. (Each *mesure* began with the left foot, the steps being made with alternate feet throughout.) This sequence is easier to comprehend in a diagram like that below in Figure 8.1, where the groups of steps in the same box are possible alternatives; those in brackets are optional.

ss	ddddd	(ss)	rrr	b
	ddd		r	
	d			

Figure 8.1. "Theoretical" step sequences of *basse dance mesures.*

That at least is the scheme as described; but when we turn to the appended examples, we find some elaborations and alternatives, as shown in Figure 8.2.

(ss d r)	ss	ddddd	(ss)	rrr	b
		ddd		r d r	
		d		r	

Figure 8.2. Alternative step sequences for *mesures.*

Commonly, *mesures* of just two kinds alternate, but sometimes a third type of *mesure* is introduced. This may be simply a matter of changing the numbers of the steps already present, or it may involve adding the prefix *ss d r* to one of the two kinds of *mesure* already present.

Music for the Fifteenth-Century Basse Dance

Toulouze and *Brussels* present the tunes of their *basses dances* in the same way, as a series of equal notes (breves) (see Fig. 8.4). This line of music is interpreted as representing the tenor part, around which other musical parts could be arranged or improvised, as round a cantus firmus. Some idea of how this would work is shown by the numerous polyphonic settings (under various names) of *La Spagna,* which is also the tune for the *basse dance Castille la novelle* (*Toulouze,* no. 10).[6] What does not emerge, and is not implied by intermediate cadences within any *basse dance* tune, is any structure involving strains of music matching the *mesures* to which the written text pays so much attention. In most other dance types sections of music and measures of dance closely correspond, but not in the *basse dance.* Instead, the music and the steps each have their own structure, which move in parallel but seldom exactly coincide except at the beginning and the end of the dance.

Steps and music are nevertheless held in register with each other by their common rhythm. Each full step of the dance (rating *pas simples* at only half of one full step each) corresponds to one breve of the tune. These notes are divisible into six counts, and this introduces an attractive dotted rhythm into the dance. Thus, the four elements of a *pas double* are distributed as follows, where "and" represents either the closing or the passing through of the moving foot (see Figure 8.3).

1	2	3	4	5	6
step		step	step		and

Figure 8.3. One *pas double*.

In the absence of scribal or printer's errors, the number of "notes" determines the number of "steps" in every dance. An example is given in Figure 8.4.[7]

Florentine: 45 notes in 5 *mesures*

R	b	ss	dddd	rrr	b
		ss	d	rrr	b
		ss	dddd	rrr	b
		ss	d	rrr	b
		ss	ddd[dd]	rrr	b

Figure 8.4. Basse dance *Florentine* from *S'ensuit l'art et instruction de bien dancer*, Toulouze, c. 1495. From facsimile edition, *Dossier Basses-Dances*. Geneva: Minkoff, 1985. By permission of Éditions Minkoff.

This same dance is given a different step sequence by *Brussels* (no. 38), in six instead of five *mesures* (see Figure 8.5).

R	b	ss	ddd	rrr	b
		ss	d	rdr	b
		ss	ddd	rrr	b
		ss	d	rdr	b
		ss	ddd	rrr	b
		ss	d	rdr	b

Figure 8.5. *Basse dance Florentine* from *Brussels*, no. 38.

There are ten other instances where *Toulouze* and *Brussels* offer significantly different step sequences for dances that have the same name and tune. This brings to mind the following statement in *Brussels:* "To dance a *basse dance* correctly, two things are needed: first, to know the number of steps in each *basse dance* and, second, how to make them *in that number*" (my emphasis).[8] The examples in the back of the booklet were there to help the reader cope with this problem; nevertheless, it is evident that the step sequences given by *Toulouze* and *Brussels* were advisory rather than mandatory. An expert dancer could presumably even devise his own. The choice of steps fell to the male dancer, who must therefore be ready (if required) to guide his partner through the sequence he had chosen. Equally, a competent female dancer should be able to follow her partner's lead.

The "Nancy Dances"

We can now return to Nancy. The first dance listed is *Basse dance de Bourgogne*, which is shown in Figure 8.6. (There is no initial *R b*, perhaps because this was a standard feature that could be taken as read.)

sss	ddddd	sss *to the right side*	b
sss	d	sss *to the right side*	b

Figure 8.6. *Basse dance de Bourgogne* from *Nancy*.

In its broad structure this resembles the dances we have already examined in *Toulouze* and *Brussels*; first, the two *mesures* only differ in the number of *pas doubles*, and second, the longer of the two goes first. In detail, however, there are significant differences. *Pas simples* are found in threes instead of twos and can be taken to the side. If the music was like that found in *Toulouze* and *Brussels*, we could imagine these *pas simples* as taking just two counts each and being danced in a hemiola to the six counts implicit in one note of the tenor.

This interpretation is certainly reinforced by a passage in the next dance, [*Basse dance*] *de la royne de cessile*, shown in Figure 8.7.

sss	dddd	sault *forwards*	d *to the left*	sss *to the right*	rrr	[b]
sss	d			sss *drawn back*	rrr	b

Figure 8.7. *Basse dance de la royne de cessile* from *Nancy*.

In the first *mesure* a *pas double* to the left is balanced by three *pas simples* to the right. The *pas double* comprises three small steps in a dotted rhythm; three *pas simples* danced in a hemiola would provide an elegant variation for the return. Another novelty in this dance is the introduction of a *sault*. *Sault* means "jump," but both its magnitude and its form are ill-defined. It could be a hop on one foot, a leap from one foot to the other, or a bounce on two feet, amongst other possibilities. It has been claimed that, by definition, a *sault* could not actually occur in a *basse dance*,[9] but this is to assume that it was a major movement in its own right. We may compare what happens in the equivalent Italian dance, the *bassadanza*, where both hops and leaps are described that are clearly no more than embellishments on the preceding step, being made on the upbeat (count 6).[10] Thus, the *sault* here is likely to be a small low leap onto the right foot incorporated into the last count of the fourth *pas double*, achieving an elegant transfer of weight that leaves the left foot free for a further *pas double* going to the left.

Other dances in this collection introduce further novelties: *pas menus* (probably quick steps taking half the time of *pas simples* and always in groups of three); one or two *levées* (of uncertain form, perhaps a raising of the foot made in place instead of stepping); and groups of three *saults* (perhaps sprung points on alternate feet, despite being found in one of the *basses dances*). The "Nancy dances" are much freer in their floor pattern and in their step sequences than the other *basses dances* that are known to us. We cannot tell if this "freedom" is related to their relatively early date, or if it is because the French royal court drew its repertoire from regions in north and central France that do not otherwise feature in our written sources.

The Sixteenth Century

Louis XI of France defeated Charles the Bold, Duke of Burgundy, in 1477. Thereafter, the cultural pre-eminence of the Burgundian court gradually declined, and this gave scope for the wider adoption of a different tradition of *basse dance*, apparently based in the south of France. In its fully developed form this sixteenth-century style is attested by three sources. The first is a parchment roll bearing the step sequences of fifty-four dances, signed by someone called Stribaldi in 1517 and now in Turin (Table 8.2, no. 10).[11] (At that time Turin lay in the Duchy of Savoy.) The second is a comic poem written in macaronic Latin[12] by Antonius Arena, instructing his fellow students in the art of dancing, that being the only way for them to meet respectable young women (Table 8.2, no. 12).[13] This was published in Lyon, apparently in 1528. Arena is valuable for a good deal of comment on the social niceties of dancing the *basse dance*, but his descriptions of *basse dance* steps are so distorted by his comic muse and constrained by the exigencies of the verse that they were already described as being incomprehensible in the sixteenth century! Attached to the poem is an appendix giving step sequences for thirty-three *basses dances* (increased to fifty-nine in the second edition). The third source was an updated edition of the "Teach Yourself" booklet that we have already met, probably printed in Lyon, perhaps by Jacques Moderne, conjecturally c. 1535 (Table 8.2, no. 13).[14] Despite the uncertainty of this attribution, the volume is still usually referred to as "Moderne." The text is marred by editorial blunders and printers' errors, but is still of much value, and it is followed by a listing of the step sequences for 172 *basses dances* (some of them repeated in variant versions). These three sources are in close agreement, having many dances in common and sharing three noteworthy innovations: introduction of the *basse dance commune* (standard *basse dance*); new conventions for the composition of *mesures*, especially in *basses dances incommunes* (non-standard *basses dances*); completion of both types of *basse dance* by addition of a separate twelve-step section, called variously *moitié*, *résidu*, or *retour* (or, in a single example already in *Toulouze*, *demie*).

Basse Dance Commune

The appearance of the *basse dance commune* was a revolutionary development both in the demands (or lack thereof) placed on the performers and in the meter of the accompanying music. First of all, the *mesures* of which the *basse dance commune* was composed all comprised sequences of either eight or four full steps, corresponding to matching strains in the music, as shown in Figure 8.8.

R	b	ss	d	rdr	b	
		ss	ddd	rdr	b	
		ss	d	r	b	
		b	d	r	b	} *moitié*
		ss	ddd	rdr	b	

Figure 8.8. *Basse dance commune.*

While this was not the first time that *basses dances* organized in this way had made an appearance in the relevant sources, as three dances in regular *mesures* matched by similar music can be found in *Brussels* where they constitute a group connected with the Duchy of Cleves (Kleve),[15] they now became mainstream, as the name "*basse dance commune*" implies. Henceforth, the *basse dance commune* was the only kind of *basse dance* regularly played and danced at parties, and for the first time the ordinary dancer did not need to know more than just one sequence of steps for the *basse dance*.

Variety was maintained by using a large repertoire of alternative musical settings. It was for the *basse dance commune* that Tylman Susato's bergerettes and similar music were composed. The arrangement of the music now current led to the dancers moving to four counts instead of six as previously, though Arena implies that *pas simples* and *doubles* were generally still not closed on the final count. The relative simplicity of using a standard step sequence encouraged the more able dancers to exercise their skills by dancing variations, just as musicians would make divisions on a simple tune. We are not told where these variations were placed, but the groups of three *pas doubles* in the second *mesure* and in the *moitié* would offer obvious possibilities for ornamental treatment.

Basses Dances Incommunes

The introduction of the *basse dance commune*, however, was far from killing off the traditional style of *basse dance*. On the contrary, it prompted the proliferation of what were now called *basses dances incommunes*. As many as 142 of these (plus some variants) are to be found in *Moderne*. These were performed by advanced dancers, either in their own homes or by special request at parties, where they (the dancers) were then in some danger of being regarded as "show-offs." The *mesures* in the *basse dance incommune* now took on a new format. In the reprise section, the combination *rrr* was universally replaced by the variant *r d r*. At the same time, a *second* pair of optional *pas simples* was introduced in the second half of the *mesure*, to yield a sequence whose maximum complement was *ss r d ss r b*, but in which only the final two steps were obligatory. This yields the following scheme shown in Figure 8.9. Note that either of the optional pairs of *pas simples* could appear without the other.

ss	ddd d	(ss)	(rd)	(ss)	r	b

Figure 8.9. *Basse dance incommune.*

The arrangement of *mesures* within dances was also changed. The first *mesure* always featured a single *pas double*; three *pas doubles* were not found until the second or third *mesure*. It was not unusual for identical *mesures* to follow one another, something unheard of in the fifteenth century, as so far known. Some of the possibilities are demonstrated in *A mon retour* (*Moderne*, no. 106) in Figure 8.10.

R	b	ss	d	ss	rd		rb
		ss	ddd			ss	rb
		ss	d	ss	rd	ss	rb

Figure 8.10. *A mon retour* (*Moderne*, no. 106).

Like a number of dances in *Moderne*, *A mon retour* recurs some pages later (no. 150): see Figure 8.11.

R	b	ss	d	ss	rd	ss	rb
		ss	ddd				rb
		ss	d	ss	rd	ss	rb

Figure 8.11. *A mon retour* (*Moderne*, no. 150).

A pair of *pas simples* has now moved up from the second to the first *mesure*. Both versions are equally valid; neither need be wrong. The occurrence of such variants is probably a sign that *Moderne* has been compiled from a number of different lists.

There is little evidence for the character of the music used for *basses dances incommunes*. Such examples as exist of published arrangements all happen to be for dances that could be analyzed into regular *mesures* like those of the *basse dance commune*, and the music is of similar character.[16] This merely serves to suggest that the majority of the *incommunes* were danced to music that was significantly *dissimilar* and, we might conjecture, not too unlike that of the fifteenth-century dances. We have to leave it open whether steps were danced to a count of six, as before, or were now danced in four.

The Moitié

The *moitié* under its various names (most of which mean "the part left over") is used with both types of *basse dance, commune* and *incommune*. According to Arena the dancers halted at the end of the main part of the dance, but the piper continued playing, going back to the beginning of the music. This gave the dancers the opportunity for a *tête-à-tête*; nevertheless, the man had to be sure to keep track of the music so that, when it again reached the point where they had dropped out before, he could bring his partner back in for the *moitié*.

The *moitié* always comprises twelve full steps, but there are at least three alternative sequences. One of these is set out above (*mesures* 4–5 of *basse dance commune*—see Figure 8.8), where it forms a logical extension of the main part of the dance, performed in the same way to an extension of the same music. How the *moitié* fits with *basses dances incommunes*, however, is less than obvious, seeing that we do not know with any certainty to what kind of music those dances were themselves performed.

Spain

It should be noted that the Christian kingdoms of northern Spain (Aragon and Castile) also had a version of the *basse dance* (*baixa* or *baja* respectively). This had some idiosyncrasies of its own, but was generally conservative in its tradition and was unaffected by the sixteenth-century developments just described.[17]

The Character of the Basse Dance

The *basse dance* was essentially a dance for a single couple. More than one couple could take the floor at once if there was enough room, but there was a real danger of coming face to face with another couple and not having the room to pass. They then had either to make their traveling steps backward in order to continue, or else make the maneuver called *conversion*. This involved each dancer in moving round in a half-circle to their partner's place, she going forward and he backward, so as to end facing back the way they had come.

This whole situation shows that when a space was cleared for dancing, other people only needed to leave enough room for one couple to pass through, and this passage was through the midst of the throng and not round the outside (where one couple could have followed another). There is certainly nothing to suggest that couples ever performed the *basse dance* in procession, going one behind the other in a column. While there are plenty of contemporary pictures of couples moving in procession to music at weddings and in court ceremonial, we have no reason to believe that they were dancing as they did so.

Our written sources make it their business to record the step sequences and (if we are lucky) the tunes for individual *basses dances*, because it is these features that distinguish one from another. The floor pattern is taken for granted. Apparently, the dancers simply went up and down the room on the same track; as we have seen, when the room was crowded, no other route was possible. This may possibly clarify the function of *mesures*, seeing that they often did not correspond to matching musical phrases: they were simply convenient lengths of dance for a chamber of normal size. We are nowhere told how the dancers turned around at each end of the floor, but *conversion* would seem to be appropriate.

Dances Performed En Suite with the Basse Dance

It was common practice for a slow and solemn dance to be followed by one that was brisker and livelier. The after-dance for the *basse dance* was called *basse dance mineure.* In the fifteenth century, this opened with a sequence in *pas de brabant,* after which the dancers reverted to moving in *basse dance.* In both these sections it was possible for partners to perform solo passages alternately, thereby relaxing the extreme formality of the *basse dance* proper.[18] In Spain, the *baja* or *baixa* was followed by the *alta* (using *seguits trenchats* or "broken doubles") and then the *ioyoso,* in a broadly similar pattern. *Pas de brabant* and *seguits trenchats* are equivalent to the Italian *saltarello.* (They are not described in detail, but presumably went to lively music and probably included skips or hops; nevertheless, in a courtly dance we can be sure that such steps would not have been boisterously rustic in execution.) In the sixteenth century, *basse dance mineure* seems to have been reduced to just the *pas de brabant.* It still belonged to a three-part suite, however, as the *basse dance* proper had now been split into two parts, as already described. By the 1540s the *pas de brabant* had itself been replaced by the more vigorous *tordion,* forerunner of the galliard.

End of the Basse Dance Era

It was in the 1540s that the *basse dance* fell out of use everywhere but Spain. The *basse dance commune* was replaced as a solemn dance by the even simpler *pavane,* whereas the lively but still quite simple *tordion* was succeeded by the more energetic and ever more complex galliard. In Spain the *baja* and *alta* continued in use with little change right into the early years of the seventeenth century.

Table 8.1. The Principal Manuscripts before 1450 Containing Music for Dancing

13th century	Paris, Bibliothèque Nationale, fonds français 844: 8 *estampies royals,* 3 *danses*
mid-14th century	London, British Library, Add. 28850 (Robertsbridge fragment): at least 3 dances
late 14th century	London, British Library, Add. 29987: 8 *istampitte,* 4 *salterelli,* 3 dance-pairs
early 15th century	Faenza, Biblioteca Comunale, 117 (Faenza codex): 3 dances

Table 8.2. Sources for the *Basse Dance* 1445–1545

1   Paris, Bibliothèque Nationale, fonds français 5699, fol. IV: the Nancy dances, c. 1445

2   Paris, Bibliothèque Nationale, fonds français 476, fol. 43v: Italian description of a *bassadança francese*, c. 1475

3   Pedro de Gratia Dei, *La criança y virtuosa dottrina . . .* : description of a *baja*, c. 1489

4   *Sensuit lart et instruction de bien dancer* (pub. Toulouze, c. 1495): short treatise and details of 48 *basses dances* with tunes

5   Cervera, Arxiu Històric Comarcal, "Notacions grafiques de dances": details of 6 *baixas* and 4 *ioyosos*, c. 1496

6   Brussels, Bibliothèque Royale de Belgique, MS 9085: short treatise and details of 58 *basses dances* with tunes, c. 1500?

7   Salisbury, Cathedral Library, copy of J. B. Janua, Catholicon, first flyleaf: details of 26 *basses dances*, c. 1510?

8   New York, Public Library for the Performing Arts, Dance Division, (S) *MGZMB-Res. 72-254, fol. 31r: Italian version of a *bassa franzesse* and of another French dance, c. 1510

9   Florence, Biblioteca Medicea Laurenziana, MS Antinori 13, fol. 28v–29r: Italian version of a Spanish *baja-alta-ioyoso* suite, 1510

10 Turin, Archivio di Stato, Arch. Biscaretti, mazzo 4, no. 14: scroll with details of 54 *basses dances*, 1517

11 Robert Coplande, "The maner of dauncynge of bace daunces. . .": translation of the treatise found in sources 4 and 6, with details of 7 *bace daunces*, 1521

12 Antonius Arena, *Ad suos compagniones studiantes . . .* (1528): comic poem on dancing, with details of 33 *basses dances* (increased to 59 in a second edition)

13 *SEnsuyuent plusieurs Basses dances . . .* (pub. Moderne?, c. 1535?): updated treatise and details of 199 *basses dances* (of which 27 are repeats)

~Notes~

1. Timothy J. McGee, *Medieval Instrumental Dances* (Bloomington: Indiana University Press, 1989).

2. Peggy Dixon, "Reflections on Basse Dance Source Material: A Dancer's Review, Part I," *Historical Dance* 2, no. 5 (1986–87): 22–29; David R. Wilson, "A Further Look at the Nancy Basse Dances," *Historical Dance* 3, no. 3 (1994): 24–28.

3. Victor Scholderer, ed., *L'art et instruction de bien dancer (Michel Toulouze, Paris)* . . . (London: Royal College of Physicians, 1936; reprint, Wakefield, Yorks.: S. R. Publishers Ltd.; New York: Dance Horizons, 1971). Facsimile edition *Dossier Basses-Dances* (Geneva: Minkoff, 1985). For comment on *Toulouze*, see especially James L. Jackman, ed., *Fifteenth Century Basse Dances* (Wellesley: Wellesley College, 1964); Frederick Crane, *Materials for the Study of Fifteenth Century Basse Danse* (New York: Institute of Mediæval Music, 1968); and David R. Wilson, "The Development of French Basse Danse," *Historical Dance* 2, no. 4 (1984–85): 5–12.

4. Facsimile with commentary: *Les basses danses de Marguerite d'Autriche / Das Tanzbüchlein de Margarete von Österreich . . . Facsimile et Commentarium* (Codices Selecti, Phototypice Impressi, vols. LXXXVII & LXXXVII*. Musica Manuscripta*, 5, Graz: 1988). For other comment, see authors cited in note 3.

5. Wilson, "Development of French Basse Danse," p. 10.

6. Crane, *Materials for Study*, pp. 73–75.

7. There are forty-five notes on the stave, but note twenty-seven looks out of place; without it, the second half of the tune would then exactly match the first. Even so, only forty-two full steps are listed. The most convincing way to bring the total up to forty-four so as to match the edited tune (and the total in *Brussels*) is to add the two *pas doubles* printed here between square brackets. Editorial adjustments of this kind are quite often needed in these two documents; but even when highly plausible, they still can never be wholly certain.

8. *Brussels*, f. 2r, "Ytem pour au vray danser vne basse danse deux choses sont requises /. premierement que on sache le nombre des pas dune chascune basse danse / Secondement que on les sache marchier du nombre des pas."

9. Daniel Heartz, "The *basse dance*: its evolution *circa* 1450 to 1550," *Annales musicologiques* 6 (1958–63): 292.

10. See examples in David R. Wilson, "'Corona', a *bassa danza ala fila* by Domenico," *Historical Dance* 4, no. 1 (2004): 23–28.

11. Paul Meyer, "Rôle de chansons à danser du XVIᵉ siècle," *Romania* 23 (1894): 156–60.

12. "Macaronic" Latin is outwardly Latin in form, but with updated vocabulary derived from vernacular languages, in Arena's case principally French and Provençal.

13. For an English translation of the passages relevant to dancing, see John Guthrie and Marino Zorzi, "Rules of dancing: Antonius Arena," *Dance Research* 4, no. 2 (1986): 3–53.

14. François Lesure, "Danses et chansons à danser au debut du XVIᵉ siècle," in *Recueil de travaux offerts à M. Clovis Brunel*, vol. 2 (Paris: Société des Chartes, 1955): 176–84; reprinted in François Lesure, *Musique et musiciens français du XVIᵉ siècle* (Geneva: Minkoff, 1976): 51–59. Facsimile edition *Dossier Basses-Dances* (Geneva: Minkoff, 1985).

15. *Brussels*, nos. 30, 58, 59.

16. Heartz. "The *basse dance*," p. 316, with his note 1.

17. See the Cervera dances (Table 2, no. 5): Crane, *Materials for Study*, nos. 3, 13, 17, 18, 22, 30, 35, 60.

18. See *Toulouze*, nos. 20–21; *Brussels*, nos. 55–57.

Recommended Reading

Crane, Frederick. *Materials for the Study of the Fifteenth Century Basse Danse*. New York: Institute of Mediæval Music, 1968.

Heartz, Daniel. "The *basse dance*: its evolution *circa* 1450 to 1550." *Annales musicologiques* 6 (1958–63): 287–340.

Jackman, James L. *Fifteenth Century Basse Dances*. Wellesley: Wellesley College, 1964.

McGee, Timothy J. *Medieval Instrumental Dances*. Bloomington: Indiana University Press, 1989.

Wilson, David R., and Véronique Daniels. "The Basse Dance Handbook: Text and Context." Unpublished manuscript.

9

Choreographic Structure in Baroque Dance

Ken Pierce

The term "baroque dance" is widely used, albeit with reservations, to refer to the style of ballroom and theatrical dance that developed in late seventeenth-century France and spread, with variation, into England and other countries of Europe and the Americas. The English under the reign of Charles II were quick to learn of the French style and incorporate it into their own approach to dance. German dancing masters in the early eighteenth century bribed French dancing masters to teach them the French style. Italian dancing masters relinquished the prevailing style they had inherited from their forebears. Spaniards accepted French dances as they accepted Bourbon rule, though without relinquishing their native style. Colonial dancing masters advertised that they could teach the latest dances in the French style. The focus of this chapter is the French dance style, in particular the formal structural elements: how steps and figures fit together to make a dance, and how dance and music are related. Though some of what I write may apply to earlier or later periods, I am concerned here mainly with the period of approximately 1680 to 1730.

The categories "ballroom" and "theatrical" dance were often used by baroque dancing masters, and I use these terms as well. But these categories are not entirely distinct: in France, theater dances sometimes found their way into the ballroom, and ballroom scenes were sometimes represented onstage.[1] In England, dances were specially composed for balls held to celebrate a special occasion such as the monarch's birthday; these dances might subsequently be performed onstage, for example during entr'acte entertainments in London theaters. Thus the same dance might fall into one category or the other, depending on where it was danced and under what circumstances.

Information about choreographic structure in baroque dance derives from several sources: verbal descriptions, in treatises and libretti, that describe the steps or sequences of a dance; cast lists that provide clues about numbers and groupings of dancers; illustrations that show dancers or stage scenes including dance; and, especially, symbolic dance notations that give music, steps, and spatial patterns for dances. With the aid of treatises that describe baroque dance steps and style, and with information about the notation systems themselves, we are able to reconstruct notated baroque dances with a fair degree of precision. Musical sources, too, can provide information about dance structure, either explicitly—for example, via annotations about dancers' entrances—or implicitly, through the structure of the music itself. In some baroque dances, the choreographic structure closely reflects the musical structure. In others, the relationship between dance structure and music structure is quite complex: dance phrases may overlap music phrases, and if there are repeated sequences in the dance these may or may not correspond to musical repeats. Even though there remain important questions about the extent to which notated dances reflected what actually occurred onstage or in the ballroom, we are able to draw some conclusions about choreographic structure in baroque dance.

General Characteristics of Baroque Dances

The extant baroque dance notation systems have several elements in common.[2] All three of them show steps or movements of the feet, legs, or body; all three offer a bird's-eye view of the dancing space that shows dancers' orientations and, to some extent at least, paths across the dance space; and all three show music for the dance and how the steps and figures relate to it. These shared features point to important aspects of choreographic structure in notated baroque dances: first, the dance is based on steps or step-like units that are combined in various ways; second, each figure, that is, each section of the dance's floor pattern or path as viewed from above, has a specific spatial orientation and is an important component of choreographic design; and third, steps and figures relate to the music in a fairly well-defined way. To a large extent these characteristics are also shared by dances that were not notated. Theoretical writings of the period make it clear that steps, figures, and music are important components of baroque dance, whether onstage or in the ballroom. In theatrical dances, there is another important component, referred to by the dancing masters Claude-François Menestrier and Jacques Bonnet as "expressions," meaning either imitative or expressive gestures or actions.[3] Later we will consider theatrical dances in which such gestures or actions contribute to choreographic structure, but first let us examine in more detail how these three components—the steps and step sequences, the figures, and the music—relate to choreographic structure.

Steps and Step Sequences

Steps

Baroque dance steps are constructed by combining certain elemental movements such as ordinary walking steps, bending, rising, springing, turning, and so on in various ways, with attention to appropriate style. The simple steps thus constructed can in turn be combined to form compound steps. A *demi-coupé*, for example, involves a bend, a step from one foot to the other, and a rise, while a *pas de bourrée* consists of a *demi-coupé* followed by two walking steps on the balls of the feet, and a *demi-coupé* followed by a *pas de bourrée* can form one type of menuet step. A more complex compound step is a *pas de sissone bâtu derriere en tournant demi tour et retombé devant,* which involves a half turn, a bend on one foot, a spring, a bend on both feet, another spring, and a landing on one foot.[4] One further component of steps formed in this modular way is the direction or directions of the steps through space: many baroque dance steps have variants that travel forward, backward, or sideways, or that change direction mid-step.

We might think that this approach to step construction would lead to an infinite number of steps, or at least to many steps vying with one another for complexity (like the mid-sixteenth- to early seventeenth-century galliard step variants); but in fact we find a relatively small number of steps in common usage. Raoul-Auger Feuillet, in his treatise, *Chorégraphie*, provided tables that he claimed showed most of the steps used in dance.[5] Though it is relatively easy to find notated steps that are not among the approximately 530 steps in Feuillet's tables, the implication is that in Feuillet's day dance-making consisted in artfully combining existing steps in pleasing sequences and floor patterns, rather than in inventing new steps.[6] The evidence is clear that dancing masters thought in terms of steps and used steps as a basis for their choreography.

Typically each step-unit (whether a simple or a compound step) would occupy one measure of music in quicker dances, or one-half measure in slower dances. This points to an important aspect of baroque choreographic structure: the steps and the music move along at more or less the same pace. Though there are some instances of steps continued from one measure into the next, or of much rapid footwork compressed into a single measure, in notated dances we never find a dancer sustaining one step over several measures, or squeezing more than two or three measures' worth of steps into one measure.[7] We should probably keep these limits in mind as we read passages like Pomey's description of a danced sarabande (1671), quoted by Patricia Ranum: "Now and then he would *let a whole rhythmic unit go by*, moving no more than a statue and then, *setting off like an arrow*, he would be at the other end of the room before anyone had time to realize that he had departed."[8] The emphasized text is Ranum's, but it serves our purpose as well. If this unnotated dance at all resembled notated sarabandes, then a "whole rhythmic unit" (*une cadence entiere*) was likely to be no more than a measure, and the distance covered by the arrow-like dancer perhaps only a couple of yards.[9]

Ornamentation, Improvisation, and Dancers' Choices

Several of the elemental movements that make up baroque dance steps can be used as ornaments. For example, extra bends and rises or beats at the ankle can be added to a given step to ornament it. The legs can beat against one another during a jump (as in some Renaissance *caprioles*, or as in modern-day *cabrioles*), or the lower leg can execute a little circle (a *rond de jambe*) before taking a step. Feuillet's step tables show many steps that include such ornaments. Musicians of the period were expected to be adept at ornamenting notated music, but were dancers performing a notated dance expected to vary and ornament their steps in similar fashion? The question is complicated by uncertainties about how notated dances were recorded: whether they reflect precise intentions of the dance masters who made the dances; interpretations of those intentions by performers; or further interpretations by those preparing the notations. Notated dances, especially theatrical dances for male dancers, show plenty of ornaments: *capri-*

oles, entrechats, beaten pirouettes, ronds de jambe, and so on.[10] Because it is not uncommon to find, in the same dance, steps that are ornamented differently from one occurrence to the next (for example, pirouettes ornamented sometimes with two beats, sometimes with four), it seems that notated ornaments, whether originating from the notator, the performer, or the choreographer, were meant to be performed as written; and that the choice of ornaments was not arbitrary, but rather a part of the overall choreographic shape of a dance.

How much choice, therefore, was left to the dancers performing baroque dances? The development of dance notation may have served to limit dancers' choices, to the extent that they sought to execute dances as notated. Notation can certainly impose structure as well as record it, and notations, by regularizing the performance of dances, may have delayed the development of new choreographic approaches. Feuillet, in the preface to *Chorégraphie*, writes that he notated the most beautiful ballroom dances of Guillaume-Louis Pécour, the newest and most in vogue, "because a great number of people don't know them accurately," implying a certain degree of freedom in the ballroom, at least prior to 1700.[11] Dancers were clearly expected to modify their steps on occasion. Rameau writes that certain "lofty Contretemps" (*contre-tems sautez*; the translation is by John Essex) should only be done by those who were young or of medium height; others should moderate their steps, replacing the jumps with gentler rises "because it is not agreeable for tall Persons to jump and skip." And men were cautioned that when dancing a passepied or a figured menuet with a woman they should soften their steps to bring them into accord with their partners.[12] In a generic ballroom courante, the dancers might adjust their steps as they danced, choosing between two steps ("short" and "long") on the basis of where they were in relation to one another and how far they had traveled along the path of the dance. On curves, the dancer on the inside (the man) might do a short step, while his partner continued with long steps, making it easier for the two of them to make the turn as a couple.[13]

The basic ballroom menuet was an improvised form, in which dancers could select from among a small set of "default" menuet steps, or substitute fancier ones. The German dancing master Gottfried Taubert offered detailed descriptions of alternatives, and of ornaments that could be added to steps in the simple ballroom menuet. As Angelika Gerbes writes, "There were no basic rules guiding variations. Taubert states that they depended mainly upon sound technique and the imagination of the dancer."[14] Other dancing masters, including Rameau, Tomlinson, and Dufort, also described steps that dancers could use in place of the basic menuet steps, and the process of substitution they describe might be thought of as a way of ornamenting not steps so much as sequences of steps.

In contredanses or country dances, dancers could choose their steps according to the figure of the dance. Feuillet provided a set of guidelines for preferred steps, and his wording suggests some latitude on the part of the dancers.[15] Such latitude in choosing steps was not to everyone's liking. Pierre Rameau complained of contredanses that "there are a great many without any Design or Taste, the Figure being always the same, without any certain Steps appointed for them." He writes that he wishes that the dancing masters who create contredanses would notate them, so that they might be danced regularly, without confusion.[16]

Dance treatises offer guidelines on use of the arms, but always with the caution that the dancer must exercise taste and good judgment. It seems apparent that there was room for variety in how arms were used, for unlike the steps and positions of the feet and legs, movements of the arms were rarely notated. Arm positions and movements might be considered another sort of ornamentation, though in some instances the movement of the arms serves a practical purpose for the dancer, aiding in the execution of a step.[17] Arms may also serve to express emotion or define a character. In duos or group dances, taking hands can help clarify the choreographic structure; menuets in particular are shaped by moments of taking and letting go of hands, and taking hands can also help dancers execute given steps or figures, as when circling around one another.

Step Sequences

As we have seen, baroque dances generally include a variety of steps and step sequences. A few notated dances, like *la Gavotte du Roi*, have a severely limited step vocabulary, but for the most part only contredanses or generic ballroom dances, like courantes and menuets, offer dancers the option of repeating the same step over and over.[18] The choreographic structure of a dance is determined partly by how steps are combined into longer sequences, as each step contributes to the rhythmic pattern, spatial design, and degree of perceived activity or repose in the dance phrases. The baroque step vocabulary is such that any step can be followed by just about any other, and a dancing master's choice of step at any given moment seems to have been influenced chiefly by the immediate choreographic context, musical rhythm, and affect; the location of the current measure within the musical phrase and the dance phrase; each dancer's facing, direction of travel, and free foot; and how the current step should maintain or alter these positions. A desire to reduce the dance's vocabulary or employ movement themes or motifs does not appear to have greatly influenced the step choice of the dancing master.[19] Especially for more complicated theater dances, repetition seems not to be the norm in baroque dance. Paradoxically, it appears that the more complicated a section of dance is, the less it bears repeating.

la Bourée d'Achille.

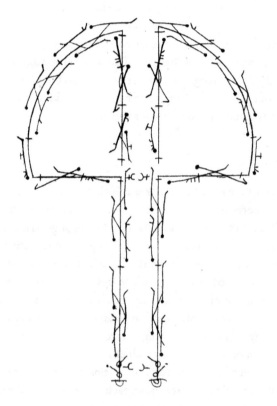

Figure 9.1. First eight bars of Pécour's *la Bourrée d'Achille*, showing the repetition of the first four steps in a mirror-symmetrical floor pattern. Courtesy of the Library of Congress, Washington, D.C.

Anne L. Witherell has identified several two-measure step "formulas" used in Pécour's ballroom dances, and similar formulas can easily be found in other notated ballroom dances.[20] But as Witherell astutely points out, Pécour's interest as a choreographer lies partly in his ability to depart from these step formulas; and Pécour is by no means alone among baroque dance masters in using unpredictability to his choreographic advantage. We also find formulaic sequences in theater dances. Kellom Tomlinson describes some of these, like the *Bouree before and behind, and behind and before, advancing in a whole Turn,* or the *Pirouette introduced by a Coupee.*[21] Many theatrical dances include a *pas de passacaille* followed by a beaten *contretemps* and *chassés* traveling backward, but as with ballroom dances, the art in using these formulaic sequences in theatrical dances lies in maintaining a suitable level of unpredictability.

Even in a dance in which there is no overall pattern of repeated steps or sequences, it is not unusual to find at least some repetition. A single step may be repeated on the other foot to form a larger choreographic unit. Or a longer sequence may be repeated "as is," or on the opposite foot, or with an altered spatial pattern. One familiar example is Pécour's ballroom dance *la Bourrée d'Achille,* which opens with the sequence *pas de bourrée, pas de bourrée, contretemps, pas grave;* most (man's side) or all (woman's side) of this sequence of steps is then repeated on the other foot, along a different path (see Figure 9.1 for the first eight measures of *la Bourrée d'Achille*).[22]

Thus, while there is variety in the sequences of steps in baroque dance, there is also uniformity, in that couples or groups of dancers generally perform the same steps at the same time. (Soloists in the center of a group may perform different steps.) The dancers may be on the same or on opposite feet, and there may be minor differences to allow for changes of direction or to switch a dancer from one foot to the other; but, generally speaking, all dancers in a couple or group dance have the same sequence of steps most of the time.

This general uniformity may help to highlight the occasional asymmetries that occur in baroque dances. It is not unusual to find short passages, typically two or four measures long, of "question and answer" exchanges, in which one dancer does a step or two, then waits while the other replies with the same step or steps. Sometimes this sequence is then repeated on the other foot, as in Pécour's ballroom dance, *les Contrefaiseurs.*[23] A related choreographic device might be called a "double question and answer": the dancers simultaneously do different steps, typically for a couple of measures, and then switch, each doing what the other has just done. In the baroque dance repertoire, the most familiar example of "question and answer" and "double question and answer" is in Pécour's ballroom dance *l'Aimable Vainqueur* (see Figure 9.2).[24]

	Question and answer		Double question and answer	
Woman:	contretemps, coupé ouvert	(rest)	2 pirouttes	balancé
Man:	(rest)	contretemps, coupé ouvert	balancé	2 pirouttes

Figure 9.2. "Question and answer," and "double question and answer," in measures 9–16 of *l'Aimable Vainqueur*, second strain, first time.

Note the difference between the choreographic use of short "question and answer" passages in baroque dance and the ballroom dances of the late Renaissance such as galliards or canaries, in which each dancer has extended solo passages, or the dances by Cesare Negri for two couples, in which first the women, then the men, wait while the others dance for an entire musical phrase, or even for an entire section. In contrast to Renaissance dances where the man and the woman may sometimes perform very different variations from one another, in baroque "question and answer" passages each dancer generally does the same steps, though in a different order. Evidently, baroque couple dances are concerned less with individual display and more with presenting moments of pleasing variety within a unified structure.

Even apart from the momentary asymmetries involved in changing from one foot to the other, we do find moments in some baroque dances in which not all the dancers perform the same steps for the entire dance. For example, we may find a "partial question and answer" in which one dancer waits while the other dancer does a step, then the first dancer does that step while the second dancer, rather than waiting, does another step entirely.[25] Or both dancers may move at the same time, but perform different steps for a measure or more, as for example in Anthony l'Abbé's choreography to the chaconne from *Galathée*, in which at one point the woman does a *tour en l'air* while the man does an *entrechat-six*.[26] Another familiar device in baroque dance is for one dancer to turn in place while another circles around him or her. Sometimes, as in a double "question and answer," the passage is repeated with the roles reversed (as in the passacaille from *Persée*); in other cases, the passage happens only once.[27] From the treatises of Menestrier and Bonnet we learn that in theatrical dances different actions might happen simultaneously, provided they are related to one another. Some dancers might deliver blows with their swords, while others parry with their shields, or a magician might summon shades by circling his wand, while the shades take on different shapes.[28]

Space and Figures

All baroque dances are made to be watched, and to be watched especially from a single direction, the front of the ballroom or stage, or even from a single viewpoint, that of the highest-ranking person in attendance. Tomlinson makes it clear that viewers mattered even for country dances: "The nice Observation of this [rule] presents to the *Beholders* an agreeable Prospect of the whole Company in Motion at once, instead of the Confusion that happens when this is neglected."[29] While theatrical dances were designed for proscenium theaters in which the centerline of the stage leads through the royal box or its equivalent, ballroom dances were designed for spaces in which the highest-ranking person present is seated front and center, along the centerline of the dance.[30] Ballroom dances typically begin and end with bows toward this "presence," and most theatrical dances also begin and end with the dancers facing downstage.[31] Thus the arrangement of the dancers in relation to the centerline of the dance is an important component of choreographic structure.

Patterns and figures in baroque dance are usually symmetrical. There are three possible types of symmetry in a plane: symmetry by translation; symmetry by reflection, or mirror symmetry; and symmetry by rotation, or axial symmetry (see Figure 9.1 for an example of mirror symmetry, Figure 9.3 for an example of translational symmetry, and Figure 9.4 for an example of axial symmetry).[32] In couple dances, whether for the ballroom or the theater, mirror and axial symmetry predominate, with only occasional instances of translational symmetry. Relative proportions of mirror and axial symmetry vary; some couple dances are entirely or almost entirely mirror-symmetrical; others are largely axial-symmetrical. Among couple dances, only the generic courante involves instead a basic figure in which the dancers progress around the dancing space, as in a Renaissance dance, although generic branles may have employed such a floor pattern as well. By contrast, in group dances we find multiple symmetries, for example, mirror symmetry across the centerline, with axial or translational symmetry within the groups on either side of center; or an axial-symmetrical arrangement of couples, with the couples in translational symmetry.[33] Most baroque dances begin and end in mirror symmetry, but among Favier's dances for *le Mariage de la Grosse Cathos*, there are three that include somewhat asymmetrical figures to start or end the dance. The danced section of the *Marche* begins with four couples in a column to the left of centerstage; they travel clockwise into a mirror-symmetrical formation. In the *Passepied*, the nine dancers begin in an arc upstage and travel clockwise and then loop back counterclockwise before arriving in mirror symmetry. At the end of the *Rigaudon*

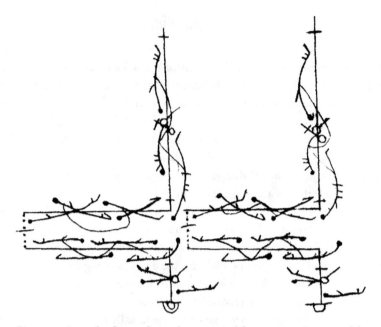

Figure 9.3. Example of a translational symmetrical floor pattern. Courtesy of the Library of Congress, Washington D.C.

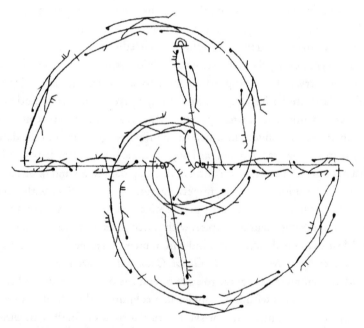

Figure 9.4. Example of an axial symmetrical floor pattern. Courtesy of the Library of Congress, Washington D.C.

Figure 9.5. The opening of Le Roussau's menuet *The Montaigü*. Edinburgh University Library, Special Collections, MS La.III.673, p. 1. By permission of Edinburgh University Library.

the five dancers follow one another along a snakelike path centerstage, ending in a symmetrical arc.[34]

Dancers traveling along mirror-symmetrical or axial-symmetrical paths will perforce be arranged symmetrically, but it is worth noting that symmetry is important both in the arrangement of dancers and in the paths along which they travel. Typically, the dancers will travel along symmetrical paths as they move from one symmetrical arrangement to another. Menestrier and Bonnet give examples of baroque dance patterns and figures: the dancers can be facing forward, back to back, in a circle, square, or cross, or X; moving in straight or curved lines, chasing or fleeing one another, or interweaving; in fact, they say, there can be as many different dance figures as there are geometric figures.[35] As an approximation, we may say that dancers moving in mirror symmetry will be on opposite feet, and those moving in axial or translational symmetry will be on the same foot. Not only the paths, but also the steps themselves, will be symmetric. Generally this is true, but we do find cases of dancers on opposite feet but moving in axial symmetry, as, for example, in *la Mariée, la Bourgogne* (sarabande), and the gigue from *Philomèle*. There are also situations, especially in figured menuets or passepieds, in which the dancers are on the same foot but in mirror-symmetrical paths, such as the opening of Pécour's *le Passepied*, or, more elaborately, in the menuet sections of F. Le Rousseau's *The Montaigü*, a couple dance in which each dancer's path traces the letters of the title, M-O-N-T-A-I-G-V (with "v" being equivalent to "u"; see Figure 9.5).[36]

Part of the choreographic interest in baroque dances lies in the choice of different floor patterns and types of symmetry for the dance, and the manner in which these succeed one another. The variety of figures, and the frequency and rhythm of changes from one figure to another, help to define the character of the dance. So do the relative frequencies of different types of symmetry, and the occurrence of "question and answer" passages or other moments that interrupt the symmetrical structure of the dance. Switches between mirror and axial symmetry help to vary the shape of the dance and keep the viewer engaged. Though it is often irrelevant to talk about narrative or dramatic meaning in baroque dance, it seems reasonable to say that axial-symmetrical sections can help convey a sense of intimacy between two dancers, whereas mirror-symmetrical sections are better suited to outward-directed, presentational passages.

In baroque dance solos, we sometimes find the sort of sequential symmetry that is so common in the Renaissance dances of Fabritio Caroso or Negri, in which a figure is performed first to one side and then to the other on the opposite foot. Feuillet provides a set of variations to *les Folies d'Espagne* that take this approach; other examples are a chaconne to music from *l'Europe Galante* that is composed entirely of sequentially symmetric figures, and a gigue by Pécour in which the first half of the dance consists of symmetrically repeated figures.[37] However, baroque solos do not necessarily adhere to any symmetrical structures of this type.

Sometimes it is difficult to determine how the figure of a notated solo is intended to relate to the centerline of the space: Beauchamps-Feuillet notation does not show a dancer's absolute position, so it is impossible to say with certainty whether a given step should be performed on the centerline or not.[38] Group dances for an odd number of dancers, like Favier's *Rigaudon*, pose an extra challenge when it comes to symmetry. For mirror-symmetrical figures, one dancer must remain on the centerline, either waiting while others dance, as in Feuillet's *Balet* for nine dancers, and during the many "echo" sections of Groscourt's *An Ecchoe;* or performing different steps, as in much of Favier's *Rigaudon;* or dropping out of the dance altogether, as in Favier's *Passepied.*[39]

Contredanses, which are group dances for an even number of couples, include a variety of short symmetrical figures, with choice of steps left partly to the dancers. The choreographic structure of a contredanse involves not only these sequences of figures, called couplets, but also the number of couplets, which may be one, two, or occasionally three, and the manner in which the dance progresses: that is, the way in which the sequence of figures is repeated first by one couple and then by others.[40] The dancers also have some choice regarding the figures of the menuet. As far as spatial patterns are concerned, the menuet is a sort of "structured improvisation": the dancers perform specified figures—of which all but the start of the first and the close of the last are axial-symmetrical—in a certain order, but they may vary the number of steps used to complete each figure, and they may repeat the basic S or Z figure an unspecified number of times, provided they remain within the bounds of good taste. Generic courantes likewise offer the dancers a choice of figures, for example oval, rectangular, or octagonal. A generic courante may be followed immediately by a "figured" courante, one with symmetrical steps and patterns as for other ballroom dances.[41]

Music

Like many styles of dance, baroque dance is performed to music, and music and dance share structural elements such as tempo, meter, and the number of measures in each strain or section of the dance. The rhythm of dance steps relates to the rhythm of the music, and steps must be timed to coincide with particular measures or beats. Though we might expect that the music for a given dance would dictate not only tempo and meter, but also the steps to be used, this is not generally the case: with the exception of menuet and courante steps, which are specific to those dance types, baroque dance steps can be adjusted to any musical type. Furthermore, sections of dance music of the same type or of different types—as, for example, two rigaudons or a bourrée and a menuet—may be combined to provide music for a single, multipartite, choreography.[42] Each section may occur only once, as in *la Bourgogne* (courante, bourrée, sarabande, passepied), or one or more sections may be repeated, as in *la Silvie* (unnamed triple meter, passepied, bourrée, passepied, bourrée).[43]

Apart from generic dances, each baroque dance, whether for ballroom or theater, is set to a specific piece of music. A baroque dance notation almost always provides the melody of the music that is to accompany the dance, with each page or section of dance notation showing the corresponding music. The choreography establishes the repeat scheme of the music, and the number of times the music is to be played. This will generally be only once or twice, as notated baroque couple dances do not require multiple repetitions of the music such as are indicated for many Renaissance dances. The exception is the contredanses, which may be played many times through depending on the number of couplets in the dance and the number of couples dancing. Generic ballroom dances— courantes and menuets—can be danced to any music of the appropriate type.[44] Thus the relation of dance to music in menuets is also improvisatory in nature: a generic menuet can be danced to any menuet tune, no matter what the musical form or the lengths of strains or phrases.[45] The only essentials are to perform the steps in time to the music, and to execute the figures without becoming flustered. In generic courantes, likewise, the dance phrasing seems to have been only loosely related to phrasing in the music.[46]

Repeat schemes in baroque dance music include binary form (AABB), rondeau form (such as ABACA or AABACAA), and sequential forms like the chaconne or the forlane, which typically consist of a series of repeated phrases of two bars (forlanes) or four bars (chaconnes and passacailles). In one dance type, *les Folies d'Espagne*, the music consists of only a single section that is repeated several times, as in the *pavaniglia* or *passo e mezzo* of the early seventeenth century.[47] A given section may consist of two almost identical, or parallel, halves, or it might include an echo of one or more measures. As noted above, it is not uncommon for music of any of these types to be played through more than once for a given dance.[48] The repeat scheme of a given piece of dance music is not hard and fast, but will depend on the structure of a particular choreography. For example, there are four extant choreographies to the same *entrée espagnole* (sarabande) from *le Bourgeois Gentilhomme*. For two of them, the music is played twice through; for the other two, it is played only once.[49] Other examples are the three extant choreographies for the sarabande from *Issé*, two of which have the repeat scheme AABB, while the third is in two sections, with repeat schemes AB and ABB.[50]

The choreographic structure of a baroque dance may or may not reflect the repeats found in the music. As was mentioned above, there are no hard and fast rules about repeated steps or step sequences in baroque dance. Many notated dances are through-composed, lacking any structural correspondence between step sequences and musical repeats. Yet there are also dances in which repeated step sequences do correspond to musical repeats, at least some of the time.[51] The sequence may be repeated unaltered, as in the opening of Pécour's *le Passepied*, in which the dancers perform the same step sequence twice in a row, corresponding to the repeated first strain of the music. Or the dancer or dancers may repeat a sequence on the opposite foot, as in the first half of Pécour's gigue for a woman, danced by Mlle. Subligny in England. A sequence of steps may be repeated, but with modified spatial pattern, as in the opening of Pécour's *la Bourrée d'Achille*[52] (see Figure 9.1). It is unusual to find a notated dance in which step sequences are fully repeated to correspond to a full repeat of the music. One dance with such a full repeat scheme is Feuillet's couple dance *la Matelotte*. The music is AABAAB, with the second strain having parallel halves. Feuillet has constructed the entire dance using only two eight-bar step sequences, one for the first strain, the other for each half of the second. He maintains choreographic interest by varying the spatial patterns and type of symmetry.[53] Another dance in which steps repeat from one playing of the music to the next is Pécour's *les Contrefaiseurs*.[54] The steps used for the second playing replicate those of the first except for the final eight measures, in which the dancers circle back to their starting places for concluding bows.

Music in rondeau form offers the possibility of repeating a step sequence at each occurrence of the musical refrain. We find an example of this approach in Pécour's *la Contredance*.[55] The music is a rondeau, played twice: ABACAAB-ACA. The dance reflects this structure, but with a twist: rather than having just one step sequence to correspond to the refrain, there are two different step sequences, one for each time through the music.[56] Among other dances that include choreographic refrains are Balon's dances *la Brissac*, *la Melanie*, and *la Transilvanie*, and Feuillet's *la Médicis*.[57]

Sequential-form music (chaconnes, passacailles, forlanes) often includes sections made of parallel halves. The dance may include repeated step sequences to match. A good example of this sort of structure is Feuillet's chaconne to music from *l'Europe Galante*, which as it happens is also a rondeau (ABACA).[58] The sixteen-bar refrain consists of two eight-bar sections, each consisting of a repeated four-bar phrase. Feuillet's dance reflects this structure: each refrain accompanies two sets of repeated (mirrored) four-bar step sequences. Interestingly, Feuillet maintains the pattern of repeated step sequences even during the couplets, though musically these do not have internal repeats: the first couplet accompanies a step sequence of eight bars and its repeat, and the second accompanies two sets of four bars and their repeats. We also find this sort of four-bar repeated step sequence, though not as consistently, in three extant choreographies to the chaconne from *Phaëton*. In Pécour's choreography for a woman there are some sections of four-bar repeated step sequences (as well as many repeated two-bar sequences);[59] in his choreography for a man about a third of the dance is built of four-bar repeated sequences.[60] The third, anonymous, choreography consists chiefly of four-bar repeated sequences.[61] Repeated steps or step sequences are relatively common in forlanes, but these do not necessarily reflect the repeats in the music. Sets of variations on *la Follia*, or *les Folies d'Espagne*, offer another familiar category of dance music that consists of a series of parallel-structured sections. Feuillet's six solo *Follia* variations for a woman reflect this structure, employing opposite-foot repeats.[62]

Imitative Dances

So far we have chiefly considered notated dances, or dances of the sort that could have been notated (with allowances for improvisation), that is, dances with steps and figures in a formal, abstract structure which has a clear relation to the music. There were, however, other types of baroque dance that were not notated, perhaps because notating them would have been too difficult, or because there was no market for notations of such dances. Among these non-notated dance types were the "imitative" dances described by the dance theorist, the abbé Jean-Baptiste Dubos, who wrote of two broad categories of baroque dance for the theater, "ordinary" and "imitative."[63] While "ordinary" dances made use of formal structural elements such as those already discussed, "imitative" dances included actions that helped define the dancer's character, and were similar to the "expressions"—imitative or expressive gestures—as described by Menestrier and Bonnet. Imitative dance might include typical movements or gestures of blacksmiths, boatmen, persons who have fallen asleep, drunks, fighters, and so on.[64] In some imitative dances, different gestures might happen simultaneously; for example, some dancers could wield swords or clubs while others parry their blows with shields.[65] Examples of imitative movements, drawn from operas by Lully, might include shivering with cold, mourning at a funeral, striking an anvil to make weapons, fighting, and so on. Lambranzi provides illustrations of many imitative dances. Figure 9.6 depicts one such dance in which two blacksmiths forge a nail in time to the music, then one dances while the other continues to forge, and finally both dance.[66]

　　As Edith Lalonger points out, dance gestures would generally be used to express a mood or sentiment rather than a precise dramatic action. She writes, "Adding definite gestures in a dance to express specific actions would be more

Figure 9.6. Blacksmith's Dance, Lambranzi, *Neue und Curieuse Theatrialische Tantz-Schul* Book II, Plate 25. Courtesy of the Library of Congress, Washington D.C., and Harvard University.

Figure 9.7. Dance of the Peasant Boys, Lambranzi, *Neue und Curieuse Theatrialische Tantz-Schul* Book I, Plate 12. Courtesy of the Library of Congress, Washington D.C., and Harvard University.

typical of the later eighteenth century."[67] Even imitative movements would most likely be used to help define the dancers' characters or to place them clearly in a particular dramatic situation, rather than to tell a story. John Weaver, in his scenario for *The Loves of Mars and Venus*, provides descriptions of some of the gestures that he and Hester Santlow used to convey emotion through dance. He refers to the final dance of the entertainment as "Pantomimic," and describes it this way: "[Venus and Vulcan] perform a *Dance* together, in which *Vulcan* expresses his *Admiration; Jealousie; Anger;* and *Despite;* And *Venus* shews *Neglect; Coquetry; Contempt;* and *Disdain*."[68] Clearly there is no elaborate narrative here, but rather a dance that explores various aspects of the confrontation between Vulcan and the adulterous Venus. Here is an example of another danced confrontation from Lambranzi, which is illustrated in Figure 9.7: "Two peasant boys begin to dance. When the air has been played once, two peasant men enter and laugh at them and blow through their noses at the same time. Since the boys do likewise the men jog them with their knees and elbows. The boys retaliate in the same manner, and so the men try to prevent their dancing. At last they become reconciled, all dance together and at the end run off with merry gestures."[69]

Apparently even imitative dances would often follow conventions of music, steps, and space seen in ordinary dances. Notated dances sometimes include imitative movements or gestures that help define the character of the dance: peasant dances show hands on hips; harlequin dances show turns of the head from side to side, as well as harlequinesque arm gestures; a dance for two bacchantes shows them striking tambourines; and Favier's dance for two drunken men includes a near-collision between the two dancers. Lambranzi's examples suggest that imitative dances were performed in time to the music, and sometimes included steps and symmetrical figures as well.[70]

Larger Structures

Whether in the ballroom or theater, a baroque dance would almost certainly have been part of a larger structure, whether at a formal ball, a private entertainment, a fairground performance, or a full-length opera. Let us look at how each individual dance might fit into the structure of a larger entertainment or event in the ballroom and in the theater.

In the ballroom, dances were performed one after another, and each dance was only a small part of the evening's dancing. Pierre Rameau described the sequence of dances at a formal ball: it would begin with branles done by the group, with each couple leading in turn; then would follow the gavotte, also danced with each couple leading in turn; then would follow couple dances, of which it appears that the majority would be courantes, menuets, or passepieds.[71] Contredanses would likely follow the couple dances. Little is known as yet about how often notated dances ("figured" dances) were danced at balls. It is conceivable that the same figured dance, perhaps one of the newest or most popular, would be danced more than once at the same ball by different couples. A ball might also include one or more interludes of theatrical dancing and music performed by courtiers or professionals. Harris-Warrick has calculated that one formal ball, at which forty couples danced, would have lasted over five hours.[72]

In the theater dances were often placed within the sequence of an extended divertissement which might include other dances along with vocal solos, duos, and choruses. Dance music was often repeated within divertissements, either directly after the initial playing; in sequence with one or more other dances; alternating with sung verses in strophic fashion; or as part of a "layer cake" or palindromic structure formed of several different pieces of vocal and dance music.[73] Thus we may find that the music for a dance that begins a divertissement is repeated in the middle or at the end of the divertissement. The choreography for the first dance would almost certainly not be repeated, however; each separate occurrence of a piece of dance music would be accompanied by different choreography, possibly for numbers or groupings of dancers different from the first time it was played.

Conclusion

We have seen how steps, figures, and music help to define and shape choreographic structure in baroque dance, and how even imitative dances sometimes share these elements. Particularly important to the character of a dance is the relationship between steps and music. Apart from generic dances, every baroque dance is set to a specific piece of music; the tempo and meter of the music determine the number of step-units per measure of dance, and the affect of the music by and large determines the affect of the dance. Each baroque dance is short: a brisk binary dance such as a bourrée or rigaudon may last less than a minute, and even the longer dances like passacailles last no more than three or four minutes.

Symmetrical spatial structures are maintained throughout most of the dance. In a couple or group dance, all dancers will generally do the same steps at the same time. Especially in dances for one or more mixed couples, the men and women will generally perform the same steps as one another. Choreographic interest may be maintained by varying the type of symmetry (generally between mirror and axial), by changing the dancers' orientations, by adjusting the frequency and rhythm of these changes of facing and symmetry, and by occasionally introducing "question and answer" passages or brief asymmetries.

All this suggests that the narrative or dramatic content of an "ordinary" baroque dance, even a lengthy passacaille, will be minimal. The story told by the dance is essentially the story told by the music: a story of a single idea or a series of related ideas, that may be restated, embellished, or looked at from various directions, but that remains essentially unitary. Multipartite choreographies may offer musical contrast, and thus the opportunity for contrasting sections within a single dance; but each section is likely to be more or less "steady-state." Even an imitative dance is likely to offer no more than a brief dramatic scenario or sketch.

ℕotes

1. Rebecca Harris-Warrick offers a very clear description of ballroom dancing at court, and of the interconnections between ballroom and theatrical dancing. See "Ballroom Dancing at the Court of Louis XIV," *Early Music* 14, no. 1 (1986): 40–49, especially pp. 47–48.

2. The systems of Lorin, Favier, and Beauchamps had all been developed by the 1680s. See chapter 1 in this volume and Ken Pierce, "Dance Notation Systems in Late 17th-Century France," *Early Music* 26, no. 2 (1998): 286–99.

3. Claude-François Menestrier, *Des ballets anciens et modernes selon les règles du théâtre* (Paris: Guignard, 1682), p. 158; Jacques Bonnet, *Histoire generale de la danse* (Paris: d'Houry, 1724), p. 61.

4. Raoul-Auger Feuillet, *Chorégraphie* (Paris, 1700), p. 81. Kellom Tomlinson provided names for some of the more common compound steps found in theatrical dance, such as the *Passacaille Step* or the *Close beating before and falling behind in the third Position, upright Spring changing to the same before, and Coupee to a Measure* (Tomlinson, *The Art of Dancing* [London, 1735], pp. 83 and 88).

5. Feuillet, *Chorégraphie*, p. 47.

6. For more on Feuillet's step tables, see Ken Pierce, "Dance Vocabulary in the Early 18th Century As Seen Through Feuillet's Step Tables," in *Proceedings of 20th Annual Conference of the Society of Dance History Scholars* (Riverside: SDHS, 1997), pp. 227–36. It is to the credit of their inventors that all three notation systems—Lorin, Favier, and Beauchamps-Feuillet—were robust enough to enable the notation of unusual steps (though admittedly Lorin's system was limited in this respect).

7. For information about the source for this dance and most of the other dances referred to in this chapter, see Meredith Ellis Little and Carol G. Marsh, *La Danse Noble:*

An Inventory of Dances and Sources (Williamstown: Broude Brothers, 1992) hereafter cited as LMC. An example of a step continued from one measure to the next is the slow *rond de jambe* (followed by a spring) in measures five and six of the last figure of Pécour's 1704 duo to music from *Persée* (LMC 2680). An example of rapid footwork within a measure is three *entrechats-six* in measure ten of l'Abbé's *Chacone of Amadis* (LMC 1840).

8. "Quelquefois il lassoit passer une cadence entiere sans se mouvoir, non plus qu'une statuë; & puis partant comme un trait, on le voyoit à l'autre bout de la sale, avant que l'on eust le loisir de s'appercevoir qu'il estoit parti" (Patricia Ranum, "Audible Rhetoric and Mute Rhetoric: The 17th-Century French Sarabande," *Early Music* 14, no. 1 [1986], pp. 22–39).

9. For a discussion of a notated sarabande, see Ken Pierce, "Uncommon Steps and Notation in the *Sarabande de Mr. de Beauchamp*," *Proceedings of 26th Annual Conference of the Society of Dance History Scholars* (n.p.: SDHS, 2003), pp. 91–98. Lambranzi describes a statue dance, an "imitative" dance (see discussion below), in which the dancers do remain motionless for long stretches. See Gregorio Lambranzi, *Neue und Curieuse Theatrialische Tantz-Schul* (Nuremberg: Wolrab, 1716), book II, plates 13–17.

10. A mid-century manuscript (the "Kinski ms.," LMC ms-110) includes a highly ornamented version of a well-known ballroom dance of the eighteenth century, *l'Aimable Vainqueur*, with the notation showing extra beats or *ronds de jambe* added to the familiar steps. See Deda Cristina Colonna, "Variation and Persistence in the Notation of the Loure 'Aimable Vainqueur,'" in *Proceedings of 21st Annual Conference of the Society of Dance History Scholars* (Riverside: SDHS, 1998), pp. 285–94, especially p. 290.

11. Feuillet, *Chorégraphie*, preface. A popular dance by the English dancing master Mr. Isaac, his *Rigaudon* (LMC 7280 and 7420), was published in two rather different notated versions, suggesting that there may have been some variability in the way it was danced.

12. J[ohn] Essex, *The Dancing Master* (London, 1728), p. 61; Pierre Rameau, *Le Maître a Danser* (Paris, 1725), p. 107.

13. Angelika Renate Gerbes, "Gottfried Taubert on Social and Theatrical Dance of the Early Eighteenth Century," Ph.D. diss., Ohio State University, 1972, pp. 187–88.

14. Ibid., p. 200. See below for further discussion on improvisation in menuets.

15. Raoul-Auger Feuillet, *Recueil de Contredances* (Paris, 1706), preface. Feuillet's approach to notating contredanses was different from Lorin's extremely prescriptive approach.

16. Essex, *The Dancing Master*, pp. 61–62; Rameau, *Le Maître*, p. 109.

17. For the use of arms as ornaments, see Francine Lancelot, "Les ornements dans la danse baroque," in *Les Gouts Réunis . . . Actes du 1er Colloque International sur la danse ancienne* (Besançon, 1982), pp. 72–78. Rameau, in *Le Maître*, describes using the arm to help in pirouettes (p. 245); Taubert describes how arms can help in *entrechats* or *caprioles* (Gerbes, "Taubert," p. 212).

18. *La Gavotte du Roi*: LMC 4920. Carol Marsh presents evidence that the rigaudon was also a generic baroque dance: see Carol G. Marsh, "French Court Dance in England, 1706–1740: A Study of the Sources," Ph.D. diss., City University of New York, 1985, pp. 231–34. Unfortunately, no descriptions of generic rigaudon choreographies have thus far been found, but as Marsh points out, a generic rigaudon must certainly have involved steps other than the *pas de rigaudon*.

19. Some scholars have written about choreographic structures corresponding to the classical rhetorical divisions of oratory. See Judith L. Schwartz, "The Passacaille in Lully's

Armide: Phrase Structure in the Choreography and the Music," *Early Music* 26, no. 2 (1998): 300–320; and Kimiko Okamoto, "Choreographic Syntax Denoting Rhetorical Structure: Analysis of French Rigaudons for a Couple," in *Structures and Metaphors in Baroque Dance: Proceedings of the Conference at the University of Surrey Roehampton, 31 March 2001* (Roehampton: Centre for Dance Research, University of Surrey, 2001), pp. 40–51.

20. Anne L. Witherell, *Louis Pécour's Recueil de dances* (Ann Arbor: UMI Research Press, 1983), p. 153.

21. Tomlinson, *The Art of Dancing*, pp. 98, 96.

22. See below for further discussion on choreographic repeats in relation to the music.

23. LMC 2200.

24. LMC 1180; another example of "double question-and-answer" is found in *la Forlana* (LMC 4800), measures 5–8 of the first figure.

25. See, for example, the last figure of LMC 4340, a musette to music from *Sémélé*.

26. LMC 1860.

27. The passacaille from *Persée* is LMC 6500. Other examples include *La Forlana* (LMC 4800), *la Médicis* (LMC 5460), *la Corsini* (LMC 2260), a menuet to music from *Omphale* (LMC 4400), a musette to music from *Callirhoé* (LMC 6160), and a duple-meter dance to music from *Sémélé* (LMC 4080).

28. Menestrier, *Des ballets anciens et modernes*, p. 167, and Bonnet, *Histoire*, p. 67.

29. Tomlinson, *The Art of Dancing*, p. 157. See also p. 159: "If a fine Picture, beautiful Fields, crystal Streams, green Trees, and imbroider'd Meadows in Landscape or Nature itself will afford such delightful Prospects, how much more must so many well shap'd *Gentlemen* and *Ladies*, richly dress'd, in the exact Performance of this Exercise [i.e., dancing], please the *Beholders*, who [the ladies and gentlemen] entertain them [the beholders] with such a Variety of Living Prospects." The exquisite illustrations of André Lorin's 1688 manuscript may also hint at the viewer's importance for contredanses.

30. Other onlookers had imperfect views. See Harris-Warrick, "Ballroom Dancing," pp. 43–45.

31. Exceptions include a solo peasant dance by Pécour (LMC 3060), a canary by Kellom Tomlinson (in *A Work Book by Kellom Tomlinson*, ed. Jennifer Shennan [Stuyvesant, N.Y.: Pendragon Press, 1992], pp. 88–91; there is no LMC number for this dance), and Feuillet's *Balet* for nine dancers (LMC 1320).

32. Feuillet writes of two sorts of figure in baroque dance, "regular" and "irregular" (*Chorégraphie*, p. 92). From his examples regular figures appear to be those that are mirror-symmetrical, while irregular figures those that are symmetrical by translation. It is not entirely clear whether he considers axial-symmetrical figures to be regular or irregular. For a discussion of symmetry, see Jennifer Thorp and Ken Pierce, "Taste and Ingenuity: Three English Chaconnes of the Early Eighteenth Century," *Historical Dance* 3, no. 3 (1994): 3–16.

33. See, for example, Feuillet's *Balet* for nine dancers (LMC 1320) and Pécour's rigaudon for four dancers (LMC 7300).

34. See Rebecca Harris-Warrick and Carol G. Marsh, *Musical Theatre at the Court of Louis XIV: Le Mariage de la Grosse Cathos* (Cambridge: Cambridge University Press, 1994), pp. 123–32, 153–70.

35. Bonnet, *Histoire*, pp. 61–62, and Menestrier, *Des ballets anciens et modernes*, p. 158. Menestrier (pp. 178–95) also provides illustrations of symmetrical figures from a ballet that took place in 1667.

36. LMC 5360, 1560, 4420, 6620, 6080. *The Montaigü* (LMC 6080) also includes a "double question and answer" (in the letter N). For more on *The Montaigü*, see Jennifer Thorp, "Spelling It Out: Le Roussau's *The Montaigue, 1720,*" in *On Common Ground 6: The Minuet in Time and Space: Proceedings of the 6th DHDS Conference, March 2007,* ed. David Parsons (Stock, Essex: Dolmetsch Historical Dance Society, 2007). One of the three choreographies composed by the Italian Gaetano Grossatesta in 1726 is a passepied in which the dancers are on opposite feet during a mirror-symmetrical figure. (Museo Civico, Raccolta Correr di Venezia, Archivio Morosini Grimani no. 245, MS 157. See p. 18 of the facsimile of the manuscript edited by Gloria Giordano, *Balletti: In occasione delle felicissime Nozze di sua Eccellenza La Signora Loredana Duodo con Sua Eccellenza il Signor Antonio Grimani Composti da Gaetano Grossatesta Maestro di Ballo in Venezia,* [Lucca: Libreria musicale italiana, 2005].)

37. LMC 4740, 1900, 5020. See Ken Pierce, "Repeated Step-sequences in Early Eighteenth Century Choreographies," in *Structures and Metaphors in Baroque Dance: Proceedings of the Conference at the University of Surrey Roehampton, 31 March 2001,* pp. 52–59 (Roehampton: Centre for Dance Research, University of Surrey, 2001), and "Choreographic Structure in Dances by Feuillet," *Proceedings of 25th Annual Conference of the Society of Dance History Scholars* (n.p.: SDHS, 2002), pp. 96–106. We occasionally find such sequential symmetry in couple dances as well, for example in the opening of the passepied section of *la Bourgogne,* where, however, the dancers remain on the same foot for the repeat of the figure.

38. Favier notation is clearer in this respect, but there is only one pertinent example, the central figure in the *Rigaudon* (see Harris-Warrick and Marsh, *Musical Theatre,* pp. 275–80). Lorin notation would likely be even less helpful than Beauchamps-Feuillet notation. (There are no Lorin-notated solos.)

39. Harris-Warrick and Marsh, *Musical Theatre,* pp. 275–80 (rigaudon) and 281–90 (passepied); LMC 1320 (*Balet*), 2560 (*Ecchoe*).

40. There are two principal ways in which contredanses may progress. For details, see Feuillet, *Recueil de Contredanses,* preface, or John Essex, *For the Further Improvement of Dancing* (London, 1710), pp. 21–23.

41. See Gerbes, "Taubert," pp. 180–83.

42. An index of multipartite choreographies may be found in Little and Marsh, *La Danse Noble,* pp. 163–64.

43. LMC 1560, 8060.

44. Presumably so could generic rigaudons (see Marsh, "French court dance," pp. 231–34). It is possible that branles were also danced to generic music, but little is known about branles in the late seventeenth-century ballroom.

45. "[I]n Effect it [the minuet] is no more than a voluntary or extemporary Piece of Performance, as has already been hinted, in Regard there is no limited Rule, as to its Length or Shortness, or the Relation to the Time of the Tune, since it may begin upon any that offers, as well within a Strain as upon the first Note or commencing thereof. It is the very same with Respect to its ending, for it matters not whether it breaks off upon the End of the first Strain of the Tune, the second, or in the Middle of either of them, provided it be in Time to the *Music*" (Tomlinson, *The Art of Dancing,* p. 137).

46. Dancers had the option of repeating a basic step sequence from four to six times, thus taking a variable number of measures to complete the basic figure (Gerbes, "Taubert," p. 181).

47. LMC 4720, 4740, 4760, 4780.

48. For more on repeated dance music see Rebecca Harris-Warrick, "Contexts for Choreographies: Notated Dances Set to the Music of Jean-Baptiste Lully," in *Jean-Baptiste*

Lully: actes du colloque, Saint Germain-en-laye and Heidelberg, 1987, ed. Jérôme de la Gorce and Herbert Schneider (Heidelberg: Laaber, 1990), pp. 433–55, and Jean-Noël Laurenti, "Les structures de distribution dans les danses de théâtre à travers les recueils de Feuillet 1704 et Gaudrau," in *Tanz und Bewegung in der Barocken Oper*, ed. Sibylle Dahms and Stephanie Schroedter (Innsbruck: StudienVerlag, 1994), pp. 45–65. With few exceptions, the music for dancing in the early eighteenth century appears to have been written expressly for dance, or for dance in alternation with song. Many of the extant notated dances use music from theatrical works by Lully, Campra, and others; but none of them prior to 1750 use music that would be considered chamber music or concert music.

49. LMC 7880, 7960, 7720, 7900.

50. LMC 7660, 7840, 7640.

51. For more on repeats in baroque dance, see Pierce, "Repeated Step-sequences," "Choreographic Structure . . . Feuillet," and "Choreographic Structure in the Dances of Claude Balon," in *Proceedings of 24th Annual Conference of the Society of Dance History Scholars* (n.p.: SDHS, 2001), pp. 101–4. Much of the material in this section is drawn from these articles.

52. LMC 6620, 5020, 1480.

53. LMC 5400. See Pierce, "Choreographic Structure . . . Feuillet," and April Lynn James, "Variations on a Matelotte," in *Proceedings of 25th Annual Conference of the Society of Dance History Scholars* (n.p.: SDHS, 2002), pp. 58–61.

54. LMC 2200.

55. LMC 2140. The title notwithstanding, this is a ballroom dance for one couple rather than a group dance.

56. For a discussion of this dance and its structure, see Witherell, *Pécour's 1700 Recueil*, pp. 95–109.

57. LMC 1640, 5480, 8140, 5460. See Pierce, "Choreographic Structure . . . Balon," and "Choreographic Structure . . . Feuillet."

58. LMC 1900.

59. LMC 2020.

60. LMC 1960.

61. LMC 1940.

62. LMC 4740.

63. Jean-Baptiste Dubos, *Reflexions critiques sur la poésie et sur la peinture*, 2 vols. (Paris: Mariette, 1719), 1: 491–96 in particular.

64. Neither Menestrier nor Bonnet says what these movements or gestures should be. (Bonnet, *Histoire*, p. 61; Menestrier, *Des Ballets*, p. 158, lists only some of these examples).

65. Menestrier, *Des Ballets*, p. 167. Bonnet gives the same passage with minor variants of wording (Bonnet, *Histoire*, p. 67).

66. Lambranzi, *Neue und Curieuse*, book II, plate 25.

67. Edith Lalonger, "J. F. Rebel's *Les Caractères de la danse*: Interpretative Choices and Their Relationship to Dance Research," in *Dance & Music in French Baroque Theatre: Sources & Interpretations*, ed. Sarah McCleave (London: Institute of Advanced Musical Studies, 1998), pp. 105–23.

68. John Weaver, *The Loves of Mars and Venus* (London, 1717), pp. 20–23. See also Richard Ralph, *The Life and Works of John Weaver* (London: Dance Books, 1985), and Moira Goff, "Coquetry and Neglect: Hester Santlow, John Weaver, and the Dramatic Entertainment of Dancing," in *Dancing in the Millenium: Proceedings of the 23rd Annual Conference of the Society of Dance History Scholars* (n.p.: SDHS: 2000), pp. 207–12.

69. Lambranzi, *Neue und Curieuse,* book I, p. 12. Translation from Lambranzi, *New and Curious School of Theatrical Dancing,* trans. Derra de Moroda (1928; reprint, Mineola, N.Y.: Dover, 2002), p. 20.

70. In addition to the taunting boys in symmetrical formation in Lambranzi, we find blacksmiths who strike an anvil for a bit, then dance (book II, plate 25 shown in Figure 9.6); peasant dancers in axial symmetry (book I, plates 7 and 8); and old women and comic masques in mirror symmetry (book I, plates 15 and 16). But there is also the statue dance of book II, plates 12–17 (see footnote 9), in which the dancers move in time to music, but without steps or symmetry.

71. Harris-Warrick, "Ballroom dancing," p. 46. Regrettably, so far we know little about the steps or figures of the branles and gavottes that opened the ball.

72. Ibid., p. 44.

73. See Harris-Warrick, "Contexts," and Laurenti, "Les structures de distribution." See also Ken Pierce and Jennifer Thorp, "The Dances in Lully's *Persée,*" *Journal of Seventeenth Century Music* 10, no. 1 (available at http://sscm-jscm.press.uiuc.edu/jscm/v10/no1/pierce.html).

Recommended Reading

Astier, Régine. "Chaconne pour une femme: *Chaconne de Phaéton,* a Performance Study." *Dance Research* 15, no. 2 (1997): 150–69.

Burgess, Geoffrey. "Ritual in the *tragédie en musique* from Lully's *Cadmus et Hermione* (1673) to Rameau's *Zoroastre* (1749)." Ph.D. diss., Cornell University, 1998. Includes discussion on questions regarding chaconne choreography.

Cohen, Selma Jean, ed. *The International Encyclopaedia of Dance.* Oxford: Oxford University Press, 1998. For general information see the articles on the individual dance types.

Harris-Warrick, Rebecca. "The Phrase Structures of Lully's Dance Music." In *Lully Studies,* ed. John Hajdu Heyer, pp. 32–56. Cambridge: Cambridge University Press, 2000.

Hilton, Wendy. *Dance and Music of Court and Theater: Selected Writings of Wendy Hilton.* Stuyvesant, N.Y.: Pendragon Press, 1997.

Lancelot, Francine. *La belle dance: catalogue raisonné.* Paris: Van Dieren, 1996.

Okamoto, Kimiko, compiler. *Structures and Metaphors in Baroque Dance: Proceedings of the Conference at the University of Surrey Roehampton, 31 March, 2001.* London: Centre for Dance Research, 2001.

Russell, Tilden A. "Minuet Form and Phraseology in *Recueils* and Manuscript Tune Books." *Journal of Musicology* 17, no. 3 (1999): 386–419.

Sadie, Stanley, and John Tyrrell, eds. *The New Grove Dictionary of Music and Musicians.* 2nd ed. London: Macmillan, 2001, or *Grove Music Online,* ed. L. Macy, www.grovemusic.com. For general information see the articles on individual dance types and on other aspects of baroque music.

Thorp, Jennifer. "The Effectiveness of the Beauchamp-Feuillet Notation System During the Eighteenth Century." In *On Common Ground 2: Continuity and Change. Proceedings of the 2nd DHDS Conference, 1998.* Salisbury: Dolmetsch Historical Dance Society, 1998, pp. 51–65.

———. "In Defence of the Danced Minuet." *Early Music* 31, no. 1 (2003): 100–109.

Part 5

Dance and the State

The three essays in part 5 all take as their starting point the view that dance is not divorced from the political process, that it does not exist in an artistic "world" apart from and uninfluenced by current events and the political realities of the society in which it is created. Whether one is looking at the figure of a dance master, at a prominent aristocratic performer, or at choreographic compositions, it is abundantly clear that the actions and resulting creative outputs are all affected by political considerations and the political process itself. In chapter 10 Katherine Tucker McGinnis devotes her attention to the Italian Cesare Negri, "one of the most successful and, to modern eyes, visible" dance masters of the Renaissance. The main reason for Negri's prominence in modern times is his dance treatise *Le gratie d'amore*, published in 1602 near the end of Negri's life. (It is instructive to compare Negri's presentation of his career with that of Guglielmo Ebreo in two redactions of his treatise more than one hundred years earlier. For Guglielmo's autobiographical passages see his *De pratica seu arte tripudii: On the Practice or Art of Dancing*], ed. and trans. Barbara Sparti [Oxford: Clarendon Press, 1993], pp. 248–54.) Negri's treatise is more than a compilation of choreographies and their music, along with instructions on how to perform the steps. Through his "autobiographical" chronicling of his professional life and a "summary of the events and people whom he considered important to contemporary readers," Negri was involved in careful self-promotion and self-marketing. Yet, in spite of this careful promotion, *Le gratie d'amore* contains no mention of the time Negri spent in the service of the French kings, an important honor in the life of any dance master. As McGinnis argues, it was political considerations that caused this otherwise strange omission.

In chapter 11 Julia Prest examines the political implications of the *ballet de cour* in mid-seventeenth-century France, and, in particular, the dance performances by Louis XIV. As Prest explains, the political potential of the *ballet de cour* was always present in the close relationship it had with the monarch, and this political element of the danced spectacle was regularly used to convey a number of different messages to the audience: the magnificence and splendor of the monarch and his strength and power; a message about the prosperity of France (especially important in times of war); and specific commentary on current events for either the court itself, the wider French populace, or for France's foreign allies or enemies. (The first two messages are also discussed in chapter 4 in part 2.) Throughout an examination of the verses in the *livrets* about Louis XIV's roles, Prest shows how a political commentary was provided for the audience that emphasized the king's exploits in war, as well as his ability to restore peace and an emphasis on Louis XIV's regal qualities of majesty, glory, and heroism. But the verses about Louis were not just the panegyric expected for a king. In these verses there were also continual allusions to Louis XIV's private life, to his marriage and to his mistresses. The tension between Louis as king, the godlike figure of Apollo, the Sun King, and Louis as a human figure, the center of court gossip, is very clear in the court ballets, and as Prest concludes, the inability of the *ballet de cour* "to uphold the image that Louis XIV and his propagandists wished to disseminate may have contributed to the genre's demise."

In chapter 12 by Linda Tomko we move to early eighteenth-century England. Through a detailed analysis of one of Mr. Isaac's birthday dances for the ballroom, *The Pastorall* (1713), Tomko focuses on how published choreographies can reflect the political views and ideals of the monarchy. This dance served to articulate Queen Anne's desire for a political process not dominated by political parties, but filled with moderate men who worked together for the good of the whole country. Isaac invokes concepts of the pastoral in his choreography not merely by the title, but also through his choice of the two dance types used, the loure and the hornpipe, his use of distinctive step-units and step sequences, and also by specific floor patterns. Tomko argues that the concept of the pastoral as a world apart, an idyllic realm, equates to Queen Anne's desire as monarch to remain above party faction and strife, and it reflects in choreographic terms her desire to return to an older mode of political conduct, to a "golden age" before the advent of political parties.

10

Your Most Humble Subject, Cesare Negri Milanese

Katherine Tucker McGinnis

In Paris, in the summer of 1587, the Milanese dancer Cesare Negri lay ill, apparently to the point of death.[1] His position as a *violon du roi* was a valuable one and several men asked for it, but the king's half sister, the Duchess d'Angoulême, advised Negri that his wife should have the right to choose his successor, thus assuring her some financial benefit after his death.[2] At that time, however, his death did not take place. Negri left the service of King Henri III of France and returned to Milan. He was undoubtedly one of the most successful and, to modern eyes, visible dancing masters in the period. He stood out in a newly professionalized occupation that had begun to appear in Italy in the fifteenth century and had expanded in the sixteenth.

The need for dancing masters paralleled changes in the function of courts and of courtiers. Social and artistic skills augmented and even replaced military ones for the nobles and other members of the elite classes. The popularity of Baldesar Castiglione's *Book of the Courtier* attests to the shift in the role of the courtier and the self-consciousness with which he fashioned himself.[3] By the time of Negri in the second half of the sixteenth century, the professional dancing master had become the ubiquitous servant of the self-improving man and woman, and a disproportionate number of those "servants" were Italian. At the top of the professional world were the dancers employed by princely and royal courts. Such was the status Negri enjoyed.

When Negri returned to Milan, he regained his position as the leading dancing master in the city and, with it, the patronage of the Spanish governors who ruled Lombardy. He taught courtiers of both Spanish and Italian extraction, trained numerous other dancers who performed as his students and then went out to spread his style of dance in other Italian and European courts, and he provided entertainments for the court and its visitors. In 1602, after half a century in his profession and fifteen years after leaving the service of the French king, Negri published *Le gratie d'amore*.[4] More than an instructional manual, although it certainly is that, Negri's treatise provides an incomparable insider's view of the world of the early dancing master. Negri described his own activities, both in Milan and throughout Italy, the dances he had composed, and the notables before whom he had performed. He named celebrated students and patrons. He self-consciously publicized his name, including his sobriquet "Il Trombone" and his reputation. He did not, surprisingly, mention his service in France. This omission stands out, anomalous in the otherwise carefully detailed self-promotion of his book. If Negri had achieved the distinction of employment by the King of France, why would he not include this honor in his autobiography? He did name dancers who served the French court and praised their success and remunerations, but of the patronage he enjoyed at the courts of Henri III, Charles IX, and Henri IV, he wrote nothing. Were the omissions evidence of lapses in Negri's memory, or did professional or political motivations underlie his reticence?

Very little information is available about members of non-elite classes in early modern Europe, but Negri is, in this regard as in so many others, exceptional. Autobiographical writing by non-humanists, other than merchants' *ricordi*, is rare. In his treatises, Negri limns not only a self-portrait, but a sketch of the professional. He does not, however, provide explicit personal information. With the exception of a single reference to his daughter Margarita, Negri wrote only of the professional activities in which he and the dancing masters whom he knew or knew of were involved. However, the machinery of both church and state operated to capture other views of these men and their families. Information in these archives, both in Milan and in France, provides answers to puzzling questions arising from Negri's omissions and permits us to sketch a simple biography of a dancer who was exemplary if unusually successful in his field. Piecing together information from archival as well as autobiographical sources will also shed light on Negri's service in France.

This clearer image of the dancer allows me to turn to the apparently deliberate gaps in the self-portrait Negri himself drew and to examine the possible reasons—professional, personal, and political—why Negri would say nothing of his activities at the French court. In describing his career as a dancer and choreographer, Negri emphasized the importance of the people whom he served as well as the impressive events in which he participated. He identified both Spanish and Italian figures in his careful enumeration of the notables before whom he danced, whom he taught, and whom he served. It is precisely this rather boastful tone that draws the attention of the modern reader to his uncharacteristic omission of the French royalty in Paris. By the standards of the day, the king of France would be too impressive a patron to ignore. As a citizen of a city under Spanish control at the end of a turbulent century, with war between Spain and France but recently ended, the political justification for Negri's reticence stands out, and in this chapter I argue for this as one explanation for his actions. A successful court dancing master would weigh political necessity against personal aggrandizement and curtail bragging about past glories if they might undermine present patronage relationships. Negri had recently participated in important festivals sponsored by both the Spanish governor and the Milanese patriciate. His principal Milanese patrons had been the Spanish governors themselves. In *Le gratie d'amore*, Negri highlighted his connections with the important people and families who had employed and patronized him and, by extension, with their associates, heirs, and successors, not with their enemies.

Negri's Career as Revealed in Le Gratie d'Amore

Of Negri's early life and family, little is known. He was born in Milan about 1536, possibly son of Girolamo.[5] He studied dancing under Pompeo Diobono and, when his master went to France in 1554, assumed responsibility for the school. For fifty years, in addition to performing, he taught members of the Milanese nobility, traveled throughout and beyond Italy for his patrons, composed dances, and, near the end of his career, published his treatise.

Negri's success seems to have been based on three things: the quality of his training under Diobono, clearly one of the premier teachers of his day, his own natural talent as a dancer and performer, and a level of ambition equal to his self-esteem. He must have been an intelligent and hard-working man. At the time Negri published, only four other Italians are known to have written and published books: Lutio Compasso, Fabritio Caroso, Prospero Lutij, and Livio Lupi da Caravaggio.[6] He traveled from Milan to Paris, apparently several times, and choreographed not only individual dances but entire entertainments. Like his countryman Belgioioso, known for the *Balet Comique de la Reyne*, he was a master at theatrical production, demonstrated by the masquerade created and presented at his own expense for the arrival of Don Juan of Austria. Negri must have been a vigorous man; he danced into his fifties.

As a product of Diobono's school, Negri's success is evidence of his master's skill as a teacher and his reputation that extended beyond the professional circles of dance. In his "Libro terzo dei grottesche," the Milanese poet Giovanni Paolo Lomazzo included an adulatory poem, "Di Pompeo Diabone."[7] Lomazzo also mentioned Diobono in his "Vita del'Auttore."[8] Negri identified several fellow dancing masters also trained by Diobono—Martino da Asso, Giovanni Battista Varade, and Pietro Francesco Rombello—implying that his readers would appreciate this association. Diobono's disciples spread his teachings far beyond Milan, and in the following generation their students extended his legacy throughout Europe.

Negri opened his autobiography with a somewhat confusing summary of his early performances. Fifty years had undoubtedly erased less memorable, possibly less successful youthful appearances. He concerned himself with those that brought him notice and honor and led to greater opportunities and connections, including the patronage of several Spanish governors. When Diobono first left for France, Negri was about eighteen. His first public performances (or the first he considered "worthy of memory") took place about two years later before Cristoforo Madrucci, the Cardinal of Trent; Ferdinando Alvarez de Toledo, the Duke of Alba; and Don Giovanni de Figaroa, each of whom governed Milan on behalf of Spain. Negri did not make clear when he danced for them or if he danced for them all at once, as seems unlikely.[9] Negri termed the next governor, the Duke of Sessa, "mio Signore, & padrone."[10] Negri neither told what dances he performed in these early years nor described the events, public or private, that brought him into contact with these men, nor did he name any others who danced with him. One asks how he gained the opportunities and the access. Presumably his association with Diobono opened important doors.

In 1561, Negri accompanied his patron, Francesco Ferdinando d'Avalos de

Aquino, Marchese of Pescara (Governor, 1560–63), to Mantua for the marriage of Duke Guglielmo Gonzaga and Eleanor of Austria (d. 1594). During the festivities, Negri danced for "many other princes." Again, it is not clear if he participated in a work choreographed by another or performed solos of his own composition. At this point, Negri not only amused his patron at home, he served as a useful ornament to the Governor's family and court. As part of Pescara's retinue, Negri promoted the reputation of both his patron and his patron's patron, Philip II, the King of Spain.

Negri continued to enjoy associations with the governors of Milan. When the Duke of Albuquerque arrived in 1564, he sent Negri to Malta with the Conte di Cifuente.[11] Negri's claim that throughout the voyage he "never for a moment" abandoned Cifuente undoubtedly derived from self-interest as well as loyalty. The expedition provided a series of outstanding opportunities for the dancer. In Genoa, he danced for Andrea Doria; in Naples and Sicily for their respective Spanish viceroys; in Malta (after the departure of the Turks) before the Grand Master; in Saragozza before the Duke of Terranova, later to be Governor of Milan; and again in Naples. His appearance in Saragozza, the Spanish Zaragoza and capital of Aragon, would be his only known performance in Spain.

In 1564, when the Habsburg princes, Rudolph and Ernest, traveled to Spain to continue their training at the court of Philip II, they passed through Milan.[12] Negri danced for them and gave them lessons, teaching them "many beautiful things."[13] At the ages of twelve and eleven, respectively, the boys would already have studied dancing, but Negri could provide master classes in the fashionable Italian style. On their return in 1571, the young men crossed Spain's northern Italian territories and Negri danced for them at a banquet in Genoa given by Giovanni Andrea Doria. Don Juan of Austria accompanied the princes. Negri traveled with the party to Ferrara and danced on the *bucintoro*, the luxurious boat on which the Este dukes entertained honored guests traveling to Ferrara.

During this period, Negri performed in Florence for Grand Duke Cosimo de' Medici, his son Francesco, and his son-in-law Paolo Giordano Orsini.[14] Francesco's name appears at least two other times in the story of Italian courtly dancing.[15] A 1559 letter from Cristiano Lamberti, possibly a musician, to Antonio Serguidi, Francesco's secretary, includes the choreography for *La caccia*, a flirtatious type of dance that is similar to *La caccia d'amore* found in Negri's 1602 *Le gratie d'amore*.[16] Lutio Compasso, whose *Ballo della gagliarda* (Florence, 1560) is believed to be the first printed Italian dancing manual, dedicated his work to Francesco de' Medici, whom he termed "Signore & Patron mio sempre osservandissimo." Negri mentions no figures with Florentine associations in *Le gratie d'amore,* with the possible exception of Sig. Donna Costantia de' Medici, to whom he dedicated the *balletto La nizzarda.*

Negri's most conspicuous service to the court began in September of 1573, when Antonio de Guzman, Marchese d'Ayamonte, became governor of Milan and Negri's patron.[17] Negri participated in a series of official celebrations. For the May 1574 visit of Don Juan of Austria, Negri danced and gave the prince dancing lessons for eight days. The instruction would have included new dances and refinements of steps and variations of the *gagliarda.* The hero of Lepanto already enjoyed a reputation as a fine and enthusiastic dancer. At the inception of the battle itself, he was reported to have broken into a spontaneous anticipatory dance, a *gagliarda.*[18] Later in May, Ayamonte brought Negri and five of his students to Vigevano again. Costumed in the style of the *mattaccino* (presumably a decorative version of armor or other type of military dress), the men performed *gagliarda* variations, a *moresca,* and passes of the *mattaccino.*[19] Negri described the event as very popular, as would be expected with an audience of military men, and stated that the princes claimed never to have seen such dexterous and agile dancing.

In the following month, Don Juan returned to Milan, accompanied by the Prince of Parma and Ottavio Gonzaga. Negri made a remarkable personal contribution to the official festive life of Milan by presenting, at his own expense, a *mascherata* of twenty-five entries.[20] Dancing included a *brando* by four kings and four queens dressed in "antique" style, a *mattaccinata* by the dwarves who accompanied them, and a "battle" by "wildmen" brandishing canes and shields. As a finale, eighty-two people danced a *brando* accompanied by the "finest musicians in Italy."

The second half of 1574 was just as busy and festive as the earlier months. In August, Charles IX of France died and his brother Henri abandoned the throne of Poland for that of France. The king, accompanied by the Dukes of Savoy, Anversa, and Ferrara (the last hoping to replace Henri as king of Poland) and the Grand Prior of France, traveled through Milanese territory.[21] Due to the strained relations between France and Spain, Henri was not given a formal entry into Milan itself; rather, Governor Ayamonte, with his noble dependents, rode out to welcome the king with festivities in a series of smaller cities of the territory. Negri and two Negri-trained dancers performed: Giovanni Stefano Faruffino with Negri at Monza and Giulio Cesare Lampugnano with Negri and Diobono-trained Martino da Asso at Mazenta. Although Negri may have served in France prior to this, it is possible that Henri noticed him for the first time.

Breaks in Negri's perhaps selective memory separate events of the next fifteen years. In October of 1582 he danced in a "most beautiful celebration" for the

Duke of Savoy at Vercelli, provided by the *castellano* of the town.[22] He remained with the Duke's party for two weeks, danced at the palace, and received rich rewards. Ten years later, his student, the nine-year-old daughter of the wealthy financier Conte Rinaldo Tettoni, performed before the visiting Duke of Mantua, Vincenzo I.

The crowning achievements of Negri's professional life took place in 1598 and 1599. In November, Margherita of Austria, the bride of Philip III, journeyed through Lombardy on her way to Spain. While the new queen traveled in state with an extensive and important retinue, official mourning occasioned by the recent death of Philip II reduced the range of acceptable celebrations. While some of the more public events planned were reduced or omitted, private entertainments were possible. The scheduled play with *intermedi*, intended for the new theater, the Salone Margherita, was cancelled. In a more intimate setting, eight of Negri's students performed *balli* and combat dances, using long swords, daggers, and poles. Later, the same group danced for other notables including the Spanish king's ambassador, Francesco, Marchese d'Ayamonte, son of Negri's late patron. Again, the young men performed more of the lively "bizzarie di balli, combattimenti, & mattaccini" (eccentric dances and weapon dances) that military men enjoyed.

The following summer provided the Milanese with an opportunity to present the theatrical events originally planned for Margherita, as the visit by Philip III's sister, the Infanta Isabella, and her popular husband, Albert of Austria, provided attractive focus for lavish entertainments. Members of the leading Milanese families performed a series of masked dances in the new theater, two of which were composed by Negri. In his treatise, Negri not only gave particulars of dress, props, and instruments, he also named the participants and included the choreography for two of the dances performed. A few days later saw the performance of Negri's *brando, Alta Regina,* for four shepherds, each carrying a cane, and four nymphs, each with a dart.[23] Dancers turned in place, changed places, took hands or arms with their partners, traveled in straight, curving, and weaving lines, and passed through fleeting geometric shapes. Shepherds and nymphs danced in pairs, together, and in alternation, repeating patterns left and right, always in symmetrical figures. Negri did not mention any use made of either canes or darts, which apparently merely formed part of the costumes and props of the scene. The dances were composed for highly trained nonprofessionals and emphasized small steps, small jumps, occasional bows, but no difficult steps. As the published edition of the play *Arminia* states, the performers were "young nobles" of Milan. Refinement and noble self-presentation would be the qualities valued. The *intermedio* finished as the eight dancers made their reverence together, ending the *brando* with grace and decorum.

In addition to information provided by his "autobiography," Negri included choreography for five dances associated with members of governors' families, thus augmenting the chronology of his self-portrait. The first choreography in *Le gratie d'amore* is *Balletto detto lo Spagnoletto*, dedicated to Giovanna della Lama, wife of Governor Alburquerque.[24] Although Alvaro de Sande was governor but seven months, Negri dedicated his *Pavaniglia alla Romana* to his daughter Isabella.[25] For Anna de Cordova, the wife of Governor Ayamonte, Negri again created a *pavaniglia*. There is no indication whether these three dances were composed for specific events or simply named to honor women Negri termed "patrona." That Negri dedicated dances to the wives of his patrons Alburquerque and Ayamonte is to be expected; he mentioned many occasions on which he served their husbands. However, the association of a dance with Sande's rule does establish Negri's presence in Milan in the brief period between the two governorships. Finally, Negri presented the *balletto*, *Il Pastor Leggiadro*, at the 1594 wedding of Governor Velasco's son and Maddalena Borgia and he dedicated *La Caccia d'Amore*, also a *balletto*, to the young man's second wife, Donna Giovanna di Cordova.

Negri's Career Beyond Le Gratie d'Amore

Not all of Negri's story is found in *Le gratie d'amore* (see Table 10.1). There remain puzzling gaps, some brief, others much longer: 1564–69, August 1571–May 1574, August 1574–October 1582, October 1582–July 1592, July 1592–December 1598. During these periods, he may have pursued some other, nonterpsichorean activity. Given his connections and his obvious ability, it is more probable that he continued teaching and performing, but perhaps in less exalted spheres, venues which, writing in 1602, he did not consider "worthy." A third possibility is that, although he continued to follow his profession, he found it impolitic to identify the patrons by whom he had been employed. There are several ways to explore these lacunae.

Official eyes of state, city, and church recorded key moments in the lives of all Milanese citizens—commercial transactions, legal activities, and domestic arrangements. In the voluminous state archives, one *fondo*, the Notarile, provides particularly important documentation of Negri's presence in Milan.[26] The Notarile is made up of wills, sales, and other civil procedures associated with the relatively prosperous middle class and above. In 1586 Negri's name appears in connection with two sales,[27] and a flurry of entries also runs from 1592 to 1597.[28] These records argue that Negri was in Milan, if not necessarily continuously, in the "gaps."

Church records include members of all socio-economic strata. After the Council of Trent (1545–63), the Catholic Church required that priests take a more pastoral role in their parishes. Priests went house to house and summarized their report in records known as the *Stati delle anime*.[29] For each *casa*, or building, the heads of household, with names, ages, occupations, and relationships of all household members, both family and servants, are listed. This material adds information on economic and social position and opens a window on dancing masters not only as professional entertainers, as Negri described, but also as citizens and family men.

In Negri's parish, San Salvatore in Xenodochio, the first collection, taken in 1576, found him in a household of nine, listed as *ballatore*, age thirty-four, and married to Isabella di Nava, twenty-four. Two daughters, Livia and Ottavia, were three and one, respectively.[30] A woman who could have been his mother or mother-in-law, Magdalena di Marchi, fifty-four,[31] lived with the couple, as did an apprentice, Francesco Bernardino di Crespi, eighteen (later included in Negri's list of famous dancers), and three children, Giovanni Jacobo di Castioni, twelve, Violante di Cepesoni, eight, and Vittoria di Lia, five. The family lived in the Casa di Clemente di Clementi, in an area across the cathedral piazza from the Governor's Palace. Typical of the housing arrangements of the day, several families lived in the Clemente house, in this case six families, totaling twenty-seven people.

In the next report, dated 1587, the family lived in the same parish, but now in the "Casa del Trombone." Negri used that sobriquet, "Detto il Trombone," after his name on the title page of *Le gratie d'amore*. This house held but one other household, for a total of seventeen souls, indicating that each family enjoyed generous living space. The Negri family had two daughters at home (Livia was gone, Ottavia now thirteen, and Margharitta two) and a son, Jacobo Filippo, four. A wetnurse, Maria di Cabij, thirty-five, had joined the family along with Elena, fourteen, a servant, and an elderly couple, Batista Crespo, fifty-one, and Lodovicha, his wife, fifty, the last two perhaps related to the apprentice of 1576.[32] Negri was now fifty and his wife thirty-eight. The ascription of age, seemingly mathematically unrelated to the years that had passed since 1576, is typical of these records. The salient fact is the apparent ownership of a house, unusual in Milan in this period, and a sign of both stability and some wealth. Over the years, the house retained this name, even after Negri's death when, in 1610, it housed his widow, her daughter and son-in-law, their dependents, and four other families.[33] Even in 1633, when it held twenty-eight people, none apparently related to Negri, in eight family units, it was still known as the Casa del Trombone.[34] At least in 1576 and 1587, Negri was in Milan during this parochial census.

In spite of patronage by the Spanish governors, Negri almost assuredly spent a significant part of his career as *violoniste* in the French court. Evidence for this is derived from both French archival materials and the poems of Giovanni Paolo Lomazzo. Numerous French records cite Negri, beginning in 1560 when his name first appears in the payment records of François II as *violon ordinare*, sent to Italy along with three other Italians, to recruit violinists.[35] He is listed in 1569 as *violon du roi*, presumably for Charles IX.[36] In 1575 he received several payments from accounts of the king's youngest brother, François d'Anjou, for wages, food, and clothing.[37] Ten years later, he was back in France as *violon de la chambre* for Henri himself.[38] At various times, Negri stood as godfather for children of court musicians.[39] Finally, in May and June of 1587 came the near-fatal illness that marked the end of his service for the French royal family. In the period 1560–87, while he served the French royal family, Negri continued his relationship with the governors of Milan. Negri's sojourn in France must have been well rewarded. By 1587, Milanese records indicate that he had achieved considerable personal wealth insofar as his family moved from an apartment in someone else's building to a *casa* of his own.

The identification as violinist rather than as dancer raises the possibility that this might be a different Negri, but the poet Giovanni Paolo Lomazzo, whose *Rime* appeared in the year of Negri's illness, clarifies this point.[40] His reference in "Di Pompeo Diabone," not merely to Diobono and other Italians in France but especially to "Il Trombone," supports the contention that Negri served French as well as Spanish and Italian masters.[41] Certainly Diobono, who held important positions in France, would have encouraged his disciple to join him and facilitated his placement at court. Lomazzo published his *Grottesche* in 1587, apparently the final year in which Negri served in France. The dancer seems to have abandoned his transalpine career and settled down. No records of Negri in France after this date have been found.

If, under Henri III, every dancer at the French court was an Italian, they were not all newcomers.[42] When Charles VIII of France invaded Italy, he complained of weather and wine but admired the festivities.[43] Well before Diobono arrived at mid-century, the flow of Italians was impressive.[44] Italian thematic ballets and *mascarades* became the fashion. Even if Negri omitted his own presence in France, he cited Lodovico Padvello, Virgilio Bracesco, Giovanni Paolo Ernandes, and Giovanni Francesco Giera as well as Diobono. Negri admired these dancers, praised their talent and skill and the rewards they received. That they served a seemingly rival court raised no criticism. But his references to these colleagues draw attention to the fact that he does not refer to his own service to three French kings.

Conclusion: Political Reality and the Dancing Master

The integration of information from the choreographies in *Le gratie d'amore*, Lomazzo's poetic references, and parish and civic records in Italy and France affords a richer, more complex picture of Negri's life and career than he himself supplied, or intended. (See Table 10.1—the times Negri spent in France are highlighted in bold.) In *Le gratie d'amore* Negri crafted a careful picture of himself. His concern was not with domestic details, but with his art, his ability and experience as a dancer, and his important connections, all information that would buttress his reputation as author of a book about dancing. This professional focus is consistent with his assumed intention to promote his book as a source of useful pedagogy and accurate reportage of his service for the rich and famous. Marketing motivated Cesare Negri. As he wrote in the dedicatory letter to Philip III, with the "heavy weight of years," he could only "move his hand and pen."[45]

If professional motives explain his emphasis on himself as artist, political factors may account for the self-censorship. A dancing master, like any other figure, acts within a social, political, and economic context. The political aspects can be summed up in the tensions between the Spanish and French. The two countries were at war throughout the first half of the century, with Milan under French rule until 1525. In the second half, religious wars (1562–1629) wracked France. Philip of Spain had married a French princess, sister of several Valois kings, including Henri III, but in spite of dynastic ties the Spanish supported the Guise family, the more extreme Catholic faction, and attempted, unsuccessfully, to prevent the Huguenot leader, Henri of Navarre, from inheriting the crown. In the very year of Negri's illness, the "War of the Three Henrys" broke out, the final struggle between Guise, Huguenot, and Valois factions. Within months, the king abandoned Paris and barricades were up in the city. Court amusements undoubtedly diminished or ceased. With the king's death in 1589, war broke out between France and Spain that lasted until 1598 when Philip agreed to remove Spanish troops from France.

Throughout this bellicose century, in spite of the political differences, numerous Italians sought and found work at the French court and Negri's career followed a common pattern in which Italian dancers moved between Italy and

France (as well as other transalpine cities and courts) as opportunity called, with no apparent regard for the tides of war. The market for Italian dancing masters was, as for other skilled artists and craftsmen of the period, European in scope, and no court was considered more generous than the French.[46]

This complicated and ambiguous political environment must have influenced Negri's decision to discard those parts of his professional life unrelated to his "faithful" service of the Spanish king and his vassals. That the political situation affected him as it does every office seeker offers another way to look at Negri's truncation of his career and omission of some seeming high points. "Luoghi e gran personaggi, dove, e dinanzi à quali hà l'auttore ballatto" (Places and grand personages where and before whom the author danced) is not a true autobiography. Negri was not recording his career for posterity or even his own satisfaction. Like every writer, he had an intended audience. He was crafting a résumé, a useful summary of the events and people whom he considered important to contemporary readers. Undoubtedly, he wished to create a less ephemeral reputation than most dancers can expect, based on the production of a physical object, the book. He reminded the reader of his activities throughout Italy and beyond, but only those in the service of Spanish governors. As a subject of Philip, in fact, a patronized servant of the Spanish governors, Negri would not wish to emphasize his presence in the Valois court.

While Negri's dedication of *Le gratie d'amore* to Philip III emphasized his lifelong and single-minded (lapses unmentioned) devotion to Spain and its rulers, both king and governors, it was not more (perhaps less) obsequious than was typical of the period and form. He spent minimal words of praise on the king, only the obligatory term "Potentissimo & Catholico." Although he claimed that the "only and principal object" of his life's work had been the king, he added, "In serving your Milanese vassals, your excellent lieutenants, and the Most Serene Rodolfo, Ernesto, and Giovanni [Juan] of Austria, I profess to have served Your Royal Person." It was the king's vassals and lieutenants, the men who ruled Milan and were in a position to help Negri, to whom he directed his efforts and attention. The abbreviation of his life's story was no more devious than omitting summer jobs on a résumé. Negri, citizen of a city no longer in control of its political destiny, responded to reality. He recalled Spanish associations because Spain was the power in Milan.

Table 10.1. Chronology Taken from Negri's *Le gratie d'amore* and Archival Sources

1536	Negri born
1554	Pompeo Diobono leaves for France and Negri takes over school
12 June 1555–13 January 1556	Rule of Ferdinando Alvarez de Toledo, Duke of Alba, before whom Negri danced (n.d.)*
June 1556–January 1557	Rule of Cristoforo Madrucci, Cardinal of Trent (governed 1556–57), before whom Negri danced (n.d.)
1557–1560	Rule of Duke of Sessa, whom he claimed as patron and before whom he danced (n.d.)
1560	**France:** *violon ordinare***
June 1560–1563	Governorship of Francesco Ferdinando d'Avalos de Aquino, Marchese of Pescara, before whom Negri danced (n.d.); went to Mantua with him for the wedding of Duke Guglielmo (n.d.); danced in Florence for Cosimo de' Medici and others (n.d.)
16 April 1564–21 August 1571	Gabriele de la Cueva, Duke of Albuquerque, governor. Negri dedicated *Balletto detto lo Spagnoletto* to the duke's wife; traveled with Cifuente to Malta, Genoa, Naples, Sicily, Saragozza (n.d.)
1564	Danced before Habsburg princes
1569	**France:** *violon du roi*
29 July 1571	Danced for Habsburg princes and Don Juan of Austria in Genoa
August 1571	Traveled with Don Juan and others and danced on *bucintoro*
September 1571–April 1572	Rule of Sande; dedicated dance to his daughter (n.d.)
17 September 1573–April 1580	Antonio de Guzman, Marchese d'Ayamonte, governor; patron of Negri; dedicated dance to de Guzman's wife (n.d.)

---

   * n.d. indicates no specific date for activity or event that took place during a broad period, such as a governorship.

   ** Boldface indicates Negri's visits to France.

6 May 1574	Danced at Vigevano before Don Juan, presented his students, and taught Don Juan for eight days
26 May 1574	Along with five disciples, Negri danced again for Don Juan at Vigevano
26 June 1574	Presented a *mascherata* for Don Juan and others
6 August 1574	Performed for Henri III at Cremona
11 August 1574	Performed for Henri III at Monza and Mazenta
1575	**France: *violon* for François d'Anjou**
13 August 1575	**France: *violon* for François d'Anjou**
27 September 1575	**France: *violon* for François d'Anjou**
1576	Living "Casa di Clemente" in the parish of San Salvatore in Xenodochio
14 May 1576	Cited in Notarile
25–26 October 1582	Danced for Duke of Savoy at Vercelli; stayed with Duke two weeks
c. 1585–1587	**France: *violon de la chambre***
27 February 1586	Cited in Notarile
29 November 1586	Cited in Notarile
1587	Living in "Casa del Trombone" in the parish of San Salvatore in Xenodochio
30 May –June 1587	**France: *violon de la chambre;* Negri ill in Paris**
13 April 1592	Cited in Notarile
10 July 1592	Negri's nine-year-old student danced for Duke of Mantua in Milan
4 December 1592–1595	Ivan de Velasco governor (also 1595–1600 and 1610–12)
23 August 1593	Cited in Notarile
4 November 1593	Cited in Notarile
21 July 1594	Negri's *Il pastor leggiadro* performed
12 August 1594	Cited in Notarile
14 September 1594	Cited in Notarile
20 September 1594	Cited in Notarile

3 October 1595	Cited in Notarile
6 June 1596	Cited in Notarile
27 September 1596	Cited in Notarile
7 October 1597	Cited in Notarile
8 December 1598	Eight of Negri's young students danced for Queen Margherita
9 December 1598	Same students danced for king's ambassador and others
18 July 1599	Negri's dances at the festivities for the Infanta and the Archduke
21 July 1599	Negri's *brando* ends the *intermedi* with *Arminia* performed for the Infanta and others
1602	Negri published *Le gratie d'amore*
1604	Negri republished *Le gratie d'amore* as *Nuove inventione di balli*
1610	Widow, daughters, son-in-law, others living in "Casa del Trombone"

Notes

1. For full citations concerning Negri and other Italian dancers who traveled to France, see my dissertation, "Moving in High Circles; Courts, Dance, Dancing Masters in Italy in the Long Sixteenth Century" (Ph.D. diss., University of North Carolina, Chapel Hill, 2001).

2. A *violon* might be employed as musician or dancer, or instruct the royal pages.

3. Baldesar Castiglione, *The Book of Courtier*, trans. George Bull (Harmondsworth: Penguin, 1981). Concerning the translation and dissemination of the book, see Peter Burke, *The Fortunes of the Courtier: the European Reception of Castiglione's Cortegiano* (University Park: Penn State University Press, 1996).

4. Cesare Negri, *Le gratie d'amore* (Milan: Pacifico Pontio and Giovanni Battista Piccaglia, 1602; facs. ed., New York: Broude Brothers, 1969; fasc. ed., Bologna: Forni, 1969). It was reisued as *Nuove inventioni di balli* (Milan: Bordone, 1604). I refer to his career summary as his "autobiography."

5. In *Le gratie d'amore* (1602), a cartouche beneath his portrait states that he is sixty-six. The portrait may have been made earlier than the publication date. The inference concerning his father is based on information in notarial records of the Archivio di Stato di Milano (hereafter ASMi), where Negri is identified as "Cesare q. Girolamo" ("Cesare son of the deceased Girolamo").

6. For full bibliographic details of these works, see the "List of Dance Treatises" at the end of this volume.

7. *Rime di Gio. Paolo Lomazzi milanese pittore, divise in sette libri. Nelle quali ad imitatione de i grotteschi usati da' pittori, ha cantato le lodi di Dio, & de le cose sacre, di prencipi, di signori* (Milan, Pontio, 1587). Lomazzo's sonnet "Di Pompeo Diabone" begins, "Tra molta gente che danzando giva [gira?], Vidi il raro Pompeo Diabone" (Among the many men who dance, I saw the rare Pompeo Diabone), "Libro terzo dei Grottesche," *Rime*, 167.

8. Lomazzo, "Libro Sesto dei Grottesche," *Rime*, 540–41.

9. Alba governed from June 1555 until January 1556; Madrucci from June 1556; Figueroa from January 1557.

10. The Duke of Sessa governed from July 1558 to June 1560 and again in 1563–64.

11. During this period, struggles against the Turks in the Mediterranean engrossed Europeans, the Spanish kings in particular. It was Philip II's half-brother, Don Juan of Austria, who led the fleet that won the Battle of Lepanto in 1571. Malta was headquarters of the Spanish corsairs and home of the Knights of St. John or Hospitalers since 1522.

12. Rudolph (1552–1612) became Holy Roman Emperor in 1576; his brother Ernest (1553–95) was made archduke in 1576.

13. Negri, *Le gratie d'amore*, p 7.

14. Negri does not mention whether he did this on his own or at the request or order of Governor Albuquerque. He includes this between the 1564 activities and those of 1571, but does not give an exact year (Negri, *Le gratie d'amore*, p. 7).

15. Francesco (1541–87) was grand duke from 1574 until his death, but Cosimo (1519–74) had given up rule to him in 1564 and Negri may have visited Florence when this transition had taken place. In 1565 Francesco married Giovanna d'Austria, and Negri's visit may have coincided with this event. Orsini (1541–85) was the husband (and murderer) of Francesco's sister, Isabella, as well as a hero at the Battle of Lepanto.

16. This letter is transcribed in Gino Corti's "Cinque balli Toscani del cinquecento," *Rivista italiana di musicologia* 12, no. 1 (1977): 73–82.

17. Guzman governed from 17 September 1573 until his death in 1580.

18. In *The Galleys of Lepanto* (New York: Scribner, 1983), Jack Beeching claims that Don Juan "danced a galliard on the gun-platform" at the moment of collision. Unfortunately, Beeching does not give a citation (p. 213).

19. The *moresca* and *mattaccino* were weapons dances. While handling and parrying weapons, either modeled on real ones or fanciful substitutions, the dancers kept up rapid footwork that involved changing places and turns.

20. G. Yvonne Kendall discusses this event, as well as the *intermedi* of 1594 and the festivities of 1599, in "Theatre, Dance and Music in Late Cinquecento Milan," *Early Music* 32, no. 1 (2004): 75–95.

21. On his return, Henri was famously entertained by the Venetians. See Bonner Mitchell, *Italian Civic Pageantry in the High Renaissance: A Descriptive Bibliography of Triumphal Entries and Selected Other Festivals for State Occasions* (Florence: Leo S. Olschki, 1979); and *The Majesty of the State; Triumphal Progresses of Foreign Sovereigns in Renaissance Italy (1494–1600)* (Florence: Leo S. Olschki, 1986). Laurie Stras provides a detailed account of Henri's trip and the entertainments given for him, with a map of his itinerary, in "'Onde havrà 'l mond'esempio et vera historia,' Musical Echoes of Henri III's Progress through Italy," *Acta Musicologica* 72, no. 1 (2000): 7–41.

22. The *castellano* was a military figure ruling on behalf of Spain.

23. Negri, *Le gratie d'amore*, pp. 291–96. The *brando* was one of the *intermedi* per-

formed with the pastoral play *Arminia* by Giambattista Visconte. The probable date of performance was 21 July (Kendall, "Theatre, Dance and Music," p. 13).

24. Alburquerque governed from 1564 to 1571.

25. Sande governed from September 1571 to April 1572.

26. Negri may appear in other records of the Archivio di Stato or Archivio Storico Civico, including the criminal records, which I have not examined.

27. ASMi, Notarile, 14252: 6509–6511 (27 February 1586) and ASMi, Notarile, 20072: 554 (29 November 1586).

28. ASMi, Notarile, 10579: 1058 (13 April 1592), 15511: 2374 (23 August 1593), 19598: 1138 (4 November 1593), 19598: 1224 (12 August 1594), 19598: 1251 (14 September 1594), 1959: 1257 (20 September 1594), 19598: 1258 (20 September 1594), 19599: 1353 (3 October 1595), 19599: 1354 (3 October 1595), 19599: 1437 (6 June 1596), 19599: 1441 (27 September 1596), and 19600: 1611 (7 October 1597).

29. These volumes are in the Archivio Storico Diocesano [hereafter ASDMi]. I would like to thank Mons. Bruno Bosatra, Director of the Archivio Storico Diocesano, who was exceptionally generous in allowing me to photocopy materials.

30. ASDMi, San Salvatore in Xenodochio, DSA 68, sect. 1.

31. She is simply identified as *madre*.

32. ASDMi, DSA, San Salvatore in Xenodochio, 68, sect. 2.

33. Ibid., 69. The son-in-law was Michael Angelo Varade, who had taken over Negri's school, here listed as a *ballarino*, age twenty-eight, possibly related to Giovanni Battista Varade whom Negri identified among the famous dancers (Negri, *Le gratie d'amore*, 6).

34. One may have been a Negri descendant: the inhabitants were Filippo Neeri (perhaps Negri), age sixty, Dorothea, ten, Carlo Francesco, *nepote*, seven, and Margarita Minla, sixty (ASDMi, DSA, San Salvatore in Xenodochio, 69).

35. François died in 1560, which may have led to Negri's return to Milan (Jeanice Brooks, *Courtly Song in Late Sixteenth-Century France:* [Chicago: University of Chicago Press, 2000], p. 515).

36. Emile Picot, *Les italiens en France au XVIe siècle* (Bordeaux: Gounouilhou, 1918). Facsimile reprint, *Memoria Bibliografica*. Vol. 25, ed. Nicola Merola (Rome: Vecchiarelli, 1995), p. 253 and n. 2.

37. Brooks, *Courtly Song*, p. 516.

38. Ibid.

39. On 22 October 1585, César DeNegri, termed *violon de la chamber du roi*, acted as godfather in the parish of St. Eustache and, on 25 May 1587, the same parish records state that he lived in the rue des Vieux Augustins (Yolande De Brossard, *Musiciens de Paris 1535–1792. Actes d'État Civil d'après Le Fichier Laborde de la Bibliothèque Nationale* [Paris: A. and J. Picard, 1965], p. 92).

40. This thesis is put forward by Laurent Guillo, who further suggests that Negri died in 1587 and the Negri whose career continued in Milan and who wrote *Le gratie d'amore* was a different Cesare Negri, possibly the son of the ailing Negri of 1587. (Laurent Guillo, "Un violon sous le bras et les pieds dans la poussière: Les violins italiens du roi Durant le voyage de Charles IX (1564–66)," in *". . . La musique, de tous les passtemps le plus beau. . . ." Hommage à Jean-Michel Vaccaro*, ed. by François Lesure and Henri Vanhulst [Paris: Klincksieck, 1998], pp. 207–33, esp. p. 231). Subsequent events suggest, as I argue, that Negri recovered, returned to Italy, and continued his career until some point between 1604 and 1610.

41. In addition to Diobono, Lomazzo named several other Italian dancing masters who had transferred to France ("Libro Terzo dei Grottesche," *Rime*, p 167).

42. Jacqueline Boucher, *Société et Mentalités autour de Henri III*, vol. 2 (Lille: Atelier Reproduction des Théses, Université de Lille 4 vols, 1981), p. 564; and *La court de Henri III. De mémoire d'homme: l'histoire* (Rennes: Ouest France, 1986), p. 101.

43. Henri Prunières, *L'Opéra italien en France avant Lulli* (1913; reprint, Paris: Honorée Champion, 1975), pp. xiii–xiv.

44. For the migration of Italians into France and related issues of anti-Italianism, see Jean-François Dubost, *La France italienne: XVIe–XVIIe siècle* ([Paris]: Aubier, 1997), as well as Boucher and Picot, and chapter 4 in this volume.

45. Negri, *Le gratie d'amore*. The dedication is in the initial, unpaged section.

46. This is not to suggest that dancers, musicians, or any other court servant were always paid in a timely or regular manner.

Recommended Reading

Boucher, Jacqueline. *Société et Mentalités autour de Henri III. Thèse presentée devant l'Université de Lyon II, le 22 Octobre 1977*, vol. 2 of 4. Lille: Atelier Reproduction des Theses, Université de Lille III, 1981. Jacqueline Boucher also abbreviated her four-volume thesis into a monograph without apparatus: *La cour de Henri III. De mémoire d'homme: l'histoire*. Rennes: Ouest France, 1986.

Dubost, Jean-François. *La France italienne: XVIe–XVIIe siècle*. [Paris]: Aubier, 1997.

Jones, Pamela. "Spectacle in Milan: Cesare Negri's Torch Dances." *Early Music* 14, no. 2 (1986): 182–96.

———. "The Relation Between Music and Dance in Cesare Negri's *Le Gratie d'Amore*." Ph.D. dissertation, King's College, London, 1988.

———. "The Editions of Cesare Negri's *Le Gratie d'Amore*: Choreographic Revisions in Printed Copies." *Studi musicali* 21, no. 1 (1992): 21–33.

Kendall, G. Yvonne. "Theatre, Dance and Music in late Cinquecento Milan." *Early Music* 32, no. 1 (2004): 74–95.

Picot, Emile. *Les italiens en France au XVIe siècle*. Bordeaux: Gounouilhan, 1918. Facsimile reprint, *Memoria Bibliografica*, vol. 25, ed. Nicola Merola. Rome: Vecchiarelli, 1995.

11

The Politics of Ballet at the Court of Louis XIV

Julia Prest

To enter the world of French court ballet (*ballet de cour*) requires a leap of faith, a broad and open mind, and a vivid imagination. It is a world of illusion and allusion, of spectacle and symbol, of marvel and mystery. More than anything else, it is a world of diversity. In this sense, French court ballet is a very baroque genre. As one critic has observed, it has more in common with modern performance art than with classical ballet.[1] Out with the tutus and in with the weird and wonderful. Alongside the diversity that is its defining characteristic, *ballet de cour* additionally underwent various developments and counter-developments in the course of its hundred-year history from the late sixteenth to the late seventeenth century. In terms of aesthetics and structuring principles, for instance, a general shift may be discerned away from an emphasis on allegory toward an emphasis on spectacle, while in terms of dance patterns and aesthetic, a parallel shift took place from horizontal (or geometric) dance to imitative dance. But many of the core features that one finds in late sixteenth-century ballets persisted throughout the history of the genre, and are present in the ballets of Louis XIV.

French court ballet can be a difficult genre to study owing to a scarcity of available sources. Most crucially of all, there is no extant choreography. It is likely that the choreography of *ballets de cour* was learned by means of imitation and not notation, and that it never existed in written form. Indeed, no choreographic notation was published in France prior to the appearance of Raoul-Auger Feuillet's *Chorégraphie, ou l'art de décrire la danse* in 1700.[2] The situation is somewhat better with regard to the music composed for court ballets, a good deal of which does remain, though much has been lost.[3] Similarly, a number of costume designs are available, as well as various examples of set design and stage machinery,[4] but the overall picture is far from complete. Furthermore, contemporary eyewitness accounts are tantalizingly short on valuable detail. In the case of ballets written during the reign of Louis XIV, our most complete source is the program (or *livret*), many of which have survived intact and are now available in a modern edition.[5]

The *Balet comique de la Reyne* (1581) is traditionally acknowledged to be the first *ballet de cour*.[6] Written to celebrate the marriage of Henri III's favorite, the Duc de Joyeuse, to the queen's sister, Mademoiselle de Vaudemont, its wider context of courtly celebration is crucial. Like this 1581 spectacle, many court ballets formed part of a much larger celebration that might include extravagant meals, fireworks, jousting, tournaments, and other more traditional forms of theater. Court ballets also had much in common with certain other courtly events and rituals, notably the Royal Entry. The *Balet comique* was, like all court ballets, a highly collaborative effort. Commonly attributed to its coordinator and choreographer, Balthazar de Beaujoyeulx (who was himself both a musician and a dancer), the *Balet comique* combined the talents of a host of other artists, including composers, musicians, costume designers, and set designers. At different times during its history, court ballet was to give greater emphasis to one or other of its principal component parts: dance, music, costume, décor, stage machinery, and, occasionally, narrative. The relatively slight importance given to plot in court ballet is one of the most important ways in which it differs from other theatrical genres such as tragedy, comedy, or even opera. Its close relationship with the monarch is another distinguishing feature of *ballet de cour* and one that is apparent from the very opening of the *Balet comique*, which features a young man who addresses the king (who was sitting in the audience) directly. Later in the ballet, Henri III receives Circé as his prisoner. In this way, the king is an active participant in the ballet at the same time that he is its principal spectator. For subsequent French monarchs to have come to dance in court ballets was thus a less radical shift than it might first appear.

This link with the French monarchy points to the political potential of court ballet. Among its other functions, ballet was thought to distract the nobility from other more threatening activities during a period when the king's authority did not go unchallenged. The great politician and first minister to Louis XIII, Richelieu, wrote regarding a courtier under Henri IV that "there was nothing to fear from him, music, carrousels and ballets being able to distract him from any thoughts that might be prejudicial to the State."[7] Louis XIV, in his memoirs written to instruct the Dauphin on the art of kingship, commented on the positive effects of such entertainments, which worked to different effect on the nobility, the people, and on foreign visitors:

> This society of pleasures, which gives to the courtiers an honest familiarity with ourselves, touches and charms them more than one can say. The people, on the other hand, enjoy a spectacle which is basically intended to please them, and all our subjects, in general, are delighted to see that we like what they like, or what they do best. This way, we hold their minds and hearts sometimes more successfully, perhaps, than by rewards and favours. In the case of foreigners, when they see that the state is otherwise flourishing and orderly, such seemingly superfluous expenses make a very advantageous impression of magnificence, power and greatness, aside from the fact that evident skill in all physical pursuits, that can only be maintained and confirmed by this, is always becoming in a prince and produces a favourable impression of what cannot be seen, by what can.[8]

Entertainment clearly has a role to play in Louis XIV's domestic and foreign policy. Moreover, the participation of the king in physical activities (of which ballet is one example) is thought to be an outward expression of his internal qualities.

Anything that is to do with a king is at a very fundamental level, political, especially in the case of Louis XIV who consciously politicized—and ritualized—almost every aspect of his life at court (down to his going to bed at night and his getting up in the morning). The political element of *ballet de cour* might take a number of forms and was used to communicate a variety of different messages to its audience. Often, as we have seen, the message was one of overt magnificence and splendor that in turn denoted the greatness of the monarch who was understood to be the driving force behind all such spectacles. At a time of peace, this message was already powerful, but at a time of war, the production of a lavish and expensive ballet also served to signify France's continued prosperity, despite the expenses necessitated by military action. To this message of monarchical greatness and wealth might be added a more specific commentary on current affairs. These messages might be intended principally for the court, the French people, or France's foreign allies or enemies. In the case of the *Balet comique*, the symbolism of the transfer of power from the fictitious evil enchantress, Circé, to the real-life Henri III is not difficult to fathom. At a time of ongoing religious conflict between Protestants and Catholics (the so-called Wars of Religion), of general instability and of widespread suffering throughout France, this portrayal of a conflict followed by its happy resolution suggested that Henri III might be able to accomplish exactly that for his country. For this reason, a large number of court ballets throughout their history feature stories of deliverance. Sadly, of course, such balletic allegories often remained remote from historical reality, an expression of wishful thinking rather than of how things really were.

Once the French court had tasted the delights of these early ballets in the late sixteenth century, they adopted the genre with enthusiasm and did not let go of it until a century later. One of its greatest enthusiasts was Louis XIII, whose decision to participate as a dancer in a number of court ballets doubtless paved the way for the more famous dancing performances of his son. In some respects, Louis XIV's use of *ballets de cour* constituted little more than a continuation of the tradition established by his father. While it is Louis XIV who is famously known today as the "Sun King," a number of French kings before him had made use of sun imagery, including Louis XIII, who, moreover, employed the symbolism of the sun in a number of ballets, as well as in Royal Entries and on medals. Like his son after him, Louis XIII danced a whole variety of roles, some of them more obviously kingly than others. In both the *Ballet de la délivrance de Renaud* (1617) and the *Ballet de Tancrède* (1619), for instance, he danced the part of the great liberator, Godefroy (the hero of Torquato Tasso's epic poem *Jerusalem Delivered*). In the *Ballet des Gaillardons* (1632), he played the highly symbolic role of the sun, spreading his life-sustaining light and warmth throughout the kingdom of France and beyond. This was precisely the type of role that Louis XIII's first minister and master of propaganda, Cardinal Richelieu, was keen to promote. However, burlesque ballet reached its peak of popularity under Louis XIII, and his first role as king was that of Pantalone, the lecherous, money-minded old man from the *commedia dell'arte* tradition. Sometimes he even performed female roles. Louis XIII's most intriguing role of all was that of chief blacksmith alongside the Duc de Luynes's incarnation of the eponymous sun-god in the *Ballet d'Apollon* (1621). On this occasion, it appears that the king was happy to allow his favorite to outperform him. What we learn from Louis XIII's ballet performances is that they were often but not systematically exploited for their political potential.

The same may be said about Louis XIV's dancing roles, which are our chief concern here. As we have seen, *ballet de cour* is a fundamentally performative and spectacular genre, in which dance, music, costume, and décor take precedence over any textual component. The development of the printed ballet program under Louis XIII added a fascinating new textual dimension to the mix, and one that was to prove especially important under Louis XIV. The program, distributed among audience members and sometimes sent to foreign courts, included the names of the performers in each ballet entry and their roles, brief descriptions of the action, transcriptions of any songs that were included (the major divisions within ballets were usually marked by a sung *récit*), and, most importantly, verses (*vers*) for the courtly dancers. It is these verses that provide a key to understanding how each role was intended to be interpreted by its audience (though they do not, of course, tell us how the audience really did respond). The author of almost all of the ballet verses written under Louis XIV was the court poet Isaac de Benserade (1613–91), whose involvement with ballets coincided almost exactly with Louis XIV's career as a dancer in those same ballets. Benserade's verses are an intriguing phenomenon for a number of reasons. First, their function within the unfolding of the entertainment is ambiguous: at no point were the verses read aloud, yet they were intended to be read silently by the spectator as the ballet progressed. Thus their impact in performance was wholly dependent on the individual audience member. Their content is also ambiguous, combining commentary on the performer's role within the entertainment and on his or her real-life existence at court. Vocabulary and references associated with a dancer's role are commonly twisted to refer to the dancer, often by means of a pun. Ultimately, the verses teach us, the true identity of the performer is of greater interest than his or her role, a fact that highlights the self-consciousness of the court ballet genre and sets it apart from other forms of theater. Very much a product of the moment, the *ballet de cour* was a forum for in-jokes and gossip, most of which alluded to male-female relations among courtiers. As will be seen, even Louis XIV's love life was not exempt from such commentary. The function of the verses written for roles played by Louis XIV is especially difficult to pin down: alongside comments on the king's amorous pursuits, we also find remarks that uphold his more conventional image as glorious, superlative king. Often propagandist in content, Benserade's verses do not, however, fall neatly into the category of pro-Louis rhetoric. Unlike the Latin inscriptions that appeared on commemorative medals and triumphal arches, Benserade's ballet texts prioritized wit and entertainment over the explicit expression of a political agenda. Just as court ballet was exempt from following the so-called "rules" of French classical theater, so also did it enjoy a greater degree of freedom than most other activities that involved the king so directly.

Louis's first appearance in a court ballet was in the *Ballet de Cassandre* in 1651, when he was only twelve years old. This was also the first ballet for which Benserade wrote the verses. The context for this ballet is arguably more important than its flimsy content. It was written and performed during the Regency of Louis's mother, Anne of Austria, in the middle of the civil war known as the Fronde, during which the power of the crown was contested by the Paris Parliament and by a number of prominent and discontented noblemen. It is widely believed that Louis's experience of the Fronde during his youth had a profound effect upon him personally and upon his chosen method of government when he became king. His youthful experience of exile from and quasi-imprisonment in Paris, for instance, is thought to account for his aversion to the capital and for his subsequent establishment of the court at Versailles. Most important, perhaps, the Fronde had graphically demonstrated to Louis that monarchical power was in fact precarious, and throughout his early reign Louis XIV famously sought to make his own power as stable as possible by reducing the power of the nobility and adopting a form of centralized government that has since been termed "absolute." The *Ballet de Cassandre* represents a rather feeble attempt at joviality and at asserting Louis's future power at a time when it was far from assured. Louis's two roles in this ballet were as a knight in Cassandra's service and as a dancer from the region of Poitou. In one instance his verses comment on how evident his noble grandeur already is, while in the other his future victorious reign is anticipated. Later the same year, Louis played a string of roles (both male and female) in the more substantial *Ballet des Fêtes de Bacchus*. The verses for Louis's role as a fortune-teller, notably, predict his future glory and hail him as the one who will bring peace to France after the Fronde.

Louis's most overtly symbolic and political role to date was in the *Ballet de la Nuit* in 1653 in which, having appeared in several minor roles earlier on, he appeared as the rising sun at the ballet's close. Performed in the immediate aftermath of the Fronde, the very conceit of the *Ballet de la Nuit* symbolizes an end to darkness and the beginning of a new era, itself represented by the young king (whose majority had been declared on 7 September 1651). The whole ballet is preparation for Louis's glorious final appearance in his magnificent costume bedecked with gold and jewels. (See Figure 11.1 for Louis XIV costumed as the "Sun King.") Other great names associated with *ballet de cour* were featured as dancers in this work, including the choreographer and musician Pierre Beauchamps (d. 1705) and Jean-Baptiste Lully (1632–87), best known as a composer but also a talented dancer. Beauchamps was Louis XIV's own dancing instructor and chief choreographer of his ballets, while Lully composed much of the music for subsequent ballets. The appearance of professional dancers alongside the courtly amateurs is significant: it points toward the increasing professionalization of dance that was to take place over the next decade and beyond. It is also representative of a striking absence of hierarchy in the genre (at least during the time of Louis XIV). Little distinction is made between the professional

Figure 11.1. Louis XIV as Apollo in *Le ballet de la nuit*, 1653. By permission of the Bibliothèque Nationale, Paris.

dancers and their courtly colleagues in terms of the roles they performed, though it is significant that verses were only written for the dancing nobility. In addition to the social hierarchy, the sexual hierarchy was broken down in these ballets, as more and more female dancers (both courtly and professional) appeared on stage.

During the remainder of the 1650s and throughout the 1660s, Louis XIV continued to perform regularly in court ballets. As one would expect, his verses tend to highlight his kingly qualities of majesty, glory, and heroism, regardless of the role he was performing. In this way, we see that Benserade emphasizes the (supposed) reality of life at court and on the battlefield over the poetic fiction of the ballet, a priority typical of and unique to the genre. As the verses for his role as an academic in the *Ballet des Noces de Pélée et de Thétis* (1654) remind us, whatever role he played, Louis was the center of attention at all times: "We do not notice anybody dancing but him."[9] Thus assured in his true status as king of France, Louis supposedly enjoyed the liberty to take on seemingly inappropriate as well as appropriate roles. Many of his verses include passing references to current political affairs, notably the on-going war with Spain. As peace with Spain became a possibility and then a reality, Louis's verses hailed him no longer as a ferocious warrior but as a gifted peacemaker. In his first ballet appearance following the Treaty of the Pyrenees (that signaled the end of the war between France and Spain) and his resultant marriage to Maria Theresa of Spain, for instance, Louis's verses revisit recent events, emphasizing his warring exploits as well as his ability to bring about peace. The self-consciousness of these verses is revealed in their specific reference to posterity (*la posterité*). If Benserade's verses do not constitute an explicit contribution to the crafting of Louis XIV's official image, they certainly resonate with that image as it was being established by other methods.[10]

What is perhaps most surprising about the verses for Louis XIV is that alongside this political commentary, we find repeated allusions to the king's private life. This extraordinary juxtaposition is nicely illustrated in the verses written for his role as a knight of the old order in the *Ballet de l'Impatience* (1661): "Whenever he dances or whenever he fights, as soon as he appears / We notice above everything else his heroic grandeur."[11] That dancing and fighting are here presented as being different yet interchangeable is highly significant: it suggests both that dance might have a political role to play in creating and sustaining Louis XIV's official image and that court ballet is ultimately less concerned with foreign policy than with the king's more private pursuits. Most private of all was his susceptibility to sexual love. In early ballets, it was Louis's nascent love (or, more accurately, desire) that was remarked upon. As he grew older and his desire became a reality, the tone of Benserade's commentary also evolved. After many insinuations, the occasion of Louis XIV's marriage offered a legitimate opportunity to comment on the subject of love, notably in the large-scale opera-ballet *Hercule amoureux* (1662). Indeed, this is one of the most politically charged ballets of the period owing largely to its context as a belated celebration of the royal wedding and, as it turned out, of the birth of the Dauphin. Louis's appearance as the House of France opposite his wife's projected incarnation of the House of Austria (in the event, Maria Theresa was unable to perform this role as she was pregnant) is an obvious means of performing the political importance of their marriage, while dressing it up in the clothes of love.

The following year, however, Benserade's verses allude to a more problematic subject: that of Louis's mistresses. In both the *Ballet des Arts* (1663) and the *Ballet des Muses* (1666), Louis XIV appeared as a shepherd alongside his preferred mistress, Mlle de la Vallière, who played a shepherdess. In both instances the verses for Mlle de la Vallière allude to her relationship with the king, which we must assume was common knowledge at court. In the verses for Louis's appearance as a shepherd in the *Ballet des Arts*, we are reassured that Louis will not be so distracted by a shepherdess (Mlle de la Vallière) as to forget his duty. The message is clear: although Louis XIV is visibly a pleasure-seeking king (especially when dancing), his kingly responsibilities are his first priority. What is less clear is how accurate a reflection of reality these verses were. Benserade's insistence is perhaps a little defensive. A sense of the king's appreciation of the female sex was heightened by some of the roles he played, including his appearance as Apollo surrounded by the Muses played by nine young ladies of the court in the first entry of the *Ballet des Noces de Pelée et de Thétis* (1654). And, as we have already seen, more women performed in the ballets of Louis XIV than ever before.

Thus Benserade's descriptions of Louis XIV as a hero are inevitably colored by a preoccupation with gallantry and male-female relations that characterizes these ballets. The two are not necessarily mutually exclusive, but it is significant that Louis's fondness for women does not feature in more formal accounts of the reign. Like Louis's official encomiasts, Benserade experimented with different methods of praising his hero. The most common method in the early part of Louis's reign was to liken him to earlier heroes. In the *Ballet de la Naissance de Vénus* (1665), for instance, Louis, playing the role of Alexander the Great, is repeatedly likened to the historical Alexander. In the *Ballet des Muses*, Louis XIV is likened to his heroic role of Cyrus, and again to Alexander the Great. In the first stanza, Benserade insists that Louis XIV (the copy) is the equal of these mythic heroes (the originals), while in the second, it is suggested that

Louis in fact surpasses his models in greatness and perfection. The most daring (and dangerous) of all such comparisons is when Benserade likens Louis XIV to God himself. He writes apropos of Louis's role as the sun toward the end of *Hercule amoureux:*

> This star looks very like his creator,
> And if we were not afraid to sound irreverent
> We would worship this beautiful copy,
> Such is its resemblance to the original.[12]

These words are not unlike many others that were written about Louis XIV during his reign. The difference lies with their context. In court ballet, it is the same person who is being presented as superlative and godlike on the one hand and all too human on the other. While the physical presence of Louis XIV at these ballets (both as an audience member and especially as a dancer) was intended to assert his unparalleled qualities, it may in fact have served to undermine them. The danger lies precisely in the coexistence of court gossip and encomium, of entertainment and a political agenda. One is familiar and private, while the other is formal and public. Louis XIV's performances in court ballets may thus be understood as the literal embodiment of an inescapable tension between the king and the man. While this tension was arguably present in all the machinery put in place to generate and uphold the image of the Sun King, it was most apparent in court ballets. And, as Louis XIV sought increasingly to impose his image on the world, the divergence between the man and his role of king became ever greater.

The court ballet's inability to uphold the image that Louis XIV and his propagandists wished to disseminate may have contributed to the genre's demise. Louis XIV, and with him Benserade, abandoned *ballet de cour* in 1669, after the performances of the *Ballet de Flore*. In his early thirties, Louis XIV was now beyond his physical prime and less able to meet the demands of a discipline that was becoming increasingly professionalized. Under Louis XIV, more and more professional dancers appeared in court ballets, performing more and more difficult steps. Such was the king's desire to maintain high standards of dance in France that he had founded the Royal Academy of Dance in 1661, which comprised thirteen professionals, many of whom were regular performers in court ballets. At the same time that the court was loosening its grip on dance, experiments were taking place in the French theater that would shortly lead to the birth of French opera. A burgeoning interest in opera was not limited to the public sphere, and we note throughout the 1660s the inclusion in court ballets of ever greater amounts of vocal music. The *Ballet de Flore*, for instance, features an extensive amount of vocal music by Lully, including solos and choruses. Only three years after the *Ballet de Flore*, Lully took over the Royal Academy of Music and embarked on the final stage of his career as a composer of operas. Given Lully's background in music and dance, it is no surprise that French opera was to accord ballet a prominent role in its structure and aesthetic. Heavily influenced by *ballet de cour*, French opera was nonetheless a very different genre owing to its emphasis on vocal music, plot development, greater unity of tone, and the fact that it was performed uniquely by professionals. Court ballet had apparently outlasted its usefulness, and so it was that the early reign of Louis XIV saw both the heyday of the genre and its disappearance.

Notes

1. Mark Franko, *Dance as Text: Ideologies of the Baroque Body* (Cambridge: Cambridge University Press, 1993), p. 1.

2. It is thought that Feuillet's system is none other than a plagiarized version of a system of notation devised by Pierre Beauchamps. Another system of notation, recently decoded, features in the manuscript of a masquerade ballet dated 1688—see Rebecca Harris-Warrick and Carol G. Marsh, *Musical Theatre at the Court of Louis XIV*: Le Mariage de la Grosse Cathos (Cambridge: Cambridge University Press, 1994).

3. Alongside the complete works of Lully, one notable source is David J. Buch, *Dance Music from the* Ballets de cour 1575–1651: *Historical Commentary, Source Study, and Transcriptions from the Philidor Manuscripts* (Stuyvesant, N.Y.: Pendragon Press, 1993).

4. Many of these are reproduced in Marie-Françoise Christout, *Le Ballet de Cour au XVIIe siècle: Iconographie thématique* (Geneva: Minkoff, 1987).

5. *Benserade: Ballets pour Louis XIV,* ed. by Marie-Claude Canova-Green (Toulouse: Société de Littératures Classiques, 1997), 2 vols. It is to this edition, in which the original spelling is retained, that I shall refer throughout my discussion. The English translations are my own.

6. This work did not, of course, spring from nowhere and scholars occasionally put forward other contenders for the title of first *ballet de cour,* including the *Paradis d'amour* (1572) and the *Ballet des Polonais* (1673). For a discussion of all three works see chapter 4 in this volume by Margaret M. McGowan, "Dance in Sixteenth- and Early Seventeenth-Century France."

7. "Il n'y avoit rien à craindre de son humeur, la musique, des carrousels et des ballets étant capables de le diverter des pensées qui pourroient être préjudiciables à l'Etat," *Mémoires du Cardinal de Richelieu,* 10 vols. (Paris: Renouard, 1907), 1: 39.

8. "Cette société de plaisirs, qui donne aux personnes de la cour une honnête familiarité avec nous, les touche et les charme plus qu'on ne peut dire. Les peuples, d'un autre côté, se plaisent au spectacle, où au fond on a toujours pour but de leur plaire; et tous nos sujets, en général, sont ravis de voir que nous aimons ce qu'ils aiment, ou à quoi ils réussissent le mieux. Par là nous tenons leur esprit et leur cœur, quelquefois plus fortement peutêtre, que par les récompenses et les bienfaits; et à l'égard des étrangers, dans un Etat qu'ils

voient florissant d'ailleurs et bien réglé, ce qui se consume en ces dépenses qui peuvent passer pour superflues, fait sur eux une impression très avantageuse de magnificence, de puissance, de richesse et de grandeur, sans compter encore que l'adresse en tous les exercises du corps, qui ne peut être entretenue et confirmée que par là, est toujours de bonne grace à un prince, et fait juger avantageusement, par ce qu'on voit, de ce qu'on ne voit pas" (Louis XIV, *Mémoires pour l'instruction du Dauphin*, ed. Pierre Goubert [Paris: Imprimerie Nationale, 1992], p. 135). Interestingly, he then goes on to warn of the dangers of being *too* skilled at such pastimes, of appearing to prioritize pleasure over business.

9. "On ne s'apperçoit pas que d'autres que luy dansent," 1: 205.

10. For an introduction to the subject of Louis XIV's official image and its creation, see Peter Burke, *The Fabrication of Louis XIV* (New Haven: Yale University Press, 1992).

11. "Qu'il dance, ou qu'il combate, aussi-tost qu'il paroist / L'on voit par dessus tout sa grandeur heroïque," 2: 513.

12. "Cet Astre à son Autheur ne ressemble pas mal, / Et si l'on ne craignoit de passer pour impie, / L'on pourroit adorer cette belle Copie / Tant elle aproche prés de son Original," 2: 594.

Recommended Reading

Boase, Alan. "Leçons sur le ballet de cour." *Neohelicon: Acta Comparationis Litterarum Universarum* 7, no. 1 (1979): 61–144.

Canova-Green, Marie-Claude. "La Parole écrite et chantée dans le ballet de cour." In *La Rochefoucauld; Mithridate; Frères et sœurs; Les Muses sœurs*, ed. Claire Carlin, pp. 319–27. Tübingen: Narr, 1998.

Christout, Marie-Françoise. *Le Ballet de cour de Louis XIV, 1643–1672: mises en scène*. Paris: Picard, 1967.

———. "Louis XIV et le ballet de cour ou le plus illustre des danseurs (1651–1670)." *Revue d'Histoire du théâtre* 3, 215 (2002): 153–78.

Franko, Mark. "Majestic Drag: Monarchical Performativity and the King's Body Theatrical." *Drama Review* 47, no. 2 (2003): 71–87.

Jeschke, Claudia. "From *Ballet de Cour* to *Ballet en Action*: The Transformation of Dance Aesthetics and Performance at the End of the Seventeenth and Beginning of the Eighteenth Centuries." *Theatre History Studies* 11 (1991): 107–22.

McGowan, Margaret M. *L'art du Ballet de cour en France, 1581–1643*. Paris: CNRS, 1963.

Prest, Julia. "Conflicting Signals: Images of Louis XIV in Benserade's Ballets." In *Culture and Conflict in 17th-century France and Ireland*, ed. Sarah Alyn Stacey and Véronique Desnain, pp. 227–41. Dublin: Four Courts Press, 2004.

———. "Cross-Casting in French Court Ballet: Monstrous Aberration or Theatrical Convention?" *Romance Studies* 21, no. 3 (November 2003): 157–68.

———. "Dancing King: Louis XIV's Roles in Molière's *Comédies-ballets*, from Court to Town." *The Seventeenth Century* 16, no. 2 (2001): 283–98.

———. "The Gendering of the Court Ballet Audience: Cross-Casting and the Emergence of the Female Ballet Dancer." *Seventeenth Century French Studies* 24 (2002): 127–34.

Silin, Charles. *Benserade and His Ballets de Cour*. Baltimore: Johns Hopkins University Press, 1940.

12

Mr. Isaac's The Pastorall and Issues of "Party"

Linda J. Tomko

❧

As early as the 1960s in Europe, North America, and Japan, the early music movement helped to galvanize academic interest in the study and reembodiment of dances that dated from the European Renaissance forward, and that were either no longer practiced or never recorded for re-viewing via photography or moving-image media. Dance practitioners and scholars have worked diligently to put into motion the principles, ranges of movement, musical relationships, and approaches to expression that period sources illuminate. Stage performance, frequently with the collaboration of period music ensembles, has been by far the predominant mode in which the rich findings from this research have been published. From the vantage of the early twenty-first century, the positivism of such a "reconstruction" approach looms large. This article takes the position that reembodiment techniques can yield valuable insights about compositional strategies and movement practices. They can as well uncover and discern ways in which choreographies conceptualize and put forward views of being, knowledge, and social engagement with others. These several kinds of gains can be coupled with historical analysis to illuminate ways in which early eighteenth-century English society negotiated debates, asserted identities, and produced cultural meanings—or at least did so for the elite strata and aspiring middling classes who pursued and consumed social and theatrical dancing. This article explores a 1713 choreography entitled *The Pastorall* for ways in which it produced cultural meanings in England near the end of Queen Anne's reign (1702–14), particularly with regard to the advent of party politics and shifting notions about how political process should proceed. This discussion aims as well to upend a vein of modernist analysis that, applied to eighteenth-century dance practices as to those of the twentieth century, has long treated dance as autonomous and regarded dances that make "topical references" as lesser in significance than those addressing "universal" themes.

Created by the English dancing master Mr. Isaac, *The Pastorall* is a ballroom choreography in the French noble style for a man and a woman. Its two sections, a loure followed by a spirited hornpipe, are set to music by James Paisible, a composer whose music Isaac had tapped previously for numerous choreographies. The dance was recorded in period Beauchamps-Feuillet notation by Mr. [E]. Pemberton and published in 1713 in London by Walsh and Hare.[1] According to the title page, it was "Mr. Isaac's New Dance made for Her Majestys BirthDay 1713." This attribution should be accepted with initial caution. Isaac was a prolific choreographer, and attribution phrases were both a recurring and changing feature of the title pages for his published dances. Some of his earliest dances for Queen Anne were published in 1706 in "A Collection of Ball-Dances Perform'd at Court." Subsequent title pages, assigned to new as well as reprinted choreographies, boasted "A New Dance Compos'd by Mr Isaac Perform'd at Court on Her Majesties Birthday," and still later, "Mr Isaac's New Dance Made for Her Majestys BirthDay."[2] Distinctions can be made between performance at court on the royal birthday and choreographies created in honor of or to mark the event but not necessarily performed at court, nor on or confined to, the actual birthdate.[3] Reporting news of the 1713 royal birthday celebration at court, the periodical *The Daily Courant* confirms that "in the Evening there was a Ball in the great Room behind the Drawing-Room, where several Persons of the first Quality Danced, and several foreign Gentlemen of the first Rank," but without naming the dances performed.[4] *The Pastorall* was published toward the end of Queen Anne's reign, one of a number of dances that appeared only under the attribution "Mr Isaac's New Dance Made for Her Majestys BirthDay." That the publisher visibly sought to link the dance to the prestigious royal orbit is clear from the attribution, as is the pattern of this attempted linkage over some seven years and as many dances. This gives us grounds in the twenty-first century to ask whether the dance articulated in choreographic notation registers views or positions taken by Queen Anne, and if so, how it did this.[5]

Review of the titles given to Isaac's birthday-connected dances show a general pattern of naming dances for political or royal personages and high political figures (*The Gloucester, The Spanheim,* even one referring to the queen as a girl, *The Princess*), or for specific dance and music types, such as *The Rigadoon* and *The Rondeau*. And at least one of the birthday-connected dances is named in reference to a major policy achievement of Anne's reign. Isaac's 1707 dance *The Union* appeared in the same year that England concluded the Act of Union in 1707 that bound together England and Scotland in the new entity Great Britain. I have argued elsewhere for ways in which the naming and, further, the choreography of *The Union* contributed to the reconceptualization then crucial for England to imagine itself anew; a new nation at that juncture—a new "imagined community," to use Benedict Anderson's term.[6] Because it references neither specific persons nor particular political initiatives, the titling of *The Pastorall* is seemingly at odds with the pattern(s) observed for naming other birthday-connected dances. Scrutiny of some period English investments in notions and instances of pastoral poetry and drama, however, suggests that *The Pastorall* as title and choreography offers potent connections to, and comment upon, a shift in the conduct of English politics.

What Was Pastoral for Queen Anne's England?

Like theories of politics and conceptions of the human body, the idea or ideas comprising things "pastoral" need to be historicized for the particular periods in which they are addressed. David Halperin enacted this approach with *Before Pastoral,* his study of Theocritus's idylls that also distinguished modern ideas about pastoral. In much earlier works, the wide-ranging yet closely argued studies of pastoral poetry and drama, Walter Greg and J. E. Congleton called out continuities and change in what counted for, or was deemed, pastoral in Western literatures of the ancient, Renaissance, and early modern periods. In a study of readers and commentaries on Virgil's eclogues, Annabel Patterson has argued cogently about the frameworks that notions of pastoral offered to intellectuals and artists—from Virgil's time to Valéry's—for interpreting and engaging with period issues and ideologies. Ellen Harris, focusing closely on Handel's musical production in England, has shown at length the different approaches taken toward pastoral drama and opera in Germany, Italy, and England of the late seventeenth and early eighteenth centuries. Findings in these several areas make it very clear just how fundamental were the works of Virgil and Theocritus as sources for Italian Renaissance humanists who renewed the interest in pastoral topics in the early sixteenth century. At the same time, it is clear just how powerful were the Italian Renaissance constructions of pastoral—especially those of Tasso's *Aminta* and Guarini's *Il Pastor Fido*, although other writers also offered examples—as models and stimulus to presentation of staged pastoral drama at various points across the seventeenth century in England. By the early eighteenth century, debate flourished among English writers about the proper nature of pastoral, including the question of which were the proper authorities to consult in creating new pastorals: the "ancients" on the one hand—that is, Virgil and Theocritus—or actual experience and English ways on the other. English debate drew heavily on theories forwarded by French critics across the channel, particularly Rapin and Fontenelle, yet the example of English poet Edmund Spenser's *Shepherd's Calendar* from the early seventeenth century continued to afford a competing conception.

What qualities or features or sources, then, made something pastoral for English readers, writers, and viewers in the early eighteenth century? Typically, shepherds were featured characters in pastoral writings; lands distant in time and imagination (Sicily, Arcadia as somewhere in the Peloponnesus, even seaside locations) were frequent settings; the notion of a Golden Age (a past point in time, a golden age of love) was often voiced; tragicomic action was deemed appropriate (and thus governed completely by the rules of neither tragedy nor comedy); and discussions about love, as well as circuits of unreciprocated affection, frequently supplied themes and the conflict which plays were to unravel. Given the late seventeenth-century value placed on decorum, that is, characters acting in proportion to their given identities whether in written or performed guise, song and competition in singing were frequently assigned to shepherd characters, who could be viewed as fulfilling occupations that actually allowed them leisure time for singing. This assignment certainly boosted the attraction of pastoral topoi for musical renderings. But whether shepherds were to be idealized types or realistic depictions of present-day shepherds was a source of debate. Linked to this was the kind of diction and expression expected of pastoral characters. In both these areas, the example of Spenser's *Shepherd's Calendar* fueled the interest by one stream of English writers in introducing rustic, unmistakably English characters and speech drawn from or resembling regional English dialect. At issue also was whether to try to retain the easy flow of Italian versification in new English compositions, and here the sheer skill of English writers affected the reception given to new work.[7]

By the second decade of eighteenth century, construals and constructions of pastoral ideas circulated in several different domains of cultural production in England, including poetry, staged drama, and competing practices of Italian and English opera. Because their timing falls quite close to the period in which Isaac's *The Pastorall* was published, I focus on two particular instances of pastoral production that vibrantly maintained the currency and visibility of pastoral notions in public eyes: the London production of Handel's *Il Pastor Fido*, and the Pope-Philips quarrel over pastoral poetry.

Paſtoral Topics in Musical Theater and Handel's *Il Paſtor Fido*

In early eighteenth-century England, pastoral topics continued to attract interest and spurred efforts by producers to present them in musical theater forms. This interest intersected the vivid audience engagement of the day with regard to, and the competition between, Italian and English opera. Opera at this juncture was coming to mean a through-composed work, fully sung, either in Italian, in which language the repertoire was already rich but also continuing to grow, or in English in a newly emerging repertoire. Both the Italian and English opera thus differed from earlier English dramatic opera, in which music was regularly composed and included but for which the spoken word continued to drive the action (the principal actors did not sing), and in which spectacular sets and machine effects figured importantly.[8] Music historian Ellen Harris contends that of several lines of musical-theater presentation explored in early eighteenth-century England, pastoral topics truly succeeded only in the form of masques. Masques used choruses as important structural elements, and included dance as well as song; masques also used smaller forces and were shorter in length than operas.[9] Significantly, early eighteenth-century masques almost never stood alone as independently produced entities. They were programmed as entr'actes or endpieces in performances devoted to spoken drama.[10] Thus the 1696 masque *Mars and Venus*, with libretto by Peter Motteux, composed by Gottfried Finger and John Eccles, saw the stage as an afterpiece, appearing three times with two different plays in 1704, while Motteux's and Eccles's 1701 *Acis and Galatea* was produced fourteen times as an endpiece for twelve different plays. Similar use was made of Nahum Tate and Henry Purcell's *Dido and Aeneas*, produced for a girls' school at a date before December 1689. Sections from this masque were "placed piecemeal throughout" the spoken drama *Measure for Measure* in 1700. In 1704, *Dido and Aeneas* as a continuous entity was presented as the afterpiece masque for two different plays, *The Anatomist* and *The Man of Mode*.[11] Harris speculates that the relative success of pastoral masques may have encouraged continuing efforts by others to produce operatic pastorals as independent entities.[12] Substantial forays in this vein included the 1705 production of *The Loves of Ergasto*, in 1706 *The Temple of Love*, and in 1708 *Love's Triumph*.[13] All three failed quickly.

It has to be noted that decisions to produce these works played into competition between the managements of the newly constructed Haymarket Theatre and that of Drury Lane Theatre. As they jockeyed to win viewers, scheduling of individual works shifted, and indeed collaborators sometimes changed employment and allegiances as well. The programming of pastoral operas represented an attempt to finger a vein of production fare that attracted audiences, but it was one that did not succeed. Dramatic opera was played out by 1710, according to Harris. Imported Italian opera gained increasing favor, first with works sung in complete or partial translation into English (*Arsinoe*, 1705; *Camilla*, 1706), and by 1710 with operas whose books, composition, and singing was done completely by Italians.[14] It bested attempts at English opera (all sung, in English) that included the 1707 *Rosamund* and the 1712 *Calypso and Telemachus*.

London in the first decades of the eighteenth century thus weathered a struggle between Italian and English-language opera. Italian heroic opera thrived, while English-language compositions lost out in the end. Interest in pastoral topics continued but found successful production only in formats that served as entr'acte or endpiece vehicles. It was in this context that George Frideric Handel presented his first two works for the London stage. The inaugural production was his 1711 heroic opera *Rinaldo*, the second his 1712 *Il Pastor Fido*. Both were sung in Italian. *Rinaldo* succeeded handily. *Il Pastor Fido* failed. Harris maintains that Handel was still steeped in the conventions of Italian pastoral that he had absorbed for the previous several years living in Italy and working there in the reformist circles of the Arcadian Academy, composing numerous cantatas. He composed *Il Pastor Fido* as a work small in scale (half the length of *Rinaldo*), of a consistent vocal range rather than wide range of vocal color, with no chorus and frequent use of continuo arias, to cite but a few features. He had not yet acquainted himself with the English situation regarding pastoral topics and conventions. Per Harris, London audiences expected Italian opera to be in the grand style, and the simplicity and consistency of action (or lack of surprises) that Handel brought to bear in the style of Italian pastorals did not match audience expectations.[15] The same year, John Hughes and J. Galliard produced the above-mentioned *Calypso and Telemachus*, which Harris identifies as a pastoral. It failed. Six years later, Handel composed *Acis and Galatea* for a private performance at Cannons, residence of the Duke of Chandos. Writers in the "neoclassical" school of pastoral poetry (discussed below) created the libretto for the production.[16] This 1718 work attempted a much smaller scale than the earlier *Il Pastor Fido*, and Harris terms it a masque. *Acis and Galatea* fielded a chorus, did not include continuo arias, and used da capo arias to further meaning rather than as conventional elements. And it construed the monster Polyphemus in a humorous way, as a buffoon. The 1718 *Acis and Galatea* won approval from its private audience.[17] From this point until 1732, Handel turned his attention to other forms and topics. What this sketch of the lay of London musical-theater land indicates, however, is that pastoral topics continued to attract the attention of English cultural producers in the early eighteenth century. And it signals that literary and theater workers and audiences were concerned to articulate national differences in construing and constructing pastorals (as well as notions of what opera should be). Pastoral topics and methods in musical theater constituted a cultural manifold that was much on the ears and lips of London musical theatergoers and supporters during Queen Anne's reign.

The Pope-Philips Quarrel

The quarrel between Alexander Pope and Ambrose Philips over pastoral poetry was widely known and conducted through several kinds of print vehicles. The camp aligning with Pope, which twentieth-century critic Congleton terms the "neoclassicists,"[18] included William Walsh and writers Jonathan Swift and Jonathan Gay. In many respects Pope's position followed that of earlier French writer Rapin, which honored the ancients as providing the standard for pastoral poetry. However, Pope and colleagues much preferred Tasso's *Aminta* to Guarini's *Il Pastor Fido*, finding the former replete with appropriate simplicity.[19] Pope approved literary imitation, though not outright plagiarism, of the ancients by writers of new pastoral poems. Regarding some key issues, he took the view that shepherds could be included in pastoral poetry as they may be conceived to have been—thus, not necessarily treated with present-day realism; he reminded poets that pastoral is an image of what they call the Golden Age; and that if poems included rural affairs, this should seem to be done by accident rather than study. Pope condemned the writing of allegorical eclogues (pastoral dialogues) by Mantuan and Spenser, and further objected to Spenser's calendar motif, use of allegory, and crafted dialect in the *Shepherd's Calendar*. He directed his ire toward contemporary eighteenth-century poet Ambrose Philips, standard bearer for the opposing alignment that Congleton terms "rationalists." The "rationalist" group counted Joseph Addison, Richard Steele, the Abbot Fraguier, and Thomas Tickell among its numbers. Regarding some key issues, the group took the position that England was a "proper scene for pastoral," giving one indication of its conviction that pastoral could and should speak to the specific experience of the English rural life. Thus, the authority of the ancients counted for relatively less, and English swains, English superstition, even English locales and scenery were deemed appropriate for the characters, matter, and setting of pastorals. While different members in the group differed on the need to more or less accurately depict actual conditions of shepherds' lives, the use of mythological characters was downplayed by all. Spenser's use of dialect-like language received positive reception among this group, and indeed, Tickell named Theocritus, Virgil, Spenser, and Philips as the leading pastoral poets.[20] Members of the "rationalist" group, too, contributed in print to the contest and scathing debate over pastoral issues. Philips published a set of pastoral poetry in 1708 and Pope a set in 1709, each in the style advocated by their groups. As the debate about their differences escalated, Addison commented sarcastically in a 1710 contribution to *The Tatler* on the seemingly recurrent musical theater interest in neoclassical pastoral themes. He mockingly welcomed the season for pastorals. In a 1712 *Spectator* issue he praises and calls attention to Philips's poetry and recommends him to other pastoral poets as a model. Tickell advanced arguments further, setting out the "English" school position with contributions to five issues of the periodical *The Guardian*, all in April 1713. Pope criticized Philips soon after in issue 40 of *The Guardian*.[21] John Gay ridiculed the rationalist approach in his 1714 "Proeme to the Courteous Reader" and his 1714 *Shepherd's Week*.[22] Pope set out the neoclassical position at length when he published in 1717 his *Discourse on Pastoral Poetry*. With this his voice carried the day. Subsequently, rationalist approaches gained ascendancy.

It is germane here to remember that Handel composed music for the 1718 *Acis and Galatea* in connection with writers from the neoclassical school who collaborated on the libretto; Harris notes that from 1713 to the production of *Acis* "the composer and the Scriblerians were in close association."[23] Here two independent kinds of inquiry into things pastoral intersected for a time. Several years prior to the end of Queen Anne's reign, these musical theater and literary projects were bent on re/fashioning pastoral topics and structures for English audiences. At the time that the notated score for Isaac's *The Pastorall* reached print in 1713, the stakes for performance production were high, and debates about pastoral were hot and immediate.

Pastoral References in The Pastorall's Choreography

The investments in pastoral by poets and musical theater production contributed to a cultural manifold from which ideas about pastoral circulated, enactments took the stage, and printed instances drew from and returned to. I argue that Isaac's *The Pastorall* referenced this manifold in choreographic and musical terms, and that the referencing acted to comment upon the rise of party politics. More explicitly, I suggest, the birthday-connected dance served to articulate a point of view taken by Queen Anne, against party, in nostalgia for a golden age of moderate men and moderate means.

How did Isaac's dance invoke notions of the pastoral? The record provided through the 1713 published Beauchamps-Feuillet notation score shows that the dance observes the conventions of noble-style dancing established in France in the second half of the seventeenth century. The style was emulated across Europe; English dancing masters and theorists were particularly avid students of it but also contributed to and extended the tradition choreographically. The notated pages of the score replicate the rectangular shape of typical period ballrooms, and they also graph the spatial coordinates of the social situation, in which the highest-ranking person in attendance was expected to take the best seat for viewing. This socially elevated person, the Presence, sat at the "top" of the room, represented by the top of the notated page. The dancers in *The Pastorall* commence moving at the bottom of the room—the bottom of the page—and advance toward this Presence. The dancers carve space and trace paths using various kinds of symmetry. They relate to each other visually and spatially, but they maintain orientation to the Presence. Their footwork is specified by the marks that are placed along the spatial tracks. The arm gestures that they use, while capable of being notated, seldom were recorded on published scores, and that is the case for *The Pastorall*. In this as in most other noble-style dances, bodily contact between the dancing couple is limited to handholds specified at various points in the choreography. As the dance concludes, the dancers retreat to the bottom of the room. Although not notated here, nor usually notated, in the ballroom context honors (formal bows) to the Presence would bracket the dance.

Isaac's *The Pastorall* moves to a tune that deploys two different meters: first a $\frac{6}{4}$ meter, marked "grave" beneath the music staff; then a $\frac{3}{2}$ meter hornpipe. This binary form is typical of many ballroom dances, and the tune repeats in an AABB scheme within each section. The dance movement, however, is through composed. The opening $\frac{6}{4}$ section resembles the "loure" dance and music type in several respects. The meter itself is typical of many loures, though a number of loures also exist in triple meter notation. Loure tunes in $\frac{6}{4}$ time[24] are typified by a short-long upbeat pattern and a *"sautillant"* (bouncy) rhythm | ♩. ♪ ♩ |. And, their choreographies pair two dance step-units with single bars of $\frac{6}{4}$ music, which requires that the tune move at a considerably slower rate than do gigues, also notated in $\frac{6}{4}$ but pairing one dance step-unit with one bar of music. The Pastorall's $\frac{6}{4}$ tune occasionally uses the *sautillant* rhythm, and then characteristically for a half-bar, but the tune also frequently deploys pairs of half notes and quarter notes | ♩ ♩ ♩ ♩ | in single $\frac{6}{4}$ bars. Three of the first four bars of the dance music employ this long-short long-short coupling. Here and elsewhere in the dance they contribute to a kind of pendulum feel: energy is first suspended, then let loose, caught again in suspension, released again suddenly. The figuration is clearly different from typical *sautillant* patterns, yet the pendular propulsion it creates resonates with the languid quality that musicologists Meredith Little and Natalie Jenne attribute to loures. Importantly, The Pastorall's dance notation shows two step-units of movement paired with each $\frac{6}{4}$ bar of the tune. Here the dance quite clearly acts like a loure.[25] The impact created by the tune's figuration and the 2:1 pairing of dance and music units leads me to term this section of the tune and dance a loure.[26]

Pervading The Pastorall's loure and hornpipe are steps and spatial patterns that can be readily seen in other noble-style choreographies. At the same time, however, the loure contributes to a pastoral feel that the dance's title summons up through the use of two distinctive step-units and some syntactical choices, that is, decisions about sequencing. The distinctive step units both appear in the first couplet of the choreography.[27] (See Figure 12.1.) Bar four calls for a quirky "pop-up" step that requires the dancers to bend and rise on the toes in fourth position on beat one, then on the next two beats to bend on two feet, spring from both feet into the air, and land on a single foot, the other held in the air (the second half of the measure calls for a *pas de bourrée* of two movements or "true" *pas de bourrée*).[28] The rising and bending, then rising and springing, in the first part of the measure happens quickly in the vertical plane; this is followed in the second half of the measure with a "true" *pas de bourrée* step that propels the dancers through space, emphasizing the covering of ground. The contrast in step units points up the suddenness and agility of the "pop-up" step, which appears infrequently in noble-style dances. That it confers pastoral connotations is confirmed by its use in two dances by Guillaume-Louis Pécour published in France in 1713. In the *Muszette à Deux* danced by Prévost and Guiot in *Callirhoé*, "pop-up" steps commence the choreographic passages set to both the first A and repeat of the B strain of the tune. In the *Entrée pour un Berger et une Bergere* danced by Dumoulin and Guiot in *Semelée*, "pop-up" steps open the dance in bar one and are repeated again in bar five.[29] A second distinctive step appears in bar seven of The Pastorall's first couplet. Here the dancers perform a *pas de bourrée ouvert* step-unit, the notation for which adds double dots to the foot indication for the first two steps that accomplish transfer of weight. The

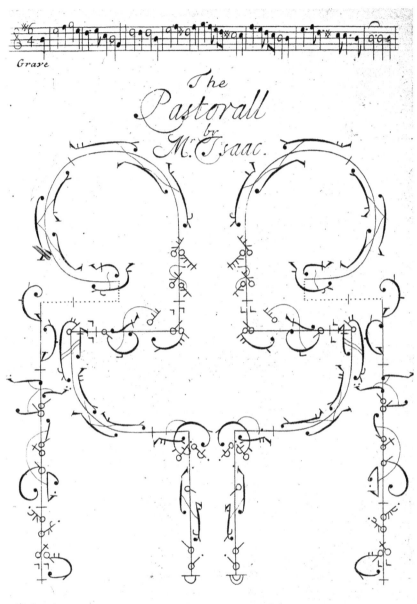

Figure 12.1. Couplet 1 from Mr. Isaac's *The Pastorall*. Courtesy of the Library of Congress, Washington, D.C.

dots signal that the dancers should bear the body's full weight on the toes; in the absence of any signs signaling bends or rises, the dots confirm that the dancers remain on the toes as measure six concludes. The second half of measure seven calls for a variation on a *pas de bourrée emboité* step-unit. No signs are placed on the movement lines of this step-unit to signal bending or rising; therefore an appropriate interpretation of the entire dance measure is to render it on the toes, or at the same unchanging level in space. Whereas the "pop-up" step found four bars earlier is still elegant in its quicksilver changes of level, the time spent on the toes for five successive transfers of weight in bar seven feels and looks clumsier by comparison. It inverts the elegance of the noble style, conveying a more rustic and less elevated, perhaps even bucolic effect.

These distinctive step-units are framed in four-bar sequences that themselves provide contrasting distributions of dancer energies. The first four bars of couplet one are filled with step-units that mobilize single springs from one foot to another, and also the *pas assemblé*. A spring occurs in bar one, following the half-turn pirouette; and twice in bar two, as the concluding element in the true *pas de bourrée* and then as a leap turning the body ninety degrees to face the partner while the second foot remains suspended in the air. Springs occur twice in bar three, following the *tombé* and then as *pas assemblé*. Springs pepper bar four, discussed above. This string of springs contrasts with step-units in bars five through eight, which stress smooth, balancing steps and channelings of the body's energy. Bar five leads into a one-footed balance via *pas coupé avec ouverture de jambe*; bar six calls for balancing steps that move backward in space, two *pas coupés simples*. The same-level, full-footed stepping of bar seven is discussed above. Bar eight turns the dancers ninety degrees to face each other via a pirouette on the toes of both feet; then the cadence is sealed by a change of energy and spring onto one foot, with the second foot closing in the air behind the first. Choreographically, the springiness of bars one to four contrast with the more sustained balances of bars five to eight. The repetition of steps at the start and conclusion of this couplet vocabulary further points up the shift in dynamics that have occurred across the eight-bar strain. The notation calls for the dancers to use all of the eighth bar to accomplish a pirouette on two feet followed by a spring, actions to which the first dance measure allocated only half a bar of music. The springiness of the lexicon in the first part of these eight bars frames the quirky "pop-up" step, and the measured ongoingness of the latter half calls attention to the unusual "full-footed" *pas de bourrées* embedded therein.

The Pastorall shifts seamlessly in meter and affect at the start of couplet nine. The hornpipe classification of the $\frac{3}{2}$ meter tune is spelled out beneath the musical staff at this point. Hornpipes are unique to English dances in the noble

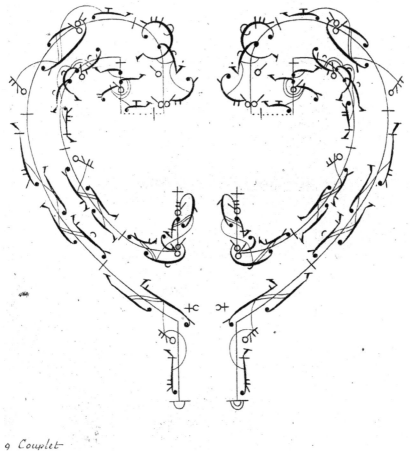

Figure 12.2. Couplet 9 from Mr. Isaac's *The Pastorall*. Courtesy of the Library of Congress, Washington, D.C.

style, and Isaac's choreography surges with a vivacity enabled by the opportunities for rhythmic variation that the meter affords.[30] Like the loure, *The Pastorall's* hornpipe signals pastoral connections by deploying distinctive step vocabulary and mobilizing a particular spatial pattern. Couplets nine and ten make use of what can be termed a "limping step" to establish pastoral affect. (Couplet nine is shown in Figure 12.2.) The limp, a somewhat ungainly maneuver, weds a step on the toe, a *demi-coupé*, with a closely following step or *pas marché* on the full foot, perhaps with a bent knee. In essence a *pas coupé simple* (without a slide), the step-unit changes level midway through its course rather than smoothly transferring weight so as to sink at the conclusion of the step-unit. This injects a peculiar, stopped quality to the ongoing flow of movement that is so characteristic of the hornpipe; it creates the impression of limping. This limping occurs in couplet nine at the conclusion of the hornpipe's first measure. In the first bar of couplet ten, the two dancers turn to face each other, take hands, and limp away from the Presence, traveling sideways toward the bottom of the room via three of these variant *pas coupés simples* in succession. In the latter part of bar four in couplet ten, a single limping-step occurs again.

The limping step is allusive. I propose that it can be read as playfully suggesting the idea of being "wounded by love," a notion well developed by the courtship motif of seventeenth-century pastoral poetry, drama, and musical theater. Further, it resonates directly with classical mythology, another contributor to the English cultural manifold of pastoral constructs. In Roman mythology, the god Vertumnus loved Pomona, a nymph fully absorbed with the cultivated woods and fruits that comprised her daily landscape. Despite his efforts, however, Vertumnus failed to win her attention and love. One day, while disguised, he told Pomona the story of Iphis, who loved but was spurned by Anaxaretes. Iphis finally hanged himself in despair on the gate to her garden that he had so often draped with floral offerings. He was wounded by love in the most mortal sense. Chancing to view the funeral procession for Iphis from her window, Anaxeretes turned to stone. Quick of wit, Pomona quickly seized the parallel between her situation and that of Anaxeretes, and when Vertumnus revealed his disguise, she accepted his love.[31] The pastoral connection thus suggested by the limping step in couplets nine and ten is compounded when viewed in connection with the spatial pattern for couplet nine, which traces the shape of a heart (see Figure 12.2). Certainly, the taste for allegory among one camp of English pastoral poets would make the reference immediately comprehensible in 1713 London. I note that the elliptical patterns found in many courante choreographies bear some resemblance to this shape, without necessarily signaling things pastoral. Indeed, step-units and many spatial patterns in the French noble-style of dancing are generally not unique to a single dance type (with minuet steps and the "Z" figure for giving and taking hands in the minuet providing a consistent, but not total, exception). But invoked here, in a dance entitled *The Pastorall*, the heart-shaped spatial form links strongly to period constructions of pastoral poetry and drama that foreground dialogues and debates about love.

These then are particular step-units, syntactical choices, and a spatial pattern that inflect Isaac's loure and hornpipe and help to develop a pastoral feel to the choreography. What implications and cultural meanings flowed from mobilizing such choreographic devices and titling the dance with those very words, *The Pastorall*?

What's in the Name?

Historians have hesitated to make too much of the titles for dances that are captured in Beauchamps-Feuillet notation. They walk carefully—and rightly so—in many cases. Titles are seen to pick up and echo the titles of current operas; or they are seen to function as dedications honoring prominent persons; or to make glancing reference to political figures. It is in this last light, especially, that titles have been viewed as "topical," indicating things of fleeting rather than enduring significance, particular and local rather than of universal import. The hierarchy of valuation traced out by this opposition between topical and universal is one that has been typical of modernist scholarship in the twentieth century, in which the arts are positioned as an empyrean realm apart, a domain of the aesthetic strongly separated from the political. I suggest that the titling of *The Pastorall*, like the titling of Isaac's birthday dance *The Union*, gives the twenty-first-century reader of period dances good cause to explore a more complicated relationship between choreographic production and political endeavor in Queen Anne's time.

If a purely topical reading were applied to Isaac's *The Pastorall*, one might think that the dance's title playfully referenced Handel's *Il Pastor Fido*. That work was performed at the Queen's Theatre three times each in November and December 1712, and again in February 1713.[32] Isaac's dance was published in 1713; the timing would have been completely right. But as noted earlier, *Il Pastor Fido* failed with audiences. This topical reference offers an unlikely explanation. Perhaps Isaac's title gestured toward the Pope-Philips dispute about the proper criteria for pastoral poetry. The Queen's 6 February birthday, the occasion prompting the publication of Isaac's dance, clearly predated the April 1713 numbers of *The Guardian* in which Philips published his series of essays about pastoral poetry, as well as Pope's rejoinder in the 27 April, number 40, issue of the same periodical. The debate had been joined before these dates, however, so the topical reference could retain some credibility. More compelling, I argue, is a view that credits the vivid circulation of pastoral constructs via poetry and musical theater experiments as supplying a cultural manifold which Isaac's dance tapped, both in coding the choreography and signaling the queen's point of view about the turn toward party alignments politics in early eighteenth-century English politics.

I utilize R.O. Bucholz's work on court ceremony during Queen Anne's reign to argue that the titling of Isaac's *The Pastorall* may relate to the problem of party agitation.[33] In the late seventeenth and early eighteenth centuries, political parties emerged in England as a new mode of political conduct, only recently having gained legitimacy. Yet the queen remained steadfastly opposed to faction and party, and she strongly expressed her preference for moderate men and measures. In this she continued a conception of politics and polity that had still been strong in the days preceding the Civil War. That was the notion of the polity as a homogenous entity, much on the model of the admired "commonweal" or "one unified world of values," as Steven Zwicker and Kevin Sharpe elegantly put it. In this model, rival divisions could, and did, compete to articulate "ideals for the whole commonwealth, not representations of rival programs within it."[34] But models of politics changed in England in the later seventeenth century; parties gained legitimacy as recognized alignments, and contest among them was seen as a viable mode of political conduct. Whigs and Tories combined efforts to press for the Glorious Revolution in 1688, after which the Tories gained ascendancy. The 1690s saw intensification of party conflict, and this was the milieu in which Anne matured before she took the throne upon the death of William III in 1702. She inclined initially toward the Tories, but that party did not echo her support for the war on the continent—England's participation in the War of the Spanish Succession—nor her program to achieve the union of Scotland with England. She had to make concessions to the Whigs to win the necessary funding for the war. Two major shifts in party power occurred during her reign. The Whigs swept into Parliamentary power in the 1708 elections when a failed Jacobite rebellion in London cast negative light on the Tories, one segment of which did indeed support return of the Pretender. But the Whigs lost the Queen's confidence in 1710, and in the elections that followed, the Tories swept in again. In the next years, party conflict remained high with regard to ending the War of Spanish Succession and settling the terms of what would be the 1713 Peace of Utrecht.[35]

In all this Queen Anne took the position that the monarch should be above party. Much quoted by historians is her fervent desire "to keep me out of ye power of ye Mercyless men of both partys."[36] She consistently called for moderate men and mixed ministries; she chose ministers whom she believed could steer a course and bridge the differences between the parties. She deeply resented those occasions when party men sought to turn to their account her own investment in royal ceremony. For as Bucholz has persuasively argued, Anne made conscious and fairly adroit use of court ceremony to shore up her position as monarch and to demonstrate her separation from factions, at least at the start of her reign. She reinstated early on the making of royal progresses to the West country, and also public thanksgivings for military victories. Such celebrations gained particular visibility, given England's nearly constant engagement in the war on the continent during her reign. She also revived the custom on touching for scrofula—many believed the monarch's touch could heal the disease—and during court seasons touched some 200 people twice a week. She observed fifteen saints days and twelve collar days with processions from the privy gallery to the Chapel Royal at St. James, and processed as well most Sundays.[37] Also, the royal birthdays were marked annually with festivities that included various mixtures of song, poetry, plays, dancing, and instrumental music. This reinvigoration did not persist at full throttle, and she reduced it substantially after 1708. Bucholz suggests that the queen pulled back in part in response to the Whig ascendancy that began in 1705, as party members pressed her to turn certain public ceremonies to partisan account. The death of her spouse, Prince George, in October 1708 led her to declare a lengthy mourning period that she lifted only at Christmas in 1710. Anne may very well have relished reduction in court ceremony during the mourning period as a means by which to evade Whig partisan pressure. The situation improved after 1710 with the fall of the Whigs and the new ministry under Robert Harley. Celebrations of the queen's accession and coronation days returned to the court schedule; twice a week during the London season Anne resumed "drawing room" nights, which attracted sizeable crowds; and the 1711 royal birthday was celebrated more fully. Although she was not well in the last years of her rule, Anne "appeared at each of her subsequent birthdays."[38]

Queen Anne clearly made vehicles of the royal birthday celebrations in her deployment of court ritual and ceremony. The Isaac dances whose title pages advertised their connection with the Queen's birthday thus assume added significance in this light. Birthday-linked dances that can be dated to the earlier part of the reign frequently named political figures but also sometimes served as indexes of royal concerns, such as *The Union* and *The Marlborough*.[39] Beginning in 1708, notated choreographies circulating as birthday-related dances more frequently bore names of dance types, or titles that emphasized the queen's status.[40] *The Royal Portuguez* of 1709 likely refers to the visit of the Portuguese ambassador of the same year, and two dances cite political figures or families. Of these, *The Northumberland*, published circa 1711, is set to music that could have been composed as early as 1699; thus the publication date of the dance may not reflect the dance's earliest performance and circulation. *The Godolphin*, published in 1714 at the end of Anne's reign, is dedicated to Lady Harriot Godolphin, the granddaughter of Anne's early adviser and treasurer, Sidney Godolphin.[41] The birthday-linked dances published from 1708 onward do, on the whole, steer away from naming specific political figures or events. The titling of the 1713 *The Pastorall* sustains this pattern. But titling of *The Pastorall* and the choreographic devices it puts into play may also continue to reference things political by the very locus and topos toward which the name and the movement devices move. The notion of pastoral as a realm apart, even a realm of innocence, an idyllic space, one in which certain peaceful moderation prevails, is congruent with Queen Anne's desire to remain above faction and party strife as the leader of the realm. Isaac's dance enacts dimensions of pastoral by the very title it bears, by the deployment of particular step vocabulary amidst the very familiar noble-style dancing that it utilizes, and by the staging of a heart-shaped floor pattern in couplet nine that deepens and compounds pastoral images of being "wounded by love" that the step vocabulary introduces. At the end of her reign, Queen Anne still longed for mixed ministries and moderate men.[42] Circulating for sale as a dance notation, asserting connection with the royal birthday through its titling and advertising, *The Pastorall* can be read as articulating a pastoral word apart, registering a political "hoped for" in choreographic terms, a desideratum of clear concern to the reigning monarch. And this set of pastoral codes would be indeed legible when, and as, it tapped into a dynamic cultural manifold of pastoral constructions and construals that both English poets and musical theater people were advancing in London in the same period.

It is not known who determined the titling of *The Pastorall*. The nature of the choreographic devices employed by Isaac, however, leads me to strongly suspect that he knew of the intended title, whether it was he, the notator, publisher, or other person(s) who made the decision. What is quite crucial, however, is the overt claim of connection with the royal birthday that the published dance score makes, asserting the composition's relevance to the queen's circuit of ceremony and representation, indeed, thereby even inserting itself into that circuit. The claim makes visible a view that the choreography and the publication mobilize a cultural efficacy different in kind from the aesthetic pleasure that they also might engender, or the momentary delight in grasping topical allusion that they might afford. *The Pastorall*, as dance and as publication offered for sale, bodies forth a capacity for making cultural meaning. And, without claiming to be exhaustive, the meanings presented here contributed to the highly charged issue of party contest and the queen's eschewal of it. We may fairly appraise *The Pastorall* as a composition and publication different in production and circulation from the modernist model that positions dance and art as occupying a realm apart, divorced from the conduct and discourse of politics.

Notes

1. See the copy held by the Library of Congress, now available via the Library's website, www.loc.gov, located therein in the American Memory Collection, subcategory Dance Manuals, "An American Ballroom Companion: Dance Instruction Manuals."

2. The six dances published in the 1706 *A Collection of Ball-Dances Perform'd at Court*, including *The Richmond* and *The Spanheim*, were also published subsequently with attributions 2 and 3. Other dances of later publication date, like *The Gloucester* and *The Royall*, appeared with the second and third attributions. *The Rigadoon Royal*, *The Royal Ann*, and a number of other dances, including *The Pastorall*, appeared under the third attribution only. For particular dances with their specific title page attributions see Meredith Ellis Little and Carol G. Marsh, *La Danse Noble: An Inventory of Dances and Sources* (Williamstown: Broude Brothers, 1992).

3. Carol Marsh notes, "There is no reason to doubt that the birthday dances, one each year from 1707 through 1714, and the two dances for the years 1715 and 1716 were composed shortly before publication." ("French Court Dance in England, 1706–1740; A Study of the Sources," Ph.D diss., City University of New York, 1985, pp. 170–71).

4. *The Daily Courant*, 9 February 1713. *The British Mercury*, 11 February 1712/13, reports, "Last Friday, being the Anniversary of her Majesty's Birth, the same was observ'd with all Demonstrations of Joy. The Nobility, Gentry, and foreign Ministers, made a splendid Appearance, and there was a Ball at night."

5. Here I pursue a question related to music historian Richard Leppert's analysis of the portraits Johan Zoffany painted for English colonials in eighteenth-century India, scrutinizing "ways in which art itself participates in the establishment and transmission" of a culture and its values, but with my caveat that artistic practices could and did contest and challenge as well as confirm values and norms. (Richard Leppert, "Music, Domestic Life and Cultural Chauvinism: Images of British Subjects at Home in India," in *Music and Society: The Politics of Composition, Performance and Reception*, ed. Richard Leppert and Susan McClary [Cambridge: Cambridge University Press, 1987], pp. 63–104, quotation from p. 102.)

6. Benedict Anderson, *Imagined Communities: Reflections on the Origin and Spread of Nationalism*, rev. ed. (New York: Verso, 1991).

7. My understanding of pastoral is indebted to David M. Halperin, *Before Pastoral: Theocritus and the Ancient Tradition of Bucolic Poetry* (New Haven: Yale University Press,

1983); Ellen T. Harris, *Handel and the Pastoral Tradition* (London: Oxford University Press, 1980); Ellen T. Harris, *Handel as Orpheus: Voice and Desire in the Chamber Cantatas* (Cambridge: Harvard University Press, 2001); Walter W. Greg, *Pastoral Poetry & Pastoral Drama: A Literary Inquiry, with Special Reference to the Pre-Restoration Stage in England* (New York: Russell & Russell, 1959); James Edmund Congleton, *Theories of Pastoral Poetry in England 1684–1798* (Gainesville: University of Florida Press, 1952); and Annabel Patterson, *Pastoral and Ideology; Virgil to Valéry* (Berkelely: University of California Press, 1987). Patterson sees greater similarity between positions taken by Rapin and Fontenelle than do other writers who stress the two's differences.

8. Robert Hume offers pithy explanation of the differences between genres and the terms that theater historians frequently use to describe them: "Used in its broadest sense, 'opera' simply means drama with a considerable amount of added music, or a masque. During the 1690s some writers seem to make a distinction between 'opera' and 'masque' basically in terms of scale. Blockbuster Dorset Garden productions such as *Psyche* and *Circe* were 'operas,' while shorter or less elaborate productions amounted merely to 'masques.'" Further, re *Arsinoe*, 1705, "though translated into English, it was 'Italian opera' in the sense that it contained no spoken dialogue and it presented none of the fancy scenic and machine effects long associated with English opera as staged by Betterton." And, "For the sake of clarity, I will use 'English opera' or 'semi-opera' to designate full-length works on the mixed model [half music, half drama]; 'masque' to describe shorter works of the English sort; and 'Italian opera' (whether sung in English or Italian) to refer to works that were all sung" ("Opera in London, 1695–1706," in *British Theatre and the Other Arts, 1660–1800,* ed. Shirley Strum Kenny, pp. 67–91 [Washington, D.C.: Folger Books, published by Associated University Presses, 1984], quotation page 69). I acknowledge difference between Hume and Harris in their appraisals of English masques. Hume, page 83, says, "There are almost no masques after 1700. *Peleus and Thetis*—interpolated into Granville's *The Jew of Venice* in January 1701 at Lincoln's Inn Fields—is probably the last of the breed." Harris sees the masque tradition as continuing longer. It strikes me that Hume cares about scenic and machine effects and thus views masques as different from semi-operas in terms of their reduced scale, whereas Harris focuses on how the action drives forward in a production—through song or through spoken dialogue, and in what proportions—while also noting measures of scale. I note the importance of genre analysis for these authors (still) in the 1980s. I am interested in the several ways in which musical theater (with its greater and lesser amounts of music, and with action driven through speech and/or song) took up pastoral issues and topics.

9. Harris, *Handel and the Pastoral Tradition,* pp. 190, 193, 196, 202; Hume, "Opera in London 1695–1706," p. 69.

10. Harris, *Handel and the Pastoral Tradition,* p. 193.

11. See ibid., p. 195, for *Mars and Venus* and *Acis and Galatea,* p. 193 for treatment of *Dido* in 1700, and pp. 137–38 for *Dido* in 1704. Curtis Price summarizes dating dilemmas for the "first known" *Dido* performance in "Dido and Aeneas," *Grove Music Online* (accessed 12 September 2006), http://www.grovemusic.com/shared/views/article.html?section=opera.006883.

12. Harris, *Handel and the Pastoral Tradition,* p. 197

13. Hume, "Opera in London, 1695–1706," pp. 84–85; Harris, *Handel and the Pastoral Tradition,* p. 189.

14. Hume, "Opera in London, 1695–1706," pp. 84–87; Harris, *Handel and the Pastoral Tradition,* pp. 193–95, 197–98.

15. Harris, *Handel and the Pastoral Tradition*, pp. 177–82, 192–93.

16. Ibid., p. 199.

17. Ibid., pp. 202, 207.

18. Congleton, *Theories of Pastoral Poetry*, p. 75.

19. Harris, *Handel and the Pastoral Tradition*, p. 192.

20. Congleton, *Theories of Pastoral Poetry*, p. 89.

21. *The Guardian* numbers 22, 23, 28, 30, 32 are Tickell's. See John Calhoun Stephens, ed., *The Guardian* (Lexington: University Press of Kentucky, 1982), pp. 26, 29, 105–9, 122–24, 128–30, 135–38.

22. Congleton, *Theories of Pastoral Poetry*, pp. 84–85; Harris, *Handel and the Pastoral Tradition*, p. 200.

23. Harris, *Handel and the Pastoral Tradition*, pp. 200, 198.

24. Meredith Little and Natalie Jenne, *Dance and the Music of J. S. Bach* (Blooming-ton: Indiana University Press, 1991), pp. 185–88. Pécour's *Aimable Vainqueur* (1701) is a well-known example of a loure tune notated in triple meter. See Julie Andrijeski, "The Elusive Loure," *Proceedings of the 21st Annual Conference of the Society of Dance History Scholars* (Riverside: SDHS, 1998), pp. 295–300.

25. The entrée grave dance type, notated in duple meter, would also pair two-step units to one measure of music, but is not an interpretive option here. See Wendy Hilton, *Dance and Music of Court and Theater: Selected Writings of Wendy Hilton* (Stuyvesant, N. Y.: Pendragon Press, 1997), pp. 154, 258.

26. Little and Marsh equate the tune with a loure; see *La Danse Noble*, p. 61.

27. Pemberton's notation for *The Pastorall* assigns "couplet" numbers to given quanti-ties of choreographic material, together with their musical notation, rendered symbolical-ly in the score. Some couplets occupy a full page of the notated score, but some pages con-tain two couplets. Couplets are numbered sequentially, with no break made when the dance and music type shifts from loure to hornpipe.

28. Wendy Hilton writes, "According to Rameau, this is the 'true' pas de bourrée. It has two 'movements' and three single steps: a demi-coupé, a pas marché, and a demi-jeté" (*Dance and Music of Court and Theater*, p. 183). Rameau indicates that this *pas de bourrée* is of an older or earlier usage (*Abbregé de la Nouvelle Methode dans L'Art d'Ecrire ou de Tracer Toutes Sortes de Danses de Villes* [Paris, 1725; facsimile ed., Farnborough, England: Gregg International Publishers 1972], p. 49).

29. The dances may be found in *Nouveau Recüeil de Dance de Bal et celle de Ballet con-tenant un tres grand nombres des meilleures Entrées de Ballet de la Composition de Mr. Pecour . . . Recüeillies et mises au jour. Par Mr. Gaudrau Me. De Dance* (Paris, [1713]).

30. Sometimes a single step-unit occupies a single bar of $\frac{3}{2}$ hornpipe music. At other times, when step-units are read across two bars of hornpipe music, three step-units occu-py two bars of music. Bars two and three of *The Pastorall's* hornpipe offers an example. Bar two calls for a *pas de bourrée* that concludes with a hop on beat three; bar three calls for a spring onto the raised foot on beat one, followed on beats two and three by a sideward *pas de bourrée* that concludes with a sliding action. Perspective gained from performing such step-actions suggests that the concluding hop in measure two of *The Pastorall* can be paired with bar three's opening spring and performed as a two-beat *contretemps-balonné* step sequence, one that is familiar indeed in noble-style choreographies. Seen from this perspective the six beats in two contiguous bars of hornpipe music can be paired quite log-ically with three step-units or step sequences, each of which is allocated two beats (*pas de bourrée; contretemps-balonnée; pas de bourrée*), even though the notated lines of liaison

within each dance measure would seem to signal one step-unit per measure. The alternation across a hornpipe choreography between the 1:1 and 2:3 ratios of musical bars to dance units generates the dance type's characteristic excitement and rhythmic vitality.

31. Thomas Bulfinch, *Bulfinch's Mythology* (New York: Modern Library, 1998), pp. 73–77.

32. Performed as *The Faithful Shepherd*, 22, 26, 29 November; 3, 6, 27 December; 21 February; all at the Queen's Theatre (Emmett L. Avery, *The London Stage 1660–1800: A Calendar, Part 2, 1700–1729* [Carbondale: Southern Illinois University Press, 1960], pp. 287–91 and 294–96).

33. R. O. Bucholz, "'Nothing But Ceremony': Queen Anne and the Limitations of Royal Ritual," *Journal of British Studies* 30, no. 3 (1991): 288–323. Patterson in *Pastoral and Ideology*, pp. 206–14, argues that the Pope-Philips quarrel about pastoral poetry can be understood in terms of positions the writers took with regard to the thorny issue of succession. While I link *The Pastorall* to the very issue of party and faction, I concur with Patterson that pastoral constructs could and did afford opportunities for engagement with period ideological struggles.

34. See Steven N. Zwicker, "Lines of Authority: Politics and Literary Culture in the Restoration," in *Politics of Discourse: the Literature and History of Seventeenth-Century England*, ed. Kevin Sharpe and Steven N. Zwicker (Berkeley: University of California Press, 1987), pp. 230–70. Quotation is from the volume editors' "Politics of Discourse: Introduction," p. 6.

35. This is necessarily a condensed discussion of emergent party politics. For a fuller treatment see Edward Gregg, *Queen Anne* (New Haven: Yale University Press, 2001); Bucholz, "'Nothing But Ceremony'"; Sharpe and Zwicker, "Politics of Discourse, Introduction," pp. 1–20; and Mark Kishlansky, *A Monarchy Transformed: Britain 1603–1714* (London: Penguin Books, 1996).

36. Gregg, *Queen Anne*, p. 134, quoting Beatrice Curtis Brown, ed., *The Letters and Diplomatic Instructions of Queen Anne* (London, 1935; reprint, 1968), p. 172: the Queen to Godolphin, 11 July [1705], Windsor. Kishlansky, *A Monarchy Transformed*, quotes the same statement with slightly different wording, p. 319.

37. Regarding collar days, Bucholz in "'Nothing But Ceremony,'" p. 318, cites E. Chamberlayne's explanation in *Anglia Notitia* (1699): "Twelve days in the year, being high and principal Festivals, His Majesty after Divine Service, attended with his principal Nobility, adorned with their Collars of Esses, in a grave solemn manner at the Altar offers a sum of Gold to God, in Signum Specialis dominii, that by his Grace he is King, and holdeth all of him."

38. This discussion draws appreciatively from Bucholz, "'Nothing But Ceremony,'" pp. 288–323, quotation p. 304.

39. Carol Marsh was early among scholars to link titles to persons and events ("French Court Dance in England," pp. 171–75).

40. Dances with their dates of publication: *The Saltarella* (1708), *The Royal Portuguez* (1709), *The Royall Galliarde* (1710), *The Northumberland* [1711], *The Rigadoon Royal* (1711), *The Royal Ann* (1712), *The Pastorall* (1713), *The Godolphin* (1714). Ibid., pp. 161–62.

41. Gregg, *Queen Anne*, p. 116; Marsh, "French Court Dance in England," p. 171.

42. See Gregg, *Queen Anne*, pp. 321, 332.

Recommended Reading

Hilton, Wendy. *Dance and Music of Court and Theater: Selected Writings of Wendy Hilton.* Stuyvesant, N.Y.: Pendragon Press, 1997.

Leppert, Richard. *The Sight of Sound: Music, Representation, and the History of the Body.* Berkeley: University of California Press, 1993.

Little, Meredith, and Natalie Jenne. *Dance and the Music of J.S. Bach.* Bloomington: Indiana University Press, 1991.

Patterson, Annabel. *Pastoral and Ideology: Virgil to Valéry.* Berkeley: University of California Press, 1987.

Thorp, Jennifer. "Your Honor'd and Obedient Servant: Patronage and Dance in London c. 1700–1735." *Dance Research* 15, no. 2 (1997): 84–98.

———. "Style or Stylus? Mr Isaac's Dance Notators in the Early Eighteenth Century." In *On Common Ground 1: Proceedings of the Dolmetsch Historical Dance Society Conference, February 1996.* Salisbury: DHDS, 1996, pp. 53–67.

Tomko, Linda J. "Issues of Nation in Isaac's *The Union*." *Dance Research* 15, no. 2 (1997): 99–125.

Part 6

Dance, Society, and the Cosmos

The attitude of the Christian Church toward dancing, a topic first encountered in chapter 2, reappears in chapter 14, in Alessandro Arcangeli's examination of the moral attitudes to dance from the late medieval to the early modern period. In his essay Arcangeli explores how dance was regarded by various sections of society, attitudes which varied across the spectrum from enthusiastic approval to uncompromising condemnation. Arcangeli arranges his discussion by concentrating on the writing about dance from the three major fields of moral theology and philosophy, law, and medicine. As Arcangeli demonstrates, legal tracts in praise of dance drew on classical precedents, such as the work of Lucian, as did the writers of moral literature who argued for a more balanced view of dancing, or those authors who argued in defense of dance. The latter group of writers were continuing a philosophic tradition from Plato and Pythagoras, and it is Plato's writings on dance that are addressed in chapter 13 by Graham Pont, in his exploration of Plato's philosophy of the dance. While Plato's life falls outside the timeframe of this collection, his philosophy continued to have a profound influence on Western thought and on writings about dance and attitudes toward it right up to the seventeenth century, as is discussed in Arcangeli's essay. Plato believed that education in music and dance (the ancient Greeks saw the two arts as one) was essential for society, as it would give to the young the required social and survival skills, as well as the necessary sense of a harmony of spirit, that is, the harmony of a well-balanced, mature personality, and also the harmony of the "well formed figure and of a well-ordered society and its larger environment." It was this harmony that would enable its possessor to recognize the beauty and order of the cosmos, since for Plato the cosmos could be interpreted as a measured dance. Human dance was an imitation of this celestial dance, the "dance of the stars." For Plato the organization of the *polis*, the city-state or "body politic," was the same as organizing and conducting a choral dance, since both were reflections of the measured dance of the heavens, and both exhibited the harmony and order of the macrocosm in the human world.

The influence of Plato's philosophy on three Renaissance art forms all concerned with the manipulation and ordering of patterns in space—dance, garden design and architecture—is the subject of chapter 15 by Jennifer Nevile. All three arts shared similar design principles, and through their use of order and proportion all three reflected the numerical order of the cosmos. While the aural representation of the cosmic ratios (1:2, 2:3, and 3:4) as expressed in fifteenth-century Italian dance practice is discussed in chapter 7, this final chapter concentrates on the depiction of the cosmos by geometric figures, such as squares, circles, and triangles, shapes which had divine connotations. Those who saw these geometric figures, whether while walking through a garden, watching a court ballet, or observing a building, were all being reminded of the nature of God and the order of the cosmos. Thus all three arts had a moral effect on viewers.

13

Plato's Philosophy of Dance

Graham Pont

The ancient Greeks considered dance to be one of their most important arts, and Plato, their greatest philosopher, was no exception. His writings, which include some of the earliest Greek theoretical literature on music and dance, have permanently influenced Western thought and practice and remain the historical foundation of modern science, philosophy, and pedagogy of dance. Many of these ideas, however, are much older than the Greeks, who inherited them from Asian cultures and went on to develop their own forms and conceptions of dance in poetry, song, drama, social ceremony, and religious ritual, as well as in architecture and the decorative arts.

For the Greeks and most other early societies, the choral or group circle dance was of special significance, as it was based on the cyclical movement of the stars.[1] Since remote pre-historical times, the celestial system had been accepted as an ideal model of human behavior and society. Training for the choral dance was a principal exercise for the young Greek—so essential, indeed, that Plato identified the uneducated person (*apaideutos*) as one who was lacking in choral art or "danceless" (*achoreutos*).[2]

Plato is also remembered as the creator of higher education in the West and founder of the first university, the Academy at Athens (c. 385 BC–529 AD). He also designed the first curriculum of academic studies, which originally consisted of just four mathematical arts—arithmetic, geometry, astronomy, and music. After Plato's death the Academy introduced three preliminary studies of verbal arts—grammar, rhetoric, and dialectic (or logic)—thus completing the classical system of the seven liberal arts.

In this syllabus of general education, which passed down to the Roman Empire and its successors, there is no mention at all of dance: dance studies appear to have been entirely omitted from higher education, both ancient and modern, before finally gaining academic recognition in the second half of the twentieth century.[3] Even during this period of enlightenment, many educators—including my own teachers in philosophy—would have been surprised at the very suggestion of university courses and research in dance, let alone a *philosophy* of dance! For hundreds of years academic philosophers have studied Plato's writings, which abound in references to dances and dancing, without seeing any need to explore this side of his thought in their own teaching and research.

How, then, are we to explain the apparent anomaly in Plato's theory and practice as regards dance? On the one hand, he insists to the last that dance is essential for education and culture; but, on the other, he and most of his academic followers seem to have entirely omitted dance from higher studies. In addressing this problem, we must remember that the classical Greeks did not usually think of dance as a separate discipline but rather as a component of the larger art they called *mousike*—the arts of the Muses, which also included song, poetry, drama, declamation, and instrumental music.[4] *Mousike* originally referred to these practical or performing arts; but, during the sixth century BC, the Greeks developed an interest in theoretical and speculative music, a line of inquiry which is particularly associated with Pythagoras (c. 530–497 BC) and his disciples. The school established by Pythagoras at Croton, in southern Italy, is remembered primarily for its mathematical analysis of musical consonances and scales, the practice of music therapy and their speculations on the "Harmony of the Spheres"—a theory developed from Babylonian-Egyptian origins that the visible relationships of the planets could be explained on the analogy with the mathematics of the musical scale.

Since dance was then part of "music," its concepts were naturally involved in the development of theoretical and speculative music, which eventually became the final discipline of Plato's mathematical arts. So Plato's philosophy of dance is part of his general philosophy of music and much of what he has to say about music, therefore, applies equally to dance (even if the implication is not always made explicit). An examination of his complete system of education reveals that music and dance perform a central role throughout, beginning with the student's mastery of the practical arts in early life and proceeding to the higher intellectual education which terminates in the study of theoretical music. This course of studies was meant to introduce the student to a philosophical worldview in which the mathematics of music and dance emerge as the key to understanding the *Kosmos* or universal system.[5]

Again following very ancient precedents, the Greeks viewed the cosmos as a hierarchy of similarly ordered systems, ranging from the human soul and body, to the family and the city-state: all of these were part of the "Microcosm" or smaller order and this in turn was seen as a reflection in miniature of the "Macrocosm," the celestial system of Earth, Sun, Moon, stars, and planets. Linking the system at every level was the unifying principle of "Harmony," a concept fundamental to the Greek philosophy of music and dance. The term *armonia* was originally used in joinery and other arts to refer to the process of binding, joining, or fitting together;[6] but, in the philosophy of the Pythagoreans—and particularly that of Plato—the harmony of the cosmos (or "music of the spheres") became a system of mathematical ratios which, they believed, was found in the structure of the musical scale as well as the entire world-system. This universal harmony came to be formulated as the "analogy of the Macrocosm and the Microcosm": the technical term *analogia*, a central concept of Greek mathematics, meant "identity (or similarity) of ratios." All these concepts are fundamental to Plato's philosophy of music and, therefore, necessary to understanding his philosophy of dance.

Music and Dance in Early Education

Plato (c. 429–347 BC), who was born at the end of the glorious Periclean Age, considered that Athens and its culture were already in decline by the early fourth century and could be saved only by the creation of a new enlightened ruling class of "philosopher-kings." To achieve this end he wrote the *Republic* and the *Laws*, outlining the organization of his ideal Greek polis or city-state and including a comprehensive system of education designed to produce the philosophically enlightened statesmen who, like Pericles, could rule the polis in the best interests of all its citizens.

This system of education (*paideia*) is divided into two stages, the "first" (or early) education—the traditional training of children in music and gymnastic—and the higher or academic education in the mathematical arts (preceded, later on, by the verbal arts). The early education was a pre-rational formation of the young mind and body through training in two integrated *technics:*[7] music and gymnastic. While the most important statements of this schooling are found in the *Republic* and *Laws*,[8] the method expounded therein is entirely traditional.[9]

To appreciate the depth, breadth, and thoroughness of this early training, it is imperative to grasp the full significance of *mousike*—the family of performing arts or *technics* patronized by the Muses. Deriving possibly from a troop of singers and musicians in the service of Osiris (the Bacchus or Dionysos of ancient Egypt), the Muses emerged in early Greek religion as the daughters of Zeus, most powerful of the gods, and Mnemosyne, the Mother of Memory. They were usually pictured as a group of handmaidens dancing in the train of Apollo, the god of the arts, medicine, music, poetry, and eloquence. Though the number of the Muses and their specific roles varied through time, they eventually came to personify a ninefold division of the musical arts: Thalia (comedy), Melpomene (tragedy), Clio (history), Calliope (heroic epic), Euterpe (flute music), Erato (lyric and amatory poetry—sometimes also dance), Polyhymnia (mimic art), Eurania (astronomy), and finally Terpsichore (choral song and dance).[10] Thus the Muses vividly represent the range of specific skills which the young Greek had to master in his early education; while "Apollo musagetes" (leader of the Muses) represents the ideal synthesis of all those arts in the well-formed Greek.

When Plato declares that "education is first given through Apollo and the Muses,"[11] he implies that the natural movements of the growing child are carefully molded, corrected, and beautified by some years of basic training in the musical or performing arts—principally dancing, singing, playing the flute and lyre, poetry, and dramatic recitation (of Homer and other approved poets). This was an integrated physical, moral, aesthetic and religious education, the technical and ideological foundation of Greek personal and social culture. Plato reaffirmed the ancient tradition in concluding that "the whole choric art is . . . the whole of education."[12] The practical test of a citizen's early education was his ability to participate in the singing and dancing of the Tragedy.

Early education in Greece paid close attention to dance, which was practised in civil forms in the school and music studio and in more military applications at the gymnasium and palaestra. Through dance (which included posture, deportment, gesture, facial expression, and other bodily movement), the young Greek learned not only to be quick, strong, agile, dexterous, and graceful but (most importantly) to imitate and internalize the characteristic rhythms, movements, and attitudes of the ideally noble Hellene, in peace and war. In this way he acquired the essential rudiments of the quality and virtue of *arete*—the many-sided excellence of style, manner, and accomplishment that was regularly exhibited and honored in national festivals such as the Olympian and Pythian games (the latter, held at Delphi, also included musical competitions—instrumental playing, singing, acting, reciting, and so on). These competitive festivals encouraged and maintained standards of all-round excellence, which were permanently recorded in sculpture and painting: generally speaking, the images of gods and heroes displayed them in noble and graceful posture[13]—in other words, in a position drawn from or resembling serious dance (such as the stately *emmeleia* of the tragic drama or the manly *pyrrhic* dance in armor).[14]

Thus, through early education in music and dance, the young Greek acquired not only a range of social and survival skills, but also a pervasive sense of *harmony*—not only of the inner, spiritual harmony of a well-balanced personality but also that of the well-formed figure and of a well-ordered society and its larger environment. So it would be natural for a Greek to see the annual procession of the seasons as a round dance (the dance of the *Horae* or "Hours"); and similarly, for Plato to view the art of politics, the royal art of managing the *polis*, as akin to the orchestration of a tribal dance in harmonious array. In Plato's thought, the management of the *polis* or "body politic" was virtually equivalent to conducting the choral dance of the entire citizenry.[15] That innate perception of harmony ultimately extended to the beauty and order of the cosmos as a whole.

Higher Education and the Cosmic Dance

Although the practical art of dance has no formal role in Plato's system of higher education, the science of cosmic dance is finally revealed as the most important subject of inquiry for the finished graduate. It is no exaggeration to say that the curriculum of Plato's "encyclopedia" of the mathematical arts was designed to prepare the philosopher or scientist for a rational understanding of the Pythagorean "harmony of the spheres" which, in Plato's last thoughts on the subject, is explicitly identified as the grand dance of the Macrocosm.

The "encyclopedia" (*enkyklios paideia* or "cycle of learning") was originally an integrated curriculum of the four mathematical arts organized by a logic that was undoubtedly Pythagorean in origin and aim (the modern sense of "encyclopedia" arose when Plato's successors at the Academy recognized the need for reference books to support the teaching). For the Pythagoreans arithmetic is the fundamental study, the science of numbers which they conceived as metaphysical units, the atoms of all things. Combinations and aggregations of these units form lines, planes, and solids, whose laws are studied in the next mathematical art: geometry. The Pythagoreans had originally assumed that any form or object must consist of a finite number of units and, therefore, that geometry would be a subset or application of arithmetic; but the proof of "Pythagoras's Theorem" (which was certainly not discovered by the Master himself) demonstrated that the hypotenuse of the right-angled isosceles triangle was incommensurable with the other two sides and could not, therefore, consist of a finite number of units. The classic proof revealed that some geometrical dimensions could not be measured arithmetically and that some numbers cannot be simple integers, units, or whole numbers. To preserve the logical sequence of his curriculum, Plato had to insert an additional study of irrational numbers. These new numbers would also be necessary for the scientific measurement of real music and dancing.[16]

The third mathematical art is Astronomy (or Cosmology), the study of the cosmos (another conception ascribed to Pythagoras): here again, Plato envisaged this third art as a subset or logical application of the preceding one: that is, geometry as applied to analyzing the motions of the "spheres" or celestial bodies. According to the Pythagoreans, this analysis will reveal the universal harmony: that is, the series of musical ratios that define the structure of the cosmos and preserve it from dissolving into disharmony and chaos. Thus the fourth and final discipline of the mathematical curriculum is Music and its subject-matter the "Harmony of the Spheres." Music, for the Pythagoreans, was the key to understanding the universe; but the music studied at the end of the higher education was not the practical art of song and dance but the mathematical theory of *musica speculativa*. This remained the core study of astronomy until the "untuning of the sky" in the seventeenth century.[17]

The encyclopedic curriculum is outlined in the *Republic* and the *Laws*,[18] though in the latter work Plato appears to place less emphasis on the final training in music. The content and rationale of the curriculum, however, are reviewed again in the *Epinomis*, an unfinished summary of Plato's general philosophy which obviously emanated from the Academy, even though Plato's authorship has been questioned. The *Epinomis* reads very much like an appendix to the *Laws* and the continuity of argument is so strong that many students, including the present writer, have accepted the *Epinomis* as a genuine writing of Plato and his final philosophical testament. If this attribution is correct, then the *Epinomis* (991A-B) reveals the secret of Plato's harmonic system, the "analogy" or musical module of 6:8:9:12: this set of interlocking ratios specifies the proportions of the structural intervals of the musical scale, of the octave (1:2), the fifth (2:3), and the fourth (3:4).[19] Pythagoras, on his deathbed, is said to have urged his followers to apply themselves to the study of the monochord, the instrument on which these and other musical ratios can be accurately demonstrated and measured. The Pythagorean Plato appears to have followed this precedent and injunction in finally revealing the module necessary for the tuning of the musical scale and understanding the harmony of the universe as a whole.[20]

The *Epinomis* is also critically important for understanding the role of dance in Plato's philosophy. The dialogue represents a very one-sided discussion by an Athenian "visitor" (presumably Plato himself) with two friends, Clinias (a Cretan) and Megillus (a Lacedaemonian). The subject is the nature of "wisdom" and the studies necessary for its acquisition. The principal speaker begins by emphasizing the difficulty of such studies, "the so-called arts, forms of understanding, or other such fancied sciences" which only a few mortals can properly master.[21] He briefly refers to the practical arts which are necessary to life but cannot by themselves lead to real wisdom, such as agriculture, cookery, hunting, the constructive arts, medicine, law, navigation, and warfare (and, presumably, dance). He then poses the central question of whether there is a "single science" without which "man would become the most thoughtless and foolish of creatures."[22]

The Athenian immediately identifies that single science as "the knowledge of number," a gift of the gods: "if number were banished from mankind, we could never become wise."[23] That science, of course, is arithmetic, the first of Plato's mathematical arts and the one which is absolutely necessary, in his view, for rational thought and expression and the attainment of virtue, goodness, and happiness. Number, furthermore, is necessary for the effective employment of all the practical arts, particularly dance and music, as "all musical effects manifestly depend on the numeration of motions and tones."[24] The Athenian then confirms the importance of arithmetic to dance and music in general with an extraordinary generalization: "[U]nregulated, disorderly, ungainly, unrhythmical, tuneless movement, and all else that partakes of evil, is destitute of number, and of this a man who means to die happy must be convinced."[25]

To appreciate the true sweep of this highly compressed statement, we must remember the aesthetic and moral role of dance in the early education, as well as the essential musical discipline of precisely measured movement in the body in general and the voice in particular. But where did we obtain the idea of rhythm and measure in the first place? The Athenian's answer is that, having endowed mankind with the "faculty of understanding," God placed before our eyes the vast panorama of the Macrocosm and its orderly, perennial motions:

"What fairer spectacle is there for a man than the face of day, from which he can then pass, still retaining his power of vision, to the view of night, where all will appear so different? Now as Uranus [Heaven] never ceases rolling all these objects round, day after day, and night after night, neither does he ever cease teaching men the lore of one and two."[26] It was from the sublime cosmic dance that humanity acquired the art of number, before coming to recognize the different motions of the Sun and Moon, and finally to address the difficult problem of relating the measures of the lunar month and the solar year.

The Athenian now proceeds to expound a general cosmology, an animistic theory of the Macrocosm in which the celestial bodies are seen as living beings "endowed with the fairest of bodies and the happiest and best of souls."[27] These heavenly beings are formed mainly of the element Fire and demonstrate their superior intelligence by moving in a procession that is fixed, regular, and completely uniform; whereas the earthly beings, including mankind, are made predominantly of the grosser element Earth, and their movements are much less orderly and intelligent. Lacking true wisdom and understanding, the earthly beings misinterpreted the grand uniformity of the cosmic spectacle: they assumed that uniformity and regularity were the result of mindlessness; whereas the "fairer, better, more welcome interpretation" would recognize the eternally regular motions as a sure sign of intelligence in the heavenly bodies, especially the stars: "They are the fairest of all sights to the eye, and as they move through the figures of the fairest and most glorious of dances they accomplish their duty to all living creatures."[28]

Thus the visiting Athenian enunciates a basic premise of Plato's mature cosmology and a conception of central importance to his philosophy of dance. The visible motions of both the Macrocosm and the Microcosm are conceived and perceived as the more or less orderly movements of sentient beings. *It now emerges that Plato's interpretation of the entire visible world depends absolutely on the concept of measured dance, that is, the mathematics of cosmic choreography.* So, far from being ignored in ancient higher education, the subject of dance—in particular, the mathematical theory of the cosmic dance—occupies a very special position in Plato's pedagogy, as the ultimate study and crowning vision of the encyclopedically trained philosopher. The Athenian confirms this conclusion by proceeding to review, for the third and last time in the Platonic literature, the ideal curriculum of the four mathematical arts and their role in preparing the student for the rational understanding of the cosmos.

Plato's view of the cosmos as a measured dance profoundly influenced Renaissance thought. In Thomas Elyot's treatise on education, for example, the chapter on dance begins with a restatement of the Platonic worldview.

> The interpreters of Plato do think that the wonderful and incomprehensible order of the celestial bodies, I mean stars and planets, and their motions harmonical, gave to them that intensity and by the deep search of reason behold their courses, in the sundry diversities of number and time, a form of imitation of a semblable motion, which they called dancing or saltation; wherefore, the more near they approached to that temperance and subtle modulation of the said superior bodies, the more perfect and commendable is their dancing, which is most like to the truth of any opinion that I have hitherto found.[29]

The ancient belief that human dance was an imitation of the celestial dance, and that both reflected an order based on harmony and reason, remained a commonplace of neo-classical thought until the age of Newton.[30]

Ethos and Education in Music, Dance, and Architecture

According to the traditional system of education, the young Greek was trained in the music and dance of his own tribe or ethnic or linguistic group. By Plato's time the different styles of music, dance, and other arts practiced in Greece had been classified into a number of "modes" associated with the various peoples who had invaded and occupied the Grecian territories after the Mycenaean period. Plato's preferred mode or style was that of the Dorians: the Dorian or Doric style, in all the arts, was considered to be noble, manly, dignified, and restrained. Given the ephemeral nature of the performing arts, our best available evidence of this and other Hellenic styles survives in the plastic and constructive arts. By the sixth century BC the styles of Greek monumental architecture were classified according to these tribal or ethnic distinctions into three principal modes (*genera*): the prestigious Dorian or Doric; the Ionic (a more feminine style from eastern Greece); and the Corinthian, an elaborate variant of the Ionic which appeared during the late fifth century BC.[31]

The crucial connection between the architectural and the musical genera is found in the concepts of "mode" and "ethos."[32] The Greek theorists recognized that each tribe or ethnic tradition had its own distinctive style or mode of poetry, song, music, dance, architecture, and other arts; and, having distinguished the regional or ethnic modes in the musical and plastic arts, they tried to codify the specific ethos or character of each mode. Accordingly, they identified a characteristic ethos in Dorian music and architecture—a character found in the pitch, tuning, and rhythm of Dorian music (and *a fortiori* dance), as well as in the construction and decoration of the Dorian or Doric style of architecture.

Certain features of this regional or ethnic character were eventually defined in precise measures: in the proportions of the Dorian musical scale (*harmonia*) and rhythm and in the forms and proportions of Doric architecture. Much of this distinctive ethos, however, could only be described subjectively; and it is highly significant that the contemporary descriptions of the Dorian tuning system were very similar to those applied to Dorian architecture, such as "manly," "majestic," "sombre," "distinguished," and "dignified." Plato's greatest pupil Aristotle summed up the consensus of the experts: "and about the Doristi [Dorian] harmonia all agree, as being steadiest and having above all masculine ethos."[33]

Having identified three different scales used by the Greeks—the Diatonic, the Chromatic, and the Enharmonic[34]—the theorists arrived at very exact measures for each tuning system, as well as attempting a general description of their respective ethos or character. Thus they formulated the "Ethos of the Genera": the diatonic genus as "natural, masculine and more austere"; the Chromatic as "sweet and plaintive," and Enharmonic as "exciting and gentle."[35] They also measured the specific rhythms of song and dance in metrical "feet" divided into long and short (double and single) units and tried to define the ethos of each rhythmic pattern, as noble or ignoble,[36] serious or gay, tragic or comic, et cetera. The motivation for such inquiries was not just the Greek passion for science, speculation, and classification; the subject of musical ethos was of great practical importance in early education. In the *Republic* Socrates asserts rhetorically that "education in music is most important because rhythm and harmonia penetrate deeply into the inmost soul and exercise strongest influence upon it, by bringing with them and imparting beauty, if one is rightly trained, or the contrary."[37]

Though firm evidence is lacking, the Greeks seem to have maintained very similar attitudes toward the moral and spiritual effects of their sacred architecture (which perhaps they saw, as Goethe has suggested, as "frozen music"). In trying to codify the ethos of the genera in temple building, they formulated precise canonic measures, supposedly derived either from the Macrocosm and/or the Microcosm (ideally, the same harmonic ratios would hold for both). Since there are no surviving Greek treatises on architecture, our best information on this subject comes from the Roman author M. Vitruvius Pollio, who makes it clear that the column of the Greek temple was carefully modeled on the proportions of the human microcosm: the Dorian on an heroic male and the Ionic on an idealized woman.[38] These ratios or modules were the vital link between the musical arts and architecture. The connection is made explicit in the dance-like posture of the graceful female figures that support the canopy of the Erectheum at Athens.[39] The theory of Ethos and the classification of the various Hellenic modes are essential to understanding Plato's important contributions to the philosophy of music and dance education.

Plato's Multicultural Music and Dance

The traditional early education had been developed to inculcate the ethos of a specific tribe, culture, or region of Greece—Dorian, Aeolian, Phrygian, Lydian, and so on. But with the growing power of Athens during the fifth century and its dominance over other city-states, there emerged the need for a "pan-Hellenic" mode expressive of Greek culture in general and, therefore, suitable for use throughout the Athenian Empire. Having made peace with Persia in 448 BC, Athens became the political capital and artistic center of the Empire and, guided by Pericles, entered its Golden Age. In 447 BC Pericles began the rebuilding of the Acropolis, which had been devastated by the Persians. The new monuments included the Parthenon and the Propylaea in the Doric style and the Erechtheum and temple of Athena Nike in the Ionic, thus creating an artistic synthesis more representative of the wider Empire.[40]

Similarly, Plato was affected by the new imperial ethos, as well as being profoundly influenced by the inquiring life and noble death of Socrates (399 BC). It was Socrates who communicated to him the teachings of the eminent music theorist Damon, teacher and friend of Pericles. According to Damon, "[S]ong and dance necessarily arise when the soul is in some way moved: liberal and beautiful songs create a similar soul, and the reverse kind create a reverse kind of soul."[41] Plato accepted this premise and reaffirmed the traditional role of music (and dance) in early education—but with a very important change which is also ascribed to Damon: given the existence of the Athenian empire, which now incorporated a number of different cultures, he realized that none of the traditional Greek musics was entirely suited to become the official mode of a pan-Hellenic or multicultural system of education. So, following Damon, Plato critically evaluated the ethos of the regional modes, mainly from a moral and political standpoint, and agreed that the manly and majestic Dorian mode (the best for inculcating temperance) had to be tempered or modified to accommodate something of the foreign ethos. After careful consideration of what was required of this new synthesis, Plato agreed that the Dorian style should be blended with the song and dance of the Phrygians, which was described as "inspired," "enthusiastic," "exciting," and "emotional" and suitable for encouraging bravery.[42] This wilder ethos was associated with the worship of Dionysos, god of wine and fertility, whose cult had evolved from savage orgies into popular annual festivals or *Dionysia*: these more civilized celebrations in turn gave rise during the fifth century to the classical drama for which the great theaters were erected under the patronage of Dionysos to become the scene for the presentation of Greece's finest tragedies.

Plato confined himself to enunciating only the general principles of this musical innovation but it is clear that, in the interests of justice, morality, and the quality of Greek life, his main aim was to reconcile the Dorian cult of Apollo with the Phrygian cult of Dionysos in a new multicultural ethos which balanced the severity and restraint of the Dorian mode with the bolder spirit and initiative of the Phrygian mode.[43] According to Aristotle, the Dorian and Phrygian scales were the two principal "species" of tunings and "all the other systems are classed either in the Dorian or in the Phrygian."[44] In that case, Plato's combining of the Dorian and Phrygian modes in a single *harmonia* would, in effect, be laying the musical foundation of a united Greece.[45] This *harmonia* was not just a tuning system but an ethos, attitude, or general mode of behavior—a harmony of opposite characters.[46]

With the great precedent of Egypt always in mind, Plato hoped to reform and permanently stabilize the Greek psyche and body politic through carefully censored education in music and dance—but in a novel mode. This, he was sure, would continue to instill the old Apollonian respect for rational order, harmony, and tradition while also cultivating the advantages of our irrational and intuitive faculties[47]—the magical Dionysiac power to transcend accepted forms and ideas—thus regularly infusing citizen and polis with fresh inspiration, creative energy, and the cathartic renewal of soul and spirit.

Notes

1. James Miller, *Measures of Wisdom; The Cosmic Dance in Classical and Christian Antiquity* (Toronto: University of Toronto Press, 1986), pp. 19–55; Françoise S. Carter, "Celestial Dance: a Search for Perfection," *Dance Research* 5, no. 2 (1987): 3–17.

2. *Apaideutos achoreutos*: see Miller, *Measures of Wisdom*, pp. 14ff.

3. Cf. Francis Sparshott, "The Missing Art of Dance," *Dance Chronicle* 6, no. 3 (1983): 164–83.

4. The Greek concept of *techne mousike* (the art[s] of the Muses) captured the imagination of Renaissance intellectuals, like the poets, artists, musicians, and choreographers who formed the Academy of Poetry and Music in 1571, led by Antoine de Baïf. The Academy was concerned with the recreation of Greek *mousike* on the sixteenth-century stage, where the text, music, dance steps, and gestures would all be closely related parts of an integrated whole. (See chapter 4 in this volume for further discussion of the Academy and its choreographic experiments.)

5. *Kosmos* was the beautiful order of the universe and its imitation at the human level, including man-made structures, organizations, and so on.

6. Solon Michaelides, *The Music of Ancient Greece; An Encyclopaedia* (London: Faber, 1978), pp. 127ff.

7. The Greeks used the term *techne* to refer to any skill, art, or craft such as those practiced by the carpenter, mechanic, and athlete; the poet, playwright, dancer, and musician; the doctor, lawyer, and architect; the general, the businessman, and the politician.

8. Plato, *Republic* III. 403–4, 410–12; *Laws* VII. 813ff. See Benjamin Jowett, trans., *The Dialogues of Plato*, 4 vols. (Oxford: Clarendon Press, 1871), *Republic*, vol. 2, pp. 229ff. and *Laws*, vol. 4, pp. 326ff.

9. Plato, *Republic* II. 376 (Jowett, *Dialogues*, vol. 2, p. 200).

10. See George M. A. Haufmann and John R. T. Pollard, "Muses," in *The Oxford Classical Dictionary*, 2nd ed. (Oxford: Oxford University Press, 1970), p. 704.

11. Plato, *Laws* II. 654 (Jowett, *Dialogues*, vol. 4, p. 174).

12. Ibid., II. 672 (Jowett, *Dialogues*, vol. 4, p. 194).

13. Cf. Athenaeus: "the statues made by the artists of old are relics of the ancient mode of dancing." *The Deipnosophists*, XIV. 629, trans. Charles Burton Gulick (Cambridge, Mass.: Harvard University Press, 1950), 6: 393.

14. Plato, *Laws* VII. 813–15 (Jowett, *Dialogues*, vol. 4, pp. 326–29).

15. Cf. ibid., II. 669–70(Jowett, *Dialogues*, vol. 4, pp. 190–92).

16. For an important study of irrational numbers in Plato's music theory see Ernest G. McClain, *The Pythagorean Plato: Prelude to the Song Itself* (Stony Brook, N.Y.: Nicholas Hays, 1978).

17. John Hollander, *The Untuning of the Sky; Ideas of Music in English Poetry 1500–1700* (Princeton: Princeton University Press, 1961).

18. Plato, *Republic* VII. 525–34 (Jowett, *Dialogues*, vol. 2, pp. 359–70); *Laws* VII. 817–23 (Jowett, *Dialogues*, vol. 4, pp. 331–37).

19. For a discussion on how the fifteenth-century Italian dance masters used these ratios as the basis of their dance practice, see chapter 7 in this volume, "The Relationship between Dance and Music in Fifteenth-Century Italian Dance Practice."

20. On this difficult passage see McClain, *Pythagorean Plato*, pp. 8ff.

21. Plato, *Epinomis* 974–76. See Raymond Klibansky, ed., *Plato Philebus and Epinomis*, trans. A. E. Taylor (London: Thomas Nelson and Sons, 1956), pp. 222–25.

22. Plato, *Epinomis* 976 (Klibansky, p. 227).

23. Ibid., 977 (Klibansky, p. 227).

24. Ibid., 978 (Klibansky, p. 228).

25. Ibid., 978 (Klibansky, p. 228).

26. Ibid., 978 (Klibansky, p. 229). Cf. Warren D. Anderson, *Ethos and Education in Greek Music: The Evidence of Poetry and Philosophy* (Cambridge, Mass.: Harvard University Press, 1966), pp. 68–69.

27. Plato, *Epinomis* 981 (Klibansky, p. 234).

28. Ibid., 982 (Klibansky, p. 236).

29. Thomas Elyot, *The Book Named the Governor* (1531), ed. S. E. Lehmberg (London: Dent, 1962), p. 73.

30. See James Miller, "The Philosophical Background of Renaissance Dance," *York Dance Review* 5 (1976): 3–15, esp. pp. 10–11; and Hollander, *Untuning of the Sky*, chapter 1, pp. 13ff., and chapter 2.

31. Ever since then these *genera* (later called "orders") have been standard technical terms of architectural theorists and historians, who have often overlooked the important fact that these linguistic-ethnic classifications were also used in (and were possibly derived from) music theory.

32. Warren D. Anderson, *Ethos and Education*, p. 39 and chapter 3. Edward A.

Lippman, *Musical Thought in Ancient Greece* (New York: Columbia University Press, 1964), pp. 69ff.

33. Michaelides, *Music of Ancient Greece*, p. 111.

34. Ibid., pp. 111–12.

35. Ibid., p. 112.

36. Plato, *Laws* VII. 815–16 (Jowett, *Dialogues*, vol. 4, pp. 328–30).

37. Plato, *Republic* III. 401, as translated in Michaelides, *Music of Ancient Greece*, p. 110. Cf. Jowett, *Dialogues*, vol. 2, pp. 227–28.

38. Vitruvius, *De Architectura Libri Decem*, IV.i, iii–vii. See Vitruvius, *Ten Books on Architecture*, trans. Ingrid D. Rowland (New York: Cambridge University Press, 1999), pp. 54ff.

39. For a detailed analysis of the imitation of the human figure in Greek architecture, see Joseph Rykwert, *The Dancing Column: On Order in Architecture* (Cambridge, Mass.: MIT Press, 1996), esp. chapter 4, "Gender and Column."

40. The Propylaea is built externally in the Doric order but has some Ionic columns inside.

41. Kathleen Freeman, *Ancilla to the Pre-socratic Philosophers: A Complete Translation of the Fragments in Diels, Fragmente der Vorsokratiker* (Oxford: Blackwell, 1952), p. 71. Cf. Plato, *Republic* III. 400–402. Cf. Jowett, *Dialogues*, vol. 2, pp. 225–29.

42. Michaelides, *Music of Ancient Greece*, pp. 111–12. Cf. Lippman, *Musical Thought*, pp. 71ff.

43. Plato, *Republic* III. 399 (Jowett, *Dialogues*, vol. 2, pp. 224–25).

44. Michaelides, *Music of Ancient Greece*, pp. 127–28.

45. Lippman, *Musical Thought*, pp. 63–64.

46. Plato, *Republic* III. 399; cf. *Republic* 410–11 (Jowett, *Dialogues*, vol. 2, pp. 224–25; 237–39). On this important point, see Giovanni Comotti, *Music in Greek and Roman Culture*, trans. Rosaria V. Munson (Baltimore: Johns Hopkins University Press, 1989), pp. 30ff. Cf. *Republic* IV. 424, where Socrates quotes another principle of Damon's that is assumed by Plato: "when modes of music change, the fundamental laws of the State always change with them" (Jowett, *Dialogues*, vol. 2, p. 251). See also Anderson, *Ethos and Education*, p. 75.

47. E.R. Dodds, *The Greeks and the Irrational* (Berkeley: University of California Press, 1951), esp. pp. 76ff., 210ff., 271ff..

Recommended Reading

Berghaus, Günter. "Neoplatonic and Pythagorean Notions of World Harmony and Unity and their Influence on Renaissance Dance Theory." *Dance Research* 10, no. 2 (1992): 43–70.

Carter, Françoise. "Celestial Dance: A Search for Perfection." *Dance Research* 5, no. 2 (1987): 3–17.

———. "Number Symbolism and Renaissance Choreography." *Dance Research* 10, no. 1 (1992): 21–39.

Harap, Louis. "Some Hellenic Ideas on Music and Character." *Musical Quarterly* 24 (1938): 153–68.

Heninger, S. K. Jr. *Touches of Sweet Harmony: Pythagorean Cosmology and Renaissance Poetics*. San Marino, Calif.: Huntington Library, 1974.

Miller, James L. *Measures of Wisdom. The Cosmic Dance in Classical and Christian Antiquity*. Toronto: University of Toronto Press, 1986.

Moyer, Ann E. *Musica Scientia: Musical Scholarship in the Italian Renaissance*. Ithaca: Cornell University Press, 1992.

Pont, Graham. "Dance in Ancient Greek Culture." In *Music and Dance*, ed. David Tunley, pp. 15–23. Perth: Musicological Society of Australia, 1982.

Thesiger, Sarah. "The *Orchestra* of Sir John Davies and the Image of the Dance." *Journal of the Warburg and Courtauld Institutes* 36 (1973): 277–304.

14

Moral Views on Dance

Alessandro Arcangeli

A Cultural Frame for the Dancing Body

The development of dance research scholarship over the past few decades has attracted renewed attention not only in the historical practice of Renaissance and baroque dance but also in the cultural history of dance during the same period. Only a few generations ago, this topic would have appeared marginal if not eccentric in relation to the dominant historical discourses; however, multiple changes in current research, in both the subject matter covered and the style of approach, have moved the cultural history of dance closer to the focus of interest of many scholars. In particular, several doctoral projects from a variety of countries and different disciplines, which have been published in studies over the past fifteen years, have investigated the attitudes expressed by early modern writers both for and against dance.[1] Even though the number of sources from which one could reconstruct such history is potentially very wide and their nature highly diverse, the secondary material now available allows for a reasonably informed attempt at a synthesis.

The first issue we need to clarify is exactly how the historical sources discussed dance; that is, was dance considered in any specific, narrow meaning, with reference to contemporary practice? All the signs point in the opposite direction and suggest that, as a subject of intellectual enquiry and cultural evaluation, dance was considered as a total phenomenon. While moralists undoubtedly paid some attention to the distinction between performing and watching, a specifically theatrical sense of the word was not prominent in their vocabulary and mental tool kit. Dancing was mainly regarded as an activity in which people engaged: it was therefore principally a question of social dancing. As for the social background of its participants, explicit reference to the aristocracy, the bourgeoisie, or the common people is rare, although there may be texts in which for a particular reason the writer specifically discusses courts and courtiers, or villages and villeins.[2] On the whole, a distinction between different social contexts is not central in the analysis of contemporary writers, who tend to regard the spectrum of dance forms as variations within a single species. These features are valid across the linguistic diversity of European culture; they are applicable to all the terms which early modern writers tended to favour: *chorea* and *saltatio* in Latin, as well as *danse* and *bal* in French, with all their parallels in the other vernaculars.

Let us now introduce the variety of disciplines which showed significant attention to dance and left some record of their assessment of its practice. Before the reorganization of the university curriculum introduced by the revolution in scientific thought, early modern European universities had inherited from their medieval predecessors a curriculum which consisted of a methodologic introduction (the "arts"), followed by the choice of one of three main faculties, the disciplines which were recognized as having a higher hierarchical status and provided the required professional competence in different walks of life: theology, law, and medicine. Given their role in the academic life of the time, we will start by outlining the context in which each of these three disciplines considered dance, as this will give us, first, an idea of why each discipline found dance a relevant topic of discussion and, second, what aspects of the dance practice were actually considered significant enough to merit comment. This does not mean that academic writing and the specific context of the university will be at the center of our analysis: they will only provide the structure of a discourse whose participants were more diverse, and included, for instance, dancing masters and literary writers.

Theology: Dance as Virtue, Dance as Vice

Moral theology and philosophy play a dominant role in the story, since dance was essentially an activity which had to be considered as appropriate or inappropriate for human beings, and therefore for many writers and readers alike its assessment within the background of ethical rules bore more importance than other aspects (for instance, its aesthetics). All the modern scholars who studied the subject have pointed out that judgments on dance during the period under consideration tended to cluster around the two extreme positions of enthusiastic approval or uncompromising condemnation, almost as if a middle ground were not tenable. The Renaissance is well known as an epoch in which the art of dance was refined and praised; however, it was the same period which witnessed harsh moral criticism, not only from the protagonists of the Reformation and Counter-Reformation, but earlier at the time of the flourishing of late medieval preaching, which drew on classical and early Christian sources for this adverse attitude toward dance. Such contrast has been summarized as a tension between "the ideal for the Christian and the ideal for the gentleman,"[3] or, more graphically, by portraying dance as being "quartered, cut up" by this tension which pulls it in opposite directions.[4]

Wholesale condemnation of dance is a known characteristic in the clerico-monastic tradition of the Western Church. A medieval adage, with precedents in the preaching of the early Church Fathers, claimed that dance was a devilish invention, an imagery which was still alive during the Reformation and found its way across the Atlantic via the Puritans. While it now may not seem a very meaningful charge, it acquires richer connotations if set in its cultural context. Most medieval and early modern writers would have agreed with modern anthropologists in giving dance some ritual origin. However, the stress for Christian authors was on the pagan nature of that activity, as if dance were a way of worshipping idols. The biblical image of the dance around the golden calf was a ubiquitous example and proof for such a link (one of its best known visual occurrences is a woodcut in the editions of Sebastian Brant's *Ship of Fools*).[5] The interpretation of the nature of contemporary social gatherings as ritual idol worship is obviously highly partisan and can hardly be taken seriously today, if we look at the many recreational reasons that must have driven people to participate in dancing parties. However, popular feasts were undoubtedly a form of social ritual, a fact which perhaps makes the clerical interpretation at the time look less bizarre. Furthermore, a specific offense was frequently seen in the timing of dance gatherings, almost directly competing with religious service, and in any case polluting the Lord's day with profane amusement. Medieval preachers had already fought against these elements of social dancing, and some protagonists of the Reformation intervened by adding a new nuance to it; that is, the folk dances that were regularly held on the feasts of Catholic saints were viewed as a popish rite linked to the ceremonial and idolatrous nature of Catholicism.

Dance was commonly associated with two capital vices, gluttony and lust, and as such was seen as a manifestation of disorderly behavior, a lack of physical control (excessive eating and drinking, and illicit or unruly sex) which mirrored a lack of control of one's own passions. Its twinning with the transgression of codes of sexual behavior arose from concerns that dancing was usually performed by men and women together,[6] and that the search and courting of a partner was one of its main intended purposes. After all, the courting between partners was regularly at center-stage from the perspective of the mimetic function of the dance, either in the sophisticated choreographic patterns of fifteenth-century Italian *balli* or in the often lamented, bawdy mimicry of sexual intercourse in comic performances and/or in folk dancing. This viewpoint acquires thicker meaning if seen in the context of the tradition of Christian warning against the flesh and suspicion toward anything that had to do with women. To the religious sensitivity of clerics and pious writers of a troubled epoch, there was more than enough to equate social dancing with a sin, or at least with an occasion for frequent sin, even when they did not go further and present it as one of the most abominable sins. It would not come as a surprise, then, to hear that some of these critics advocated a complete ban on dance, from Catholic Italy, where in 1580 one of Carlo Borromeo's closest collaborators tried to get a universal decree prohibiting dance and theater on Sundays and religious holidays approved by the pope, to Calvinist Geneva or Puritan New England. We should always remember, though, that, generally speaking, prohibitionism encountered little success: the 1580 ban did not obtain approval from Rome, and even the fierce campaign conducted by the Calvinist preachers in the Netherlands has been summarized by its scholar as "another battle fought and lost."[7]

Although harsh censorship of dance was widespread, it was not the sole attitude to dance found in the contemporary moral literature. On the contrary, a tradition with no lesser pedigree—considering that it dated back to classical Greece—recommended a balanced view, which praised honest and moderate dancing. The context of this orientation is interesting in itself, since it associates dance not with the other "performing arts," such as music and theater, as we ordinarily tend to do today, but rather with the world of play and leisure. In the fourth century BC, Aristotle listed a specific virtue, *eutrapelia*, as the art of amusing oneself and one's interlocutors by avoiding both excessive laughter and excessive seriousness. The concept of *eutrapelia* continued in medieval and Renaissance writings, such as the systematic theological compilations known as *summae*, one example of which was the influential piece written by Thomas Aquinas (II/II, 168). Aquinas's work presented a balanced orientation in praise of moderate recreation, of which dancing was cited as the most frequent and obvious example.[8] This balanced view also structured the assessment of dancing within Catholic *summae* for confessors (handbooks on sins and the recommended penitence), both before and after the Reformation: if dance was regularly discussed as a frequent occasion for sin, it was not usually regarded as blameworthy per se, but rather for the manner and circumstances in which it was performed.

It is worthwhile to sketch the structure of a moral discussion of dance and of its forms of argumentation as they appeared in most of the sources from the period. According to the dominant rhetorical rules, an argument could be proved by recourse to three types of evidence: authorities, reasons, and examples. The Scripture naturally provided the main authority; however, reference to dancing in the Bible is neither frequent nor easy to interpret, suggesting to most of its readers the presence of both good and bad examples (David and Salome offering the two most obvious, contrasting cases). Typical arguments by reason included educational and/or physical benefits, custom (we have always done so; why should we stop now?), the statement that if a practice is abused it should be amended, not abolished altogether, and finally, the rejection of all the above arguments by the insistence on sin, and on the display of links between dance, drunkenness, and folly. Evidence argued by example was regularly included within sermons and took the form of narratives in which dancing was normally punished by harsh divine retribution, unless repentance and reform intervened in time.[9]

Let us move to a case study and examine a representative text. In 1606 Jean Boiseul, a reformed pastor in La Rochelle, published his *Traitté contre les danses* ("Treatise against dancing"). The scene is clearly set: we are at the heart of Protestant France, toward the beginning of the century in which, after bloody civil wars, the reformed confession was legally authorized in a predominantly Catholic country. The pamphlet of Boiseul makes use of the set series of proofs we mentioned above: dancing is presented as condemned by the Scripture, by theologians, by Church councils and civil laws, and even by pagan writers; the arguments in its defense are rejected, and the conclusions support a total ban of the practice in the Huguenot community. Boiseul's text is, however, more interesting for its vocabulary and nuances. It is full of topoi characteristic of the type of pastoral literature to which it belongs. Thus, dance is a side effect of gluttony ("après la panse vient la danse" [after the paunch the dance comes], a proverb went).[10] Dance is also presented as the amusement and rite of witches, to the extent that several times throughout the book dance is accorded a power of "bewitching" (*ensorceler*): dancers are bewitched, and in their turn enchant the onlookers.[11] Furthermore, "what possesses them is a folly: a sage, sensible and serious man who sees them turning, vaulting and stamping in the dance—one foot here one foot there, one down one up, marching now forwards, then backwards, sometimes to one side, then to the other side—what else would he say they are if not all mad?"[12] Above all, women get the blame. They make a vain and dangerous display of their *grace* (grace), *disposition* (disposition), and *gentilesse* (gentility).[13] If we look carefully at the connotations of the latter series of terms, we discover that the main concern of the reformed vicar is not the disorderly movement of the limbs the reader could find caricatured in the previous passage, as Boiseul cannot deny the gracefulness of the dancing body. Throughout his text key words are *affeterie* (affectation), *artifice* (artifice), *contenance* (countenance), and *mesure* (measure), signaling to the reader that his critique is attacking the unnatural affectation of a demeanor that is anything but spontaneous, and which he finds so "perfectly and oddly synchronized" to the sound of music.[14]

If we want to assess what was specific to the cultural attitudes toward dance, and what depended on wider orientations and value systems, a comparison with what was said of a neighboring discipline may prove instructive. If, by contrast with dance, we look for what the same or similar authors wrote on music, most of the moral concern of the authors will vanish. In lieu of the censure of dance, we find an almost ubiquitous praise for music. Furthermore, singers and players do not ordinarily share the bad reputation or chastisement which stigmatize dancers (usually female) in preachers' *exempla*. Boiseul further proves the case, by repeatedly charging dance with the aggravating circumstance of making a dishonest use of music.[15]

Needless to say, on the opposite front many authors left us passionate texts in praise of dance. One of their most characteristic commonplaces was cosmic harmony, which human dancing mirrored on earth. A philosophical tradition which had its roots in Platonic and Pythagorean thought believed in the existence of an arithmetical, geometrical, and musical order, which explained both the origin of the world and its deepest meaning. Even Renaissance astronomers were influenced by the idea of dancing and music-making stars and planets; the topos was consistently exploited both in writing and on stage. Since contemporary political discourse in praise of absolute monarchy and social hierarchy made use of the same imagery, the aesthetics of dance and ballet was supported by a strong cultural background, whose legitimacy it confirmed in return.[16]

Law: Power and Justice

It is interesting to note that a number of authors of tracts in praise of dance belonged to the legal professions. To a certain extent this may just be a coincidence: here is a social group from which we have inherited considerable documentation, and which may have engaged in social dancing to the same extent as many other of their contemporaries. However, a professional training in arguing a case, combined with the secular—rather than clerical—nature of their trade, may have helped to orientate a number of lawyers toward writing apologies for the art. A tentative list may present some surprises. In early sixteenth-century Provence it is a judge, Antonius Arena, who wrote a macaronic poem, in which instructions on how to dance a *basse dance* were mixed with playful rules of courtesy; and he addressed it to his fellow students of law in Avignon.[17] Later in the same century and further north in France, a similar combination of dance tutoring and inculcation of social norms was proposed by Jean Tabourot (alias Thoinot Arbeau). In this case, while the author was a canon, his fictional pupil in the dialogue was again a student of law.[18] The most frequently quoted apology for dance in Western history, the dialogue *The Dance* by the Greek satyrical writer Lucian (second century AD), was adapted during the sixteenth century by two jurists, Jean Pirrhus d'Angleberme and Rinaldo Corso.[19] The latter's *Dialogo del ballo* (1555) was set in a minor Italian court (Correggio) on the appropriate occasion of Carnival, and a few generations later Corso's treatise was in turn plagiarized by another juriconsult, Filippo degli Alessandri from Narni.[20] Finally, John Davies, the author of the poem *Orchestra* (1596), one of the most remarkable variations on the topos of cosmic dance, was a student of English common law (and one awaiting a highly successful career).[21]

However, this enthusiastic company could by no means represent the whole legal side of the story, as the relation between dance and law is manifold.[22] At the opposite end of the spectrum to tolerance, there were the attempts to outlaw dance in early modern Europe (and North America). Some theological writing took the middle ground, particularly that writing which by its nature was very close to ecclesiastical law, specifically the discipline of cases of consciousness by which individual sins were assessed. (We have seen that even the literature on penance tended to consider dancing per se as neutral, and condemned only its excesses.) This moderate tone is also predominant in a specific juristic dissertation, discussed at the University of Wittenberg in 1730.[23] The fact that this dissertation originated from the birthplace of the Reformation is significant: within the variety of forms of early modern Christianity, the Lutheran Church is undoubtedly the one that showed more consistently a tolerant attitude toward dancing and other current pastimes. The same tolerance on the whole prevailed in the orientation of secular authorities, who undertook occasional campaigns of moralization and regulation of popular culture, but ultimately preferred to leave the common people with their amusements, rather than risk the provocation of social unrest by trying to ban them.

The topic of recreation, with which dance was so often associated, offers us the opportunity to mention a specific tradition of juristic writing, the fifteenth-century Italian treatise on games (*de ludo*).[24] In the context of a predominant preoccupation with gambling and its financial consequences, some authors considered the wider spectrum of leisure activities and offered an evaluation of dance which was in line with the assessment provided by contemporary moralists and theologians.

Medicine: To Be or Not To Be Fit

The third type of discourse which remains to be analyzed is medicine.[25] That dance benefits human health was generally acknowledged. Even the art's arch-enemies—as we could duly consider the French Reformed Churches—in their official treatise on the subject (1579) did not deny it; they only remarked that agility was a vain aim to pursue, and that the faithful should care about their souls more than about their bodies.[26]

From the medical perspective dance was interpreted as a form of physical exercise. This classification should not be taken for granted, as obviously different genres of dance require physical efforts of varying magnitude. As a consequence, and perhaps more than in other types of sources, medical texts were able to discuss dance in a more detailed manner, recommending some dance forms while warning the reader about others. Naturally enough, in order to produce some physical effect, dancing had to be significantly lively, and it is no surprise, therefore, to find the galliard quoted more often in this context than dances of processional type such as the pavane. At the other extreme, based on both a mixture of moral and medical perspectives, some dances were clearly perceived as too quick and springy, as was often argued about couples spinning in the *volta*, and, in later centuries, the waltz,[27] who were bound to be afflicted by vertigo.

Alternatively, and consistent with the basic tenets of humoral theory, different dance types could be prescribed for people of differing temperament. One of the most explicit texts in this area is written in 1607 by John Lowin (Roscio), a former actor converted to a Puritan persuasion, who recommends, according to one's constitution, "such dances as doe strongly stirre the body," or "that dancing . . . which exerciseth the bodie in a meane measure of agitations," or "not . . . any kind of dancing."[28]

Like moralists, physicians had some caveats to give to their patients and/or readers, in matter of circumstances of place, time, and other conditions which would affect the outcome of the exercise. The main concern here was not to interfere with the process of digestion (a rule dancing parties regularly broke after banquets); one should also preferably dance in the open air and avoid extreme weather conditions.

While the first systematic studies of physical exercise were inspired by humanism and mainly concerned with ancient gymnastics, a series of medical treatises subsequently began to pay more attention to contemporary sports and pastimes. This is the case for a number of French physicians, notably Jérôme de Monteux (1557), Joseph Duchesne (1606), Pierre Gontier (1668), and Michel Bicaise (1669), as all of them praised most of the genres of dancing that were fashionable at their time, providing sometimes lists of dance names and sometimes detailed and enthusiastic explanations of the physical benefit these dances could provide.

So far we have encountered dance in relation with comparatively healthy bodies, in the context of what was commonly perceived as a preventive part of medicine (hygiene). We also find dance associated with specific diseases, although dance's roles as a symptom, or as a means of cure, easily overlap and become confused. This is the case for tarantism, the example of music and dance therapy most frequently quoted during the early modern period, which, however, at the same time, offered a display of disorderly bodily movement that confirm the moralists' general prejudice against dance.[29]

Conclusion

It goes without saying that the three disciplinary contexts we have surveyed only cover part of the contemporary cultural scene, and the reader may find interesting parallels elsewhere in this volume, where iconography or literature are discussed. It may be worth noting that the same period witnessed early developments of an anthropological perspective: dance and music were often observed and registered as important features of native cultures by travelers to the new worlds in the age of discoveries, while comparative sketches could also be given of the contrasting dancing traditions of the different European nations.[30]

In this overview, we have not so far suggested explicit patterns of change through time. There are certainly recognizable cultural facts an observer can notice as present at some point during the period under discussion, while absent or modified at other times. For instance, the moral discourse concerning the dance performance—the subject of moral deliberation being the dancer—was prominent until the first decades of the seventeenth century, when social dance and folk recreations were under scrutiny. By the second half of the seventeenth century, however, a stream of theologians (particularly within French Catholicism) had started to group going to a ballet together with going to the theater, to an opera, or a concert, so that the previous focus on the dance performer changed to a focus on the experience of the audience. Writing on dance also becomes unoriginal and out of touch with contemporary social trends; but it is worth registering that its focus has partially changed. In the early modern period historians also date a gradual process of widening the gap between elite and popular culture, with increasingly separate and differentiated social gatherings and forms of recreation.[31] The most obvious consequence of which was an increased control from above over the behavior of the working classes.

The significant refining of the art of dance made any moral critique centered on the caricature of disorderly movement progressively redundant. In fact, around 1600 the case of Boiseul, and other similar texts, clearly exemplified a specific concern for an over-sophisticated demeanor. This does not mean that contemporary culture expressed a unanimous reaction against patterns of behavior originating on the dancing floor. The story of the Jesuits is a telling and different one: the religious order which was protagonist of many battles fought by the Counter-Reformation Church was also the most experimental in adopting forms of ballet within the educational activities of its colleges.

The legacy of the Renaissance and baroque era is thus a complex one. The period witnessed a variety of dancing practices and of cultural responses to them. A moral perspective prevailed and proved influential also within the legal and medical discourses. Each author's social milieu and ideological orientation influenced him to portray dance in one of either two opposing ways: as a disorderly behavior which equated human beings to beasts, or as a noble and edifying practice which inserted them within a political and cosmic order. Similar ambiguity characterized the consideration of dance from the perspectives of health and law. However, its beneficial role as a form of physical exercise was rarely challenged, and any radical attempt to simply ban dancing from the civilized world was destined to fail.

Notes

1. Anne Wéry, *La danse écartelée de la fin du Moyen Âge à l'âge classique* (Paris: Champion, 1992); Alessandro Arcangeli, "Dance under Trial: The Moral Debate, 1200–1600," *Dance Research* 12, no. 2 (1994): 127–55, and *Davide o Salomè? Il dibattito europeo sul-*

la danza nella prima età moderna (Rome: Viella, 2000); Ann Wagner, *Adversaries of Dance: From the Puritans to the Present* (Urbana: University of Illinois Press, 1997).

2. It would be simplistic, though, to assume from the learned elite only sycophantic praise for the powerful and blame for the underdog. Some writers, in fact, express a significantly different orientation.

3. Wagner, *Adversaries of Dance*, p. 20 (and throughout her book).

4. Wéry, *La danse écartelée* (that is the meaning of the title of this study).

5. Sebastian Brant, *Das Narrenschiff* (Basel, 1493), sig. K3v.

6. Early modern sources labeled the universal fact of men and women dancing together as "mixed," "promiscuous," or with more elaborate terms, such as the learned Hellenism "gynaecandrical." The last two terms appear in [Increase Mather], *An Arrow against Profane and Promiscuous Dancing* (Boston: S. Green, 1684; text also at http://www.covenanter.org/IMather/arrowagainstmixtdancing.htm); similarly, five years later, the title of Johannes Joachimus Zentgravius, *De choreis gynaeco-andricis*, thesis defended by Johannes Jacobus Windenius (Strasbourg: J. Welperus, 1689).

7. Frederick Naerebout, "Another Battle Fought and Lost: Seventeenth-Century Dutch *Predikanten* and the Dance," *Laban Centre Working Papers in Dance Studies* 2 (1989): 18–43; for Borromeo: Arcangeli, *Davide o Salomè?*, p. 121. On New England: Bruce C. Daniels, *Puritans at Play: Leisure and Recreation in Colonial New England* (Basingstoke: Palgrave Macmillan, 1995), pp. 189–218 (also informative on the eighteenth-century developments of social dancing); Wagner, *Adversaries of Dance*.

8. On *eutrapelia* see Alessandro Arcangeli, *Recreation in the Renaissance: Attitudes towards Leisure and Pastimes in European Culture, c. 1425–1675* (Basingstoke: Palgrave Macmillan, 2003), pp. 50–52; for the occurrence of the term in Domenico da Piacenza's dance treatise see Jennifer Nevile, *The Eloquent Body: Dance and Humanist Culture in Fifteenth-Century Italy* (Bloomington: Indiana University Press, 2004), pp. 89–90.

9. Alessandro Arcangeli, "Dance and Punishment," *Dance Research* 10, no. 2 (1992): 30–42 (for *exempla*), and *Davide o Salomè?*, esp. pp. 189–218.

10. Jean Boiseul, *Traitté contre les danses* (La Rochelle: heirs of H. Haultin, 1606), p. 43 (cf. also 35); see Wéry, *La danse écartelée*, and Arcangeli, *Davide o Salomè?*

11. Boiseul, *Traitté contre les danses*, p. 50 ("sont les jeu & ceremonies des sorciers & du diable avec eux"); for occurrences of *ensorceler* (and related forms): pp. 6, 16, 20, 21, 35, 43, and 44; elsewhere in the text reference is also made to contemporary witch trials (p. 14).

12. Ibid., p. 12: "C'est une folie qui les tient: un homme sage d'un sens rassis & grave—les voyant tourner, virer & trepigner en la dance, pied ça, pied la, pied bas, pied haut, marcher tantost en avant, tantost en arriere, tantost d'un costé, tantost de l'autre—qui dira-il sinon que se sont tous des fols?" Wéry, *La danse écartelée* can be usefully consulted for some of the vocabulary (see for instance p. 298 for *trépigner*).

13. Boiseul, *Traitté contre les danses*, p. 10.

14. Ibid., p. 5 ("compassé si justement et curieusement").

15. Ibid., pp. 17–20, 38, 41.

16. Sarah Thesiger, "The *Orchestra* of Sir John Davies and the Image of the Dance," *Journal of the Warburg and Courtauld Institutes* 36 (1973): 277–304.

17. Antonius Arena, "Rules of Dancing: Antonius Arena," trans. John Guthrie and Marino Zorzi, *Dance Research* 4, no. 2 (1986): 3–53; W. Thomas Marrocco and Marie-Laure Merveille, "Antonius Arena: Master of Law and Dance of the Renaissance," *Studi musicali* 18, no. 1 (1989): 19–48.

18. Thoinot Arbeau, *Orchesography*, trans. Mary Stewart Evans, reprinted, with introduction and notes by Julia Sutton (New York: Dover, 1967).

19. On the former, see Arcangeli, *Davide o Salomè?* p. 113; for the latter: Rinaldo Corso, *Dialogo del ballo* (Venice: S. Bordogna, 1555), reprinted with introduction by Alessandro Arcangeli (Verona: AMIS, 1987).

20. Marina Nordera, "'La maniera che la dama doverà usare ballando': la donna che danza tra XV e XVII secolo," in *La danza in Europa tra Rinascimento e Barocco*, ed. by Maurizio Padovan (Rome: Associazione Italiana per la Musica e la Danza Antiche, 1995), pp. 17–26; Arcangeli, *Davide o Salomè?* pp. 117–18.

21. For a rich analysis see Thesiger, "The *Orchestra* of Sir John Davies."

22. Alessandro Arcangeli, "Dance and Law," in *Terpsichore, 1450–1900: Proceedings of the International Dance Conference, Ghent, April 2000*, ed. Barbara Ravelhofer (Ghent: Institute for Historical Dance Practice, 2000), pp. 51–64.

23. Gebhardus Christianus Bastineller, *Dissertatio inauguralis iuridica de eo quod iustum est circa saltationes*, thesis defended by Ioannes Daniel Kettnerus (Wittenberg: A. Kobersteinius, 1730).

24. Arcangeli, *Recreation in the Renaissance*, pp. 189–218.

25. Alessandro Arcangeli, "Dance and Health: The Renaissance Physicians' View," *Dance Research* 18, no. 1 (2000): 3–30.

26. [Lambert Daneau], *Traité des danses, auquel est amplement resolue la question, à sçavoir s'il est permis aux chrestiens de danser* ([Geneva: F. Estienne], 1580), pp. 75–76 (on this important work, see Wéry, *La danse écartelée*).

27. Rémi Hess, *La valse: révolution du couple en Europe* (Paris: Métailié, 1989).

28. Arcangeli, "Dance under Trial," p. 142.

29. Boiseul's treatise mentions tarantism from this perspective (Boiseul, *Traitté contre les danses*, p. 16). For a recent historical survey of tarantism, see *Music as Medicine*, ed. Peregrine Horden (Aldershot: Ashgate, 2000), part 4 (with essays by David Gentilcore, Pilar León Sanz, and Karen Lüdtke).

30. Arcangeli, *Davide o Salomè?* pp. 289–320, and, for a physician's survey of European practice, "Dance and Health," pp. 25–26.

31. The classic study of these developments is Peter Burke, *Popular Culture in Early Modern Europe* (1978; reprint, Aldershot: Scolar, 1994).

Recommended Reading

Arcangeli, Alessandro. *Davide o Salomè? Il dibattito europeo sulla danza nella prima età moderna*. Rome: Viella, 2000.

Baskerville, Mary Pennino. "Terpsichore Reviled: Antidance Tracts in Elizabethan England." *Sixteenth-Century Journal* 22, no. 3 (1991): 475–93.

Brainard, Ingrid. "Sir John Davies' *Orchestra* as a Dance Historical Source." In *Songs of the Dove and the Nightingale: Sacred and Secular Music c.900—c.1600*, ed. Greta Mary Hair and Robyn E. Smith, pp. 176–212. Sydney: Currency Press, 1994.

Carter, Françoise. "Dance as a Moral Exercise." In *Guglielmo Ebreo da Pesaro e la danza nelle corti italiane del xv secolo*, ed. Maurizio Padovan, pp. 169–79. Pisa: Pacini, 1990.

Gstrein, Rainer. "' . . . welches warlich bey einer wolbestelten Policy ist warzunehmen und auffs allerscharffeste zu verbieten . . .': Austößige Tänze im 17 Jahrhundert." In *Morgenröte des Barock: Tanz im 17 Jahrhundert,* ed. Uwe Schlottermüller and Maria Richter, pp. 71–80. Freiburg: Fa-gisis, 2004.

Wagner, Ann. *Adversaries of Dance: From the Puritans to the Present.* Urbana: University of Illinois Press, 1997.

15

Order, Proportion, and Geometric Forms: The Cosmic Structure of Dance, Grand Gardens, and Architecture during the Renaissance

Jennifer Nevile

Dance is an art form that is concerned with the manipulation, controlling, and ordering of space. Dance creates patterns in space: patterns which form and re-form and trace out shapes in the air and on the ground. Therefore, throughout the fifteenth, sixteenth, and seventeenth centuries dance shared a common heritage with other artistic practices that were also concerned with the manipulation and ordering of patterns in space, especially garden design and architecture.[1] Throughout the fifteenth to seventeenth centuries these arts shared similar design principles: order and proportion, geometrical forms and figures, and symmetry. In garden design and architecture human skill and knowledge transformed the matter of nature into an artificial human order, but this was still an order that reflected the numerical order of the cosmos. Human ingenuity shaped and proportioned the raw materials of building—stone, wood, marble—into beautiful, ordered forms, just as the skills and craftsmanship of human artistic endeavor shaped, re-created, and ornamented the existing natural landscape.

Dance was also seen as both a natural activity and as an art, a product of human ingenuity and skill. For the fifteenth-century Italian dance master Guglielmo Ebreo da Pesaro dance was part of the natural world, an activity that occurred when people moved together with measured steps that were in harmony with one another. Dance moved into the realm of an art when music was played and the dancers adjusted their steps to fit the music.[2] It is through this act that human skill enters the equation, and natural dancing becomes part of the art of dance. In the latter scenario the dancers are imitating a natural activity, but human skill and knowledge transform this natural activity, or order, into a man-made human order. For Guglielmo dance is a natural practice, and innate ability in this practice is found in people in varying degrees. But for this natural practice to be truly perfect it needs the refining layer of human application and skill, of training and education. And when the natural activity of dancing became an art it too reflected the order of the cosmos.

That the kinetic and horticultural arts shared similar design principles was well recognized at the time. For example, Sir Hugh Plat published several gardening books in the early seventeenth century. In one of these, *The Garden of Eden*, Plat says: "I shall not trouble the Reader with any curious rules for shaping and fashioning of a *Garden* or *Orchard*. . . . Every Drawer or Embroider, nay, (almost) *each Dancing-Master* [my emphasis], may pretend to such niceties."[3] As far as Plat was concerned, both choreographers and garden designers created artifacts which were constructed according to the same design principles.[4] When writing his treatise on gardens in the second decade of the seventeenth century,[5] the French royal gardener Claude Mollet used the same language to discuss garden design as was used by other writers to describe dancing and drawing.[6] In contemporary descriptions of gardens and of dances the term "figure" was used to refer to the patterns in both art forms.[7] For example, in a work from 1607 Elie Vinet recommends that "a garden is more beautiful if it is laid out in figures, such as coats of arms, wheels, rosettes, squares, triangles and so on."[8] In this chapter the operation and expression of these basic design principles in the arts of dance, horticultural design, and architecture will be explored.

Order and Proportion

In all of these arts the fundamental principle was order and measure, that is, the same order and proportion on which the cosmos was thought to be constructed. The overwhelming importance of order in the fifteenth- and sixteenth-century garden was the characteristic that distinguished them from the gardens of earlier centuries. Nature was seen as a reflection of the cosmic order, and therefore was inherently ordered, and so the art of garden design had to "imitate not only nature's outward appearance but also its underlying order."[9] This underlying order was understood to be rendered more perfect by the cultivation of the trees and plants in the garden, and in the addition of sculpture, ornaments, water features, mounds, and grottoes. In the topiary work, labyrinths, and in trellis constructions, natural materials—plants, vines, and trees—were cultivated into geometric figures like spheres or pyramids, or into shapes reminiscent of sculpture like ships or human figures, or into natural shapes like animals. One fifteenth-century garden is described as having topiary in the form of "ships, temples, vases, giants, men, women, dragons, centaurs, putti, various animals and birds, jousters, philosophers, a pope [and] cardinals."[10]

In his treatise on architecture, *De re aedificatoria*, Leon Battista Alberti argued that it was the responsibility of the architect to design and construct an ordered environment, since "without order there can be nothing commodious, graceful or noble."[11] As far as Alberti was concerned the proportions that were found in beautiful and elegant buildings were the same ratios found in music, dance, arithmetic, geometry, and astronomy.[12] Filarete endorses Alberti's conception of the discipline of architecture. A good (that is, knowledgeable) architect will "strive to make his building good and beautiful,"[13] and the way he will achieve this is by following the "laws of nature": the proportions which order the cosmos.[14] For Filarete the proportions that he uses most frequently in designing his ideal city are 1:1, 1:2, and 2:3, and then the ratios of 3:4 and 1:4,[15] all of which fall within the small set of Pythagorean ratios that represented the numerical reality of the cosmos.

Alberti recommends that when designing a piazza or open area like a garden, the ratio of width to length that the architect should use is the 1:1 ratio of the square, or the musical consonances of the fifth 2:3, or the fourth 3:4.[16] Furthermore, flat surfaces like the paving in a church should be decorated with the same musical proportions and geometric shapes: "I strongly approve of patterning the pavement with musical and geometric lines and shapes, so that the mind may receive stimuli from every side."[17] For Alberti the "natural excellence and perfection" of a building, that "excit[ed] the mind" of its viewers, and caused immediate sympathy with it, was the fact that the building was a representation of the cosmos.[18] The architect, through the use of geometric figures such as the circle and the square and by the utilization of the Pythagorean proportions, could create buildings, and indeed whole cities, that were three-dimensional representations of the divine world. It was this visual representation of divine beauty to which a city's inhabitants would naturally respond, causing them to desire virtue and to imitate the divine order that they saw before them in their city buildings.

The cosmos could be represented by "many different models based upon the several disciplines of the quadrivium."[19] One of these models was geometric figures, while another was the "visual depiction of ratios between numbers."[20] The cosmic order was expressed in the art of dance using both these models: the numerical proportions that ordered the cosmos and also the geometric figures created by the dancers during the course of a choreography. The aural representation of the cosmic ratios were expressed in dance through the ratios between the relative speeds of the four *misure*. This subject is discussed in chapter 7 in this volume, "The Relationship between Dance and Music in Fifteenth-Century Italian Dance Practice." The use of geometric figures in dance, as well as in garden design and architecture, is the focus of the following section.

Geometric Figures

The dances of the elite, those that were recorded in the dance treatises and which were performed at court spectacles, were more than entertainment. In fact it was the "movements and the geometric patterns" that made Renaissance court dance "both graceful and more significant than a simple social ritual. The patterns inscribed on the floor of the ballroom or stage were not haphazard; they had divine effects."[21] These were the same geometric patterns which were present in the formal gardens, and which were also seen as having a moral effect on those who walked through them. The "geometric forms which recur so frequently in these designs for plant-beds—shapes such as the square (traditionally a symbol of earth and its elements), the circle (a symbol of heaven and divinity), the regular polygons and the triangle (a symbol of fire)—had to sustain complex astrological and magical-esoteric connotations."[22] For example, in 1623 John Taylor visited the garden at Wilton, which he described as follows:

> circular, triangular, quadrangular, orbicular, oval, and every way curiously and chargeably conceited: there he hath made walks, hedges and arbours . . . planting them and placing them in such admirable art-like fashions, *resembling both divine and moral remembrances* [my emphasis], as three arbours standing in a triangle, having each a recourse to a greater arbour in the midst, resemble three in one and one in three.[23]

The geometric order in the gardens was primarily created by the geometry of the compartments, the small beds out of which the garden was constructed, but also by the use of quadrilateral—and in the seventeenth century bilateral—symmetry, the central paths which bisected each other at right angles, and the trees planted in straight lines, all of which created a strong rectilinear character. The earliest extant garden design of the sixteenth century is a sketch for a small garden by Baldessare Peruzzi from the 1520s.[24] The designs in the square compartments are geometric, segments of squares and circles. One garden in Europe that exemplifies the geometric nature of Renaissance gardens is the famous botanical garden at Padua, which was designed as a square within two concentric circles, the former being divided into four smaller squares by two perpendicular central paths. The four smaller squares were themselves divided into triangular, circular, and square beds, while the triangular shape was also formed by the eight segments between the arc of the inner circle and each side of the four smaller squares. An early description of this garden written by the Venetian Marco Guazzo in 1546 emphasizes the use of these three principal geometric figures.

In the grand gardens the concern for straight lines and regular geometric shapes extended from the largest design units down to the smallest components, as it did in the Medici villa L'Ambrogiana (begun after 1587) with its wide central avenue with symmetrical units on either side of it, as seen in Figure 15.1. Not only does each compartment have its own geometrical space, but each section is divided into four quarters.[25] Even the large trees in the beds at the back of the garden are planted in straight lines. The beds, which were filled with flowering plants of different colors and shapes, were divided again into squares, circles, triangles, all delineated by paths. (Details of the garden compartments can be seen in Figure 15.2.)

Circles, squares, triangles, and rectangles were all present in the patterns formed by the dancers as the result of conscious decisions on the part of the dance masters, both in Italy and in France. Geometric patterns lay at the heart

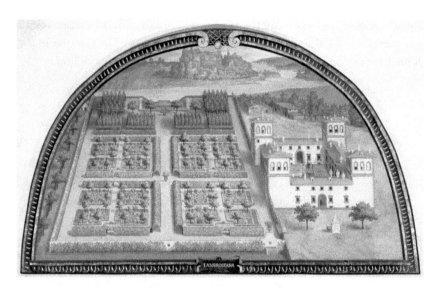

Figure 15.1. The villa *L'Ambrogiana* by Giusto Utens, 1599. Museo di Firenze com'era. Scala/ Art Resource, New York.

Figure 15.2. Detail of the villa *L'Ambrogiana* by Giusto Utens, 1599. Museo di Firenze com'era. Scala / Art Resource, New York.

of the French court spectacles from the mid-sixteenth to the early seventeenth century, such as the Valois fêtes, *Le Ballet des Polonais* (1573), and *Le Balet Comique de la Reyne* (1581).[26] As Thomas Greene comments: "The geometric character of the dance figures participates in what could be termed the quadrivial sublime of the early modern period, which assigned cosmic patterns and effects to arithmetic, geometric, astronomic (or astrological), and musical relations."[27] The climax of the 1581 ballet was a dance with forty geometric figures. The description of this part of the ballet leaves the reader with an impression of "a brilliant series of successive geometric patterns always dissolving before another reforms, like the patterns in the *Ballet des Polonais*."[28] In his description of *Le Balet Comique* the choreographer, Balthazar de Beaujoyeulx, emphasizes the geometric nature of these forty figures.[29]

> [T]hey danced the Grand Ballet with forty passages or geometric figures. These were all exact and well-planned in their forms, sometimes square, sometimes round, in several diverse fashions; then in triangles accompanied by a small square, and other small figures. These figures were no sooner formed by the Naiads . . . than the four Dryads . . . arrived to change the shape, so that as one ended the other began. . . . The spectators thought that Archimedes could not have understood geometric proportions any better than the princesses and the ladies performed them in this Ballet.[30]

The practice of composing dances comprised of geometric figures continued into the seventeenth century, as illustrated by both the descriptions of the English court masque dances, and also by the notebook of a French dancing master who worked in Brussels circa 1614–19.[31] This manuscript contains numerous drawings of figures for five to sixteen dancers. Many of these 450-plus figures are geometric shapes: squares, circles, triangles, pyramids, or lozenge shapes.[32]

The sixteenth-century Italian dances were not constructed as a series of geometric figures as were the dances from the French court spectacles. Yet the geometric shapes of squares, circles, and triangles were still present in these dances. The anonymous mid-sixteenth-century *balletto, La Battaglia,* is for three couples arranged in a square, with the men in a line facing their partners who stand opposite them.[33] For the first half of this dance the square formation is emphasized as first the six dancers and then each couple move toward and then away from each other, always returning to their places on the two sides of the square. The final floor pattern in the first half of the dance creates a circle in the center of the square, as each dancer moves toward his or her partner before circling around each other and then returning to his or her original starting position on the perimeter of the square. The second half of the dance emphasizes circular patterns, as it begins with the three men walking around the dance

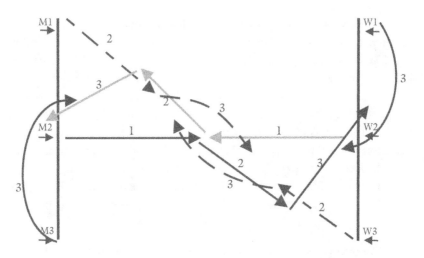

Figure 15.3. Floor pattern of first three changes in the hay from the *balletto Dolce Amoroso Foco.*

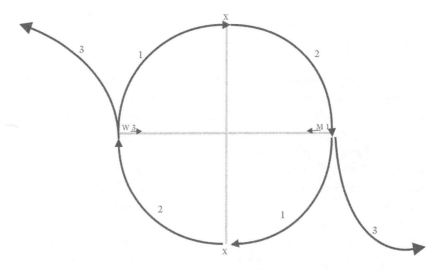

Figure 15.4. The circle and cross floor pattern created by the hay along a straight line from the *balletto Dolce Amoroso Foco.*

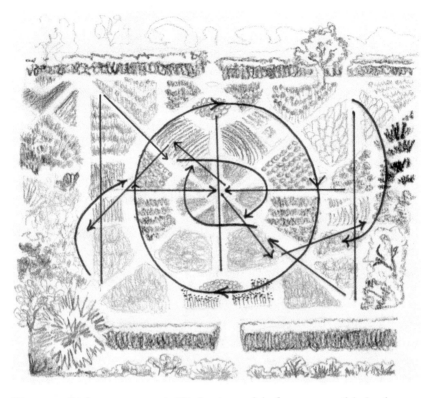

Figure 15.5. Garden compartment in *L'Ambrogiana* and the floor patterns of the hay from the *balletto Dolce Amoroso Foco*. Drawn by F. Nevile.

space in a large circle while the three women do the same maneuver in the opposite direction.

The similarity between the patterns of the garden compartments and those of the choreographies can be illustrated by comparing the garden at L'Ambrogiana with the sixteenth-century *balletto, Dolce Amoroso Foco*.[34] In this dance, also for three couples, the men stand in a line down one side of the room, the ladies facing them down the other side. The first part of the dance emphasizes the straight lines with all the movement being along the original axes or an axis perpendicular to it, created when the couples change places. The second half of the dance is a hay which creates patterns that are those of the compartments. The middle couple start the hay and change places on the perpendicular axis. They then move diagonally to change places with the last woman and first man. They then move along the original axis to change places with the remaining two dancers. (The path created is shown in Figure 15.3.) This path is very similar to those in the top left compartments of L'Ambrogiana (see Figure 15.2). After six steps all the dancers are in a straight line across the width of the hall. The hay continues in a straight line, with each change of place creating a circular figure like that found in the top right compartment of L'Ambrogiana. (See Figure 15.5 for a drawing of the dance floor patterns superimposed over the outline of the garden compartment.) Holding right then left hands alternately, each couple traces a 90 degree arc to create a straight line along the length of the hall. During the next step they trace another 90 degree arc to complete their half of the circle and to form a straight line across the width of the hall. (See Figure 15.4.) Thus the circle is traced out by the dancers' bodies, and the cross inside the circle by the movement of their linked hands.

One of the major contributing factors to the ordered, rectilinear nature of the formal gardens was the use of the square. The compartments, while often having circular forms within them, were invariably square. This shape was further emphasized by the planting of large trees in each corner of the compartment, as in the Villa Petraia and L'Ambrogiana. This characteristic of the Renaissance garden also found expression in the patterns created by the dancers as they progressed through the figures of a dance. The figure of a square delineated by a dancer at each corner was a common formation in Renaissance dance, either as an initial pattern or as a formation kept throughout the dance, as in Cesare Negri's *balletto*, *Battaglia*, a dance for two couples which begins and ends in a square.[35] This dance also contains several hays in which the square dissolves into a straight line, then back into a square, then into a line again but on an axis perpendicular to the previous one.

Squareness also found expression in the patterns created by the dancers as they progressed through the figures of a dance. One example is the fifteenth-century dance, *Anello*, in which the choreography emphasizes the pattern of squares within circles. This dance begins with the two couples facing one another in a square. The whole dance then consists of the four performers changing places and moving around the outside of the other couple to create circles. The "problem" of squaring the circle, that is, changing a circle into a square, had occupied mathematicians since the time of Pythagoras. The circle, with no beginning or end, symbolized perfection and the deity, and the square symbolized the physical world. Therefore, the "problem" of squaring the circle was a problem of how to change the divine into earthly material.[36]

Furthermore, in the choreographies the harmony and proportion of the straight walks of espaliered fruit trees or yew were transmuted into the long, forward-moving floor tracks of the fifteenth-century *balli* and *bassadanze*, and the common circular figure which was often interspersed with the rectilinear patterns. (I am referring here to the figure which is created when a couple takes

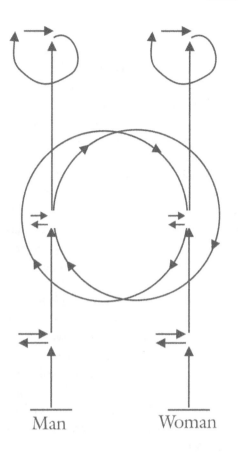

Figure 15.6. Floor track of the *bassadanza Lauro*.

Man   Woman

left or right hands and they move around each other tracing out a circle as they go.) One example of this type of floor pattern is the *bassadanza, Lauro*, which was choreographed by Lorenzo de' Medici. Many of the *bassadanze* and *balli* share this type of floor pattern. Figure 15.6 shows the starting position of the two performers and the path they traverse during the course of the dance. In this particular dance the couple only move forward, with a pause in the middle of the choreography to describe a circle. The floor track is very similar to the gardens with their long straight central avenue, often interspersed with a circle around which the four compartments are arranged, for example, the Medici villa Petraia, or the Medici villa Poggio a Caiano.[37] In other dances the performers move forward *and* backward from the starting position, but usually still in straight lines. As Claudia Lazzaro remarks: "Throughout the Renaissance, a central avenue traversed the garden, often covered with a pergola. . . . Movement from one end of the garden to the other, but not excursions to either side, was encouraged by such an axis."[38] In the *bassadanza, Lauro*, the two performers move from one end of the dance space to the other, with only a few small "excursions to either side" with the *riprese*. One should note that two of the four groups of sideways steps occur in the central circular space, created by the couple taking hands and walking around each other. Thus half of the sideways movements are used to reinforce the circle in the middle of the long, straight path.

The same geometric figures also formed the basis of architectural design. For Alberti an ordered environment was one in which the buildings, squares, indeed the whole city was designed and laid out according to the geometric figures that are found in Nature, and which underlie the whole cosmos. And it was from the judicious selection and management of these geometric shapes, as well as their numerical expressions in the proportions of a building, room, or column, that the beauty of a building resided.[39] The ideal shape of a church building as a whole should imitate the basic geometric shapes: the circles, squares, rectangles, or polygonal figures like the hexagon that can be circumscribed by a circle and which are also found in nature.[40]

Often architects designed both the house and the garden. Alberti himself recommended that the garden was the concern of the architect just as much as the house was, because the same geometric figures should be employed in gardens as in buildings.[41] It was no accident that the great garden designers of the fifteenth and sixteenth centuries were also the famous architects of the day; for example, Francesco di Giorgio Martini, Giuliano da Sangallo, and Bramante. In the designs of Francesco di Giorgio, for example, the compartments of the gardens are very similar to the rooms of the houses. The sixteenth-century architects, Sebastiano Serlio and Giorgio Vasari the Younger, included in their treatises designs for garden compartments, all of which used geometric shapes in many complex variations. Serlio's designs particularly were widely known across Europe during the sixteenth century.[42] The ordered and compartmentalized gardens in sixteenth-century Italy often resembled the plans for ideal cities which appeared at the same time, for example the Boboli garden in Florence which was begun in 1550, and the plan of an ideal city by Pietro Cattaneo, published in 1554.[43] The association of the architect with garden design still continued in the early seventeenth century. When Giovan Battista Ferrari published his treatise on flowers in 1633 he still assumed that "an architect will draw up the plan for the projected garden" and the designs for the compartments.[44] Furthermore, Ferrari also insisted upon a harmony between "architectural interiors," such as geometric floor designs and the designs for the garden.[45] Thus the principles outlined by Alberti almost one hundred and fifty years earlier still continued to inform important writings on horticulture even though, as we see in the following section, the geometric character of the designs was changing.[46]

France and the Seventeenth Century

In the first half of the seventeenth century changes occurred in the design and patterning of both court choreographies and gardens. The geometric character of the figures, the squares, circles, triangles, and hexagons, and the rectilinear aspect of the compartments which were so prominent in the European grand gardens of the previous two centuries, disappeared and were replaced by curvilinear patterns, "S"-shaped curves, arabesques,[47] arcs, and embroidery-like scroll patterns in both the choreographies and in gardens. In this case it was French designers and choreographers who initiated these changes. Claude Mollet claimed that he was the first person to introduce the new *parterres de broderie* to French gardens. One of the earliest gardens in which we know this occurred is the palace at Fontainebleau, renovated by Claude Mollet in the 1590s under the instructions of Henri IV. A general plan of the palace and gardens from c. 1600 has survived, which shows that the beds were still laid out in geometrical patterns. In 1614, however, another plan was made of Fontainebleau by Alexandre Francini. In this design all the parterres are of the new scroll-like designs: the geometric shapes of the previous century have gone.[48] Even in France, however, the introduction of these new designs was not universal, as the older patterns still persisted. For example, in the book of garden designs published in 1629 by D. Loris, *Le Thresor des Parterres de l'Univers*, the patterns are square in their proportions and strongly resemble the sixteenth-century geometric designs and knots, rather than the new curvilinear *parterres de broderie*.[49] In Italy the new French designs and concepts were particularly slow to be adopted. In Francesco Pona's treatise of 1622, *Il Paradiso de' Fiori*, the author recommends that if there is a choice then a garden should be arranged in "four perfect squares,"[50] the standard format of the fifteenth- and sixteenth-century garden.[51] Even eleven years later in 1633 in Giovan Battista Ferrari's treatise, the flower beds are either square or rectangular and geometric designs still predominate over curvilinear ones for the interior of the beds.[52]

One of the best examples of these changed patterns is the château and garden at Vaux-le-Vicomte, constructed from 1656 to 1661, and at which, in August 1661, an extravagant fête was held for Louis XIV and his court. Many of the features of the layout of the building, the decoration of the rooms within the building, and the garden itself "parallelled, in a general way, certain key elements of the ballet."[53] For example, bilateral symmetry was becoming increasingly common in the court ballets of the mid-seventeenth century as well as in architecture and garden design at the time.[54] It is now probably impossible to know for certain whether there was any direct exchange of ideas or collaboration between the choreographers at the French court and the garden, architectural, and decorative designers there, and how the flow of ideas developed among these different groups. However, all these groups worked for the French crown and thus would have seen how design elements were shaped and presented in the court spectacles. This was certainly the case for the three designers of Vaux-le-Vicomte: Louis Le Vau, who was responsible for the architectural design; André Le Nôtre, who was responsible for the gardens; and Charles Le Brun, who designed the decorations on the walls and ceiling of the château.[55] Furthermore, at the same time Pierre Beauchamps was developing his system of dance notation and working as ballet master at the Opéra, his colleague, Jean Berain, was the chief designer, producing costume and set designs for the Opéra.[56] Berain also worked in a court milieu, as he had artistic control over court spectacles from 1674 to 1711 and was garden designer to the king. He also worked as a decorative designer and engraver, publishing engravings of his arabesques throughout his life.[57] Thus it is difficult to imagine that ideas and discussions were not exchanged between these two men during the time they worked together at the Opéra.

Conclusion

During the fifteenth to seventeenth centuries dance shared similar design principles with garden design and architecture. Through order and proportion all three arts reflected the numerical order of the cosmos, while the geometric patterns common to all three had divine connotations. By reminding those watching of the nature of God, these geometric figures had a moral effect, whether on the citizens of an ordered and designed city, the viewers of a court ballet, or those looking out on the compartments, labyrinths, and central avenues of a grand garden. In the seventeenth century the strong geometric patterning changed, but the shared design principles between dance and garden design continued. While the patterns had changed, the participation of the art of dance in contemporary intellectual and artistic culture remained, just as it had done for the previous two centuries.

Notes

1. Short sections of this chapter appeared in my earlier article, "Dance and the Garden: Moving and Static Choreography in Renaissance Europe," *Renaissance Quarterly* 52, no. 3 (1999): 805–36.

2. Guglielmo Ebreo da Pesaro, *Guilielmi Hebraei pisauriensis de practica seu arte tripudii vulgare opusculum, incipit,* 1463, Paris, Bibliothèque Nationale, MS fonds it. 973, f. 18v–19r (hereafter cited as Pg).

3. Hugh Plat, *The Garden of Eden* (London, 1654), pp. 31–32.

4. For examples of other early modern English authors who saw analogies between the designs used in gardens and in other arts, see Mary E. Hazard, *Elizabethan Silent Language* (Lincoln: University of Nebraska Press, 2000), pp. 38–40.

5. The treatise, *Théâtre des plans et jardinages,* was published posthumously in 1652. (David Coffin, *Gardens and Gardening in Papal Rome* [Princeton: Princeton University Press, 1991], p. 160).

6. Sarah Cohen, *Art, Dance, and the Body in French Culture of the Ancien Régime* (Cambridge: Cambridge University Press, 2000), p. 94.

7. Ibid., p. 93.

8. Kenneth Woodbridge, *Princely Gardens: The Origins and Development of the French Formal Style* (London: Thames and Hudson, 1986), p. 97.

9. Claudio Lazzaro, *The Italian Renaissance Garden: From the Conventions of Planting, Design, and Ornament to the Grand Gardens of Sixteenth-Century Central Italy* (New Haven: Yale University Press, 1990), p. 8.

10. Ibid., p. 49.

11. Leon Battista Alberti, *On the Art of Building in Ten Books,* trans. Joseph Rykwert, Neil Leach, and Robert Tavernor (Cambridge, Mass.: MIT Press, 1988), p. 191.

12. Ibid., p. 305.

13. Filarete, *Filarete's Treatise on Architecture, Being the Treatise by Antonio di Piero Averlino, Known as Filarete,* trans. John R. Spencer (New Haven: Yale University Press, 1965), vol. I, p. 16.

14. Ibid., vol. I, p. 5.

15. John R. Spencer, introduction to *Treatise on Architecture,* by Filarete, vol. I, p. xxii.

16. Alberti, *Art of Building,* p. 306.

17. Ibid., p. 220.

18. Ibid., p. 302.

19. S. K. Heninger Jr., *The Cosmographical Glass: Renaissance Diagrams of the Universe* (San Marino, Calif.: Huntington Library, 1977), p. 143.

20. Ibid., p. 143.

21. Margaret M. McGowan, *Ideal Forms in the Age of Ronsard* (Berkeley: University of California Press, 1985), p. 224.

22. Lucia Tomasi Tongiorgi, "Geometric Schemes for Plant Beds and Gardens: A Contribution to the History of the Garden in the Sixteenth and Seventeenth Centuries," in *World Art. Themes of Unity in Diversity (Acts of the XXVI International Congress of the History of Art),* I, ed. Irving Lavin (University Park: Penn State University Press, 1989), p. 212.

23. Roy Strong, *The Renaissance Garden in England* (London: Thames and Hudson, 1979), p. 122.

24. Lazzaro, *Italian Renaissance Garden,* p. 38. The sketch by Peruzzi is also reproduced on page 38.

25. For further examples of gardens laid out in four compartments, see David Coffin, *Gardens and Gardening in Papal Rome,* pp. 174–75.

26. See chapter 4 in this volume for an extensive discussion on dance at the sixteenth-century French court.

27. Thomas M. Greene, "The King's One Body in the *Balet Comique de la Royne*," *Yale French Studies* 86 (1994): 92.

28. Thomas M. Greene, "Labyrinth Dances in the French and English Renaissance," *Renaissance Quarterly* 54, no. 4.2 (2001): 1422.

29. A facsimile edition of Beaujoyeulx's description was published in 1982. (Balthazar de Beaujoyeulx, *Le balet comique*, 1581. Facsimile edition edited and introduction by Margaret M. McGowan [Binghamton, N.Y.: Medieval and Renaissance Texts and Studies, 1982]).

30. The translation is by Thomas Greene based on the translation by Carol and Lander MacClintock from *Le Balet Comique de la Royne* (n.p.: American Institute of Musicology, 1971), and is taken from Greene, "The King's One Body," p. 92.

31. Stockholm, Kungliga Bibliotek, Cod. Holm S 253.

32. For more information on this manuscript, and an extensive discussion of the figures recorded in it, see Jennifer Nevile, "Dance Patterns of the Early Seventeenth Century: The Stockholm Manuscript and *Le Ballet de Monseigneur de Vendosme*," *Dance Research* 18 no. 2, (2000): 186–203, and Margaret M. McGowan, *L'art du Ballet du cour en France, 1581–1643* (Paris: CNRS, 1963), pp. 69–84.

33. Florence, Biblioteca Nazionale Centrale, Codex Magliabecchiana-Strozziano XIX 31.

34. Fabritio Caroso, *Il ballarino*, Venice, 1581. Facsimile edition, New York: Broude Brothers, 1967, pp. 174r–174v.

35. Cesare Negri, *Le gratie d'amore*, Milan, 1602. Facsimile edition, New York: Broude Brothers, 1969, pp. 257–63.

36. For more details, see S. K. Heninger Jr., *Touches of Sweet Harmony: Pythagorean Cosmology and Renaissance Poetics* (San Marino, Calif.: Huntington Library, 1974), p. 111.

37. See Lazzaro, *Italian Renaissance Garden*, pp. 85 and 42 for colored reproductions of Guisto Utens's paintings of these two gardens from 1599, and p. 72 for a detail of the four square compartments, central avenue, and circular bed in the center of the avenue of Poggio a Caiano.

38. Ibid., p. 80.

39. Alberti, *Art of Building*, p. 303.

40. Ibid., p. 196.

41. Ibid., p. 300.

42. Lazzaro, *Italian Renaissance Garden*, pp. 38–41.

43. Ibid., p. 44.

44. Coffin, *Gardens and Gardening in Papal Rome*, p. 175.

45. Ibid., p. 175.

46. Alberti's Latin treatise on architecture is thought to have been finished around 1450, when he presented it to Pope Nicholas V. The treatise then circulated in manuscript copies, and may have even been translated into Italian before it was printed in 1486. (Joseph Rykwert, "Introduction," in *On the Art of Building in Ten Books*, trans. Joseph Rykwert, Neil Leach, and Robert Tavernor [Cambridge, Mass.: MIT Press, 1988], p. xvi).

47. Arabesques were ornamental designs painted on the inside walls of the houses of the elite. "The engravings of arabesques published widely in the latter half of the seventeenth century . . . particularly resemble the dance in its notated form, and it is likely that the taste for one enhanced the taste for the other in the print market of Paris." (Cohen, *Art, Dance and the Body*, p. 89. For further discussion on the similarities between arabesque designs and choreographic patterns in France in the second half of the seventeenth century, see ibid., pp. 97–133.)

48. Sten Karling, "The Importance of André Mollet and His Family for the Development of the French Formal Garden," in *The French Formal Garden*, ed. Elisabeth B. Macdougall and F. Hamilton Hazlehurst (Washington, D.C.: Dumbarton Oaks, 1974), pp. 8–10.

49. Christopher Thacker, *The History of Gardens* (Berkeley: University of California Press, 1985), p. 145.

50. Coffin, *Gardens and Gardening in Papal Rome*, p. 174.

51. For a discussion of when these changes arrived in England, see Nevile, "Dance and the Garden," pp. 827–33.

52. Coffin, *Gardens and Gardening in Papal Rome*, p. 175.

53. Cohen, *Art, Dance, and the Body*, p. 64. For a wide-ranging discussion of Vaux-le-Vicomte and how the architectural, decorative, and garden design all contributed toward creating a spectacle of a physical movement through time and space, just as did court ballet, see Cohen, *Art, Dance, and the Body*, pp. 55–67.

54. Ibid., p. 64. For a discussion of symmetry in baroque dance see chapter 9 in this volume.

55. Cohen, *Art, Dance, and the Body*, p. 55.

56. Ibid., p. 119.

57. Ibid., pp. 110–11.

Recommended Reading

Carter, Françoise. "Neoplatonism and Cosmic Dance." *Renaissance Bulletin* 23 (1996): 11–25.

Cohen, Sarah. *Art, Dance, and the Body in French Culture of the Ancien Régime*. Cambridge: Cambridge University Press, 2000.

Greene, Thomas M. "Labyrinth Dances in the French and English Renaissance." *Renaissance Quarterly* 54, no. 4.2 (2001): 1403–66.

Johnson, A. W. *Ben Jonson: Poetry and Architecture*. Oxford: Clarendon Press, 1994, esp. chaps. 5–6, pp. 115–75.

Lazzaro, Claudia. *The Italian Renaissance Garden: From the Conventions of Planting, Design, and Ornament to the Grand Gardens of Sixteenth-Century Central Italy*. New Haven: Yale University Press, 1990.

Van Orden, Kate. *Music, Discipline, and Arms in Early Modern France*. Chicago: University of Chicago Press, 2005, chap. 2, pp. 37–80.

List of Dance Treatises and Manuscripts, Modern Editions, and Translations

After 1700 the publication of dance treatises and notated choreographies increased rapidly. It is beyond the scope of this collection to include every single publication from this period. Therefore, only the dance publications from this period that are cited in the essays are included in this list. For a comprehensive catalogue readers are advised to consult the following monographs: Judith L. Schwartz and Christena L. Schlundt, *French Court Dance and Dance Music: A Guide to Primary Source Writings 1643–1789* (Stuyvesant, N.Y.: Pendragon Press, 1987); Meredith Ellis Little and Carol G. Marsh, *La Danse Noble: An Inventory of Dances and Sources* (Williamstown: Broude Brothers, 1992); Francine Lancelot, *La belle dance: catalogue raisonné* (Paris: Van Dieren, 1996).

Fifteenth- and Early Sixteenth-Century Italy

Cornazano, Antonio. *Libro dell'arte del danzare.* Rome, Biblioteca Apostolica Vaticana, Codex Capponiano, 203. English translation by Madeleine Inglehearn and Peggy Forsyth, *The Book on the Art of Dancing: Antonio Cornazano.* London: Dance Books, 1981. English translation of the choreographies in David R. Wilson, *101 Italian Dances (c. 1450–c. 1550): A Critical Translation.* Cambridge: Early Dance Circle, 1999.

Domenico da Piacenza, *De arte saltandj & choreas ducendj De la arte di ballare et danzare,* Paris, Bibliothèque Nationale, MS fonds it. 972. English translation of the choreographies in Wilson, *101 Italian Dances.* Transcription of entire treatise in *Domenico of Piacenza (Paris, Bibliothèque Nationale, MS ital. 972),* edited by David R. Wilson. Cambridge: Early Dance Circle, 1988.

Florence, Biblioteca Nazionale Centrale, Codex Palatini.

Foligno, Seminario Vescovile, Biblioteca Jacobilli, MS D.I.42.

Guglielmo Ebreo, *Ghuglielmi ebrej pisauriensis de praticha seu arte tripudi vulghare opusculum, feliciter incipit,* New York, New York Public Library, Dance Collection, *MG-ZMB-Res. 72–254. English translation of the choreographies in Wilson, *101 Italian Dances.*

Guglielmo Ebreo, *Ghuglielmi hebrei pisauriensis de practicha seu arte tripudij vulghare opusculum feliciter incipit,* Florence, Biblioteca Nazionale Centrale, Codex Magliabecchiana-

Strozziano XIX 88. English translation of the choreographies in Wilson, *101 Italian Dances.*

Guglielmo Ebreo, *Qui chominca elibro de bali Ghugliemus ebreis pisauriensis de praticha seu arte tripudii volghare opusculum,* Florence, Biblioteca Medicea-Laurenziana, Codex Antinori, A13. English translation of the choreographies in Wilson, *101 Italian Dances.*

[Guglielmo Ebreo], Siena, Biblioteca Comunale, Codex L. V. 29. English translation of the choreographies in Wilson, *101 Italian Dances.*

[Guglielmo Ebreo], Modena, Biblioteca Estense, Codex Ital. 82, α. J. 94.

Guglielmo Ebreo da Pesaro, *Domini Iohannis Ambrosii pisauriensis de pratica seu arte tripudii vulgare opusculum faeliciter incipit,* Paris, Bibliothèque Nationale, MS fonds it. 476. English translation of the choreographies in Wilson, *101 Italian Dances.*

Guglielmo Ebreo da Pesaro, *Guilielmi Hebraei pisauriensis de practica seu arte tripudii vulgare opusculum, incipit,* 1463. Paris, Bibliothèque Nationale, MS fonds it. 973. Edited and translated into English by Barbara Sparti, *De practica seu arte tripudii: On the Practice or Art of Dancing.* Oxford: Clarendon Press, 1993.

Il Papa, New York Public Library, *MGZMB-Res. 72–254. For a transcription by Joseph Casazza and Elizabeth Cain, see www.nypl.org/research/lpa/dan/ilpapa.html.

Nuremberg, Germanisches Nationalmuseum, MS 8842/GS 1589. Seven Italian *balli* and one *bassadanza* as performed at a ball in Bologna and described in a letter of 1517.

Venice, Biblioteca Nazionale Marciana, It. II 34 (=4906), f. 105.

Viterbo, Archivio di Stato di Viterbo, Notarile de Montefiascone, Protocollo 11.

Fifteenth- and Sixteenth-Century France

Arbeau, Thoinot. *Orchésographie.* Langres, 1588. Facsimile edition of 1596 printing, Geneva: Minkoff, 1972. Translated by Mary Steward Evans, 1948. Reprinted with an introduction and notes by Julia Sutton, New York: Dover Publications, 1967.

Arena, Antonius, *Ad suos compagniones studiantes.* c. 1529. English translation in John Guthrie and Marino Zorzi, "Rules of Dancing: Antonius Arena." *Dance Research* 4, no. 2 (1986): 3–53.

Beaujoyeulx, Balthazar de. *Le Balet Comique de la Reyne.* 1581. Facsimile edition edited by Margaret M. McGowan. Binghamton, N.Y.: Center for Medieval and Early Renaissance Studies, 1982.

Brussels, Bibliothèque Royale de Belgique, MS 9085. *Le manuscrit dit des Basses Danses de la Bibliothèque de Bourgogne.* Facsimile edition and commentary: *Les basses danses de Marguerite d'Autriche / Das Tanzbüchlein de Margarete von Österreich . . . Facsimile et Commentarium* (Codices Selecti, Phototypice Impressi, vols. LXXXVII & LXXXVII*. *Musica Manuscripta,* 5, Graz: 1988). Transcript and edition in David Wilson and Véronique Daniels, "The Basse Dance Handbook: Text and Context," unpublished manuscript.

Paris, Bibliothèque Nationale, fonds français 5699, f. 1v: the "Nancy" dances, c.1445.

S'ensuit l'art et instruction de bien dancer. Paris, Michel Toulouze, n.d. Facsimile edition, Geneva: Minkoff, 1985.

S'ensuyvent plusieurs basses dances, n.d. pub. Moderne? c.1535? Facsimile edition, Geneva: Minkoff, 1985.

Tuccaro, Arcangelo. *Trois dialogues de l'exercice de sauter, et voltiger en l'air.* Paris, 1599.

Turin, Archivio di Stato, Archivi Biscaretti, Mazzo 4, no. 14. "Stribaldi," 1517.

Fifteenth- and Sixteenth-Century Spain

Cervera, Arxiu Històric Comarcal, unnumbered ms. (late fifteenth century).

Reglas de danzar (sixteenth century). Original now lost. Nineteenth-century copy in Madrid, Biblioteca Nacional, MS Barbieri 14059/2.

Fifteenth- and Sixteenth-Century England

Coplande, Robert. trans. *The maner of dauncynge of bace daunces*, 1521. Oxford, Bodleian Library, Douce B. 507, f. 16r–16v.

Gresley of Drakelow papers. Derbyshire Record Office, D77 box 38, pp. 51–79. A transcription of this material is found in David Fallows, "The Gresley Dance Collection, c. 1500," *RMA Research Chronicle* 29 (1996): 1–20.

Oxford, Bodleian Library, MS Rawlinson Poet. 108, f. 10r–11v. A commonplace book copied c. 1563–1566. Transcription and discussion in David R. Wilson, "Dancing in the Inns of Court." *Historical Dance* 2, no. 5 (1986/87): 3–16, and Ian Payne, *The Almain in Britain, c.1549–c.1675: A Dance Manual from Manuscript Sources*. Aldershot: Ashgate, 2003.

Salisbury, Cathedral Library, copy of J. B. de Janua, *Catholicon*, 1497, first flyleaf: details of 26 *basses dances, c.*1510?

Taunton, Somerset Record Office, DD/WO 55/7, Item 36. The choreographies of eight "olde Measures" copied by Jo[hn] Willoughby of Payhembury, Devon in 1594. Transcription and discussion in Payne, *The Almain in Britain*.

Mid-Sixteenth- to Early Seventeenth-Century Italy

Caroso, Fabritio. *Il ballarino*. Venice 1581. Facsimile edition, New York: Broude Brothers, 1967.

Caroso, Fabritio. *Nobilità di dame*. Venice, 1600. Facsimile editions, New York: Broude Brothers, 1967, and Bologna: Forni, 1980. Edited and translated into English by Julia Sutton as *Courtly Dance of the Renaissance: A New Translation and Edition of the Nobiltà di Dame 1600. Fabritio Caroso*. New York: Dover, 1995.

Cavalieri, Emilio de'. *O che nuovo miracolo* for the final *intermedio* of *La Pellegrina*, 1589. Choreographic description and music recorded in Cristofano Malvezzi, *Intermedii et concerti fatti per la commedia rappresentata in Firenze nelle nozze del serenissimo don Ferdinando Medici, e madama Christina di Loreno, gran duchi di Toscana*. Venice: G. Vincenti, 1591.

Compasso, Lutio. *Ballo della gagliarda*, Florence 1560. Facsimile edition, Freiburg: Fa-gisis, 1995.

Corso, Rinaldo. *Dialogo del ballo*. Venice: S. Bordogna, 1555. Reprinted with introduction by Alessandro Arcangeli. Verona: AMIS, 1987.

Florence, Archivio di Stato, Carte Strozziane, I, 22, f. 138r–140v. Description of a choreography called *La caccia* in a letter dated 1559. Transcription in Gino Corti, "Cinque balli Toscani del cinquecento," *Rivista italiana di musicologia* 12, no. 1 (1977): 73–82.

Florence, Biblioteca Nazionale, MS Codex Magliabecchiana-Strozziano XIX, 31, f. 1–6. Four anonymous *balli*. Transcription in Gino Corti, "Cinque balli Toscani del cinquecento."

Jacobilli, Ludovico. *Modo di ballare*, c. 1615. Foligno, Biblioteca Jacobilli, A.III.19, f. 102–4.

Lupi da Caravaggio, Livio. *Mutanze di gagliarda, tordiglione, passo è mezzo, canari* (Palermo: Carrara, 1600).

Lutij di Sulmona, Prospero. *Opera bellissima nella quale si contengono molte partite, et passeggi di gagliarda* (Perugia: Pietropaolo Orlando, 1589).

Mancini, Giulio. *Del origin et nobiltà da ballo,* c. 1615. Biblioteca Apostolica Vaticana, MS Barb. Lat. 4315, f. 157–186.

Negri, Cesare. *Le gratie d'amore,* Milan, 1602. Facsimile editions, New York: Broude Brothers, 1969, and Bologna: Forni, 1969. English translation by G. Yvonne Kendall, *"Le Gratie d'Amore* 1602 by Cesare Negri: Translation and Commentary." D.M.A. thesis, Stanford University, 1985.

Negri, Cesare. *Nuove inventioni di balli,* 1604. Re-edition of *Le gratie d'amore.*

Rome, Biblioteca Vaticana Apostolica, Chigi S. V. 6 (3), f. 24r–33v. Anonymous collection of thirteen choreographies. Transcipion in Fabio Carboni, Barbara Sparti, and Agostino Ziino, *"Balli* To Dance and Play in a Sixteenth-Century Miscellany," in *Music Observed: Studies in Memory of William C. Holmes,* edited by Colleen Reardon and Susan Parisi. Warren, Mich.: Harmonie Park Press, 2004, pp. 44–51.

Santucci, Ercole. *Mastro da ballo,* 1614. Facsimile edition, Hildesheim: Georg Olms, 2004.

Seventeenth-Century France

De Lauze, François. *Apologie de la danse,* London, 1623. Facsimile edition, Geneva: Minkoff, 1977. English translation by Joan Wildeblood. London: F. Muller, 1952.

Instruction pour dancer les dances cy apres nommez. Darmstadt, Hessische Hochschul- und Landesbibliothek, HS 304. Facsimile and transcription, Instruction pour dancer: *An Anonymous Manuscript.* Edited and introduced by Angene Feves et al. Freiburg: Fagisis, 2000.

Lorin, André. *Livre de la contredance du roy présenté à sa majesté par André Lorin . . . ,* 1688. Paris, Bibliothèque Nationale, MS fr. 1698. Description this and the following manuscript in Jean-Michel Guilcher, "André Lorin et l'invention de l'écriture chorégraphie," *Revue de la société d'histoire du théâtre* 21 (1969): 257–58.

Lorin, André. *Livre de contredance présenté au roy par André Lorin . . . ,* 1685. Paris, Bibliothèque Nationale, MS fr. 1697.

Menestrier, Claude-François. *Des ballets anciens et modernes selon les règles du théâtre,* 1682. Facsimile edition, Geneva: Minkoff, 1972.

Montagut, B. de. *Louange de la Danse,* edited by Barbara Ravelhofer. Cambridge: Renaissance Texts from Manuscripts, 2000.

Pure, Michel de. *Idée des spectacles anciens et nouveaux,* 1668. Facsimile edition, Geneva: Minkoff, 1972.

Saint-Hubert, M de. *La manière de composer et faire réussir les ballets.* Paris, 1641. Facsimile edition, Geneva: Minkoff, 1993. English translation by Andrée Bergens, "How to Compose a Successful Ballet." *Dance Perspectives* 20 (1964): 26–37.

Stockholm, Kungliga Biblioteket, Cod. Holm S. 253.

Seventeenth- and Eighteenth-Century Spain

Esquivel Navarro, Juan de. *Discursos sobre el arte del dancado.* Seville, 1642. Facsimile edition, Madrid: Hauser y Menet, 1947. English translation by Lynn Matluck Brooks, *The Art of Dancing in Seventeenth-Century Spain: Juan de Esquivel Navarro and His World.* Lewisburg, Pa.: Bucknell University Press; London: Associated University Presses, 2003.

Jaque, Juan Antonio. *Libro de danzar.* Original manuscript of twenty-five folios now lost.

Two nineteenth-century copies in Madrid, Biblioteca Nacional, MS Barbieri 14059/15, and Madrid, Biblioteca Nacional, MS 18580/5. Modern edition in José Subirá, "'Libro de danzar', de don Baltasar de Rojas Pantoja, compuesto por el maestro Juan Antonio Jaque (s. XVII)," *Anuario musical* 5 (1950): 190–98.

Madrid, Biblioteca Nacional, MS Barbieri 14059/12 "Xácara" (probably from the eighteenth century). Instructions for the *jácara*. Transcription of the Barbieri copy is found in Maurice Esses, *Dance and Instrumental* Diferencias *in Spain during the 17th and Early 18th Centuries*. Stuyvesant, N.Y.: Pendragon Press, 1992, vol. 3, part 4, note 302.

Tarragó, Jatot. Barcelona, Biblioteca Central, a single parchment leaf, probably early seventeenth century. Contains brief choreographic notes on eighteen or nineteen dances. Discussed in Frederick Crane, *Materials for the Study*, pp. 27–29.

Seventeenth-Century England

London, British Library, MS Harley 367, f. 178r–179v. Transcription and discussion in David R. Wilson, "Dancing in the Inns of Court." *Historical Dance* 2, no. 5 (1986/87): 3–16, and Ian Payne, *The Almain in Britain, c.1549–c.1675: A Dance Manual from Manuscript Sources*. Aldershot: Ashgate, 2003.

London, British Library, MS Rawlinson D. 864, f. 199r–199v, copied c. 1630. Transcription and discussion in Wilson, "Dancing in the Inns of Court," and Payne, *The Almain in Britain*.

London, Inner Temple Library, Inner Temple Records, vol. 27 f. 3r–6v, "The Measures as they are danced in the Inner Temple Hall." Written down by Butler Buggins c. 1672–1675. Transcription and discussion in Wilson, "Dancing in the Inns of Court," and Payne, *The Almain in Britain*.

London, Royal College of Music, MS 1119, f. 1r–2v, copied no earlier than the 1670s. Transcription and discussion in Wilson, "Dancing in the Inns of Court," and Payne, *The Almain in Britain*.

Oxford, Bodleian Library, MS Douce 280, f. 66(a)v–66(b)v, probably c. 1606–1609. Transcription and discussion in Wilson, "Dancing in the Inns of Court," and Payne, *The Almain in Britain*.

Playford, John. *The English Dancing Master or, Plaine and easie Rules for the Dancing of Country Dances, with the Tune to each Dance*. 1st edition, London, 1651. Reprint of the 1933 edition, edited by Hugh Mellor and Leslie Bridgewater. London: Dance Books, 1984.

Eighteenth-Century Italy

Gaetano Grossatesta, Museo Civico, Raccolta Correr di Venezia, Archivio Morosini Grimani no. 245, MS 157. Facsimile edition, *Balletti: In occasione delle felicissime Nozze di sua Eccellenza La Signora Loredana Duodo con Sua Eccellenza il Signor Antonio Grimani Composti da Gaetano Grossatesta Maestro di Ballo in Venezia, 1726*, edited by Gloria Giordano. Lucca: Libreria musicale italiana, 2005.

Eighteenth-Century France

Bonnet, Jacques. *Histoire générale de la danse*. Paris, 1724. Facsimile editions, Geneva: Minkoff, 1969, and Bologna: Forni, 1972.

Feuillet, Raoul-Auger. *Chorégraphie ou l'art de décrire la danse*. Paris: Michel Brunet, 1700.

Facsimile editions, New York: Broude Brothers, 1968, and Hildesheim: Georg Olms, 1974. English translation by John Weaver, *Orchesography or the Art of Dancing*, 1706.

Feuillet, Raoul-Auger. *Recüeil de contredances*. Paris, 1706. Facsimile edition, New York: Broude Brothers, 1968. English translation by John Essex, *For the Further Improvement of Dancing*. London, 1710.

Feuillet, Raoul-Auger. *Receüil de dances . . . entrées de ballet de Mr. Pécour*. Paris, 1704. Facsimile editions, Farnborough: Gregg International, 1972, and Bologna: Forni, 1969.

Gaudrau. *Nouveau Recüeil de dance de bal et celle de ballet contenant un tres grand nombres des meilleures entrées de ballet de la composition de Mr. Pécour . . . Recüeillies et mises au jour Par Mr. Gaudrau Me. de dance*. Paris, [1713].

Rameau, Pierre. *Abbregé de la nouvelle méthode dans l'art d'écrire ou de traçer toutes sortes de danses de villes*. Paris, 1725. Facsimile edition, Farnborough: Gregg International, 1972.

Rameau, Pierre. *Le maître à danser*. Paris, 1725. Facsimile edition, New York: Broude Brothers, 1967. English translation by John Essex, *The Dancing Master*, 1728. English translation of the 1725 edition by Cyril W. Beaumont, *The Dancing Master*, 1931. Facsimile edition of 1931 publication, Alton: Dance Books, 2003.

Eighteenth-Century England

Essex, John. *For the Further Improvement of Dancing*. London, 1710. Facsimile editions, Farnborough: Gregg International, 1970, and New York: Dance Horizons, 1970.

Essex, John. *The Dancing Master: or the Art of Dancing Explained*. London, 1728.

Isaac. *The Pastorall Mr. Isaac's New Dance*. London, 1713.

Pemberton, E. *An Essay for the Further Improvement of Dancing. . . .* London, 1711. Facsimile editions, Farnborough: Gregg International, 1970, and New York: Dance Horizons, 1970.

Roussau, F[rançois] le. *A Collection of New Ball- and Stage Dances . . . compos'd by Several Masters*. 1720. Edinburgh, University Library, Laing MSS, La.III.163.

Roussau, F[rançois] le. *A New Collection of Dances . . . composed by Monsieur L'Abbé*. London, c. 1725. Facsimile edition, *Anthony L'Abbé, A New Collection of Dances, originally published by F. Le Roussau, London c. 1725*. In *Music for London Entertainment 1660–1800*, Series D, volume 2. London and New York: Stainer & Bell, 1991.

Shennan, Jennifer, ed. *A Work Book by Kellom Tomlinson: Commonplace Book of an Eighteenth-Century English Dancing Master, A Facsimile Edition*. Stuyvesant, N.Y.: Pendragon Press, 1992.

Tomlinson, Kellom. *The Art of Dancing*. London, 1735. Facsimile editions, New York: Dance Horizons, 1970, and Farnborough: Gregg International, 1970.

Tomlinson, Kellom. *Six Dances compos'd by Mr Kellom Tomlinson. Being a Collection of all the Yearly Dances publish'd by him from the Year 1715 to the present Year*. London, 1720. Facsimile editions, New York: Dance Horizons, 1970, and Farnborough: Gregg International, 1970.

Weaver, John. *Orchesography or the Art of Dancing*, London, 1706. Facsimile editions, New York: Broude Brothers, 1968, New York: Dance Horizons, 1971, Farnborough: Gregg International, 1971, and in Richard Ralph, *The Life and Works of John Weaver*. New York: Dance Horizons, 1985, pp. 173–285.

Eighteenth-Century Germany

Bonin, Louis. *Die neuste Art zur galanten und theatralischen Tantz-Kunst.* Frankfurt, 1711.

Lambranzi, Gregorio. *Neue und curieuse theatralische Tantz-Schul,* Nuremberg, 1716. English translation by F. Derra de Moroda in a facsimile edition, *New and Curious School of Theatrical Dancing,* London, 1928. Reprint, Mineola, N.Y.: Dover, 2002.

Pasch, Johann. *Beschreibung wahrer Tanz-Kunst.* Frankfurt, 1707.

Taubert, Gottfried. *Rechtschaffener Tantzmeister.* Leipzig, 1717.

Glossary

The glossary contains brief definitions of key terms as they are used in the essays. The definitions given here are not comprehensive, and they do not discuss every aspect of the term or concept. The glossary does not contain a definition of every dance genre and type from 1250 to 1750, only those that may be less familiar. For fuller definitions see Selma Jean Cohen, ed., *The International Encyclopaedia of Dance* (Oxford: Oxford University Press, 1998), Stanley Sadie and John Tyrrell, eds., *The New Grove Dictionary of Music and Musicians*, 2nd ed. (London: Macmillan, 2001), or *Grove Music Online*, ed. L. Macy, www.grovemusic.com. Crossreference is indicated by bold type within a definition.

arete: A virtue admired by the ancient Greeks. It encompassed excellence of style, manner, and accomplishment.

armonia: Literally "harmony." In Pythagorean and Platonic philosophy of music and dance the term referred to the unifying principle of the cosmos, that is, the system of mathematical ratios that ordered the cosmos, as well as the musical scale and the entire human world.

baixa / baja: The Aragonese and Castilian versions, respectively, of the **basse dance**.

baladin: A professional, theatrical dancer capable of performing virtuosic steps and leaps.

ballet à entrées: A choreographed theatrical work with many separate parts, each of which had its own subject and characters, that were tied only loosely to the theme of the danced spectacle as expressed in its title.

ballet de cour: A danced spectacle performed at the French court from the late sixteenth to the late seventeenth century, and at courts across Europe in the mid- to late seventeenth century. The spectacle included **recits**, choruses, and polyphonic songs, and rhyming verses printed in the **livrets**. The dancers were both courtiers and professionals. The largest *ballet de cour* could have as many as thirty separate **entrées**.

balletto: In sixteenth-century Italy a generic term for dance. Also, a specific dance genre in this century.

ballo: A generic term for dance in fifteenth-century Italy. Also one of the two genres of dances recorded in the fifteenth-century Italian dance treatises. A *ballo* was constructed of a number of short, irregular sections that differed in speed and meter. Each *ballo* was a unique arrangement of steps and floor patterns, with an individual name.

bassadanza: One of the two genres of dances recorded in the fifteenth-century Italian dance treatises. A *bassadanza* was normally only in one speed and meter. Each *bassadanza* was a unique arrangement of steps and floor patterns, with an individual name.

basse dance: A dance genre from northern Europe in the fifteenth and sixteenth century, particularly Burgundy and France. It had a limited step vocabulary of four steps. These four steps were arranged according to conventions that changed over time and from one region to another (see *mesure*).

belle danse / danse noble: In the mid-seventeenth century Michel de Pure defined *la belle danse* as "a certain finesse in movement and steps and in the whole person which cannot be expressed or taught through words." Developed from court etiquette and comportment, *la belle danse* or *danse noble* was the style of dance exemplified by the best dancers, whether that person was a courtier or a professional, both in the ballroom and in the theater (Francine Lancelot, *La belle danse: catalogue raisonné* [Paris: Van Dieren, 1996], p. xi).

breve: A unit of time in medieval and Renaissance music theory. Today a breve is often transcribed as one bar. A breve could be divided into either two or three **semibreves**. The notated music for *basse dances* were written in breves.

cantus firmus: The term used to describe a pre-existing melody that is then used as the basis for a new polyphonic composition.

carole / chorea / carol: The most popular dance type from the twelfth to the fourteenth century. It could be performed in a line, or in a circle, indoors or outdoors, and was usually accompanied by the singing of the dancers.

comédie-ballet: A seventeenth-century French theatrical spectacle combining dances, comedy (spoken dialogue), and vocal music.

continuo aria: An aria in which the vocal line is accompanied only by the small group of instruments in the continuo section of the orchestra.

couplet: This word had several slightly different meanings in the dance practice of late seventeenth and early eighteenth centuries. In Pemberton's notations the word referred to a quantity of choreographic material together with its musical notation. Usually the couplet number referred to the amount of choreographic material given on one page, but sometimes only to that on half a page. In contredanses the term referred to the amount of choreographic material that corresponded to one playing of the music. In a contredanse with more than one couplet, the first couplet would be danced by all the couples through the entire progression; then, with everyone back in place, the head couple would begin the second couplet.

da capo aria: A type of aria found predominantly in Italian operas of the first half of the eighteenth century. Arias of this type were in two parts, AB, with the A section repeated after the B section. When the A section returned the singer varied the melody by freely improvising ornaments and embellishments.

dance figure: A shape formed by the path traced out on the dance floor by the dancers. In the sixteenth century, particularly, dance figures were often geometric shapes, such as a circle, square, triangle, or lozenge, or shapes such as a cross, a half moon, a star, or letters of the alphabet. These figures were regarded as having astrological and magical connotations and divine effects. In the sixteenth and seventeenth centuries the term "figure" was also used to refer to patterns created in garden beds, including geometric shapes, coats of arms, and so on.

entrée: In the seventeenth century *ballet de cour* the term referred to a collection of dances which were unified by subject. They were considered by seventeenth-century writers to divide a ballet into scenes, as in purely spoken dramatic works.

festa / fête: A feast, holy day, celebration, banquet, or entertainment.

floor pattern: A pattern or shape formed by the movement of the dancers during the course of a dance. A choreography consists of a number of floor patterns.

floor shape: The smallest unit of shape. Several floor shapes combine to form a floor pattern.

floor track: The path of an entire dance from start to finish, that is, a sequence of floor patterns.

hemiola: The ratio 3:2. In modern musical terminology the term refers to a change in rhythm where two bars of triple meter are played as if they were three bars of duple meter. It can also refer to the rhythm set up between simultaneous lines of music, one of which is barred or accented in triple time, the other in duple time, for example, $\frac{3}{4}$ against $\frac{6}{8}$.

intermedio: From the late fifteenth century onward, when the five-act Latin comedies of Plautus and Terence were revived at the Ferrarese court, entertaining interludes were inserted between each act and before and after the comedy. These *intermedi* helped to clarify the divisions of the play into each act, as well as providing relief for the spectators. Typically an *intermedio* consisted of instrumental and vocal music, costumed dancers and actors, with increasingly elaborate scenery and stage effects as the sixteenth century progressed.

kosmos: For the ancient Greeks *kosmos* was the beautiful order of the universe and the imitation of that order at the human level.

liberal arts: The series of subjects that formed the course of academic studies. Plato's first curriculum of study consisted of the four mathematical arts, arithmetic, geometry, music, and astronomy, called the **quadrivium.** After his death three more subjects were introduced to precede the study of the **quadrivium,** that is, the three verbal arts—grammar, rhetoric, and dialectic (or logic)—called the trivium.

livret: The program of a *ballet de cour*. A *livret* contained the verses about the dancers, descriptions of the scenes, and a list of the dancers' names and the character(s) they were portraying.

macrocosm: The celestial system of the Earth, Sun, Moon, stars, and planets.

major/minor: In fifteenth-century music theory the terms "major" and "minor" referred to the division of the **semibreve** into either three or two **minima,** respectively.

mensuration: The system used in medieval and Renaissance music theory to describe the relationships between notes of one value and those of smaller or longer values, which could be either binary or ternary. The four main notes values were the long, **breve, semibreve,** and the **minima.** From the late fourteenth century onward the different relationships (or mensurations) between the **breve,** the **semibreve,** and the **minima** were represented by four symbols: ☉, ○, ℭ, ℭ. (See Figure 16.1.)

mesure: In the *basse dance* repertoire a *mesure* was a grouping of steps according to certain conventions. A series of *mesures* made up a *basse dance*.

microcosm: The systems found on earth that were ordered in the same ratios as the cosmos (or **macrocosm**). These systems included the human soul and body, the family, the city-state, music, and dance.

perfect major ⊙	breve = 3 semibreves semibreve = 3 minima
perfect minor ○	breve = 3 semibreves semibreve = 2 minima
imperfect major ₵	breve = 2 semibreves semibreve = 3 minima
imperfect minor C	breve = 2 semibreves semibreve = 2 minima

Figure 16.1. Division of the breve and semibreve

minima: A short unit of time in medieval and Renaissance music theory. A minima was either one-half or one-third the length of a **semibreve**.

misura: Literally a measure, a rule, a method, or a proportion. In fifteenth-century Italian dance practice the word was used in a number of slightly different ways, all of which embodied the idea of proportion: a proportioning of the space around the dancer's body through the movements of her or his body, a proportioning of the ground on which the floor patterns were traced out, and a proportioning of the music. *Misura* was also the word used to describe the four different combinations of meter and speed that were found in the **balli**, that is, *bassadanza misura, quadernaria misura, saltarello misura,* and *piva misura*.

misura el tereno: A "direction" or "rule" that applied to movements of the body while dancing. These movements should always keep to the mean and avoid the extremes of movement.

moitié / résidu / retour: Literally "the part left over." An additional grouping of twelve steps that was added to the end of a **basse dance** in the sixteenth century. These twelve steps could be arranged in three different sequences.

moresca / moresque: A dance genre performed by both courtiers and dance masters, with elaborate costumes, masks, and scenery. In the fifteenth and sixteenth centuries *moresche* often included danced combat and other pantomimic dancing. Often the dancers represented allegorical or mythological figures, or exotic characters such as wild men.

mousike: For the ancient Greeks *mousike* referred to what we would now call the performing arts, that is, music—both vocal and instrumental—dance, poetry, drama, and declamation.

musica humana: The same musical proportions, or ratios, of **musica mundana**, but found in the human body, thereby uniting the human soul with the cosmos.

musica instrumentalis: The audible pitches (what we now call music) produced by human instruments and voices.

musica mundana / musica speculativa: The music of the cosmos, or the heavenly spheres, inaudible to human ears. The series of ratios that define the structure of the cosmos and preserve it from dissolving into disharmony and chaos.

parterre de broderie: In horticulture "parterre" referred to the garden beds planted out with flowers or herbs. "Parterre de broderie," therefore, were the new patterns formed by these plantings in the garden beds from the late sixteenth century onward. These patterns were curvilinear, with "S"-shaped curves, arcs, and embroidery-like scroll patterns.

perfect / imperfect: In fifteenth-century music theory the terms "perfect" and "imperfect" referred to the division of the **breve** into either three or two **semibreves,** respectively.

pieces en machines / machine plays: Seventeenth- and eighteenth-century dramatic productions, such as an opera or a *ballet de cour,* which required elaborate and complicated stage machinery to produce the desired supernatural and magical effects.

piffero: A wind musician, particularly one who played the shawm. *Pifferi* was the term used to refer to the "dance band" that accompanied dancing in the fifteenth century, that is, two or three shawms and a brass instrument with a slide mechanism.

quadrivium: See the **liberal arts.**

recit: Used in France in the seventeenth and eighteenth century, this term generically referred to a whole composition, or part thereof, for a solo voice or instrument. In the *ballet de cour recits* were solo vocal pieces inserted at the beginning of each section of the ballet to provide a commentary on the ensuring action. *Recits* were considered to divide a ballet into acts.

semibreve: A unit of time in medieval and Renaissance music theory. A semibreve was either one-half or one-third the length of a **breve.** Semibreves could be divided into either two or three **minima.**

techne: The term used by the ancient Greeks to refer to any skill, art, or craft, for example, practiced by a carpenter, mechanic, athlete, poet, playwright, dancer, musician, doctor, lawyer, or architect.

tripudium: A Latin word meaning "dancing," "a measured stamping." Also the term for a dance genre from the time of the Roman republic that was danced by men and performed on festive occasions. In the thirteenth and fourteenth centuries the word was used to refer to a dance or dancing that occurred at peace celebrations. It could have been danced by men and women.

Bibliography

Manuscripts

See also the list of dance treatises, manuscripts, modern editions, and translations.

Calendar of State Papers, Elizabeth, 1580–81.

Florence, Biblioteca Nazionale, Magl. VII 1121.

London, Public Record Office, LC/7/3

London: Westminster Archives centre, parish registers of St. Clement Danes, vol. 30: marriages 1716–1754.

Milan, Archivio di Stato di Milano, Notarile.

Milan, Archivio Storico Diocesano.

Paris, Bibliothèque de l'Arsenal, MS 6544, IV.

Paris, Bibliothèque-Musée de la Comédie-Française, Archives.

Paris, Bibliothèque Nationale, Fonds du Conservatoire, Rés. F. 516: *Les Ballets Des Jesuistes Composé par Messieurs Beauchant Desmatins et Collasse Recueillie par Philidor L'aisné en 1690*. (Philidor's 1690 ms. copy of Beauchamps's score for *Le Collier de perles* is available online through http://gallica.bnf.fr, Notice no. FRBNF39748343.)

Paris, Bibliothèque Nationale, Fonds du Conservatoire, *Les Fâcheux*. (Philidor's 1681 ms. copy of Beauchamps's score of *Les Fâcheux* is available online through http://gallica.bnf.fr, Notice no. FRBNF39749767.)

Paris, Bibliothèque Nationale, ms. Clairambault 808.

Paris, Bibliothèque Nationale, ms. lat. 7324, Henri Bate, *Nativitas magistri Henrici Mechliniensis*.

Paris, Bibliothèque Nationale, ms. n.a. 6532: Claude and François Parfaict, *Histoire de l'Académie Royale de Musique*.

Paris, Bibliothèque Nationale, Mélanges Colbert 264.

Paris, *Sujet de la comédie italienne intitulée le Collier de perles, mêlée de ballets et de musique*, 1672. (Available online at http://gallica.bnf.fr, Notice no. FRBNF33616342.)

Printed Works

Abromeit, Klaus. "Lambranzi's *Theatralische Tantz-Schul:* Commedia dell'arte and French Noble Style." *Studi musicali* 25, nos. 1–2 (1996): 317–28.

Akkerman, Nadine N. W., and Paul R. Selin. "A Stuart Masque in Holland: *Ballet de La Haye* (1665)." *Ben Jonson Journal* 11 (2004): 207–58.

———. "A Stuart Masque in Holland: *Ballet de La Haye* (1665) Commentary, Part 2." *Ben Jonson Journal* 12 (2005): 141–64.

Alberti, Leon Battista. *Della pittura,* trans. with introduction and notes by John R. Spencer. London: Routledge and Kegan Paul, 1956.

———. *On the Art of Building in Ten Books.* Trans. Joseph Rykwert, Neil Leach, and Robert Tavernor. Cambridge, Mass.: MIT Press, 1988.

Alexander, Jonathan J. G. "Dancing in the Streets." *Journal of the Walters Art Gallery* 54 (1996): 147–62.

Alm, Irene. "Winged Feet and Mute Eloquence: Dance in Seventeenth-Century Venetian Opera." Ed. Wendy Heller and Rebecca Harris-Warrick. *Cambridge Opera Journal* 15, no. 3 (2003): 216–80.

Anderson, Benedict. *Imagined Communities: Reflections on the Origin and Spread of Nationalism,* rev. ed. New York: Verso, 1991.

Anderson, Gordon Athol, ed. *Notre-Dame and Related Conductus: Opera Omnia. Pars octava: 1pt—The Latin Rondeau Répertoire.* Henryville, Pa.: Institute of Mediaeval Music, 1979.

Anderson, Warren D. *Ethos and Education in Greek Music: The Evidence of Poetry and Philosophy.* Cambridge, Mass.: Harvard University Press, 1966.

Andrijeski, Julie. "The Elusive Loure." In *Proceedings of the 21st Annual Conference of the Society of Dance History Scholars,* pp. 295–300. Riverside: SDHS, 1998.

Anglo, Sydney. *Spectacle, Pageantry and Early Tudor Policy,* 2nd ed. Oxford: Clarendon Press, 1997.

Arcangeli, Alessandro. "Carnival in Medieval Sermons." *European Medieval Drama* 1 (1997): 199–209.

———. "Dance and Health: The Renaissance Physicians' View." *Dance Research* 18, no. 1 (2000): 3–30.

———. "Dance and Law." In *Terpsichore 1450–1900: Proceedings of the International Dance Conference, Ghent, April 2000,* ed. Barbara Ravelhofer, pp. 51–64. Ghent: Institute for Historical Dance Practice, 2000.

———. "Dance and Punishment." *Dance Research* 10, no. 2 (1992): 30–42.

———. "Dance under Trial: The Moral Debate, 1200–1600." *Dance Research* 12, no. 2 (1994): 127–55.

———. *Davide o Salomè? Il dibattito europeo sulla danza nella prima età moderna.* Rome: Viella, 2000.

———. *Recreation in the Renaissance: Attitudes towards Leisure and Pastimes in European Culture, c. 1425–1675.* Basingstoke: Palgrave Macmillan, 2003.

Archer, Ian W. *The Pursuit of Stability: Social Relations in Elizabethan London.* Cambridge: Cambridge University Press, 1991.

Aristotle. *The Ethics of Aristotle: The Nicomachean Ethics.* Trans. J. A. K. Thomson, rev. Hugh Tredennick. Harmondsworth: Penguin, 1976.

Arnold, Janet. "Costume for Masques and Other Entertainments c1500–1650." *Historical Dance* 3, no. 2 (1993): 3–20.

Ashbee, Andrew, and David Lasocki et al. (comp). *A Biographical Dictionary of English Court Musicians 1485–1714*, 2 vols. Aldershot: Ashgate, 1998.

Astier [Kunzle], Régine. "Académie Royale de Danse." In *International Encyclopedia of Dance*, 1: 3–5. Oxford: Oxford University Press, 1998.

———. "Chaconne pour une femme: *Chaconne de Phaéton*, A Performance Study." *Dance Research* 15, no. 2 (1997): 150–69.

———. "Louis XIV, 'Premier Danseur.'" In *The Sun King: The Ascendancy of French Culture during the Reign of Louis XIV*, ed. David Lee Rubin, pp. 73–102. Washington: Folger Shakespeare Library; Toronto: Associated University Presses, 1992.

———. "Pierre Beauchamps and the Ballets de Collège." *Dance Chronicle* 6, no. 2 (1983): 138–63.

———. "Pierre Beauchamp: The Illustrious Unknown Choreographer, Part I." *Dance Scope* 8, no. 2 (1974): 32–45.

———. "Pierre Beauchamp: The Illustrious Unknown Choreographer, Part II." *Dance Scope* 9, no. 1 (1975): 31–44.

Athenaeus. *The Deipnosophists*. Trans. Charles Burton Gulick. Cambridge, Mass.: Harvard University Press, 1950.

Auld, Louis. "The Unity of Molière's Comedy-Ballets: A Study of Their Structure, Meanings, and Values." Ph.D. diss., Bryn Mawr College, 1968.

Avery, Emmet L., ed. *The London Stage 1660–1800: A Calendar, Part 2 1700–1729*. Carbondale: Southern Illinois University Press, 1960.

Baïf, Antoine de. *Euvres en rime*, 5 vols. Paris: A. Lemerre, 1881–1890.

Baldwin, John. *Aristocratic Life in Medieval France: The Romances of Jean Renart and Gerbert de Montreuil, 1190–1230*. Baltimore: Johns Hopkins University Press, 2000.

Balthazar de Beaujoyeulx. *Le balet comique*, 1581. Facsimile edition. Ed. and with an introduction by Margaret M. McGowan. Binghamton, N.Y.: Medieval and Renaissance Texts and Studies, 1982.

Barlow, Jeremy, ed. *The Complete Country Dance Tunes from Playford's Dancing Master (1651-ca. 1728)*. London: Faber Music, 1985.

———. "'Mockmusick' and the Survival of Antimasque Traditions in the Restoration Theatre." In *The Restoration of Charles II: Public Order, Theatre and Dance*, ed. David R. Wilson, pp. 15–19. Cambridge: Early Dance Circle, 2002.

———. "Tunes in *The English Dancing Master* 1651: John Playford's Accidental Misprints?" In *On Common Ground 3: John Playford and The English Dancing Master 1651: Proceedings of the 3rd DHDS Conference, March 2001*, ed. David Parsons, pp. 21–34. Stock, Essex: Dolmetsch Historical Dance Society, 2001.

Baschet, Armand. *La diplomatie vénitienne*. Paris: H. Plon, 1862.

Baskerville, Mary Pennino. "Terpsichore Reviled: Antidance Tracts in Elizabethan England." *Sixteenth-Century Journal* 22, no. 3 (1991): 475–93.

Bastineller, Gebhardus Christianus. *Dissertatio inauguralis iuridica de eo quod iustum est circa saltationes*. Thesis defended by Ioannes Daniel Kettnerus. Wittenberg: A. Kobersteinius, 1730.

Baxandall, Michael. *Giotto and the Orators: Humanist Observers of Painting in Italy and the Discovery of Pictorial Composition, 1350–1450*. Oxford: Clarendon Press, 1971.

———. *Painting and Experience in Fifteenth-Century Italy. A Primer in the Social History of Pictorial Style*. Oxford: Oxford University Press, 1974.

Beeching, Jack. *The Galleys of Lepanto*. New York: Scribner, 1983.

Béguin, Sylvie. *Le château de Fontainebleau*. Paris, 1960.

Benoit, Marcelle. *Musiques de cour: Chapelle, Chambre, Écurie (1661–1733)*. Paris: Picard, 1971.

Berger, Anna Maria Busse. *Mensuration and Proportion Signs. Origins and Evolution*. Oxford: Clarendon Press, 1993.

Berghaus, Günter. "Neoplatonic and Pythagorean Notions of World Harmony and Unity and Their Influence on Renaissance Dance Theory." *Dance Research* 10, no. 2 (1992): 43–70.

Berlioz, Jacques. "Exempla as a Source for the History of Women." In *Medieval Women and the Sources of Medieval History*, ed. Joel T. Rosenthal, pp. 37–50. Athens: University of Georgia Press, 1990.

Berlioz, Jacques, and Marie-Anne Polo de Beaulieu. *Les exempla médiévaux: Nouvelles perspectives*. Paris: Honoré Champion Éditeur, 1998.

Biller, Peter, and A. J. Minnis, eds. *Handling Sin: Confession in the Middle Ages*. York: University of York, York Medieval Press, 1998.

Biow, Douglas. "Reflections on Humanism and Professions in Renaissance Italy and the Humanities Today." *Rinascimento* 43 (2003): 333–53.

Black, Robert. "École et société à Florence aux XIVe et XVe siècles: Le témoignage des *ricordanze*." *Annales: Histoire, Sciences sociales* 59, no. 4 (2004): 827–46.

Boase, Alan. "Leçons sur le ballet de cour." *Neohelicon: Acta Comparationis Litterarum Universarum* 7, no. 1 (1979): 61–144.

Boiseul, Jean. *Traitté contre les danses*. La Rochelle: heirs of H. Haultin, 1606.

Bonniffet, Pierre. "Esquisses du ballet humaniste (1572–1581)." *Cahiers de l'Institut de Recherches et d'Histoire Musicale des Etats de Savoie* 1 (1992): 15–49.

Boucher, Jacqueline. *La court de Henri III. De mémoire d'homme: l'histoire*. Rennes: Ouest France, 1986.

——. *Société et Mentalités autour de Henri III. Thèse presentée devant l'Université de Lyon II, le 22 Octobre 1977*, 4 vols. Lille: Atelier Reproduction des Theses, Université de Lille III, 1981.

Bouquet-Boyer, Marie-Thérèse, ed. *Le ballet aux XVIe et XVIIe siècles en France et à la cour de Savoie*. Geneva: Slatkine, 1992.

Bourdeille, Pierre de, seigneur de Brantôme. *Oeuvres complètes*, 8 vols. Ed. Louis Jean Nicolas Monmerqué. Paris, 1822.

Boyden, David D. *The History of Violin Playing from Its Origins to 1761, and Its Relationship to the Violin and Violin Music*. Oxford: Oxford University Press, 1965.

Brainard, Ingrid. "The Art of Courtly Dancing in Transition: Nürnberg, Germ. Nat. Mus. MS 8842, a Hitherto Unknown German Dance Source." In *Crossroads of Medieval Civilization: The City of Regensburg and Its Intellectual Milieu*, ed. Edelgard E. DuBruck and Karl Heinz Göller, pp. 61–79. Detroit: Michigan Consortium for Medieval and Early Modern Studies, 1984.

——. "Medieval Dance." In *International Encyclopaedia of Dance*, 4: 347–50. Oxford: Oxford University Press, 1998.

——. "New Dances for the Ball: The Annual Collections of France and England in the 18th Century." *Early Music* 14, no. 2 (1986): 164–73.

——. "The Role of the Dancing Master in Fifteenth-Century Courtly Society." *Fifteenth-Century Studies* 2 (1979): 21–44.

——. "Sir John Davies' *Orchestra* as a Dance Historical Source." In *Songs of the Dove and the Nightingale: Sacred and Secular Music c. 900–c. 1600*, ed. Greta Mary Hair and Robyn E. Smith, pp. 176–212. Sydney: Currency Press, 1994.

Brant, Sebastian. *Das Narrenschiff.* Basel, 1493.

Bremond, Claude, Jacques Le Goff, and Jean-Claude Schmitt. *L'"exemplum."* Turnhout: Brepols, 1982.

Bridgeman, Jane. "Ambrogio Lorenzetti's 'Dancing Maidens': A Case of Mistaken Identity." *Apollo* 133, no. 350 (1991): 245–51.

Britland, Karen. "An Under-Stated Mother-in-Law: Marie de Médicis and the Last Caroline Court Masque." In *Women and Culture at the Courts of the Stuart Queens,* ed. Clare McManus, pp. 204–23. Houndsmills: Palgrave Macmillan, 2003.

Bromyard, John. *Summa predicantium.* Venice, 1636.

Brooks, Jeanice. *Courtly Song in Late Sixteenth-Century France.* Chicago: University of Chicago Press, 2000.

Brooks, Lynn Matluck. *The Art of Dancing in Seventeenth-Century Spain: Juan de Esquivel Navarro and His World.* Lewisburg, Pa.: Bucknell University Press; London: Associated University Press, 2003.

———. "Cosmic Imagery in the Religious Dances of Seville's Golden Age." In *Proceedings of 14th Annual Conference of Society of Dance History Scholars, February 1991,* pp. 82–94. Riverside: SDHS, 1991.

———. "Court, Church, and Province: Dancing in the Netherlands, Seventeenth and Eighteenth Centuries." *Dance Research Journal* 20, no. 1 (1988): 19–27.

———. *The Dances of the Processions of Seville in Spain's Golden Age.* Kassel: Reichenberger, 1988.

Brooks, William, ed. *Le Théâtre et l'opéra vus par les gazetiers Robinet et Laurent, 1670–1678: Papers on French Seventeenth-Century Literature.* Paris, 1993.

Brossard, Yolande De. *Musiciens de Paris 1535–1792. Actes d'État Civil d'après Le Fichier Laborde de la Bibliothèque Nationale.* Paris: A. and J. Picard, 1965.

Brown, Beatrice Curtis, ed. *The Letters and Diplomatic Instructions of Queen Anne.* London, 1935; reprint, 1968.

Brown, Elizabeth A. R., and Nancy Freeman Regalado. "*La grant feste:* Philip the Fair's Celebration at the Knighting of His Sons in Paris at Pentecost of 1313." In *City and Spectacle in Medieval Europe,* ed. Barbara A. Hanawalt and Kathryn L. Ryerson, pp. 56–86. Minneapolis: University of Minnesota Press, 1994.

Brown, Howard M. *Instrumental Music Printed before 1600. A Bibliography.* Cambridge, Mass.: Harvard University Press, 1965.

Brown, Richard. "The Politics of Magnificence in Ferrara 1450–1505: A Study in the Socio-political Implications of Renaissance Spectacle." Ph.D. diss., University of Edinburgh, 1982.

———. "The Reception of Anna Sforza in Ferrara, February 1491." *Renaissance Studies* 2, no. 2 (1988): 231–39.

Bryce, Judith. "Performing for Strangers: Women, Dance, and Music in Quattrocento Florence." *Renaissance Quarterly* 54, no. 4.1 (2001): 1074–1107.

Buch, David J. *Dance Music from the* Ballets de cour *1575–1651: Historical Commentary, Source Study, and Transcriptions from the Philidor Manuscripts.* Stuyvesant, N.Y.: Pendragon Press, 1993.

Bucholz, R. O. "'Nothing But Ceremony': Queen Anne and the Limitations of Royal Ritual." *Journal of British Studies* 30, no. 3 (1991): 288–323.

Bulfinch, Thomas. *Bulfinch's Mythology.* New York: Modern Library, 1998.

Burden, Michael. *Henry Purcell's Operas: The Complete Texts.* Oxford: Oxford University Press, 2000.

Burgess, Geoffrey. "The Chaccone and the Representation of Sovereign Power in Lully's *Amadis* (1684) and Charpentier's *Medée* (1693)." In *Dance & Music in French Baroque Theatre: Sources & Interpretations*, ed. Sarah McCleave, pp. 81–104. London: Institute of Advanced Musical Studies, King's College London, 1998.

———. "Ritual in the *tragédie en musique* from Lully's *Cadmus et Hermione* (1673) to Rameau's *Zoroastre* (1749)." Ph.D. diss., Cornell University, 1998.

Burke, Peter. *The Fabrication of Louis XIV*. New Haven: Yale University Press, 1992.

———. *The Fortunes of the Courtier: The European Reception of Castiglione's Cortegiano*. University Park: Penn State University Press, 1996.

———. *Popular Culture in Early Modern Europe*. 1978. Reprint, Aldershot: Scolar, 1994.

Bussels, Stijn. "*Le Balet de Princes Indiens* (1634)." In *Terpsichore 1450–1900: Proceedings of the International Dance Conference, Ghent, April 2000*, ed. Barbara Ravelhofer, pp. 105–14. Ghent: Institute for Historical Dance Practice, 2000.

Caldwell, John. "Some Observations on the Four *misure*." In *Terpsichore 1450–1900: Proceedings of the International Dance Conference, Ghent, April 2000*, ed. Barbara Ravelhofer, pp. 9–10. Ghent: Institute for Historical Dance Practice, 2000.

Cano, David Sanchez. "Dances for the Royal Festivities in Madrid in the Sixteenth and Seventeenth Centuries." *Dance Research* 23, no. 2 (2005): 123–52.

Canova-Green, Marie-Claude, ed. *Benserade: Ballets pour Louis XIV*. 2 vols. Toulouse: Société de Littératures Classiques, 1997.

———. "Dance and Ritual: The *Ballet des nations* at the Court of Louis XIII." *Renaissance Studies* 9, no. 4 (1995): 395–403.

———. "La Parole écrite et chantée dans le ballet de cour." In *La Rochefoucauld; Mithridate; Frères et sœurs; Les Muses sœurs*, ed. Claire Carlin, pp. 319–27. Tübingen: Narr, 1998.

Capellanus, Andreas. *The Art of Courtly Love*, trans. John Jay Parry. New York: Norton, 1969.

Carboni, Fabio, Barbara Sparti, and Agostino Ziino. "*Balli* To Dance and Play in a Sixteenth-Century Miscellany." In *Music Observed: Studies in Memory of William C. Holmes*, ed. Colleen Reardon and Susan Parisi, pp. 31–54. Warren, Mich.: Harmonie Park Press, 2004.

Carpenter, Nan Cooke. *Music in the Medieval and Renaissance Universities*. Norman: University of Oklahoma Press, 1958.

Carter, Françoise. "Celestial Dance: A Search for Perfection." *Dance Research* 5, no. 2 (1987): 3–17.

———. "Dance as a Moral Exercise." In *Guglielmo Ebreo da Pesaro e la danza nelle corti italiane del xv secolo*, ed. Maurizio Padovan, pp. 169–79. Pisa: Pacini, 1990.

———. "Neoplatonism and Cosmic Dance." *Renaissance Bulletin* 23 (1996): 11–25.

———. "Number Symbolism and Renaissance Choreography." *Dance Research* 10, no. 1 (1992): 21–39.

Carter, Tim. *Monteverdi's Musical Theatre*. New Haven: Yale University Press, 2002.

Castelnau, Michel de, sieur de Mauvissière. *Mémoires de Michel de Castelnau*. Ed. J. Michaud et J. J. F. Poujoulat. Paris: Adolphe Everat, 1838.

Castiglione, Baldesar. *The Book of the Courtier*. Trans. George Bull. Harmondsworth: Penguin, 1981.

Chailley, Jacques. "La danse religieuse au Moyen Age." In *Arts Liberaux et Philosophie au Moyen Age: Actes du IVe Congrès International de Philosophie Médiévale, Montreal, 1967*, pp. 357–80. Montreal: Institut d'Études Médiévales, 1969.

Chatenet, Monique. *La cour de France au XVIe siècle: vie sociale et architecture*. Paris: Picard, 2000.

Chevalley, Sylvie. "Le 'Registre d'Hubert' 1672–1673: Étude critique." *Revue d'histoire du théâtre* 25 (1973): 12–67.

Chiarle, Angelo, ed. *Atti: L'arte della danza ai tempi di Claudio Monteverdi*. Turin: Istituto per i Beni Musicali in Piemonte, 1996.

Christout, Marie-Françoise. *Le Ballet de cour au XVIIe siècle: Iconographie thématique*. Geneva: Minkoff, 1987.

———. *Le Ballet de cour de Louis XIV, 1643–1672: mises en scène*. Paris: Picard, 1967.

———. "Louis XIV et le ballet de cour ou le plus illustre des danseurs (1651–1670)." *Revue d'histoire du théâtre* 3, 215 (2002): 153–78.

Cibber, Colley. *An Apology for the Life of Colley Cibber, Comedian*. London: printed by John Watts for the author, 1740.

Cimber, L. *Archives curieuses de l'histoire de France*. Paris: Beauvais, 1836.

Cobban, Alan B. *The Medieval Universities: Their Development and Organization*. London: Methuen, 1975.

Coeyman, Barbara. "Lully's Influence on the Organization and Performance of the 'Ballet de Cour' after 1672." In *Jean-Baptiste Lully*, ed. Jérôme la Gorce and Herbert Schneider, pp. 517–28. Heidelburg: Laaber, 1990.

———. "Opera and Ballet in Seventeenth-Century French Theaters: Case Studies of the Salle des Machines and the Palais Royal Theater." In *Opera and Context: Essays on Historical Staging from the Late Renaissance to the Time of Puccini*, ed. Mark A. Radice, pp. 37–71. Portland: Amadeus Press, 1998.

———. "Sites of Indoor Musical-Theatrical Production at Versailles." *Eighteenth-Century Life* 17 (1993): 55–67.

———. "Social Dance in the 1688 *Feste de Versailles*: Architecture and Performance Context." *Early Music* 26, no. 2 (1998): 264–82.

Coffin, David. *Gardens and Gardening in Papal Rome*. Princeton: Princeton University Press, 1991.

Cohen, Sarah. *Art, Dance, and the Body in French Culture of the Ancien Régime*. Cambridge: Cambridge University Press, 2000.

Cohen, Selma Jean, ed. *The International Encyclopaedia of Dance*. Oxford: Oxford University Press, 1998.

Coldwell, Charles P. "Angelo Gardano's *Balletti Moderni* and its Relation to Cesare Negri's *Le Gratie d'Amore*." *Journal of the Lute Society of America* 16 (1983): 57–102.

Le Colloque de Fontainebleau, Paris, 1972 (Catalogue).

Colonna, Deda Cristina. "Variation and Persistence in the Notation of the Loure 'Aimable Vainqueur.'" In *Proceedings of 21st Annual Conference of the Society of Dance History Scholars*, pp. 285–94. Riverside: SHDS, 1998.

Comotti, Giovanni. *Music in Greek and Roman Culture*. Trans. Rosaria V. Munson. Baltimore: Johns Hopkins University Press, 1989.

A Comparison between the Two Stages. London, 1702.

Congleton, James Edmund. *Theories of Pastoral Poetry in England 1684–1798*. Gainesville: University of Florida Press, 1952.

Cooman, Ingeborg de. "Dances and Ballet in Seventeenth-Century Theatre of the Southern Netherlands." In *Terpsichore 1450–1900: Proceedings of the International Dance Conference, Ghent, April 2000*, ed. Barbara Ravelhofer, pp. 115–29. Ghent: Institute for Historical Dance Practice, 2000.

Il corago, o vero alcune osservazioni per metter bene in scena le composizioni drammatiche. Ed. P. Fabbri and A. Pompilio. Florence: Leo S. Olschki, 1983.

Corti, Gino. "Cinque balli Toscani del cinquecento." *Rivista italiana di musicologia* 12, no. 1 (1977): 73–82.

Couton, Georges, ed. *Œuvres complètes de Molière*, 2 vols. Paris: NRF/Gallimard, 1971.

Crane, Frederick. *Materials for the Study of the Fifteenth Century Basse Danse.* New York: Institute of Mediæval Music, 1968.

Cruickshank, Diana. "Circling the Square." In *On Common Ground 3: John Playford and the* The English Dancing Master *1651: Proceedings of the 3rd DHDS conference March 2001,* ed. David Parsons, pp. 35–42. Stock, Essex: Dolmetsch Historical Dance Society, 2001.

d'Albenas, Béranger de la Tour. *Choréide, autrement, louenge du bal.* Lyon, 1556.

D'Accone, Frank A. *The Civic Muse: Music and Musicians in Siena during the Middle Ages and the Renaissance.* Chicago: University of Chicago Press, 1997.

———. "Lorenzo the Magnificent and Music." In *Lorenzo il Magnifico e il suo mondo,* ed. Gian Carlo Garfagnini, pp. 259–90. Florence: Leo S. Olschki, 1994.

Dan, Père P. *Le Trésor des merveilles de la maison royale de Fontainebleau.* Paris, 1642.

Daneau, Lambert. *Traité des danses, auquel est amplement resolue la question, à sçavoir s'il est permis aux chrestiens de danser.* Geneva: F. Estienne, 1580.

Daniels, Bruce C. *Puritans at Play: Leisure and Recreation in Colonial New England.* Basingstoke: Palgrave Macmillan, 1995.

Dartois-Lapeyre, Françoise. "Comédie-ballet." In *Dictionnaire de la musique en France aux XVIe et XVIIe siècles,* ed. Marcelle Benoit, p. 166. Paris: Fayard, 1992.

d'Avray, David L. *The Preaching of the Friars: Sermons Diffused from Paris before 1300.* Oxford: Clarendon Press, 1985.

Daye, Anne. "The Banqueting House, Whitehall: A Site Specific to Dance." *Historical Dance* 4, no. 1 (2004): 3–22.

———. "From Word to Movement." *Historical Dance* 2, no. 4 (1984/5): 14–23.

———. "Skill and Invention in the Renaissance Ballroom." *Historical Dance* 2, no. 6 (1988/1991): 12–15.

———. "Taking the Measure of Dance Steps 1650–1700, through the Publications of John Playford." In *On Common Ground 3: John Playford and* The English Dancing Master *1651: Proceedings of the 3rd DHDS Conference March 2001,* ed. David Parsons, pp. 13–20. Stock, Essex: Dolmetsch Historical Dance Society, 2001.

———. "Theatre Dance in the Private and Public Domains of Stuart and Commonwealth London, 1625–1685." In *The Restoration of Charles II: Public Order, Theatre and Dance: Proceedings of a Conference, London February 2002,* ed. David R. Wilson, pp. 11–14. Cambridge: Early Dance Circle, 2002.

———. "A Valentine for the King." *Dance Research* 15, no 2 (1997): 63–83.

———. "'Youthful Revels, Masks, and Courtly Sighs': An Introductory Study of the Revels within the Stuart Masque." *Historical Dance* 3, no. 4 (1996): 5–22.

Daye, Anne, and Jeremy Barlow. "The Shock of the New: Ben Jonson's Antimasque of Witches 1609." In *On Common Ground 4: Reconstruction and Re-creation in Dance before 1850: Proceedings of the 4th DHDS Conference, March 2003,* ed. David Parsons, pp. 83–94. Stock, Essex: Dolmetsch Historical Dance Society, 2003.

Deierkauf-Holsboer, S. Wilma. *Le Théâtre du Marais.* 2 vols. Paris: Nizet, 1954.

Denifle, Heinrich, and Émile Chatelain, eds. *Chartularium Universitatis Parisiensis.* 4 vols. Paris: Delalain, 1889–97.

Devero, Lisa C. "The Court Dance of Louis XIV as Exemplified by Feuillet's *Chorégraphie* (1700) and How the Court Dance and Ceremonial Ball Were Used as Forms of Political and Socialization." PhD diss., New York University, 1991.

Dixon, Peggy. "Reflections on Basse Dance Source Material: A Dancer's Review, Part I." *Historical Dance* 2, no. 5 (1986–87): 22–29.

Dobbins, Frank. *Music in Renaissance Lyons.* Oxford: Clarendon Press, 1992.

Dodds, E. R. *The Greeks and the Irrational.* Berkeley: University of California Press, 1951.

Dorat, Jean. *Magnificentissimi spectaculi.* Paris, 1573.

Dorvane, Jeannine. "Ballet de Collège." In *International Encyclopedia of Dance,* 1: 282–85. New York: Oxford University Press, 1998.

Downes, John. *Roscius Anglicanus.* London, 1708.

Dubos, Jean-Baptise. *Réflexions critiques sur la poésie et sur la peinture.* 2 vols. Paris, 1719. Reprint, Geneva: Slatkine, 1967.

Dubost, Jean-François. *La France italienne: XVIe–XVIIe siècle.* Paris: Aubier, 1997.

Earp, Lawrence. "Genre in the Fourteenth-Century French Chanson: The Virelai and the Dance Song." *Musica Disciplina* 45 (1991): 123–41.

L'École de Fontainebleau: Grand Palais, Paris, 1972 (Catalogue).

Ehrmann, Jean. *Antoine Caron: peintre des fêtes et des massacres.* Paris: Flammarion, 1986.

Elyot, Thomas. *The Book Named the Governor* (1531). Ed. S. E. Lehmberg. London: J. M. Dent and Sons, 1962.

Esses, Maurice. *Dance and Instrumental* Diferencias *in Spain during the 17th and early 18th Centuries.* 3 vols. Stuyvesant, N.Y.: Pendragon Press, 1992.

Fallows, David. *Dufay.* London: J. M. Dent and Sons, 1987.

———. "The Gresely Dance Collection, c. 1500." *RMA Research Chronicle* 29 (1996): 1–20.

Fama, Marianovella. "Gregorio Lambranzi: un 'maestro di ballo' da Venezia a Norimberga." *Biblioteca teatrale nuova serie* no. 8 (1987): 61–82.

Fenlon, Iain. "The Claims of Choreography—Women Courtiers and Danced Spectacle in Late Sixteenth-Century Paris and Ferrara." In *Frauen und Musik im Europa des 16 Jahrhunderts: Infrastrukturen-Aktivitaten-Motivationem,* ed. Nicole Schwindt, pp. 75–89. Kassel: Barenreiter, 2005.

———. "Guarini de' Sommi and the Pre-History of the Italian Danced Spectacle." In *Leone de' Sommi and the Performing Arts,* ed. Ahuva Belkin, pp. 49–65. Tel Aviv: Tel Aviv University, 1997.

Ferguson, Ian. "Some Notes on the Beauchamps Family." *Dancing Times* 72, no. 854 (November 1981): 107.

Fermor, Sharon. "Movement and Gender in Sixteenth-Century Italian Painting." In *The Body Imaged: The Human Form and Visual Culture since the Renaissance,* ed. Kathleen Adler and Marcia Pointon, pp. 129–45. Cambridge: Cambridge University Press, 1993.

———. "On the Question of Pictorial 'Evidence' for Fifteenth-Century Dance Technique." *Dance Research* 5, no. 2 (1987): 18–32.

———. "Poetry in Motion: Beauty in Movement and the Renaissance Concept of *leggiardrìa*." In *Concepts of Beauty in Renaissance Art,* ed. Francis Ames-Lewis and Mary Rogers, pp. 124–33. Aldershot: Ashgate, 1998.

———. "Studies in the Depiction of the Moving Figure in Italian Renaissance Art, Art Criticism and Dance Theory." Ph.D. diss., London: Warburg Institute, University of London, 1990.

Feves, Angene. Introduction to Instruction pour dancer: *An Anonymous Manuscript,* ed. Angene Feves et al. Freiburg: Fa-gisis, 2000.

Filarete. *Filarete's Treatise on Architecture, Being the Treatise by Antonio di Piero Averlino, Known as Filarete.* Trans. with introduction by John R. Spencer. 2 vols. New Haven: Yale University Press, 1965.

Forrest, John. *The History of Morris Dancing, 1458–1750.* Toronto: University of Toronto Press, 1999.

Fortini-Brown, Patricia. *Private Lives in Renaissance Venice: Art, Architecture, and the Family.* New Haven: Yale University Press, 2004.

Foster, Susan Leigh. "Dancing the Body Politic: Manner and Mimesis in Eighteenth-Century Ballet." In *From the Royal to the Republican Body: Incorporating the Political in Seventeenth- and Eighteenth-Century France,* ed. Sara E. Melzer and Kathryn Norberg, pp. 162–81. Berkeley: University of California Press, 1998.

Francalanci, Andrea. "The '*Copia di M° Giorgio e del guideo di ballare basse danze e balletti*' as found in the New York Public Library." *Basler Jahrbuch für Historiche Musikpraxis* 14 (1990): 87–179.

———. "Le tre grazie della 'Primavera' del Botticelli: La danza fra allegoria e realtà storica." *Medioevo e Rinascimento* 6th series, 3 (1992): 23–37.

Franko, Mark. *Dance as Text: Ideologies of the Baroque Body.* Cambridge: Cambridge University Press, 1993.

———. *The Dancing Body in Renaissance Choreography (c. 1416–1589).* Birmingham, Ala.: Summa Publications, 1986.

———. "Double Bodies: Androgyny and Power in the Performances of Louis XIV." *Drama Review* 38 (1994): 71–82.

———. "Figural Inversions of Louis XIV's Dancing Body." In *Acting on the Past: Historical Performances Across the Disciplines,* ed. Mark Franko and Annette Richards, pp. 35–51. Hanover, N.H.: Wesleyan University Press and University Press of New England, 2000.

———. "The King Cross-Dressed: Power and Force in Royal Ballets." In *From the Royal to the Republican Body: Incorporating the Political in Seventeenth- and Eighteenth-Century France,* ed. Sara E. Melzer and Kathryn Norberg, pp. 64–84. Berkeley: University of California Press, 1998.

———. "Majestic Drag: Monarchical Performativity and the King's Body Theatrical." *Drama Review* 47, no. 2 (2003): 71–87.

Freeman, Kathleen. *Ancilla to the Pre-socratic Philosophers: A Complete Translation of the Fragments in Diels, Fragmente der Vorsokratiker.* Oxford: Blackwell, 1952.

Galli, Quirino. "Una danzografia in un protocollo notarile a Montefiascone nella seconda metà del xv secolo." In *Arte e accademia: Ricerche studi attività '89,* pp. 121–43. Viterbo: Accademia di Belle Arti "Lorenzo da Viterbo," 1989.

Gallo, F. Alberto. "L'autobiografia artistica di Giovanni Ambrosio (Guglielmo Ebreo) da Pesaro." *Studi musicali* 12, no. 2 (1983): 189–202.

———. "Il 'ballare lombardo' (circa 1435–1475)." *Studi musicali* 8 (1979): 61–84.

Garlick, Fiona. "Dances to Evoke the King: The Majestic Genre Chez Louis XIV." *Dance Research* 15, no. 2 (1997): 10–34.

———. "A Measure of Decorum: Social Order and the Dance Suite in the Reign of Louis XIV." PhD diss., University of New South Wales, 1992.

Gerbes, Angelika R. "Eighteenth Century [*sic*] Dance Instruction: The Course of Study Advocated by Gottfried Taubert." *Dance Research* 10, no. 1 (1992): 40–52.

———. "Gottfried Taubert on Social and Theatrical Dance of the Early Eighteenth Century." Ph.D. diss., Ohio State University, 1972.

Giordano, Gloria. "Balli Veneziani in notazione coreografica." *La danza italiana* 7 (1989): 31–49.

———. "Gaetano Grossatesta, an Eighteenth-Century Italian Choreographer and Impresario, Part One: The Dancer-Choreographer in Northern Italy." *Dance Chronicle* 23, no. 1 (2000): 1–28.

———. "Gaetano Grossatesta, an Eighteenth-Century Italian Choreographer and Impresario, Part Two: The Choreographer-Impresario in Naples." *Dance Chronicle* 23, no. 2 (2000): 133–91.

———. "A Venetian Festa in Feuillet Notation." *Dance Research* 15, no. 2 (1997): 126–41.

Godefroy, D. *Le Cérémonial François.* 2 vols. Paris, 1649.

Goff, Moira. "'*Actions, Manners* and *Passions*': Entr'acte Dancing on the London Stage, 1700–1737." *Early Music* 26, no. 2 (1998): 213–28.

———. "'The Art of Dancing, Demonstrated by Characters and Figures': French and English Sources for Court and Theatre Dance, 1700–1750." *British Library Journal* 21, no. 2 (1995): 202–31.

———. "Art and Nature Join'd: Hester Santlow and the Development of Dancing on the London Stage, 1700–1737." Ph.D. diss., University of Kent at Canterbury, 2000.

———. "Coquetry and Neglect: Hester Santlow, John Weaver, and the Dramatic Entertainment of Dancing." In *Dancing in the Millenium: Proceedings of the 23rd Annual Conference of the Society of Dance History Scholars*, pp. 207–12. N.p.: SDHS: 2000.

———. "Dancing-Masters in Early Eighteenth-Century London." *Historical Dance* 3, no. 3 (1994): 17–22.

———. "Edmund Pemberton, Dancing-Master and Publisher." *Dance Research* 11, no. 1 (1993): 52–81.

———. "Shadwell, Saint-André and the 'Curious Dancing' in *Psyche*." In *The Restoration of Charles II: Public Order, Theatre and Dance*, ed. David R. Wilson, pp. 25–33. Cambridge: Early Dance Circle, 2002.

———. "Steps, Gestures and Expressive Dancing: Magri, Ferrère, and John Weaver." In *The Grotesque Dancer on the Eighteenth-Century Stage: Gennaro Magri and his World*, ed. Rebecca Harris-Warrick and Bruce Alan Brown, pp. 199–230. Madison: University of Wisconsin Press, 2005.

———. "Trumpets and Flutes: Music and Dance in John Weaver's *The Loves of Mars and Venus*." In *Proceedings of Sound Moves: An International Conference on Music and Dance, Roehampton University, London, 5–6 November 2005*, pp. 62–69. http://www .roehampton.ac.uk/SoundMoves.

Goff, Moira, and Jennifer Thorp. "Dance Notations Published in England *c.* 1700–1740 and Related Manuscript Material." *Dance Research* 9, no. 2 (1991): 32–50.

Goldine, Nicole. "Henri Bate, chanoine et chantre de la cathédrale Saint Lambert à Liège et théoricien de la musique (1246-après 1310)." *Revue Belge de Musicologie* 18 (1964): 10–27.

Gorce, Jérôme de la. "*Le Collier de perles* et la musique de Pierre Beauchamps." In *Histoire, Humanisme et Hymnologie, Mélanges offerts au Professeur Edith Weber*, ed. Pierre Guillot and Louis Jambot, pp. 99–107. Paris: University of Paris-Sorbonne Press, 1997.

———. "Guillaume-Louis Pecour: A Biographical Essay." Trans. Margaret M. McGowan. *Dance Research* 8, no. 2 (1990): 3–26.

Gougaud, L. "La danse dans les églises." *Revue Historique Ecclésiastique* 15 (1914): 5–22, 229–45.

Gouk, Penelope. *Music, Science, and Natural Magic in Seventeenth-Century England*. New Haven: Yale University Press, 1999.

Graham, Victor E., and W. McAllister Johnson. *The Royal Tour of France by Charles IX and Catherine de' Medici, Festivals and Entries, 1564–66*. Toronto: Toronto University Press, 1979.

Grayson, Cecil, ed. *Francesco Guicciardini: Selected Writings*. Trans. Margaret Grayson. Oxford: Oxford University Press, 1965.

Greene, Richard L. "Introduction." In *The Early English Carols*, 2nd rev. ed., ed. Richard L. Greene, pp. xxi–clxxii. Oxford: Clarendon Press, 1977.

Greene, Thomas M. "The King's One Body in the *Balet Comique de la Royne*." *Yale French Studies* no. 86 (1994): 75–93.

———. "Labyrinth Dances in the French and English Renaissance." *Renaissance Quarterly* 54, no. 4.2 (2001): 1403–66.

Greg, Walter W. *Pastoral Poetry & Pastoral Drama: A Literary Inquiry, with Special Reference to the Pre-Restoration Stage in England*. New York: Russell & Russell, 1959.

Gregg, Edward. *Queen Anne*. New Haven: Yale University Press, 2001.

Grocheio, Johannes de. *Concerning Music: De musica*. Trans. Albert Seay. Colorado Springs: Colorado College Music Press, 1967.

Grodecki, Catherine. *Documents du minutier central des notaires de Paris. Histoire de l'art au XVIe siècle, 1500–1600*. 2 vols. Paris: Archives Nationales, 1986.

———. *Les travaux de Philibert Delorme pour Henri II et son entourage*. Paris: Librairie des Arts et Métiers-Éditions Jacques Laget, 2000.

Gstrein, Rainer. "' . . . welches warlich bey einer wolbestelten Policey ist warzunehmen und auffs allerscharffeste zu verbieten . . . ': Austößige Tänze im 17 Jahrhundert." In *Morgenröte des Barock: Tanz im 17 Jahrhundert*, ed. Uwe Schlottermüller and Maria Richter, pp. 71–80. Freiburg: Fa-gisis, 2004.

Guerzoni, Guido. "*Liberalitas, Magnificentia*, Splendor: The Classic Origins of Italian Renaissance Lifestyles." In *Economic Engagements with Art*, Annual Supplement to Volume 31 of *History of Political Economy*. Ed. Neil De Marchi and Craufurd D. W. Goodwin, pp. 332–78. Durham, N.C.: Duke University Press, 1999.

Guidobaldi, Nicoletta. *La musica di Federico: Immagini e suoni alla corte di Urbino*. Florence: Leo S. Olschki, 1995.

Guiffrey, Georges, ed. *Cronique de François Ier de ce nom*. Paris: J. Renouard, 1860.

Guilcher, Jean-Michel. "André Lorin et l'invention de l'écriture chorégraphie." *Revue de la société d'histoire du théâtre* 21 (1969): 256–64.

———. *La contredanse et les renouvellements de la danse française*. Paris: Mouton, 1969.

Guillo, Laurent. "Un violon sous le bras et les pieds dans la poussière: Les violins italiens du roi durant le voyage de Charles IX (1564–66)." In " . . . *La musique, de tous les passtemps le plus beu* . . . " *Hommage à Jean-Michel Vaccaro*, ed. François Lesure and Henri Vanhulst, pp. 207–33. Paris: Klincksieck, 1998.

Gundersheimer, Werner L., ed. *Art and Life at the Court of Ercole I d'Este: The* De triumphis religionis *of Giovanni Sabadino degli Arienti*. Geneva: Librairie Droz, 1972.

Guthrie, John, and Marino Zorzi, trans. "Rules of Dancing: Antonius Arena." *Dance Research* 4, no. 2 (1986): 3–53.

Hale, David George. *The Body Politic: A Political Metaphor in Renaissance English Literature*. The Hague: Mouton, 1971.

Halperin, David M. *Before Pastoral: Theocritus and the Ancient Tradition of Bucolic Poetry*. New Haven: Yale University Press, 1983.

Harap, Louis. "Some Hellenic Ideas on Music and Character." *Musical Quarterly* 24 (1938): 153–68.

Harding, Ann. *An Investigation into the Use and Meaning of Medieval German Dancing Terms.* Göppingen: Alfred Kümmerle, 1973.

Harris, Ellen T. *Handel and the Pastoral Tradition.* London: Oxford University Press, 1980.

———. *Handel as Orpheus: Voice and Desire in the Chamber Cantatas.* Cambridge: Harvard University Press, 2001.

Harris-Warrick, Rebecca. "Ballroom dancing at the court of Louis XIV." *Early Music* 14, no. 1 (1986): 40–49.

———. "Contexts for Choreographies: Notated Dances Set to the Music of Jean-Baptiste Lully." In *Jean-Baptiste Lully: Actes du colloque, Saint Germain-en-laye and Heidelberg, 1987*, ed. Jérôme de la Gorce and Herbert Schneider, pp. 433–55. Heidelberg: Laaber, 1990.

———. "Interpreting Pendulum Markings for French Baroque Dances." *Historical Performance* 6, no. 1 (1993): 9–22.

———. "*La Mariée:* The History of a French Court Dance." In *Jean-Baptiste Lully and the Music of the French Baroque: Essays in Honor of James R. Anthony,* ed. John Hajdu Heyer, pp. 239–57. Cambridge: Cambridge University Press, 1989.

———. "The Phrase Structures of Lully's Dance Music." In *Lully Studies,* ed. John Hajdu Heyer, pp. 32–56. Cambridge: Cambridge University Press, 2000.

———. "Recovering the Lullian Divertissement." In *Dance & Music in French Baroque Theatre: Sources & Interpretations,* ed. Sarah McCleave, pp. 55–80. London: Institute of Advanced Musical Studies, King's College London, 1998.

———. "*Toute Danse Doit Exprimer, Peindre . . . :* Finding the Drama in the Operatic Divertissement." *Basler Jahrbuch für Historische Musikpraxis* 23 (1999): 187–210.

Harris-Warrick, Rebecca, and Bruce Alan Brown, eds. *The Grotesque Dancer on the Eighteenth-Century Stage: Gennaro Magri and His World.* Madison: University of Wisconsin Press, 2005.

Harris-Warrick, Rebecca, and Carol G. Marsh. *Musical Theatre at the Court of Louis XIV: Le Mariage de la Grosse Cathos.* Cambridge: Cambridge University Press, 1994.

Haskins, Charles Homer. "The University of Paris in the Sermons of the Thirteenth Century." *American Historical Review* 10 (1904): 1–27.

Haufmann, George M. A., and John R. T. Pollard. "Muses." In *The Oxford Classical Dictionary,* 2nd ed., p. 704. Oxford: Oxford University Press, 1970.

Hazard, Mary E. *Elizabethan Silent Language.* Lincoln: University of Nebraska Press, 2000.

Heartz, Daniel. "The *basse dance:* its evolution *circa* 1450 to 1550." *Annales musicologiques* 6 (1958–63): 287–340.

———. *Pierre Attaingnant, Royal Printer of Music: A Historical Study and Bibliographical Catalogue.* Berkeley: University of California Press, 1969.

———. "A Venetian Dancing Master Teaches the Forlana: Lambranzi's *Balli Teatrali.*" *Journal of Musicology* 17, no. 1 (1999): 136–51.

Heninger Jr., S. K. *The Cosmographical Glass: Renaissance Diagrams of the Universe.* San Marino, Calif.: Huntington Library, 1977.

———. *Touches of Sweet Harmony: Pythagorean Cosmology and Renaissance Poetics.* San Marino, Calif.: Huntington Library, 1974.

Héroard, Jean. *Journal sur l'enfance et la jeunesse de Louis XIII, 1601–1628.* 2 vols. Ed. E. Soulié and E. de Barthélemy. Librairie de Firmin Didot: Paris, 1868.

Hess, Rémi. *La valse: révolution du couple en Europe*. Paris: A. M. Métailié, 1989.

Highfill, Philip H., Kalman A. Burnim, and Edward A. Langhans, eds. *A Biographical Dictionary of Actors, Actresses, Musicians, Dancers, Managers, and Other Stage Personnel in London 1660–1800*. 16 vols. Carbondale: South Illinois University Press, 1973–93.

Hillemacher, Frédéric. *Galerie historique des portraits des comédiens de la troupe de Molière*. Lyon, 1869.

Hilton, Wendy. *Dance of Court and Theatre: The French Noble Style, 1690–1725*. London: Dance Books, 1981.

———. *Dance and Music of Court and Theater: Selected Writings of Wendy Hilton*. Stuyvesant, N.Y.: Pendragon Press, 1997.

———. "Dances to Music by Jean-Baptiste Lully." *Early Music* 14, no. 1 (1986): 51–63.

Hollander, John. *The Untuning of the Sky; Ideas of Music in English Poetry 1500–1700*. Princeton: Princeton University Press, 1961.

Horden, Peregrine, ed. *Music as Medicine*. Aldershot: Ashgate, 2000.

Houle, George, ed. *Le Ballet des Fâcheux: Beauchamp's Music for Moliere's Comedy*. Bloomington: Indiana University Press, 1991.

Howard, Skiles. *The Politics of Courtly Dancing in Early Modern England*. Amherst: University of Massachusetts Press, 1998.

Hume, Robert. "Opera in London, 1695–1706." In *British Theatre and the Other Arts, 1660–1800*, ed. Shirley Strum Kenny, pp. 67–91. Washington, D.C.: Folger Books, published by Associated University Presses, 1984.

Inglehearn, Madeleine. "Swedish Sword Dances in the 16th and 17th Centuries." *Early Music* 14, no. 3 (1986): 367–72.

Jack, Sybil M. "The Revels Accounts: This Insubstantial Pageant Faded Leaves not a Wrack Behind?" *Renaissance Studies* 9, no. 1 (1995): 1–17.

Jackman, James L., ed. *Fifteenth Century Basse Dances*. Wellesley: Wellesley College, 1964.

James, April Lynn. "Variations on a Matelotte." In *Proceedings of 25th Annual Conference of the Society of Dance History Scholars*, pp. 58–61. N.p.: SDHS, 2002.

Janequin, Clément. *La guerre*. In *Chansons Polyphoniques*, vol. 1, ed. A. Tillman Merritt and François Lesure, p. 23–53. Monaco: L'Oiseau-Lyre, 1983.

Jeschke, Claudia. "From *Ballet de Cour* to *Ballet en Action*: The Transformation of Dance Aesthetics and Performance at the End of the Seventeenth and Beginning of the Eighteenth Centuries." *Theatre History Studies* 11 (1991): 107–22.

Johnson, A. W. *Ben Jonson: Poetry and Architecture*. Oxford: Clarendon Press, 1994.

Jones, Pamela. "The Editions of Cesare Negri's *Le Gratie D'Amore*: Choreographic Revisions in Printed Copies." *Studi musicali* 21, no. 1 (1992): 21–33.

———. "The Relation Between Music and Dance in Cesare Negri's *Le Gratie d'Amore*." Ph.D. diss., Kings College, London, 1988.

———. "Spectacle in Milan: Cesare Negri's Torch Dances." *Early Music* 14, no. 2 (1986): 182–96.

Jurgens, Madeleine, and Elizabeth Maxfield-Miller, eds. *Cent ans de recherches sur Molière*. Paris: Imprimerie Nationale, 1963.

Kaeuper, Richard W., and Elspeth Kennedy. *The Book of Chivalry of Geoffroi de Charny: Text, Context, and Translation*. Philadelphia: University of Pennsylvania Press, 1996.

Karling, Sten. "The Importance of André Mollet and His Family for the Development of the French Formal Garden." In *The French Formal Garden*, ed. Elisabeth B. Macdougall and F. Hamilton Hazlehurst, pp. 1–25. Washington, D.C.: Dumbarton Oaks, 1974.

Kendall, G. Yvonne. "'Le Gratie d'Amore' 1602 by Cesare Negri: Translation and Commentary." DMA thesis, Stanford University, 1985.

———. "Ornamentation and Improvisation in Sixteenth-Century Dance." In *Improvisation in the Arts of the Middle Ages and Renaissance*, ed. Timothy J. McGee, pp. 170–90. Kalamazoo, Mich.: Medieval Institute, 2003.

———. "Rhythm, Meter and *Tactus* in 16th-Century Italian Court Dance: Reconstruction from a Theoretical Base." *Dance Research* 8, no. 1 (1990): 3–27.

———. "Theatre, Dance and Music in late Cinquecento Milan." *Early Music* 32, no. 1 (2004): 74–95.

Kent, F. W. *Lorenzo de' Medici and the Art of Magnificence.* Baltimore: Johns Hopkins University Press, 2004.

Kibre, Pearl. *Scholarly Privileges in the Middle Ages: The Rights, Privileges, and Immunities of Scholars and Universities at Bologna, Padua, Paris, and Oxford.* Cambridge, Mass.: Medieval Academy of America, 1962.

Kirkendale, Warren. *L'aria di Fiorenza, id est Il ballo del Gran Duca.* Florence: Leo S. Olschki, 1972.

Kishlansky, Mark. *A Monarchy Transformed: Britain 1603–1714.* London: Penguin Books, 1996.

Knowles, James. "The 'Running Masque' Recovered: A Masque for the Marquess of Buckingham (c. 1619–20)." *English Manuscript Studies* 8 (2000): 79–135.

Kolsky, Stephen. "Graceful Performances: The Social and Political Context of Music and Dance in the *Cortegiano*." *Italian Studies* 53 (1998): 1–19.

Kühne, H., and E. Stengel, eds. *Maître Elie's Überarbeitung der ältesten französischen Übertragung von Ovid's Ars Amatoria.* Ausgaben und Abhandlungen aus dem Gebiete der Romanischen Philologie 47 (1882).

L'Estoile, Pierre de. *Mémoires-Journaux, 1574–1611.* 11 vols. Ed. G. Brunet et al. Paris: Librairie des bibliophiles, 1875–83.

L'Orme, Philibert de. *Nouvelles inventions pour bien bastir et à petits fraiz.* Paris: F. Morel, 1561. Facsimile edition, ed. J.-M. Pérouse de Montclos. Paris: Léonce Laget, 1988.

La Bruyère, Jean de. *Les Caractères de Théophraste, traduits du grec, avec Les Caractères ou les mœurs de ce siècle.* (1692). Ed. Robert Pignarre. Reprint, Paris: Garnier-Flammarion, 1965.

Labalme, Patricia H., and Laura Sanguinetti White (with Linda Carroll, trans.). "How to (and How Not to) Get Married in Sixteenth-Century Venice (Selections from the Diaries of Marin Sanudo)." *Renaissance Quarterly* 52, no. 1 (1999): 43–72.

Laborde, Léon de. *Les comptes des bâtiments du roi, 1528–71.* 2 vols. Paris: J. Baur, 1887–80.

Lalonger, Edith. "Les chaconnes d'Arlequin conservées en notation Feuillet." In *Arlequin danseur au tournant du XVIIIᵉ siècle: atelier rencontre et recherche, Nantes, 14–15 mai 2004*, pp. 13–17. Paris, Annales de l'Association pour un Centre de Recherche sur les Arts du Spectacle au XVIIᵉ et XVIIIᵉ siècles, no. 1, June 2005.

———. "J. F. Rebel's *Les Caractères de la danse*: Interpretive Choices and Their Relationship to Dance Research." In *Dance & Music in French Baroque Theatre: Sources & Interpretations*, ed. Sarah McCleave, pp. 105–23. London: Institute of Advanced Musical Studies, 1998.

Lancelot, Francine. *La belle dance: catalogue raisonné.* Paris: Van Dieren, 1996.

———. "Les ornements dans la danse baroque." In *Les Gouts Réunis . . . Actes du 1er Colloque International sur la danse ancienne*, pp. 72–78. Besançon, 1982.

Laurenti, Jean-Noël. "Les structures de distribution dans les danses de théâtre à travers les recueils de Feuillet 1704 et Gaudrau." In *Tanz und Bewegung in der Barocken Oper*, ed. Sibylle Dahms and Stephanie Schroedter, pp. 45–65. Innsbruck: StudienVerlag, 1994.

Laven, Mary. *Virgins of Venice: Enclosed Lives and Broken Vows in the Renaissance Convent*. London: Viking, 2002.

Lazzaro, Claudio. *The Italian Renaissance Garden: From the Conventions of Planting, Design, and Ornament to the Grand Gardens of Sixteenth-Century Central Italy*. New Haven: Yale University Press, 1990.

Lecomte, Nathalie. "Beauchamps, Pierre." In *Dictionnaire de la musique en France aux XVIe et XVIIe siècles*, edited by Marcelle Benoit, pp. 61–62. Paris: Fayard, 1992.

LeCoq, Anne-Marie. "Une fête à la Bastille en 1518." In *Il se rendit à Rome. Etudes offertes à André Chastel*, pp. 149–68. Paris: Flammarion, 1987.

Lehner, Marcus. "The *Cascarda*: An Italian Dance Form of the Sixteenth Century." In *Terpsichore 1450–1900: Proceedings of the International Dance Conference, Ghent, April 2000*, ed. Barbara Ravelhofer, pp. 11–20. Ghent, Institute for Historical Dance Practice, 2000.

———. *A Manual of Sixteenth-Century Italian Dance Steps*. Freiburg: Fa-gisis Musik- und Tanzedition, 1997.

Leppert, Richard. "Music, Domestic Life and Cultural Chauvinism: Images of British Subjects at Home in India." In *Music and Society: The Politics of Composition, Performance and Reception*, ed. Richard Leppert and Susan McClary, pp. 63–104. Cambridge: Cambridge University Press, 1987.

———. *The Sight of Sound: Music, Representation, and the History of the Body*. Berkeley: University of California Press, 1993.

Lesure, François. "Danses et chansons à danser au debut du XVIᵉ siècle." In *Recueil de travaux offerts à M. Clovis Brunel*, vol. 2, pp. 176–84. Paris: Société des Chartes, 1955.

———. *Musique et musiciens français du XVIᵉ siècle*. Geneva: Minkoff, 1976.

Levinson, André. "Notes sur le ballet du XVIIe siècle: les danseurs de Lully." *La Revue musicale* 4, no. 5 (1925): 44–55.

Limon, Jerzy. "The Masque of Stuart Culture." In *The Mental World of the Jacobean Court*, ed. Linda Levy Peck, pp. 209–29. Cambridge: Cambridge University Press, 1991.

Lippman, Edward A. *Musical Thought in Ancient Greece*. New York: Columbia University Press, 1964.

Little, Meredith. "Problems of Repetition and Continuity in the Dance Music of Lully's *Ballet des Arts*." In *Jean-Baptiste Lully: Acts du colloque, Saint Germain-en-laye and Heidelberg, 1987*, ed. Jérôme de la Gorce and Herbert Schneider, pp. 423–32. Heidelberg: Laaber, 1990.

Little, Meredith, and Natalie Jenne. *Dance and the Music of J. S. Bach*. Bloomington: Indiana University Press, 1991.

Little, Meredith Ellis, and Carol G. Marsh. *La Danse Noble: An Inventory of Dances and Sources*. Williamstown: Broude Brothers, 1992.

Livet, Charles-Louis. *La Muze historique*. Paris, 1877.

Lo Monaco, Mauro, and Sergio Vinciguerra. "God Save the Double!" *Dance Research* 24, no. 1 (2006): 66–69.

———. "The *Passo Doppio* and the *Contrapasso* in the Italian *Balli* of the Fifteenth-Century: Problems of Mensuration and a Conjectural Reconstruction." Trans. Diana Cruickshank. *Dance Research* 23, no. 1 (2005): 51–78.

Lomazzo, Giovanni Paolo. *Rime di Gio. Paolo Lomazzi milanese pittore, divise in sette libri*.

Nelle quali ad imitatione de i grotteschi usati da' pittori, ha cantato le lodi di Dio, & de le cose sacre, di prencipi, di signori. Milan, Pontio, 1587.

Louis XIV. *Mémoires pour l'instruction du Dauphin,* ed. Pierre Goubert. Paris: Imprimerie Nationale, 1992.

Lubkin, Gregory. *A Renaissance Court: Milan Under Galeazzo Maria Sforza.* Berkeley: University of California Press, 1994.

MacClintock, Carol, and Lander MacClintock, trans. *Le Balet Comique de la Royne.* N.p.: American Institute of Musicology, 1971.

MacHardy, Karin J. "Cultural Capital, Family Strategies and Noble Identity in Early Modern Habsburg Austria 1579–1620." *Past and Present* 163 (1999): 36–75.

Magnus, Albertus. *Beati Alberti Magni . . . Opera Omnia.* 38 vols. Ed. A. Borgnet. Paris, 1890–99.

Malvezzi, Cristofano. *Intermedii et concerti fatti per la commedia rappresentata in Firenze nelle nozze del serenissimo don Ferdinando Medici, e madama Christina di Loreno, gran duchi di Toscana.* Venice: G. Vincenti, 1591.

Marimón, J. M. Madurell. *Mensajeros barceloneses en la corte de Nápoles de Alfonso V de Aragon, 1435–1458.* Barcelona, 1963.

Marrocco, W. Thomas, and Marie-Laure Merveille. "Antonius Arena: Master of Law and Dance of the Renaissance." *Studi musicali* 18, no. 1 (1989): 19–48.

Marsh, Carol G. "French Court Dance in England, 1700–1740: A Study of Sources." Ph.D. diss., City University of New York, 1985.

———. "The Lovelace Manuscript: A Preliminary Study." In *Morgenröte des Barock. Tanz im 17. Jahrhundert,* ed. Uwe Scholttermüller and Maria Richter, pp. 81–90. Freiburg: Fa-gisis, 2004.

Martin, John Jeffries. "Introduction. The Renaissance: Between Myth and History." In *The Renaissance: Italy and Abroad,* ed. John Jeffries Martin, pp. 1–23. London: Routledge, 2003.

———, ed. *The Renaissance: Italy and Abroad.* London: Routledge, 2003.

Mas i Garcia, Carles. "Baixa Dansa in the Kingdom of Catalonia and Aragon in the 15th Century." *Historical Dance* 3, no. 1 (1992): 15–23.

Mather, Increase. *An Arrow against Profane and Promiscuous Dancing.* Boston: S. Green, 1684.

Maxfield-Miller, Elizabeth. "Louis de Mollier, musician et son homonyme Molière." *Recherches sur la musique française classique* 3 (1963): 25–38.

McArdle, Grainne. "Dance in Dublin Theatres 1729–35." In *Proceedings of 27th and 28th Annual Conferences of the Society of Dance History Scholars,* pp. 11–16. N.p.: SDHS, 2005.

McClain, Ernest G. *The Pythagorean Plato: Prelude to the Song Itself.* Stony Brook, N.Y.: Nicholas Hays, 1978.

McClary, Susan. "Unruly Passions and Courtly Dances: Technologies of the Body in Baroque Music." In *From the Royal to the Republican Body: Incorporating the Political in Seventeenth- and Eighteenth-Century France,* ed. Sara E. Melzer and Kathryn Norberg, pp. 85–112. Berkeley: University of California Press, 1998.

McCleave, Sarah. "Dancing at the English Opera: Marie Sallé's Letter to the Duchess of Richmond." *Dance Research* 17, no. 1 (1999): 22–46.

———. "English and French Theatrical Sources: The Repertoire of Marie Sallé." In *Dance & Music in French Baroque Theatre: Sources & Interpretations,* ed. Sarah McCleave, pp. 13–32. London: Institute of Advanced Musical Studies, King's College London, 1998.

McGee, Timothy J. "Dancing Masters and the Medici Court in the 15th Century." *Studi musicali* 17, no. 2 (1988): 201–24.

———. "Medieval Dances: Matching the Repertory With Grecheio's Descriptions." *Journal of Musicology* 7, no. 4 (1989): 489–517.

———. *Medieval Instrumental Dances.* Bloomington: Indiana University Press, 1989.

———. "Misleading Iconography: The Case of the 'Adimari Wedding Cassone.'" *Imago Musicae* 11–12 (1992–95): 139–57.

McGinnis, Katherine Tucker. "Material Culture, Immaterial Culture: Courtly Dancing as an Economic Motor in Early Modern Italy." In *Terpsichore 1450–1900: Proceedings of the International Dance Conference, Ghent, April 2000,* ed. Barbara Ravelhofer, pp. 21–29. Ghent: Institute for Historical Dance Practice, 2000.

———. "Moving in High Circles: Courts, Dance, and Dancing Masters in Italy in the Long Sixteenth Century." Ph.D. diss., Chapel Hill: University of North Carolina, 2001.

McGowan, Margaret M. "Une affaire de famille: les fêtes parisiennes en l'honneur d'Henri, duc d'Anjou, roi de Pologne." In *Arts du spectacle et histoire des idées,* ed. J. M. Vaccaro, pp. 9–20. Tours: Centre d'Études Superieures de la Renaissance, 1984.

———. *L'art du Ballet de cour en France, 1581–1643.* Paris: CNRS, 1963.

———. "The Art of Dance in Seventeenth-Century French *ballet de cour*: An Overview." In *Terpsichore 1450–1900: Proceedings of the International Dance Conference, Ghent, April 2000,* ed. Barbara Ravelhofer, pp. 93–104. Ghent: Institute for Historical Dance Practice, 2000.

———. "The Arts Conjoined: A Context for the Study of Music." *Early Music History* 13 (1994): 171–98.

———. "Ballets for the Bourgeois," *Dance Research* 19, no. 2 (2001): 106–26.

———. "Beaujoyeulx, Balthazar de." In *International Encyclopedia of Dance,* 1: 397–98. Oxford: Oxford University Press, 1998.

———. *The Court Ballet of Louis XIII: A Collection of Working Designs for Costumes 1615–33.* London: Victoria & Albert Museum in association with Hobhouse & Morton Morris, 1986.

———. "L'Essor du ballet à la cour de Henri III." In *Henri III, Mécène. Les lettres, les sciences et les arts sous le règne du dernier Valois.* Ed. Isabelle Conihout, Jean-François Maillard, and Guy Poirier, pp. 81–91. Paris: Presses de l'Université de Paris—Sorbonne, 2006.

———. "Festivals and the Arts in Henri III's Journey from Poland to France (1574)." In *Europa Triumphans: Court and Civic Festivals in Early Modern Europe,* 2 vols., ed. J. R. Mulryne, Helen Watanabe-O'Kelly, and Margaret Shewring, 1: 122–29. Aldershot: Ashgate, 2004.

———. "Fêtes: religious and political conflict dramatized. The role of Charles IX." In *Writers in Conflict in Sixteenth-Century France. Essays Offered in Honour of Malcolm Quainton.* Ed. Elizabeth Vinestock and David Foster. Durham: Durham University Press, 2007.

———. *Ideal Forms in the Age of Ronsard.* Berkeley: University of California Press, 1985.

———. "Introduction." In *Le Balet Comique de la Reyne, 1581.* Ed. Margaret M. McGowan. Binghamton, N.Y.: Center for Medieval and Early Renaissance Studies, 1982.

———. "Recollections of Dancing Forms from Sixteenth-Century France." *Dance Research* 21, no. 1 (2003): 10–26.

———. "A Renaissance War Dance: The Pyrrhic." *Dance Research* 3, no. 1 (1984): 29–38.

McKee, Eric. "Influences of the Early Eighteenth-Century Social Minuet on the Minuets from J. S. Bach's French Suites, BWV 812–17." *Music Analysis* 18, no. 2 (1999): 235–60.

McManus, Clare, ed. *Women and Culture at the Courts of the Stuart Queens.* Houndsmills, Basingstoke: Palgrave Macmillan, 2003.

———. *Women on the Renaissance Stage: Anna of Denmark and Female Masquing in the Stuart Court (1590–1619).* Manchester: Manchester University Press, 2002.

Mélèse, Pierre. *Répertoire analytique des documents contemporains d'information et de critique concernant le théâtre à Paris sous Louis XIV, 1659–1715.* Paris: Droz, 1934.

Meyer, Paul. "Rôle de chansons à danser du XVIᵉ siècle." *Romania* 23 (1894): 156–60.

Michaelides, Solon. *The Music of Ancient Greece: An Encyclopaedia.* London: Faber, 1978.

Michel, Artur. "The Earliest Dance Manuals." *Medievalia et Humanistica* 3 (1945): 117–31.

Milhous, Judith. "The Economics of Theatrical Dance in Eighteenth-Century London." *Theatre Journal* 55, no. 3 (2003): 481–508.

Milhous, Judith, and Robert D. Hume. "New Light on Handel and the Royal Academy of Music in 1720." *Theatre Journal* 35, no. 2 (1983): 149–67.

———. *A Register of English Theatrical Documents 1660–1737.* Carbondale: South Illinois University Press, 1991.

———. *Vice Chamberlain Coke's Theatrical Papers 1706–1715.* Carbondale: Southern Illinois University Press, 1982.

Miller, James. *Measures of Wisdom: The Cosmic Dance in Classical and Christian Antiquity.* Toronto: University of Toronto Press, 1986.

———. "The Philosophical Background of Renaissance Dance." *York Dance Review* 5 (1976): 3–15.

Minor, Andrew C., and Bonner Mitchell. *A Renaissance Entertainment: Festivities for the Marriage of Cosimo, Duke of Florence in 1539.* Columbia: University of Missouri Press, 1968.

Mitchell, Bonner. *Italian Civic Pageantry in the High Renaissance: A Descriptive Bibliography of Triumphal Entries and Selected Other Festivals for State Occasions.* Florence: Leo S. Olschki, 1979.

———. *The Majesty of the State; Triumphal Progresses of Foreign Sovereigns in Renaissance Italy (1494–1600).* Florence: Leo S. Olschki, 1986.

Mongrédien, Georges. *Recueil des textes et des documents du XVIIe siècle relatifs à Molière.* 2 vols. Paris: CNRS, 1965.

Motteux, Peter. *The Island Princess.* London, 1699.

———. *Love's Triumph, an Opera as it is perform'd at the Queen's theatre in the Hay-Market.* London, 1708.

Moyer, Ann E. *Musica Scientia: Musical Scholarship in the Italian Renaissance.* Ithaca: Cornell University Press, 1992.

Muir, Edward. *Civic Ritual in Renaissance Venice.* Princeton: Princeton University Press, 1981.

Mullally, Robert. "Dance Terminology in the Works of Machaut and Froissart." *Medium ævum* 59, no. 2 (1990): 248–59.

———. "The Editions of Antonius Arena's *Ad Suos Compagnones Studiantes.*" *Gutenburg-Jahrbuch* (1979): 146–57.

———. "Johannes de Grocheo's 'Musical Vulgaris.'" *Music & Letters* 79, no. 1 (1998): 1–26.

————. "Measure as a Choreographic Term in the Stuart Masque." *Dance Research* 16, no. 1 (1998): 67–73.

————. "More about the Measures." *Early Music* 22, no. 3 (1994): 417–38.

————. "Reconstructing the *Carole*." In *On Common Ground 4: Reconstruction and Re-creation in Dance before 1850: Proceedings of the 4th DHDS Conference, March 2003*, ed. David Parsons, pp. 79–82. Stock, Essex: Dolmetsch Historical Dance Society, 2003.

Mulryne, J. R., and Elizabeth Goldring, eds. *Court Festivals of the European Renaissance*. Aldershot: Ashgate, 2002.

Muraro, Maria Teresa. "La festa a Venezia e le sue manifestazione rappresentative: Le compagnie della calza e le *momarie*." In *Storia della cultura veneta*, 3: 315–41. Vicenza: N. Pozza, 1976.

Murray, Alexander. "Confession as a Historical Source in the Thirteenth Century." In *The Writing of History in the Middle Ages*, ed. R. H. C. Davies and J. M. Wallace-Hadrill, pp. 275–322. Oxford: Clarendon Press, 1981.

————. *Reason and Society in the Middle Ages*. Oxford: Clarendon Press, 2002.

Naerebout, Frederick. "Another Battle Fought and Lost: Seventeenth-Century Dutch *Predikanten* and the Dance." *Laban Centre Working Papers in Dance Studies* 2 (1989): 18–43.

Needham, Maureen. "Beauchamps, Pierre." In *The New Grove Dictionary of Opera*, ed. Stanley Sadie, 1: 364. London: Macmillan, 1992.

————. "Louis XIV and the Académie Royale de Danse, 1661—A Commentary and Translation." *Dance Chronicle* 20, no. 2 (1997): 173–90.

Nevile, Jennifer. "A Measure of Moral Virtue: Women, Dancing and Public Performance in Fifteenth-Century Italy." In *The Sights and Sounds of Medieval and Renaissance Music: Essays in Honour of Timothy J. McGee*, ed. Maureen Epp and Brian Power. Aldershot: Ashgate, forthcoming 2008.

————. "Cavalieri's Theatrical *Ballo* 'O che nuovo miracolo': A Reconstruction." *Dance Chronicle* 21, no. 3 (1998): 353–88.

————. "Cavalieri's Theatrical *Ballo* and the Social Dances of Caroso and Negri." *Dance Chronicle* 22, no. 1 (1999): 119–33.

————. "Dance in Early Tudor England: An Italian Connection?" *Early Music* 26, no. 2 (1998): 230–44.

————. "Dance and the Garden: Moving and Static Choreography in Renaissance Europe." *Renaissance Quarterly* 52, no. 3 (1999): 805–36.

————. "Dance and Time in Fifteenth-Century Italy." In *Art and Time*, ed. Jan Lloyd Jones et al., pp. 299–313. Melbourne: Australian Scholarly Publishing, 2007.

————. "Dance Patterns of the Early Seventeenth Century: The Stockholm Manuscript and *Le Ballet de Monseigneur de Vendosme*." *Dance Research* 18, no. 2 (2000): 186–203.

————. "Dance Steps and Music in the Gresley Manuscript." *Historical Dance* 3, no. 6 (1999): 2–19.

————. "Disorder in Order: Improvisation in Italian Choreographed Dances of the Fifteenth and Sixteenth Centuries." In *Improvisation in the Arts of the Middle Ages and Renaissance*, ed. Timothy J. McGee, pp. 145–69. Kalamazoo, Mich.: Medieval Institute, 2003.

————. "The Early Dance Manuals and the Structure of Ballet: A Basis for Italian, French and English Ballet." In *The Cambridge Companion to Ballet*, ed. Marion Kant, pp. 9–18. Cambridge: Cambridge University Press, 2007.

————. *The Eloquent Body: Dance and Humanist Culture in Fifteenth-Century Italy*. Bloomington: Indiana University Press, 2004.

Noinville, Jacques-Bernard Durey de. *Histoire du théâtre de l'Académie Royale de Musique en France*, 2nd ed. Paris, 1757. Reprint, Geneva: Minkoff, 1972.

Nordera, Marina. "'La maniera che la dama doverà usare ballando': la donna che danza tra XV e XVII secolo." In *La danza in Europa tra Rinascimento e Barocco*, ed. Maurizio Padovan, pp. 17–26. Rome: Associazione Italiana per la Musica e la Danza Antiche, 1995.

Nuitter, Charles, and Ernest Thoinan. *Les origines de l'Opéra français; d'après les minutes des notaires, les registres de la Conciergerie et les documents originaux conservés aux Archives nationales, à la Comédie, français et dans diverses collections publiques et particulières.* Paris, 1886. Reprint, New York: Da Capo Press, 1977.

O'Brien, John. *Harlequin Britain: Pantomime and Entertainment 1690–1760.* Baltimore: Johns Hopkins University Press, 2004.

Oberzaucher-Schüller, Gunhild. "L'Austria," *Musica in scena: Storia dello spettacolo musicale Vol. V, L'Arte della danza e del balletto*, ed. Alberto Basso, pp. 549–64. Turin: Unione Tipografico-Editrice Torinese, 1995.

Occhipinti, Carmelo, ed. *Carteggio d'arte degli ambasciatori estensi in Francia, 1536–1553.* Pisa: Scuola normale superiore, 2001.

Okamoto, Kimiko. "Between the Ancient and the Modern: A Study of *Danses à Deux* in Duple-Metre within Changing Aesthetics in France 1700–1733." Ph.D. diss., Roehampton University, 2005.

———. "Choreographic Syntax Denoting Rhetorical Structure: Analysis of French Rigaudons for a Couple." In *Structures and Metaphors in Baroque Dance: Proceedings of the Conference at the University of Surrey Roehampton, March 31, 2001*, pp. 40–51. Roehampton: Centre for Dance Research, University of Surrey, 2001.

———. "Discord within *Organic Unity*: Phrasal Relations Between Music and Choreography in Early Eighteenth-Century French Dance." In *Proceedings of 27th and 28th Annual Conferences of the Society of Dance History Scholars*, pp. 5–10. N.p.: SDHS, 2005.

———. "From Autonomy to Conformity: The Metrical Relationship between Music and Dance in Early Eighteenth-Century France." In *Proceedings of Sound Moves: An International Conference on Music and Dance, Roehampton University, London, 5–6 November 2005*, pp. 162–67. http://www.roehampton.ac.uk/SoundMoves.

———, comp. *Structures and Metaphors in Baroque Dance: Proceedings of the Conference at the University of Surrey Roehampton, March 31, 2001.* London: Centre for Dance Research, 2001.

Oldani, Louis J., S.J., and Victor R. Yanitelli, S.J. "Jesuit Theater in Italy: Its Entrances and Exit." *Italica* 76, no. 1 (1999): 18–32.

Oosterwijk, Sophie. "Of Corpses, Constables, and Kings: The Dance Macabre in Late Medieval and Renaissance Culture." *Journal of the British Archaeological Association* 157 (2004): 61–90.

Ossi, Massimo. "*Dalle macchine . . . la maraviglia*: Bernardo Buontalenti's *Il rapimento di Cefalo* at the Medici Theater in 1600." In *Opera and Context: Essays on Historical Staging from the Late Renaissance to the Time of Puccini*, ed. Mark A. Radice, pp. 15–35. Portland: Amadeus Press, 1998.

Oxford Dictionary of National Biography. Oxford, Oxford University Press, 2004.

Padovan, Maurizio. "Da Dante a Leonardo: La danza italiana attraverso le fonti storiche." *Danza italiana* 3 (1985): 5–37.

———, ed. *Guglielmo Ebreo da Pesaro e la danza nelle corti italiane del xv secolo.* Pisa: Pacini, 1990.

———. "Lorenzo de' Medici e la danza." *Rinascimento* 2nd ser., 32 (1992): 247–52.

Page, Christopher. *The Owl and the Nightingale: Musical Life and Ideas in France 1100–1300*. London: J. M. Dent and Sons, 1989.

———. *Voices and Instruments of the Middle Ages: Instrumental Practice and Songs in France 1100–1300*. Berkeley: University of California Press, 1986.

Palmer, Barbara D. "Court and Country: The Masque as Sociopolitical Subtext." *Medieval and Renaissance Drama in England* 7 (1995): 338–54.

Paradin, Guillaume. *Histoire de nostre temps*. Lyon, 1550.

Parfaict, Claude, and François Parfaict. *Dictionnaire des théâtres de Paris*, 7 vols. Paris, 1756. Reprint of 1767–70 edition, Geneva, 1971.

———. *Histoire de l'ancien Théâtre italien*. Paris, 1767. Reprint, New York: AMS Press, 1978.

Patterson, Annabel. *Pastoral and Ideology: Virgil to Valéry*. Berkeley: University of California Press, 1987.

Payne, Ian. *The Almain in Britain, c. 1549–c.1675: A Dance Manual from Manuscript Sources*. Aldershot: Ashgate, 2003.

Payne, T. *An Exact Description of the Two Fam'd Entertainments of Doctor Faustus*. London, 1724.

Pedersen, Olaf. *The First Universities: Studium Generale and the Origins of University Education in Europe*. Cambridge: Cambridge University Press, 1997.

Pérouse de Montclos, Jean-Marie. "Philibert de l'Orme à Paris. Le Palais de la Cité et les fêtes de 1549 et 1559." *Revue de l'art* no. 114 (1996): 9–15.

Petre, Robert. "Six New Dances by Kellom Tomlinson: A Recently Discovered Manuscript." *Early Music* 18, no. 3 (1990): 381–91.

Picot, Emile. *Les italiens en France au XVIe siècle*. Bordeaux: Gounouilhou, 1918. Facsimile reprint, *Memoria Bibliografica*, vol. 25, ed. Nicola Merola. Rome: Vecchiarelli, 1995.

Pierce, Ken. "Choreographic Structure in Dances by Feuillet." In *Proceedings of 25th Annual Conference of the Society of Dance History Scholars*, pp. 96–106. N.p.: SDHS, 2002.

———. "Choreographic Structure in the Dances of Claude Balon." In *Proceedings of 24th Annual Conference of the Society of Dance History Scholars*, pp. 101–4. N.p.: SDHS, 2001.

———. "Dance Notation Systems in Late 17th-Century France." *Early Music* 26, no. 2 (1998): 286–99.

———. "Dance Vocabulary in the Early 18th Century As Seen Through Feuillet's Step Tables." In *Proceedings of 20th Annual Conference of the Society of Dance History Scholars*, pp. 227–36. Riverside: SDHS, 1997.

———. "Repeated Step-sequences in Early Eighteenth Century Choreographies." In *Structures and Metaphors in Baroque Dance: Proceedings of the Conference at the University of Surrey Roehampton, March 31, 2001*, pp. 51–59. Roehampton: Centre for Dance Research, University of Surrey, 2001.

———. "Shepherd and Shepherdess Dances on the French Stage in the Early 18th Century." In *Proceedings of 27th and 28th Annual Conferences of the Society of Dance History Scholars*, pp. 123–34. N.p.: SDHS, 2005.

———. "Uncommon Steps and Notation in the *Sarabande de Mr. de Beauchamp*." In *Proceedings of 26th Annual Conference of the Society of Dance History Scholars*, pp. 91–98. N.p.: SDHS, 2003.

Pierce, Ken, and Jennifer Thorp. "The Dances in Lully's Persée." *Journal of Seventeenth Century Music* 10, no. 1 (available at http://sscm-jscm.press.uiuc.edu/jscm/v10/no1/pierce.html).

Pirrotta, Nino, and Elena Povoledo. *Music and Theatre from Poliziano to Monteverdi.* Trans. Karen Eales. Cambridge: Cambridge University Press, 1982.

Plat, Hugh. *The Garden of Eden.* London, 1654.

Plato, *Epinomis.* In *Plato Philebus and Epinomis.* Ed. Raymond Klibansky. Trans. A. E. Taylor. London: Thomas Nelson and Sons, 1956.

———. *Laws.* In *The Dialogues of Plato,* 4 vols. Trans. Benjamin Jowett, vol. 2. Oxford: Clarendon Press, 1871.

———. *Republic.* In *The Dialogues of Plato,* 4 vols. Trans. Benjamin Jowett, vol. 4. Oxford: Clarendon Press, 1871.

Platter, Felix. *Beloved Son Felix. The Journal of Felix Platter: A Medical Student in Montpellier in the Sixteenth Century.* Trans. Sean Jeannett. London: F. Muller, 1961.

Polk, Keith. *German Instrumental Music of the Late Middle Ages: Players, Patrons and Performance Practice.* Cambridge: Cambridge University Press, 1992.

———. "Instrumentalists and Performance Practices in Dance Music, c. 1500." In *Improvisation in the Arts of the Middle Ages and Renaissance,* ed. Timothy J. McGee, pp. 98–114. Kalamazoo, Mich.: Medieval Institute, 2003.

———. "Review of *Medieval Instrumental Dances.*" *Journal of the American Musicological Society* 44, no. 2 (1991): 324–28.

Pont, Graham. "Dance in Ancient Greek Culture." In *Music and Dance,* ed. David Tunley, pp. 15–23. Perth: Musicological Society of Australia, 1982.

Pontremoli, Alessandro. "Minica ed espressione del volto in alcuni balli di corte del xv secolo." In *Il volto e gli affetti: fisiognomica ed espressione nelle arti del Rinascimento. Atti del convegno di studi, Torino 28–29 novembre 2001,* ed. Alessandro Pontremoli, pp. 253–79. Florence: Leo S. Olschki, 2003.

Pontremoli, Alessandro, and Patrizia La Rocca. *Il ballare lombardo: Teoria e prassi coreutica nella festa di corte del xv secolo.* Milan: Vita e Pensiero, 1987.

———. *La danza a Venezia nel Rinascimento.* Vicenza: Neri Pozza, 1993.

Potter, David, and P. R. Roberts. "An Englishman's View of the Court of Henri III, 1584–1585: Richard Cook's 'Description of the Court of France.'" *French History* 2, no. 3 (1988): 312–44.

Powell, John S., ed. *Marc-Antoine Charpentier: Music for Molière's Comedies.* Madison, Wisc.: A-R Editions, 1990.

———. *Music and Theatre in France 1600–1680.* Oxford: Oxford University Press, 2000.

———. "Pierre Beauchamps, Choreographer to Molière's Troupe du Roy." *Music and Letters* 76, no. 2 (1995): 168–86.

Pradel, Abraham du. *Le Livre commode contenant les adresses de la ville de Paris, et le tresor des almanachs pour l'année Bissextile 1692.* Paris, 1692. Reprint, Geneva: Minkoff, 1973.

Prest, Julia. "Conflicting Signals: Images of Louis XIV in Benserade's Ballets." In *Culture and Conflict in 17th-century France and Ireland,* ed. Sarah Alyn Stacey and Véronique Desnain, pp. 227–41. Dublin: Four Courts Press, 2004.

———. "Cross-Casting in French Court Ballet: Monstrous Aberration or Theatrical Convention?" *Romance Studies* 21, no. 3 (November 2003): 157–68.

———. "Dancing King: Louis XIV's Roles in Molière's *Comédies-ballets,* from Court to Town." *Seventeenth Century* 16, no. 2 (2001): 283–98.

———. "The Gendering of the Court Ballet Audience: Cross-Casting and the Emergence of the Female Ballet Dancer." *Seventeenth Century French Studies* 24 (2002): 127–34.

———. *Theatre under Louis XIV: Cross-casting and the Performance of Gender in Drama, Ballet and Opera.* London: Palgrave Macmillan, 2006.

Primatice. Maître de Fontainebleau. Musée du Louvre, 22 septembre 2004–3 janvier 2005 (Catalogue).

Prina, Federica Calvino. "Nizarda! Qué danza es esa?" In L'arte della danza ai tempi di Claudio Monteverdi, Atti del convegno internazionale, Torino, 6–7 settembre 1993, ed. Angelo Chiarle, pp. 17–32. Turin: Istitutio per i Beni Musicali in Piemonte, 1996.

Pruiksma, Rose A. "Generational Conflict and the Foundation of the Académie Royale de Danse: A Re-examination." Dance Chronicle 26, no. 2 (2003): 169–87.

———. "Music, Sex, and Ethnicity: Signification in Lully's Theatrical Chaconnes." In Gender, Sexuality, and Early Music, ed. Todd M. Borgerding, pp. 227–48. New York: Routledge, 2001.

Prunières, Henri. L'Opéra italien en France avant Lulli (1913). Reprint, Paris: Honorée Champion, 1975.

Raguenet, François. Parallèle des Italiens et des Français en ce qui regarde la musique et les opéras; Défense du Parallèle des Italiens et des Français en ce qui regarde la musique et les opéras. Paris, 1702. Reprint, Geneva: Minkoff, 1976.

Ralph, Richard. The Life and Works of John Weaver. London: Dance Books, 1985.

Ranum, Orest. "Islands and the Self in a Ludovician Fête." In The Sun King: The Ascendancy of French Culture during the Reign of Louis XIV, ed. David Lee Rubin, pp. 17–27. Washington, D.C.: Folger Shakespeare Library; Toronto: Associated University Presses, 1992.

Ranum, Patricia M. "Audible Rhetoric and Mute Rhetoric: The 17th-Century French Sarabande." Early Music 14, no. 1 (1986): 22–39.

———. Portraits around Marc-Antoine Charpentier. Baltimore: Dux Femina Facti, 2004.

Ranum, Patricia M., and Catherine Cessac. "Trois favoris d'ut ré mi fa sol la': août 1672, les Comédiens français taquinent leurs confrères italiens." In Marc-Antoine Charpentier: un musicien retrouvé, ed. Catherine Cessac, pp. 209–23. Paris, 2005.

Rashdall, Hastings. The Universities of Europe in the Middle Ages. Oxford: Clarendon Press, 1936.

Ravelhofer, Barbara. "Dancing at the Court of Queen Elizabeth." In Queen Elizabeth I: Past and Present, ed. Christa Jansohn, pp. 101–15. Münster: LIT Verlag, 2004.

———. The Early Stuart Masque: Dance, Costume, and Music. Oxford: Oxford University Press, 2006.

———. "English Masques." In The Cambridge Companion to Ballet, ed. Marion Kant, pp. 32–41. Cambridge: Cambridge University Press, 2007.

———. Introduction to Louange de la Danse: In Praise of Dance, by B. de Montagut, ed. Barbara Ravelhofer, pp. 1–81. Cambridge: Renaissance Texts from Manuscripts, 2000.

Renart, Jean. The Romance of the Rose or of Guillaume de Dole, ed. Regina Psaki. New York: Garland Publishing, 1995.

Ribeiro, Aileen. Fashion and Fiction: Dress in Art and Literature in Stuart England. New Haven: Yale University Press, 2005.

Riccio, Bernardino. Le Livre de la Forest . . . contenant et explicant briefvement L'appareil: les Jeux: et le Festin de la Bastille. Paris, 1518.

Richardson, Philip J. S. "The Beauchamp Mystery: Some Fresh Light on an Old Problem." Dancing Times 37 (1946): 299–302.

Riché, Pierre. "Danses profanes et religieuses dans le haut Moyen Age." In Histoire sociale, sensibilités collectives et mentalités: Mélanges Robert Mandrou, pp. 159–67. Paris: Presses Universitaires de France, 1985.

Richelieu, Armand-Emmanuel Jean du Plessis, duc de. *Mémoires du Cardinal de Richelieu*, 10 vols. Paris: J. Renouard, 1907–37.

Ridder-Symoens, Hilde de, ed. *A History of the University in Europe, vol. I: Universities in the Middle Ages*. Cambridge: Cambridge University Press, 1992.

Rimmer, Joan. "Carole, Rondeau and Branle in Ireland 1300–1800: Part 1 The Walling of New Ross and Dance Texts in the Red Book of Ossory." *Dance Research* 7, no. 1 (1989): 20–46.

———. "Dance Elements in Trouvère Repertory." *Dance Research* 3, no. 2 (1985): 23–34.

Rock, Judith. *Terpsichore at Louis-Le-Grand: Baroque Dance on the Jesuit Stage in Paris*. St. Louis: Institute of Jesuit Sources, 1996.

Rokesth, Y. "Danses cléricales du XIIIe siècle." *Publications de la Faculté des Lettres de l'Université de Strasbourg* 106 (1947): 93–126.

Ronsard, Pierre de. *Oeuvres complètes*. Ed. Paul Laumonier. Paris: Didier, 1946.

Rottensteiner, Gudrun. "Vom 'Ballarino' zum 'Maitre à danser': Grazer Tanzmeister des 17. Jahrhunderts." In *Morgenröte des Barock. Tanz im 17. Jahrhundert*, ed. Uwe Scholtermüller and Maria Richter, pp. 181–88. Freiburg: Fa-gisis, 2004.

Russell, Tilden A. "Minuet Form and Phraseology in *Recueils* and Manuscript Tune Books." *Journal of Musicology* 17, no. 3 (1999): 386–419.

———. "The Unconventional Dance Minuet: Choreographies of the Menuet d'Exaudet." *Acta Musicologica* 64 (1992): 118–38.

Russell, Tilden A., and Dominique Bourassa. *The 'Minuet de la Cour'*. Hildesheim: Georg Olms, 2007.

Ryder, Alan. *Alfonso the Magnanimous: King of Aragon, Naples, and Sicily, 1396–1458*. Oxford: Clarendon Press, 1990.

Rykwert, Joseph. Introduction to *On the Art of Building in Ten Books*, trans. Joseph Rykwert, Neil Leach, and Robert Tavernor, pp. ix–xxi. Cambridge, Mass.: MIT Press, 1988.

———. *The Dancing Column: On Order in Architecture*. Cambridge, Mass.: MIT Press, 1996.

Sadie, Stanley, and John Tyrrell, eds. *The New Grove Dictionary of Music and Musicians*. 2nd ed. London: Macmillan, 2001.

Sahlin, Margit R. *Étude sur la carole médiévale: L'origine du mot et ses rapports avec l'église*. Uppsala: Almqvist & Wiksells, 1940.

Saint-Simon, M. le duc de. *Memoirs of Louis XIV and the Regency*, trans. Bayle St. John. 3 vols. London: Allen & Unwin, 1926.

Salmen, Walter. *Tanz im 17. und 18. Jahrhundert*. Musikgeschichte in Bildern, vol. 4. Liepzig: VEB Deutscher Verlag für Musik, 1988.

Sanudo, Marin. *I diarii di Marin Sanuto (1496–1533)*. 58 vols. Ed. Rinaldo Fulin et al., Venice: 1879–1903. Reprint, Bologna: Forni, 1969–79.

Sardoni, Alessandra. "'Ut in voce sic in gestu'. Danza e cultura barocca nei collegi gesuitici tra Roma e la Francia." *Studi musicali* 25, nos. 1–2 (1996): 303–16.

Savage, Roger. "The Staging of Courtly Theatre: 1560s to 1640s." In *Europa Triumphans: Court and Civic Festivals in Early Modern Europe*. 2 vols., ed. J. R. Mulryne, Helen Watanabe-O'Kelly, and Margaret Shewring, 1: 57–74. Aldershot: Ashgate, 2004.

Schneider, Herbert. "Structures métriques du menuet au XVIIe et au début du XVIIIe siècle." *Revue de Musicologie* 78, no. 1 (1992): 27–65.

Schwartz, Judith L. "The Passacaille in Lully's Armide: Phrase Structure in the Choreography and the Music." *Early Music* 26, no. 2 (1998): 300–320.

Schwartz, Judith L., and Christena L. Schlundt. *French Court Dance and Dance Music: A Guide to Primary Source Writings 1643–1789.* Stuyvesant, N.Y.: Pendragon Press, 1987.

Schwartz, William Leonard. "Molière's Theater in 1672–1673: Light from *Le Registre d'Hubert.*" *Publications of the Modern Language Association* 56 (1941): 395–427.

Scouten, Arthur H., ed. *The London Stage 1660–1800: A Calendar, Part 3 1729–1747.* Carbondale: Southern Illinois University Press, 1965.

Semmens, Richard. "Branles, Gavottes and Contredanses in the Later Seventeenth and Early Eighteenth Centuries." *Dance Research* 15, no. 2 (1997): 35–62.

———. *The bals publics at the Paris Opéra in the Eighteenth Century.* Hillsdale, N.Y.: Pendragon Press, 2004.

Sharpe, Kevin, and Steven N. Zwicker. "Politics of Discourse, Introduction." In *Politics of Discourse: The Literature and History of Seventeenth-Century England,* ed. Kevin Sharpe and Steven N. Zwicker, pp. 1–20. Berkeley: University of California Press, 1987.

Shennan, Jennifer, ed. *A Work Book by Kellom Tomlinson.* Stuyvesant, N.Y.: Pendragon Press, 1992.

Shepherd, Rupert. "Giovanni Sabadino degli Arienti, Ercole I d'Este and the Decoration of the Italian Renaissance Court." *Renaissance Studies* 9, no. 1 (1995): 18–57.

Silen, Karen. "Elizabeth of Spalbeek: Dancing the Passion." In *Women's Work: Making Dance in Europe before 1800,* ed. Lynn Matluck Brooks, pp. 207–27. Madison: University of Wisconsin Press, 2007.

Silin, Charles. *Benserade and His Ballets de Cour.* Baltimore: Johns Hopkins University Press, 1940.

Silver, Isidore. "Ronsard on the Marriage of Poetry, Music, and the Dance." In *Studies in the Continental Background of Renaissance English Literature: Essays Presented to John L. Lievsay,* ed. Dale B. J. Randall and George Walton Williams, pp. 155–69. Durham, N.C.: Duke University Press, 1977.

Skinner, Quentin. "Ambrogio Lorenzetti's *Buon Governo* Frescoes: Two Old Questions, Two New Answers." *Journal of the Warburg and Courtauld Institutes* 62 (1999): 1–28.

Smart, Sara. "The Württemberg Court and the Introduction of Ballet into the Empire." In *Europa Triumphans: Court and Civic Festivals in Early Modern Europe.* 2 vols. Ed. J. R. Mulryne, Helen Watanabe-O'Kelly, and Margaret Shewring, 2: 35–45. Aldershot: Ashgate, 2004.

Smith, A. William. "Dance at Mantua and in Northern Italy: The Tradition Inherited by Leone de' Sommi and His Generation." In *Leone de' Sommi and the Performing Arts,* ed. Ahuva Belkin, pp. 83–97. Tel Aviv: Tel Aviv University, 1997.

———. "Dance in Early Sixteenth-Century Venice: The *Mumaria* and Some of Its Choreographers." In *Proceedings of the 12th Annual Conference of Society of Dance History Scholars,* pp. 126–38. Riverside: SDHS, 1989.

———. Introduction to *Fifteenth-Century Dance and Music: Twelve Transcribed Italian Treatises and Collections in the Tradition of Domencio da Piacenza.* Stuyvesant, N.Y.: Pendragon Press, 1995, p. xi–xxii.

Smith, Judy, and Ian Gatiss. "What Did Prince Henry Do with His Feet on Sunday 19 August 1604?" *Early Music* 14, no. 2 (1986): 199–207.

Smith, William C. *A Bibliography of the Musical Works published by John Walsh 1695–1720.* London: Bibliographical Society, 1968.

Southern, Eileen. "A Prima Ballerina of the Fifteenth Century." In *Music and Context: Es-*

says for John M. Ward, ed. Anne Dhu Shapiro, pp. 183–97. Cambridge, Mass.: Department of Music, Harvard University, 1985.

Sparshott, Francis. "The Missing Art of Dance." *Dance Chronicle* 6, no. 3 (1983): 164–83.

Sparti, Barbara. "Dancing Couples Behind the Scenes: Recently Discovered Italian Illustrations, 1470–1550." *Imago Musicae* 13 (1996): 9–38.

———. "La 'danza barocca' è soltanto francese?" *Studi musicali* 25, nos. 1–2 (1996): 283–302.

———. "La danza come politica al tempo di Machiavelli." In *La lingua e le lingue di Machiavelli: atti del convegno internazionale di studi, Torino, 2–4 dicembre 1999,* ed. Alessandro Pontremoli, pp. 295–313. Florence: Leo S. Olschki, 2001.

———. "Improvisation and Embellishment in Popular and Art Dances in Fifteenth- and Sixteenth-Century Italy." In *Improvisation in the Arts of the Middle Ages and the Renaissance,* ed. Timothy J. McGee, pp. 117–44. Kalamazoo, Mich.: Medieval Institute, 2003.

———. Introduction to *Ballo della gagliarda,* by Lutio Compasso, Florence 1560. Facsimile edition, pp. 5–19. Freiburg: Fa-gisis, 1995.

———. Introduction to *De practica seu arte tripudii: On the Practice or Art of Dancing,* by Guglielmo Ebreo da Pesaro, ed. and trans. Barbara Sparti, pp. 3–72. Oxford: Clarendon Press, 1993.

———. Introduction to *Mastro da ballo,* 1614, by Ercole Santucci. Facsimile edition, pp. 60–69. Hildesheim: Georg Olms, 2004.

———. "Rôti Bouilli: Take Two 'el gioioso fiorito.'" *Studi musicali* 24, no. 2 (1995): 231–61.

———. "Would You Like to Dance this Frottola? Choreographic Concordances in Two Early Sixteenth-Century Tuscan Sources." *Musica Disciplina* 50 (1996): 135–65.

Spencer, John R. Introduction to *Filarete's Treatise on Architecture,* by Filarete. Trans. John R. Spencer, 1: xvii–xxxvii. New Haven: Yale University Press, 1965.

Stark, Alan. "What Steps did the Spaniards Take in the Dance?" In *Proceedings of the 14th Annual Conference of Society of Dance History Scholars,* pp. 54–64. Riverside: SDHS, 1991.

Steel, Carlos. "Introduction." In *Speculum divinorum et quorundam naturalium/Henricus Bate,* vol. 12, ed. Helmut Boese, pp. ix–xxxiii. Leuven: Leuven University Press, 1990.

Stein, Louise K. "The Musicians of the Spanish Royal Chapel and Court Entertainments, 1590–1648." In *The Royal Chapel in the Time of the Hapsburgs: Music and Court Ceremony in Early Modern Europe,* trans. Yolanda Acker, English version ed. Tess Knighton, pp. 173–94. Woodbridge: Boydell Press, 2005.

Stephens, John Calhoun, ed. *The Guardian.* Lexington: University Press of Kentucky, 1982.

Stevens, Denis. "Monteverdi's Earliest Extant Ballet." *Early Music* 14, no. 3 (1986): 358–66.

Stevens, John. *Words and Music in the Middle Ages: Song, Narrative, Dance and Drama, 1050–1350.* Cambridge: Cambridge University Press, 1986.

Stevens, John, et al. "The English Carol." In *Report of the Tenth Congress of the International Musicological Society, Ljubljana, 1967,* ed. Dragotin Cvetko, pp. 284–309. Kassel: Bärenreiter, 1970.

Stokes, James, and Ingrid Brainard. "'The olde Measures' in the West Country: John Willoughby's Manuscript." *REED Newsletter* 17, no. 2 (1992): 1–10.

Stras, Laurie. "'Onde havrà 'l mond'esempio et vera historia': Musical Echoes of Henri III's Progress through Italy." *Acta Musicologica* 72, no. 1 (2000): 7–41.

Streitberger, W. R. *Court Revels, 1485–1559.* Toronto: University of Toronto Press, 1994.

Strong, Roy. *Art and Power: Renaissance Festivals, 1450–1650.* Woodbridge: Boydell Press, 1984.

———. "Festivals for the Garter Embassy at the Court of Henri III." *Journal of the Warburg and Courtauld Institutes* 22 (1959): 60–70.

———. *The Renaissance Garden in England.* London: Thames and Hudson, 1979.

Sutton, Julia. "Cadential Formulae in Music and Dance in 16th-Century Italy." In *Proceedings of 20th Annual Conference of the Society of Dance History Scholars*, pp. 299–304. Riverside: SDHS, 1997.

———. "Lorin and Playford: Connections and Disparities." In *On Common Ground 3: John Playford and the The English Dancing Master 1651: Proceedings of the 3rd DHDS Conference, March 2001*, ed. David Parsons, pp. 135–37. Stock, Essex: Dolmetsch Historical Dance Society, 2001.

———. "Triple Pavans: Clues to Some Mysteries in 16th-Century Dance." *Early Music* 14, no. 2 (1986): 175–81.

Tamalio, Raffaele. *Federico Gonzaga alla corte di Francesco I de Francia nel carteggio privato con Mantova, 1515–1540.* Paris: Champion, 1994.

Thacker, Christopher. *The History of Gardens.* Berkeley: University of California Press, 1985.

Thesiger, Sarah. "The *Orchestra* of Sir John Davies and the Image of the Dance." *Journal of the Warburg and Courtauld Institutes* 36 (1973): 277–304.

Thierry, Edouard. *Documents sur le 'Malade imaginaire': Estat de la recette et despence.* Paris: Berger-Levrault, 1880.

Thorp, Jennifer. "An Echo of the Past? Le Roussau's Harlequin and *Le Malade Imaginaire.*" In *On Common Ground 4: Reconstruction and Re-creation in Dance before 1850: Proceedings of the 4th DHDS Conference, March 2003*, ed. David Parsons, pp. 69–78. Stock, Essex: Dolmetsch Historical Dance Society, 2003.

———. "The Effectiveness of the Beauchamp-Feuillet Notation System During the Eighteenth Century." In *On Common Ground 2: Continuity and Change. Proceedings of the 2nd DHDS Conference, 1998*, ed. David Parsons, pp. 51–65. Salisbury: Dolmetsch Historical Dance Society, 1998.

———. *Harlequin Dancing-Master: The Career of F. le Roussau.* Forthcoming.

———. "In Defence of the Danced Minuet." *Early Music* 31, no. 1 (2003): 100–109.

———. "Mr Isaac, Dancing Master." *Dance Research* 24, no. 2 (2006): 117–37.

———. "P. Siris: An Early Eighteenth-Century Dancing-Master." *Dance Research* 10, no. 2 (1992): 71–92.

———. "Pecour's *L'Allemande* 1702: How Germanic Was It?" *Eighteenth-Century Music* 1, no. 2 (2004): 183–204.

———. "Serious and Comic Dance in the Work of F. le Roussau." In *Structures and Metaphors in Baroque Dance: Proceedings of the Conference at the University of Surrey Roehampton 2001*, pp. 10–20. Roehampton: University of Surrey, 2001.

———. "Spelling it out: Le Roussau's *The Montaigue*, 1720." In *On Common Ground 6: The Minuet in Time and Space. Proceedings of the 6th DHDS Conference, March 2007*, ed. David Parsons. Stock, Essex: Dolmetsch Historical Dance Society, 2007.

———. "Style or Stylus? Mr Isaac's Dance Notators in the Early Eighteenth Century." In *On Common Ground 1: Proceedings of the DHDS Conference, February 1996*, ed. David Parsons, pp. 53–67. Salisbury: Dolmetsch Historical Dance Society, 1996.

———. "Your Honor'd and Obedient Servant: Patronage and Dance in London c. 1700–1735." *Dance Research* 15, no. 2 (1997): 84–98.

Thorp, Jennifer, and Ken Pierce. "Taste and Ingenuity: Three English Chaconnes of the Early Eighteenth Century." *Historical Dance* 3, no. 3 (1994): 3–16.

Thou, Jacques-Auguste de. *Histoire universelle*. 16 vols. London, 1734.

Tilmouth, Michael. "Music on the Travels of an English Merchant: Robert Bargrave (1628–61)." *Music & Letters* 53, no. 2 (1972): 143–59.

Tomasi, Luisa Tongiorgi. "Geometric Schemes for Plant Beds and Gardens: A Contribution to the History of the Garden in the Sixteenth and Seventeenth Centuries." In *World Art. Themes of Unity in Diversity (Acts of the XXVI International Congress of the History of Art)*, ed. Irving Lavin, 1: 211–17. University Park: Penn State University Press, 1989.

Tomko, Linda J. "Issues of Nation in Isaac's *The Union*." *Dance Research* 15, no. 2 (1997): 99–125.

Tondo, Ornella di. "'Leggiadrìa di ballo et di gesti'. Alcune osservazioni sulla danza negli intermedi e nel primo melodramma tra XVI e XVII secolo." In *L'arte della danza ai tempi di Claudio Monteverdi, Atti del convegno internazionale, Torino, 6–7 settembre 1993*, ed. Angelo Chiarle, pp. 189–226. Turin: Istitutio per i Beni Musicali in Piemonte, 1996.

Trexler, Richard C. *Public Life in Renaissance Florence*. Ithaca: Cornell University Press, 1991.

Tyard, Pontus de. *Le Solitaire second, ou prose de la musique*, Lyon, 1555.

Van Orden, Kate. *Music, Discipline, and Arms in Early Modern France*. Chicago: University of Chicago Press, 2005.

Veevers, Erica. *Images of Love and Religion: Queen Henrietta Maria and Court Entertainments*. Cambridge: Cambridge University Press, 1989.

Veronese, Alessandra. "Una *societas* ebraico-cristiano in *docendo tripudiare sonare ac cantare* nella Firenze del quattrocento." In *Guglielmo Ebreo da Pesaro e la danza nelle corti italiane del xv secolo*, ed. Maurizio Padovan, pp. 51–57. Pisa: Pacini, 1990.

Vieilleville, François de Scépeaux, sire de. *Mémoires de la vie*. Vol. 9. Ed. J. Michaud and J. J. F. Poujoulat. Paris, 1838.

Vienne, Philibert de. *Le Philosophe de Court*. Lyon, 1547. Ed. P. M. Smith. Geneva: Droz, 1990.

Viéville, Lecerf de la. *Comparaison de la musique italienne et de la musique françoise*. Paris, 1704. Reprint, Geneva: Minkoff, 1972.

Vigarello, Georges. "The Upward Training of the Body from the Age of Chivalry to Courtly Civility." In *Fragments for a History of the Human Body*, ed. Michel Feher, Ramona Naddaff, and Nadia Tazi, 2: 148–99. New York: Zone, 1989.

Vitruvius. *Ten Books on Architecture. (De Architectura Libri Decem.)* Trans. Ingrid D. Rowland. New York: Cambridge University Press, 1999.

Wagner, Ann. *Adversaries of Dance: From the Puritans to the Present*. Urbana: University of Illinois Press, 1997.

Wagner, David L., ed. *The Seven Liberal Arts in the Middle Ages*. Bloomington: Indiana University Press, 1983.

Waley, Daniel. "Ambrogio Lorenzetti's 'dancing maidens.'" *Apollo* 134 (1991): 141–42.

Walkling, Andrew. "Masque and Politics at the Restoration Court: John Crowne's *Calisto*." *Early Music* 24, no. 1 (1996): 27–62.

Walls, Peter. *Music in the English Courtly Masque, 1604–1640*. Oxford: Clarendon Press, 1995.

Ward, John M. "Apropos 'The olde Measures.'" *REED Newsletter* 18, no. 1 (1993): 2–21.

———. "The English Measure." *Early Music* 14, no. 1 (1986): 15–21.

———. "Newly Devised Measures for Jacobean Masques." *Acta Musicologica* 60, no. 2 (1988): 111–42.

Watanabe-O'Kelly, Helen. "Early Modern European Festivals—Politics and Performance, Event and Record." In *Court Festivals of the European Renaissance: Art, Politics and Performance*, ed. J. R. Mulryne and Elizabeth Goldring, pp. 15–25. Aldershot: Ashgate, 2002.

———. "The Early Modern Festival Book: Function and Form." In *Europa Triumphans: Court and Civic Festivals in Early Modern Europe*, 2 vols., ed. J. R. Mulryne, Helen Watanabe-O'Kelly, and Margaret Shewring, I: 3–17. Aldershot: Ashgate, 2004.

Wéry, Anne. *La danse écartelée de la fin du Moyen Âge à l'âge classique.* Paris: Champion, 1992.

Wilson, David R. "The Art of Transcription: A Discussion of the Issues in Transcribing Using Fifteenth-Century Italian Texts." In *On Common Ground 1: Proceedings of the DHDS Conference, February 1996*, ed. David Parsons, pp. 30–37. Salisbury: Dolmetsch Historical Dance Society, 1996.

———. "'Il Bianco Fiore' by Cesare Negri." *Historical Dance* 2, no. 5 (1986/87): 33–35.

———. "*Contrapassi* in Fifteenth-Century Italian Dance Reconsidered." *Dance Research* 24, no. I (2006): 60–65.

———. "'Corona', a *bassa danza ala fila* by Domenico." *Historical Dance* 4, no. I (2004): 23–28.

———. "'Damnes' as Described by Domenico, Cornazano and Guglielmo." *Historical Dance* 2, no. 6 (1988/1991): 3–8.

———. "Dancing in the Inns of Court." *Historical Dance* 2, no. 5 (1986–87): 3–16.

———. "The Development of French Basse Danse." *Historical Dance* 2, no. 4 (1984–85): 5–12.

———. "'Finita: et larifaccino unaltro uolta dachapo.'" *Historical Dance* 3, no. 2 (1993): 21–26.

———. "A Further Look at the Nancy Basse Dances." *Historical Dance* 3, no. 3 (1994): 24–28.

———. "'La giloxia'/'Gelosia' as Described by Domenico and Guglielmo." *Historical Dance* 3, no. I (1992): 3–9.

———. "Language in Fifteenth-Century Italian Dance Descriptions." *Historical Dance* 4, no. I (2004): 29–32.

———. *101 Italian Dances (c. 1450–c. 1510). A Critical Translation.* Cambridge: Early Dance Circle, 1999.

———. "Performing Gresley Dances: The View from the Floor." *Historical Dance* 3, no. 6 (1999): 20–22.

———. "Problems and Possible Solutions in Fifteenth-Century French Basse Dance." In *On Common Ground 4: Reconstruction and Re-creation in Dance before 1850: Proceedings of the 4th DHDS Conference, March 2003*, ed. David Parsons, pp. 45–52. Stock, Essex: Dolmetsch Historical Dance Society, 2003.

———. "Regional Traditions in the French Basse Dance." In *Proceedings of 27th and 28th Annual Conferences of the Society of Dance History Scholars*, pp. 42–48. N.p.: SDHS, 2005.

———. *The Steps Used in Court Dancing in Fifteenth-Century Italy.* 3rd rev. ed. Cambridge: David R. Wilson, 2003.

Wilson, David R., and Véronique Daniels. "The Basse Dance Handbook: Text and Context." Unpublished manuscript.

Winerock, E. F. "Dance References in the Records of Early English Drama: Alternative Sources for Non-Courtly Dancing, 1500–1650." In *Proceedings of the Society Dance History Scholars 27th and 28th Annual Conferences*, pp. 36–41. N.p.: SDHS, 2005.

Witherell, Anne L. *Louis Pécour's Recueil de dances*. Ann Arbor: UMI Research Press, 1983.

Woodbridge, Kenneth. *Princely Gardens: The Origins and Development of the French Formal Style*. London: Thames and Hudson, 1986.

Wright, Craig. *The Maze and the Warrior: Symbols in Architecture, Theology, and Music*. Cambridge, Mass.: Harvard University Press, 2001.

———. *Music and Ceremony at Notre Dame of Paris, 500–1550*. Cambridge: Cambridge University Press, 1989.

Wycherley, William. *The Gentleman Dancing-Master*. London, 1673, reprinted 1702.

Yates, Frances A. *The French Academies of the Sixteenth Century*. London: Warburg Institute, 1947.

———. *The Valois Tapestries*. London: Warburg Institute, 1959.

Young, Bert Edward, and Grace Philputt Young, eds. *Le registre de La Grange, 1659–1685, reproduit en fac-similé avec un index et une notice sur La Grange et sa part dans le théâtre de Molière*. 2 vols. Paris: Droz, 1947.

Zentgravius, Johannes Joachimus. *De choreis gynaeco-andricis*. Thesis defended by Johannes Jacobus Windenius. Strasbourg: J. Welperus, 1689.

Zwicker, Steven N. "Lines of Authority: Politics and Literary Culture in the Restoration." In *Politics of Discourse: The Literature and History of Seventeenth-Century England*, ed. Kevin Sharpe and Steven N. Zwicker, pp. 230–70. Berkeley: University of California Press, 1987.

Contributors

ALESSANDRO ARCANGELI is Associate Professor of Renaissance and Early Modern History at the University of Verona. His books include *Davide o Salomè?* which won the Premio Finale Ligure Storia-Opera Prima, *Recreation in the Renaissance,* and *Che cos'è la storia culturale.*

KATHERINE TUCKER McGINNIS is a social historian who studies the developing profession of the dancing master in early modern Italy. She is currently working on a comparative study of dancing masters in several Italian cities during the late sixteenth century.

MARGARET M. McGOWAN is Research Professor in French at the University of Sussex. She is a Fellow of the British Academy and a Commander of the British Empire. She has published over twenty articles on dance history, and her books include *L'art du ballet de court en France, Ideal Forms in the Age of Ronsard, The Court Ballet of Louis XIII,* an edition of *Le Balet comique de la Reyne,* and her latest monograph, *Dance in the Renaissance.*

JENNIFER NEVILE is an Honorary Research Fellow in Music and Music Education at the University of New South Wales. Her research on fifteenth- and sixteenth-century dance practices and their relationship with other contemporary artistic practices, as well as choreographic analysis of individual works and genres, has been published in twenty articles and book chapters. She is also the author of *The Eloquent Body: Dance and Humanist Culture in Fifteenth-Century Italy* (Indiana University Press, 2004).

KEN PIERCE directs the early dance program at the Longy School of Music, and has taught early dance at workshops throughout Europe and North America. He has performed with companies in New York and Paris, and now directs his own Boston-based company, the Ken Pierce Baroque Dance Company. His historically informed choreographies and reconstructions have been presented at festivals from Copenhagen to Vancouver.

GRAHAM PONT taught in the General Education program at the University of New South Wales for thirty years. Trained in philosophy, his principal research area has been the history and philosophy of music, the results of which have appeared in *Early Music, Goettinger Händel-Beiträge,* and *Nexus Network Journal.* He is currently completing a biography of Australia's first resident composer, Isaac Nathan (1792–1864).

JOHN S. POWELL is Professor of Music History at the University of Tulsa. He has researched the music of seventeenth-century France for the past thirty years, publishing in that time over twenty articles on various aspects of French Baroque music and editing numerous critical editions. He is also the author of *Music and French Theatre, 1600–1680.*

JULIA PREST is Assistant Professor of French at Yale University. Her publications include *Theatre under Louis XIV: Cross-Casting and the Performance of Gender in Drama, Ballet and Opera,* a critical edition of *Le Mariage forcé,* and articles on *comédie-ballet, ballet de cour,* school drama, and the court of Louis XIV.

KAREN SILEN is currently writing a dissertation on dance practice and theory in late thirteenth-century France and French Flanders, in partial fulfillment of her interdisciplinary Ph.D. at the University of California at Berkeley. Works for publication include "Medieval Dance" in *Women and Gender in Medieval Europe: An Encyclopedia,* and "Elizabeth of Spalbeek's Dance of Passion," in *Women's Work: Making Dance in Europe Before 1750.*

JENNIFER THORP is an archivist and dance historian who for several years taught baroque theater dance at the University of Middlesex and has published a number of articles on aspects of seventeenth- and eighteenth-century dance in England and France. She is the co-organizer of annual academic symposia on eighteenth-century dance and music at New College, Oxford.

LINDA J. TOMKO is Associate Professor of Dance at the University of California, Riverside. She co-directed the annual summer Workshop in Baroque Dance and its Music at Stanford University, and is the author of *Dancing Class: Gender, Ethnicity, and Social Divides in American Dance, 1890–1920* (Indiana University Press, 1999).

The late DAVID R. WILSON started researching, publishing, and performing early dance in the 1980s. His expertise and interest centered on investigations of original sources, especially Catalan, French, and Italian manuscripts of the fifteenth century. His published work has mainly concerned Italian dancing of the fifteenth and sixteenth centuries, including research on transmission of manuscripts, detailed analysis of individual dances, and an exhaustive study of the individual steps and their variants found in the fifteenth-century Italian sources, as well as a translation and edition of the 101 choreographies of this same repertory. At the time of his death a monograph on the *basse dance* in France, Spain, and England was substantially complete.

Index

Page numbers in italics indicate illustrations.